# Imaging the Arctic

This publication was made possible
by a generous grant from the
Eugene V. and Clare E. Thaw Charitable Trust,
Santa Fe

# Imaging the Arctic

Edited by J. C. H. King and Henrietta Lidchi

Published for the Trustees of the British Museum by British Museum Press

© 1998 The Trustees of the British Museum
Published by British Museum Press
A division of The British Museum Company Ltd
46 Bloomsbury Street, London WCIB 3QQ

British Library Cataloguing in Publication Data
A catalogue record for this book is available from the British Library

ISBN 0 7141 2537 7


Designed by Alan Bartram
Typeset by Wyvern 21, Bristol
Duotone origination by Bright Arts, Hong Kong
Printed and bound in Italy

# Contents

# List of Contributors

William Barr
Department of Geography, University of
Saskatchewan, Saskatoon, Sask. S7N OWD,
Canada

Karen Brewster
Commission on Inupiat History, Language
and Culture, North Slope Borough, PO Box
69, Barrow, Alaska 99723, USA

Hugh Brody
c/o The Department of Ethnography,
The British Museum, Great Russell Street,
London WC1B, Great Britain

Jim Burant
Art Acquisition and Research, Visual and
Sound Archives Division, National Archives
of Canada, 395 Wellington Street, Ottawa,
Ontario K1A 0N3, Canada

Robert J. Christopher
School of American/International Studies,
Ramapo College of New Jersey, 505 Ramapo
Valley Road, Mahwah, New Jersey
07430–1680, USA

Dorothy Harley Eber
c/o McCord Museum of Canadian History,
690 Sherbrooke St West, Montreal, Quebec
H3A 1E9, Canada

Elizabeth Edwards
Pitt Rivers Museum, South Parks Road,
Oxford OX1 3PP, Great Britain

Ann Christine Eek
Ethnographic Museum, Frederiks Gate 2,
N–0164 Oslo, Norway

William W. Fitzhugh
National Museum of Natural History,
MRC–112, Smithsonian Institution,
Washington DC 20560, USA

Paula Richardson Fleming
National Museum of Natural History,
MRC–112, Smithsonian Institution,
Washington DC 20560, USA

Peter Geller
Keewatin Community College, 504 Princeton
Drive, Thompson MB R8N OA5, Canada

Nelson H. H. Graburn
Department of Anthropology, University of
California, Berkeley, California 94720, USA

Stephen Hendrie
Makivik Corporation, 650 32nd Avenue,
6 Floor, Lachine, Quebec H8T 3K5, Canada

Bill Hess
Running Dog Publications, PO Box 69,
Barrow, Alaska, USA

Aldona Jonaitis
University of Alaska Museum, 907 Yukon
Drive, PO Box 756960, Fairbanks, Alaska
99775–6960, USA

Simeonie Keenainak
PO Box 484, Pangnirtung, NT X0A 0R0,
Canada

J. C. H. King
Department of Ethnography,
The British Museum, Great Russell Street,
London WC1B 3DG, Great Britain

Inge Kleivan
Department of Eskimology, University of
Copenhagen, 100 H Strangade, DK–1401,
Copenhagen K, Denmark

Molly Lee
University of Alaska Museum, 907 Yukon
Drive, PO Box 756960, Alaska 99775–6970,
USA

Henrietta Lidchi
Department of Ethnography,
The British Museum, Great Russell Street,
London WC1B 3DG, Great Britain

Stephen Loring
National Museum of Natural History,
MRC–112, Smithsonian Institution,
Washington DC 20560, USA

Alan Rudolph Marcus
Department of Drama, The University of
Manchester, Oxford Road, Manchester
M13 9PL, Great Britain

Eileen Norbert
Bering Strait Foundation, PO Box 1008,
Nome, Alaska 99762, USA

Zebedee Nungak
Makivik Corporation, 650 32nd Avenue, 4th
Floor, Lachine, Quebec H95 3J8, Canada

George Quviq Qulaut
Implementation Commissioner for Nunavut,
PO Box 147, Igloolik, Northwest Territories
X0A 0L0, Canada

Pamela Stern
Department of Anthropology, University of
California, Berkeley, California 94720, USA

William C. Sturtevant
National Museum of Natural History,
Smithsonian Institution, Washington DC
20560, USA

Douglas Wamsley
119 Monte Vista Avenue, Ridgewood,
New Jersey 07450, USA

Donny White
Medicine Hat Museum and Art Gallery,
1302 Bomford Crescent, Medicine Hat,
Alberta T1A 5E6, Canada

Nicholas Whitman
1251 Northwest Hill Road, Williamstown,
Massachusetts 01267, USA

Kesler E. Woodward
Department of Art, University of Alaska, Fine
Arts Complex, PO Box 755640, Fairbanks,
Alaska 99775–5640, USA

Chris B. Wooley
Chumis Cultural Resource Services, 2073
Dimond Drive, Anchorage, Alaska 99507,
USA

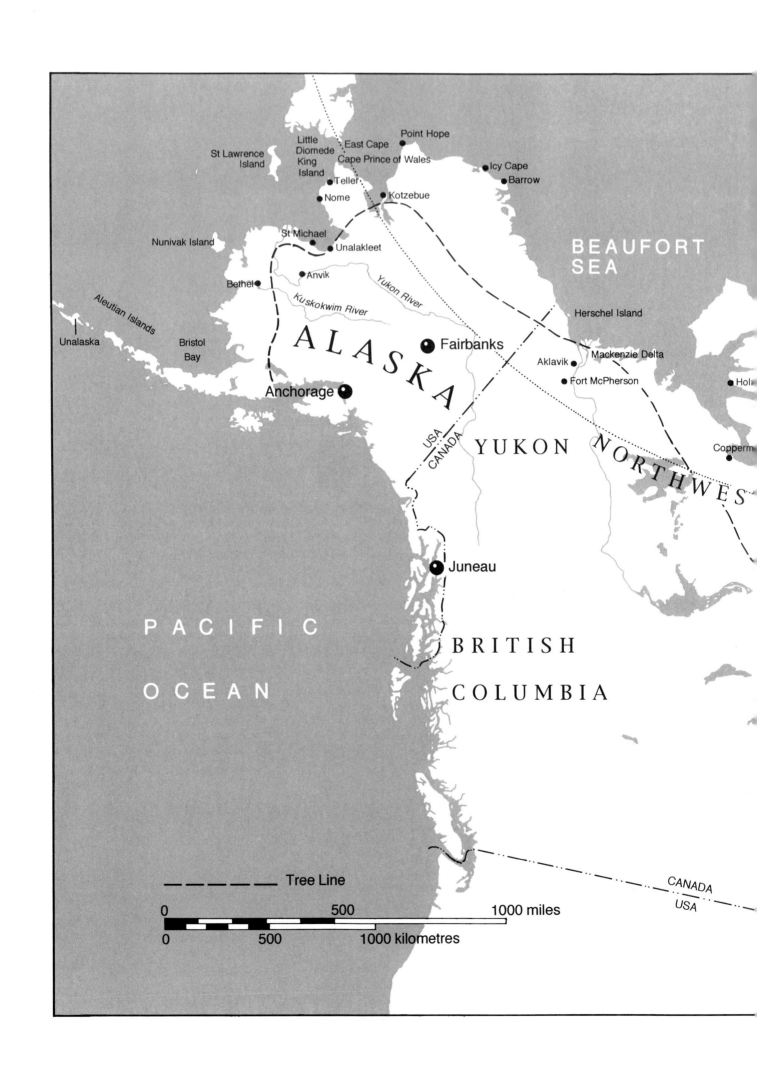

Point Hope

East Cape
Little
Diomede
King
Island

St Lawrence
Island

Cape Prince of Wales

Icy Cape

Barrow

Teller

Nome

Kotzebue

BEAUFORT
SEA

Nunivak Island

St Michael

Unalakleet

Bethel

Anvik

Kuskokwim River

Yukon River

Herschel Island

Aleutian Islands

Unalaska

Bristol
Bay

A L A S K A

Fairbanks

Mackenzie Delta

Aklavik

Fort McPherson

Hol

Anchorage

Y U K O N

N O R T H W E S

Copperm

USA
CANADA

Juneau

B R I T I S H

C O L U M B I A

P A C I F I C

O C E A N

CANADA

USA

– – – – – –  Tree Line

0                          500                          1000 miles

0            500         1000 kilometres

J. C. H. King and Henrietta Lidchi

# Introduction

The Inuit of the Arctic are capable of adopting new changes. Our ancestors and ourselves have been able to adapt to new surroundings and changes. Photography is no exception . . . During our grandparents' time there were few photographers from other countries coming to our land. Our grandparents themselves had no use for cameras, let alone having any idea what a camera was all about. As I interviewed some of the elders and asked about photographs, and what they think of them, they talked to me with great interest. Whenever they see an early photograph they talk about how time flies, and how much our culture has changed. They often start telling stories relating to the photograph. I find that when elders talk about photography they are really talking about their parents and their grandparents. They often wonder if there are any photographs of them.
(Qulaut, this volume)

The Photograph does not necessarily say *what is no longer*, but only for certain *what has been*. This distinction is decisive. In front of a photograph, our consciousness does not necessarily take the nostalgic path of memory (how many photographs are outside of individual time), but for every photograph existing in the world, the path of certainty: the Photograph's essence is to ratify what it represents. (Barthes 1984: 85).

This volume is concerned with the visual image and principally, but not solely, with still photography in the North American Arctic. Through this means it addresses many of the more recent ways in which a region and its inhabitants have been visually constructed and how these representations arise out of and relate to different fields of knowledge. In essence, then, what is being considered is the manner in which the visual *image*, intentionally or unintentionally, has utilised and contributed to the way in which the Arctic as a social, cultural and geographical space has been collectively and subjectively *imagined*.

The above quotations from Qulaut and Barthes focus attention on the significance and richness of photographs as an archival source for public and private memories – histories and reminiscences. In so doing they do not discuss photography by concentrating on the much debated link between reality and its representation, but choose instead to address positively the value of photographs through highlighting the articulation between photographs and memory. Barthes in his dialectic, subjective and influential essay on photography, *Camera Lucida* (1984), argues for a recognition of the objective and physical presence of photographs. For Barthes, as for Qulaut, the significance of photographs is located in their capacity to fix a moment and thus offer some degree of certainty – to act as a category of record of a pre-existing 'reality' or 'fact', a relationship which is analogous to that between oral myths and their written transcriptions. Yet the ambivalence, and the potential for interpretation, of photography lies in its ability to exceed this ascribed perfunctory role. Photographs do not simply recapture or re-present a former moment signifying certainty or 'the triumph of stasis over flux' (Pinney 1992: 165). They undertake this function while persistently refusing to reveal greater complexities (as transcriptions fail to adequately convey the fullness of myth), most particularly, for example, the context or the conditions of their production.

Qulaut's statement illustrates how the verisimilitude of photographs encourages webs of memories to be spun around them. On entering the social arena they have substantial performative value because, as archival keys, they may cue

Fig.1. Labrador Inuit women.

Fig.2. George Quviq Qulaut addressing the conference on the first day.

collective or personal memories. But the act of recollection or recapturing is neither wholly satisfactory nor complete. Like the individual or collective memories they often mobilise, photographs never comprehensively elucidate nor perfectly reclaim the original moment of creation. Their meanings need not be fixed. Those events depicted in photographs and replayed as memories can only ever be partially recalled (Lippard 1992a: 14). So photographs are interpreted and invested with meanings which evolve as the consequence of the interplay of competing and complementary narratives, of different categories of memories – communal histories and personal reminiscences. And it is precisely for these reasons that photographs are enthralling and seductive objects, the polymorphous and formative matter of myths and memories.

The essays in this collection seek to work through the connections between image and imagination, photography and memory. The majority of them were first presented at a conference entitled *Imagining the Arctic: The Native Photograph in Alaska, Canada and Greenland*, organised by the British Museum's Department of Ethnography (Museum of Mankind) in London in April 1996.

This conference was initially inspired by the images and imagination of the pioneering turn-of-the-century artist Geraldine Moodie. Moodie was already a successful professional photographer by the time she arrived at Cape Fullerton in the eastern Arctic in 1904. Here she created some of her most arresting and affecting images. Establishing her studio on board ship, Moodie took a series of photographs, a large number of which were of women wearing fully beaded inner parkas. She sent an album of her work to the library of the British Museum under the terms of the Copyright Deposit programme then in operation.[1] Subsequently, the album was transferred to the Department of Ethnography in the British Museum. By 1987 there had been some scholarly interest in the album,[2] but in the same year, while researching in the pictorial archive in the Department of Ethnography, George Qulaut came across a photograph that he recognised as being that of his grandmother Odelle Panimiraq, identified by Moodie as Koo-tuck-tuck. This interest and discovery prompted a re-evaluation of the significance of this album. In turn, the seeds of an idea for a conference were sown. This would be devoted to discrete collections of photographs of the Arctic. As a keynote speaker at this event, George Qulaut used memories of his grandmother as a point of departure not only to question the importance of historic photographs

of the Arctic but equally to examine contemporary photographic practices.

It was decided that the image of Koo-tuck-tuck would be used for the poster. This portrait brought together the various themes of the conference, because it can be thought of in a variety of ways. As a record, it is a testament to Moodie's presence in Cape Fullerton. As an image, it documents the style and intricacy of the beadwork on the inner parkas worn by Inuit women at the time.

But, clearly, the value of the photograph exceeds this role. This photograph is only one constituent element of a larger album, which, when viewed in its entirety, builds a familiarity with the eye and the skill of the photographer and hints at the degree of intimacy between Moodie and her sitters. The album, on being rediscovered, has acquired a heightened social value in changed circumstances. It has provoked a distinct set of communal and personal memories which have been reclaimed and recorded as a consequence (Qulaut, this volume; Eber 1994). Furthermore, by virtue of the pose and Koo-tuck-tuck's provocative stance, the photograph lends itself to a semiological reading. Raising the curtain, she appears to be tempting the viewer to enter into some deeper recesses of the image. Koo-tuck-tuck seems to be signalling that what we see is *not* all there is, but that there are further, as yet undisclosed, truths lying beyond the curtain and behind the image.

The task of this volume is not that of defining what makes certain types of photography ethnographic, nor of reassessing the relationship between photography and ethnography (Edwards 1992b), nor again of determining new ways of seeing through reshaping photographic practice (Edwards 1997). It acknowledges that the debate concerning the 'politics of representation' has revolutionised the manner in which photographs are received and discussed, affecting all those interested in photography, intellectually and practically. The volume approaches photography from a position that recognises that photography can be cast as a vehicle of truth or meaning, but equally that it is a technology used to construct certain kinds of truths about certain categories of persons (Sekula 1986; Tagg 1988; Green 1984, 1986). Whether photography is characterised primarily as a governmental technology used by the powerful on the powerless – to inform and oppress (and fetishise) (Alloula 1986; Graham-Brown 1988) – or as part of an ongoing semiological process in which conflicting and complex meanings are constructed, the end result is a 'foregrounding' of its ambivalences. Though a realist interpretation of photography can no longer be sustained, the seduction and the challenge of photography are nevertheless articulated around its invitation to be taken literally. This promise of verisimilitude is, perhaps, most potent with historical photographs which tantalisingly promise to represent the past, disclosing long-forgotten details or vanished constituent aspects of it. Paradoxically, however, it is precisely with historical photographs that the dislocations are most resonant, though it should not be assumed that these are any less pertinent to the production and consumption of contemporary photographs. Photographs do not simply scoop up raw data from the world, transfer it onto a photographic plate and serve it up to a passive recipient. Photographs communicate and circulate, they consequently require and mobilise frameworks of knowledge and interpretation (Bush & Mitchell 1994; Fleming & Luskey 1993; Silversides 1994). As Barthes indicates, one of the means through which they achieve this is by navigating temporal and spatial dislocations (Edwards 1992a: 7). Photographs are of the past, but they function in the present. The potential temporal and cultural disjunctions between the photographer and the critical reader compound the possible cultural distances between the photographer and the subject.

These essays in their various ways seek to determine, however partially, the nature of cultural work occurring within the frame, to ascertain the conditions under which photographs have gained or gain meaning and relevance, as well as seeking to uncover the distinctive view and ambitions of the individual photographers. Inevitably, these critical readings of bodies of photographs must take into account two centres of gravity, two sets of conditions of interpretation: those operative for the photographs at the time when they were taken, and those which operate today. If the image of Koo-tuck-tuck is taken as an example, it is clear that a fuller reception of this photograph is only possible in the present, when it is informed by a retroactive understanding of its conditions of production, of the life history of the photographer (White, this volume) and the sitter (Qulaut, this volume). The reader's appreciation is altered by Qulaut's paper, by the knowledge of what happened after the picture was taken. The photograph ceases to be an icon and is transformed into a partial (subjective and incomplete) record which serves to fix a fleeting encounter in two women's lives (Clifford 1986).

Though most of the essays here are concerned with historical photographs, this is never fuelled by a desire to establish a mythical past in relation to a present, nor to take what Barthes calls 'the nostalgic path of memory'. In each case the papers take on the certainty that the photographs under investigation describe a certain kind of event, that they encapsulate a grain of truth, but that this alone is not sufficient. Rather they attempt to situate the photographs within their sociopolitical contexts and alongside texts produced contemporaneously with them. As Edwards (1992a: 5) notes, 'context is, as with any historical source, crucial to the interpretation of photographs. It is not necessarily always definitive, but certainly provocative and suggestive.' Thus the papers delineate certain routes of understanding and suggest some of the possible journeys that can ease the path of interpretation. By bringing into focus the networks of knowledge that can be mobilised in and through the visual image, the various essays delineate the type of work needed to elucidate the social, cultural and political contexts in which photographs are situated and the diversity of perspectives that can be adopted to analyse them. As a whole, then, this volume allows photographs to emerge not as objective documents or vehicles of meaning so much as rich, ambiguous and embedded cultural products.

This volume does not claim to take an unusual view of the visual image, but it is unusual in its focus. Although there are many volumes which address the content and context of representation of native North Americans (for instance, Bush & Mitchell 1994, Lippard 1992b, Fleming & Luskey 1993 and Silversides 1994, to mention a few), there has not, up to the present, been a publication that has dealt solely with historic images of the Arctic. There are good reasons for dedicating a volume to this topic. In most of the history of native/non-native relations in the Americas, a dialectic has existed between metropolitan and frontier attitudes. For the urban intellectual the Indian has since the sixteenth century been a child of nature, a *naturel*, if not a noble savage or woodsman. In contrast, on the frontier moving west, Anglo-American colonisers lived in daily contact with people of whom they were rightly or wrongly frightened, if not for reasons of violence then because of perceived cultural and racial differences. Andrew Jackson, the soldier and politician most responsible for the removal of the eastern Indians, justified his attitude by the regular Indian killings of white settlers in and around Nashville, the Tennessee settlement to which he first moved in 1788. Indians as savages were for him barbarians, not noble, and not merely uncivilised, but without religion and morality.

In the United States romantic notions of the Indians re-emerged in the first half of the last century with Fenimore Cooper's leatherstocking tales, set in upper New York state, half a century or less after most of the Iroquois had been dispossessed. The other pattern, of fear, hatred and violence on the frontier, also re-emerged slightly later in the trans-Mississippian west, with corresponding stereotyping in popular literature, Wild West shows, and the eventual creation of evolutionary schemes to underpin racial attitudes. Romanticism, after the Indian engagements on the Plains in 1862–90, slowly re-established itself in the US, but around different images – especially that of the dying Indian, the last of his race, defeated by social evolution. For Eskimoan peoples there were no equivalent cycles of violence and romanticism, no clash between the urban and frontier understanding of Arctic peoples. Instead, the Eskimo was usually a heroic figure, frequently a helper and provider of food, never a hostile. In the north the symbiosis between native and non-native was particularly marked in guiding and interpreting in the fur trade, and before that in whaling. In the south, following initial contact with Indians, which included war, the provision of interpreters and help with subsistence, what remained was the process of treaty-making and inexorable settlement. In a very real sense native

peoples in the Arctic remained noble savages in a way that American Indians did not (Fienup-Riordan 1995: 8–9). There was no comparable 'fall from grace'. One consequence of this is that representation of Arctic peoples concentrated, perhaps more usually than for Indians, on the exotic, and on the use of ethnicity for the maintenance of distance.

The Arctic also, for reasons of geography, climate and history, emerged in the public imagination long after the rest of North America. In part this was because European involvement in the Arctic remained important – in Alaska until 1867, the Canadian Arctic until 1880, Labrador until 1949, and in Greenland until even more recently. It was also the last part of the Americas, apart from the Amazon, to be explored by Europeans or Americans. In a real sense the Arctic and its peoples were not part of North America until recently, and in a more general sense the Arctic functioned as a separate space in the Euro-American imagination. It also presented a distinct set of challenges and possibilities to the photographer relating both to climate and exploration (Condon 1989). Perhaps nowhere else in the world is there a single people – the speakers of Inupiaq-Inuktitut living from Bering Strait to east Greenland – spread through three countries with diverse histories. This analogy can be extended, of course, to suggest that Eskimoan peoples living from East Cape, Siberia, to Greenland, once part of the European Union, inhabit three continents. Whichever way this is regarded, the conference organisers believed that the unifying principles of the Arctic and photography would serve to ensure a varied series of presentations and essays contrasting Arctic representations with those of not only other native north Americans but also, by implication, indigenous peoples everywhere.

At the planning stage it was decided that the criteria for inclusion in the conference *Imagining the Arctic: The Native Photograph in Alaska, Canada and Greenland* should be generously interpreted so that those who demonstrated an interest in the photographic image and the Arctic could hopefully be accommodated. The conference wanted to bring together a variety of practitioners and professionals while allowing them the freedom to focus on and discuss a topic which seldom occupies centre stage. Indeed, the wealth of interest that this initiated made eventual selection a more difficult task than the organisers were prepared for. The broad scope was partly fuelled by the belief that a conference should provide a means for native and non-native participants who had different levels of engagements with images

– archivists, researchers, museum curators, photographers, community development workers and others – to come together and share information and understandings. The conference had a substantial historical focus, reflecting perhaps the wealth of archival sources of Arctic images that have yet to be comprehensively researched or published. But the conference was not confined to historical images or, indeed, to those in public collections. The book is greatly enhanced by the inclusion of the work of outstanding contemporary photographers (Hess, Keenainak, this volume) and very fortunate to be able to publish photographs from family albums (Norbert, Qulaut, this volume), though other visual images featured in this volume do come from a number of public and archival sources across the United States, Canada and Europe. Furthermore, it was decided that in order to benefit from this ninety-strong gathering of enthusiasts and specialists, participants should write succinct presentations to allow adequate space for discussion. The conference encouraged active participation from the audience, a self-selecting group of interested parties from equally diverse backgrounds who did not hesitate to pursue, extend and return to the issues that were raised in the presentations. The success of this format and the importance of these formally allocated sessions were demonstrated in the acuity and expansiveness of the debate.

The volume's organisation in part reflects that of the conference: different parts of the volume correspond to the different sessions that formed the conference. The discussions are transcribed in shortened form in the Appendix. Since each paper illustrated a number of themes and could, frequently, have been included in a number of different sessions, the ordering principles were quite broadly defined. Predictably, perhaps, the trajectory of the conference was one of narrowing down. The initial presentations were broad sweeps, historical overviews of Arctic photography, moving onto historical papers which were more focused, considering the work of particular groups of photographers, then proceeding to the work of individual photographers, before finishing with a more discursive focus and the contemporary work of Bill Hess and Simeonie Keenainak. This was one axis of selection, the other was geographical. Within the conference there was a greater degree of concentration on the eastern Canadian Arctic, with which the Museum has been associated – through acquisitions of Inuit art and material culture – for 250 years. Other contributions focused on the western Canadian Arctic, Alaska and to a much lesser extent Greenland.

Fig.3. Eileen Norbert addressing speakers during a discussion session. (Photographer: Stephen Hendrie)

The history of Arctic photography was introduced by three speakers, each with a different focus. Pamela Stern provided an overall view of photography in the western Canadian Arctic, referring in particular to images of the Copper Inuit. Nicholas Whitman spoke about photography in the eastern Arctic from an American perspective and his presentation carried the burden of detailing technological changes in photography. Douglas Wamsley examined the uses of photography during public and privately financed expeditions of the mid-nineteenth century, providing a necessarily brief, but comprehensive, overview of early Arctic photography.

Historical case studies also featured prominently. Jim Burant described the important role of photography in official Canadian expeditions and in the establishment of sovereignty at the beginning of this century. J. C. H. King introduced the work of private photographers in the commercial employment of the Hudson's Bay Company. In his contribution, which considered the context of the Western Arctic, William Fitzhugh described the work of Edward Nelson, who may be counted as the first Alaskan photographer and whose work set the scene for the Smithsonian's northern endeavours. Other historical case studies were provided by Ann Christine Eek who discussed the photography of the private explorer Roald Amundsen, lending the proceedings a Scandinavian perspective. Donny White contextualised the studio work of Geraldine Moodie, examining it as a narrative distinct from, but closely linked to, the male world of expedition photography. Kesler Woodward introduced the persuasive promotional uses to which the work of the anthropologist Stefansson and his colleagues was put.

Missionary endeavours provided a separate

Fig.4. The follow up to the *Imagining the Arctic* conference. Zebedee Nungak, President of the Makivik Corporation, with a photograph of Inuit at the Hudson's Bay Company Post at Ft. Chimo (Kujjuak), Northern Québec, taken by Lucien Turner (Smithsonian Institution) in 1883–4. (Photographed at the National Anthropological Archives, Smithsonian Institution, December 1996. Photographer: Stephen Loring)

category of case studies and perspectives on the Arctic image. Stephen Loring, in his paper, explained the importance of photography to the Moravians during their fund-raising work for Labrador missions in nineteenth-century Europe. Peter Geller detailed the use that Archibald Fleming had for photography in the creation and building of the Anglican Arctic diocese early in this century, highlighting the missionary role in the circulation of popular images of the Arctic.[3]

Indeed, the role of popular culture was taken up by others who considered the relationship between the moving image – film and video – and still photography. Robert Christopher contextualised Robert Flaherty's later cinematic work by examining his initial ideas about Indians and Inuit as voiced in his early diaries and shown in his photographic images. Henrietta Lidchi explored the work of several European photographers involved in the production of the 1932 German/American feature film *SOS Eisberg*, to posit connections between filmic and photographic images. The connection between photography and other visual images was explored by Dorothy Eber who detailed the use of laboriously posed images in the graphic work of Peter Pitseolak at Cape Dorset. Alan Marcus considered the iconic value of an image produced in *Life* magazine as a vantage point from which to explore the relationship between the suffering of the Ahiarmiut and their public image.

If the papers mentioned above were intended to reveal the 'hidden histories' of categories of photographs (Edwards 1992a: 13), other papers looked at the 'hidden motives' of the photographer, detailing their motivation in the light of their personal histories. Molly Lee's account of the work of Gladys Knight Harris allows the reader to develop an understanding of a personal

attempt to appreciate the lives of Inupiat women in Kotzebue. In her paper Inge Kleivan considers the work of the first Greenlandic photographer, John Møller, who, in contrast to the work of the Alaskan photographers, also portrayed numerous non-natives. Contributions that focused on a native perspective and drew substantially from family albums included a presentation by Chris Wooley and Karen Brewster on Inupiat photographer Marvin Peter at Barrow. The work of Charles Menadelook in the Bering Strait region was presented by Eileen Norbert, his granddaughter (with Rob Stapleton). These native photographers, with an intimacy arising from their familial and community relations, created images in marked contrast to more formal exoticising images of outsiders, although in a number of respects no less partial. A contemporary perspective was provided by Simeonie Keenainak from Pangnirtung, who contributed an account of the development of his interest in photography and selected images for the exhibition at the Museum of Mankind which coincided with the conference. In speaking of his vision as a photographer, Keenainak also outlined his belief that photography is a means of preserving the past and shaping the future. The conference sought, additionally, to qualify the absolute contrast often drawn between native and non-native photography. This was achieved in a number of ways. In his paper Bill Hess spoke of his own experience photographing Inupiat communities and his vocation of documenting Inupiat whaling culture. Here, a photographer from outside the community manages to create photographs that seem to express an exceptional closeness between photographer and subject.[4]

Distinctions between the exotic image of the outsider and propaganda uses were further questioned by Dorothy Eber and Nelson Graburn in two very different papers.[5] Dorothy Eber showed how native photographs may equally emphasise the exotic, and Nelson Graburn added critical weight to the example provided by Bill Hess: that non-native photographers may record intimate images taken from within the community. Eber detailed how Pitseolak, in addition to producing an intimate portraiture of family, used photography as a means for recording the disappearing present and as a purely technical aid in the presentation of information for watercolours, prints, and engraved ivories. Graburn introduced his own photographs, taken since 1959, with a historical account which in addition indicates the positive, but costly, benefits in continually returning images to the relevant communities. This artificial division was further questioned by

the perspective given on the role of photography in communication by Zebedee Nungak, President of the Makivik Corporation of Quebec. Nungak spoke about the impact of photography throughout the recent history of his organisation, and its cultural arm, *Avataaq*. He emphasised its potential in the future, drawing attention to the political nature of photography and its flexibility, which allowed it to be used for positive and productive purposes within this arena.

The conference discussions (Appendix, this volume) drew on the various themes found in the papers. These included: the role of photographic images in relation to other visual images (Sturtevant); the importance of photographs as a document type in the nineteenth century (Edwards); the role of photography in documenting change (Edwards); the responsibility of archives and public institutions to make their collections accessible to native communities (Fleming); the problem of conservation and preservation of archives (Fleming); and the polysemic nature of photographs (Jonaitis). It is a testament to the positive spirit of collaboration that emerged from the conference that William Sturtevant and Inge Kleivan (Sturtevant & Kleivan, this volume) discovered a common interest and fostered each other's research into what may be the first daguerreotype of an Inuit man (published in this volume). Taken in England in the 1850s, it, as yet, survives only as an engraving.

The conference was opened by a personal account with general relevance as to the importance of photography to the Inuit, and how it can be used in the construction and perpetuation of an Inuit identity. George Qulaut raised a number of issues, which were interwoven with personal reminiscences of his father and grandmother. In closing, other qualities of photography were addressed. Drawing from the conference papers, Hugh Brody emphasised the importance of the aesthetic qualities of photography while questioning their documentary value. He spoke of their silence and unreliability. Photographs draw the viewer in, by disavowing themselves, by existing in a state of verisimilitude. Going beyond the unsatisfactory dichotomies of archival/contemporary and native/non-native, he argued that neither Archibald Fleming nor Zebedee Nungak could be entirely successful in their desires to fix meaning. There could be no guarantee that future generations would read images as their authors originally intended. Brody concluded that, because of their beauty, silence and evasiveness, photographs would inevitably retain the power to mystify, delight, intrigue and compel.

## Acknowledgements

The conference was made possible through a most generous grant from the Eugene V. and Clare E. Thaw Trust of Santa Fe. The conference itself was part of a broader programme of events, also sponsored by the Eugene V. and Clare E. Thaw Trust of Santa Fe, which is leading to the opening of the Chase Manhattan Gallery of North America in the British Museum in 1998.

The photographic exhibition which accompanied the conference was made possible by a separate, much appreciated subvention from Mr and Mrs Morton I. Sosland, through the American Friends of the British Museum in New York. Dr John R. and Lady Romayne Bockstoce generously entertained participants. His Excellency the High Commissioner for Canada, Mr Royce Frith, graciously agreed to make the time to open the conference and welcome the participants. The Canadian High Commission provided assistance at both the opening and the closing of the conference. Robert Anderson, Director of the British Museum, made the final speech and spoke of the interest in photography at the British Museum, referring in particular to the work of Roger Fenton. John Mack, Keeper of the Department of Ethnography, welcomed the participants.

Many members of staff assisted with the organisation of the conference. The help of Hermione Cornwall-Jones, Jim Hamill and Phillip Taylor must be mentioned in particular. Dean Baylis, Jeni Blackmore, Alison Deeprose, Saul Peckham, Harry Persaud, Christopher Power, Frank Stansfield, Simon Tutty and Susan Vacarey all assisted in the preparation and smooth running of the conference.

In the organisation of the exhibition Leah Ottak and John MacDonald (of the Igloolik Research Centre) provided the Inuktitut translations and transcriptions. In the organisation of the conference John Bennett and Jim Taylor from *Inuktitut* magazine were extremely helpful. Thanks are also due to all who attended the conference and gave of their substantial energies to create a very productive intellectual atmosphere, in particular Michael Bravo and Diane Brenner who are not published in this volume.

## Editorial Note

The editors of this volume have not, by and large, sought to alter the ethnic nomenclature used in the papers. In general terms 'Eskimo' is a non-preferred term. It is useful, however, in providing a single term to unify the Yup'ik and Inupiat peoples of Alaska with Canadian Inuit and Greenlanders. It also retains a use in archaeology, as in 'Paleo-Eskimo', and in linguistics, as in 'Eskimo-Aleut'. In Alaskan English 'Inuit' is not a term of self-designation generally employed. However, 'Alaska Inuit' appears in specialised Canadian and European English usage, where it is seen as a useful construct in juxtaposition or contrast to 'Inuit' or 'Canadian Inuit'.

A further difficulty arises in the use of the singular or plural: 'Inuk' and 'Inuit'. In ordinary English 'Inuit' refers both to singular and plural 'person' or 'persons', and this is the sense retained here.

Readers may be struck by the diversity of styles contained in these proceedings, since the contributors are by no means uniform in their approaches to the subject. It is the editors' view that the integrity of the volume lies in the preservation of this heterogeneity, as one of the most positive elements to arise out of the conference was the variety of tones and voices that it contained. The proceedings presented here are true to the delivery and spirit of the conference. In keeping with this view, the volume also contains transcriptions of the discussion texts as an Appendix. These discussion texts are shortened and edited to allow the richness of the debate to surface on paper as it did in discussion.

Notes

1. The images in this album are part of the 2,445 photographs located in the Canadian Copyright Deposit Scheme, *A Checklist of Canadian Copyright Deposit in the British Museum: Volume V Photographs*.

2. Joan Eldridge (Moodie's granddaughter) and Donny White (see this volume) were significant amongst these.

3. Geller (1996) also contributed a review.

4. Other photographers participated in the conference, particularly Bryan Alexander, Jim Barker, Robert Stapleton, Stephen Hendrie, Sisslé Honoré and Christopher Wooley.

5. Graburn contributed reviews of the conference in 1996a.

George Quviq Qulaut

# Imagining the Arctic: Keynote Address

Qujannamiik Inuuqatikka tamaani takujunnarakkit amma qujalijugut aksukallak tamaunga tariuraaluup akianut tikititaujunnaratta.

Well, first of all I want to say thank you very much, and I am very proud to stand here at this moment behind my grandmother. I do not remember her that young, but I do remember her when she was very old. Later on I will show you a photograph of her the way I remembered her.

Before I go on, thank you for making us Inuit feel very welcome here. When I first accepted Jonathan King's invitation to give a presentation on the Arctic photography, I accepted without hesitation, since I would have no problem in talking about Inuit and photography. And that was last December. But after talking about and thinking about the photography and talking to various people from my home community, it was more complicated than I thought. As you may be aware, the Inuit of the Arctic are capable of adopting new changes. Our ancestors and ourselves have been able to adapt to new surroundings and changes. Photography is no exception. At this point I do not know where to begin. I could talk about the first illustrations that the Inuit saw for the first time, and how they felt about it, or the early photography of our grandparents, and how we feel about them today. Or today's photographs, how we use them, how they change our lives or how they hurt us. I could talk about how Inuit feel about the photograph first and themselves as photographers. I would like to touch a little bit on all of these. I am very certain that the rest of the speakers will also discuss them more. Before I go on, I would like to take this opportunity to thank all the elders of Igloolik, from my home community, and the various

people I have interviewed. Without their support and interest I would not have been able to give you the most important part of the information which I will be giving you today.

Today I would like to talk to you about my own personal experience, and the experience of the various people I have interviewed in my home community. I am not able to talk to you about the rest of the communities of Nunatsiaq, the future Nunavut. As you may be aware, the first contact in Igloolik between Inuit and *qallunaat*, which is the white man, was back in 1822 and 1823. During that time there were two wooden ships. My grandfather Itikuttjuk used to tell me stories of these two ships, but that is another story. One of the captains of the two ships was Captain Lyon, and he was a very good artist. He had made some drawings of Inuit at that time and they were engraved. One of the Inuit he had drawn was Takalikitak. About half a century later an explorer by the name of Charles Francis Hall came to Igloolik. He showed some of these drawings to the Inuit. One Inuk, Usuk, recognised her father, Takalikitak, who had passed away some years earlier. To me that could be one of the first pictures that the Inuit had seen. I could easily relate to how she had felt at that time when she had seen her father's picture. For I have been in a similar situation. My father died when I was young, and I recall clearly how I felt when I first saw a photograph of my father ten years later. It struck me a second time when a friend of mine ten years later showed me another photograph of him in Copenhagen. He showed me slides of my father taken the year I was born. Viewing the photographs and slides made me relive my boyhood years with my father. It was very emotional.

During our grandparents' time there were few

photographers from other countries coming to our land. Our grandparents themselves had no use for cameras, let alone having any idea what a camera was all about. As I interviewed some of the elders and asked about photographs, and what they think of them, they talked to me with great interest. Whenever they see an early photograph they talk about how time flies, and how much our culture has changed. They often start telling stories relating to the photograph. I find that when elders talk about photography they are really talking about their parents and their grandparents. They often wonder if there are any photographs of them. They ask if they could obtain copies. At this point I start wondering where I would look. The first place of course for me to find them would be at the Canadian National Archives, but they are very limited. I often think of the other photographers that were here before. These people were traders, missionaries, teachers and scientists and other people who had gone through Igloolik over the years. If I find some of these people I wonder if they would be willing to share their photographs with the people of Igloolik.

Today photographs are widely used in our community. I think in almost every Inuit home there are photographs of their loved ones. These photographs may be of their loved ones who had passed away, or of their relatives and families – very few scenic pictures. In Attagulatuk school hallway we have a very good collection of old and new photographs. These photographs are of people well known in our community who are no longer with us, and pictures of our elders of today. Whenever elders come to the school they use these pictures to show the youngsters their relatives, and to illustrate how much our culture has changed and how camps and communities change. My generation used the camera more on hunting trips to photograph places of importance to us or favourite hunting and fishing camps. Wild life is of course another favourite subject. We often take pictures of social events, especially during Christmas and Easter. I think cameras are used more during the spring and summer camping trips, when whole families are able to travel. I think older Inuit have different ideas about what to photograph. They would want to photograph an elder or a relative who is visiting from another community, or a hunter going on hunting trips to show how he hunts. They have other views about which animals to photograph. They would want to photograph polar bears rather than birds, seals, walrus or whales that a *qallunaat* or person of my generation might photograph, because polar bears are mystic.

I don't think I will talk to you so much of what non-Inuit photographers would want to photograph, since we have seen their work and of course we will hear from them tomorrow and the following day. Mind you, their contribution is greatly appreciated by the Inuit. Their publications are widely used in schools and cultural centres. I would very much like to thank most of the Arctic photographers who are no longer with us and a few who are with us today. They have helped us realise how important our culture is. They have created a visual image of our traditional culture which we now appreciate and use. But some photographers have hurt us very much, so much so that they have changed our lifestyle. These photographs are of seals being slaughtered off the coast of Labrador. We would never skin an animal which is half dead. To do such would bring us harm. They present an image which is not true, they have harmed us spiritually as well as economically. They are photographs that are shown out of context and do not convey the deep respect that the Inuit have for all living things.

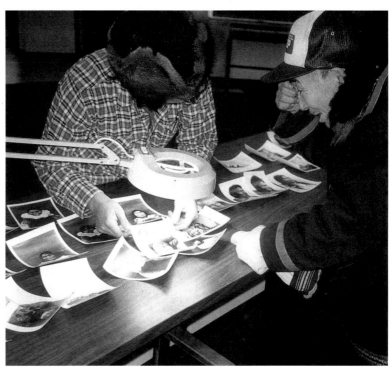

ABOVE LEFT
Fig.4. That's my wife Pat, who is here with us today, and our daughters Claire and Renée.

LEFT
Fig.5. This picture is approximately fifteen years old, a picture of my grandfather Itikuttuk and a friend of his by the name of Qungasiriktuq who came to Igloolik by snowmobile from Arctic Bay, which is approximately 400 miles away.

ABOVE
Fig.6. These photographs I have collected from the National Archives of Canada in Ottawa. I had some elders with me, and this is me with the cap on the left hand side with an elder, Joe Tasiuq, trying to identify some of these photographs. To them it's a great joy to see old photographs and trying to recognise and bring memories back. (Photographer: John MacDonald)

Fig.7. Canada Day
Celebrations: Rosie
Iqalijuq and Yvonne
Ujaralaaq.

TOP
Fig.8. This is our
daughter. It's quite
interesting that
Jonathan had taken a
similar suit to that my
daughter was wearing,
and I think it is here
in the Museum.

ABOVE
Fig.9. My aunt
Qillaq, who's now in
her seventies, in her
house.

OPPOSITE
Fig.10. Spring fishing
at Naluqqajarvik.
(Photographer: Pat
Qulaut)

Fig.1. Engraving of
Kallihirua after a
daguerreotype,
published in Prichard
(1855).

William C. Sturtevant and Inge Kleivan

# Two Early Photographs
# of an Inughuaq (Polar Eskimo)

One result of the conference 'Imagining the Arctic' was the rediscovery of the contexts for what may be the earliest photographs of an Inuk, which were taken in England rather than in the Arctic. In this case the traveller was not the photographer, but rather was the subject in the photograph. Furthermore, the Inuk man in the photograph was himself almost a missionary.

At the conference William Sturtevant showed photocopies of an engraved portrait, after a photograph, suggesting that it might represent the earliest known photograph of an Eskimo. The engraving, captioned 'Kallihirua (An Esquimaux.)' (fig.1), was published in the 1855, fourth (posthumous) edition of James Cowles Prichard's *The Natural History of Man*, as edited and enlarged by Edwin Norris. The depiction is one of sixty-two hand-coloured steel engravings in this edition that illustrate non-European types or, as Prichard's subtitle has it, 'the modifying influence of physical and moral agencies on the different tribes of the human family'. According to a statement added in brackets by Norris (p.518), 'the plate opposite is the portrait of a young Esquimaux, now a student at 'S. Augustin's' College in Canterbury. It is copied from an excellent photograph which was taken for this work.' The plate does not appear in the third, 1848, edition of Prichard's work.

The portrait of Kallihirua illustrates a short chapter by Prichard which summarily describes the distribution and physical type of the Inuit, especially by means of a misleading description quoted (pp.517–18) from Charlevoix's history of New France (1761), which says that, of all the peoples of America, these best meet the standard European idea of 'sauvages', particularly since the men have full beards that cover their faces up to

their eyes: 'They are fierce, wild, suspicious, agitated, always inclined to do harm to strangers.' But Kallihirua is shown as a clean-shaven young man with black hair and tan skin, neatly dressed in a white shirt, black tie, and black coat and waistcoat – far from the European stereotype of savages or, indeed, from the way Europeans imagined that Inuit appeared. Nearly all Prichard's other illustrations are of people in native dress (and this is the only one that is clearly based on a photograph). Did Norris add this picture simply to fill a gap in Prichard's collection of images or was he implicitly contradicting Charlevoix's description? Or perhaps he wished to illustrate the effects of conversion and an English education. There can be little doubt that Kallihirua was photographed for some such reason.

Inge Kleivan has long possessed an example of this engraving but did not know its source nor that it was based on a photograph. However, seeing the photocopy, she was immediately able to provide the context for the image. The manner in which Kallihirua came to be in England, and what is recorded of his character and personality, again contradict the imaginings of Charlevoix and others. The sources at hand are two articles by Aage Bugge based on materials he discovered during a 1958 visit to Canterbury and in several publications, including a Danish history of Arctic missions published in 1869, translated from a German publication. A very important source on Kallihirua's life is a booklet of sixty-four pages by the Revd T. B. Murray (who was well acquainted with Kallihirua in England), entitled *Kalli, the Esquimaux Christian, A Memoir*. The first edition of the last was published in London in 1856 by the Society for Promoting Christian Knowledge.[1]

Born about 1832 or 1834, Kallihirua was a young man in August 1850, living among a small group of three families of Inughuit (Polar Eskimos) in a summer camp at Cape York, at the southern end of Inughuit territory, when ships of the British naval expedition commanded by Captain Horatio T. Austin arrived. This was one of the early attempts to discover information about the expedition led by Sir John Franklin in search of the Northwest Passage, which had left England in May of 1845 but had not been heard from since early August of the same year. One of Austin's ships was the steamship HMS *Pioneer* (Lt Sherard Osborn), with an engine room that much interested Kallihirua and his relatives when they came aboard for a visit. Another Franklin search expedition under Captain William Penny, with the ships HMS *Lady Franklin* and HMS *Sophia*, joined Captain Austin's search expedition at Cape York. Carl Petersen, the Danish interpreter for Penny, aided Austin's men in communicating with the Eskimos at Cape York. In particular he helped Captain Erasmus Ommanney, in command of the ship HMS *Assistance* in Austin's group, to talk with Kallihirua and his relatives.

Kallihirua was intrigued by the visitors and offered to guide or pilot them to the location just to the north, where HMS *North Star* of the previous year's Franklin search expedition had over-wintered in 1849–50. His family agreed that he should go, partly because there was no one there that he could marry. He was told that he must have his hair cut and be dressed in English clothes provided by the ship's company of HMS *Assistance*. He readily agreed and indicated that he wished to learn English. According to Petersen,[2] he was not at all troubled by leaving his familiar surroundings and did not even say goodbye to his mother and sisters, who were present, behaving as though this departure were perfectly usual. He was called Erasmus York and was taken in hand by Captain Erasmus Ommanney and by a sergeant of marines who began to teach him to speak, read and write English. He seems to have been treated well on board and to have adapted well. The crews of the expeditions' ships, and Petersen, were very impressed by his intelligence and friendliness. He was soon able to help the British to communicate with other Inuit.

The expedition sailed west through Lancaster Sound where they found the first traces of the Franklin expedition at Cape Riley and on Beechey Island, and then overwintered in the ice in Barrow Strait, near the ships under Penny. Returning east in the summer of 1851, Captain Ommanney found the Greenland coast to be iced in, so that it would have been difficult to leave Kallihirua among his own people. In the event, he expressed a wish to go to England with the returning expedition (according to a manuscript in Canterbury cited by Bugge 1965, p.169).

About fifty years later Knud Rasmussen recorded an account from Kallihirua's people that he published under the heading 'When the "Navel" was abducted' – he gives his name as Qalaseq 'navel' in West Greenlandic, whereas the form Kallihirua evidently represents 'the big navel' in Polar Eskimo (North Greenlandic). According to this account, Qalaseq went hunting with another man, leaving his mother and his little brother and sister alone at a bird cliff with auks. One day they saw some human beings, but they turned out to be mountain spirits. A very heavy storm broke out, and they met more mountain spirits.

These strange events foreshadowed something unusual, and in the spring a big ship arrived at Cape York and Qalaseq disappeared with it. Mountain spirits never forebode anything good and it was therefore to be assumed that poor Qalaseq had found his death among the white men. In vain his old mother consulted her helping spirits but she never learned anything about the fate of her son.[3]

The 'abducted' in Rasmussen's title is evidently his own interpretation, which is supported neither by the tradition he reported nor by the contemporary accounts.

It must have been soon after Kallihirua arrived in England that he was portrayed, dressed in the uniform of Captain Ommanney's ship HMS *Assistance*, in an engraving (fig.2) published as the frontispiece to Murray's 1856 booklet, then in Murray's second edition and reprinted in the 1869 Danish history (and probably in the German original), from which it was copied by Bugge (on p.19 of his 1966 article). Below the 1856 engraving appears Kallihirua's signature and the statement 'Aged 18' (the equivalent in the second edition reads 'Aged 17'). Almost certainly this engraving was based on a photograph, now unknown, for it definitely represents the same individual as is shown in the portrait in Prichard, and the depiction of the clothing is much more likely to have been based on a photograph than on a drawing from life. Bugge, who was unaware of the Prichard illustration, thought that a daguerreotype he found in St Augustine's College (reproduced on p.165 of his 1965 article) was another portrait of Kallihirua. However, this last certainly does not represent the same individual depicted in the two portraits of Kallihirua now known. It shows someone else, much older and apparently not an Inuk.

In London the Admiralty and Captain Ommanney entrusted Kallihirua to the care of the Society for Promoting Christian Knowledge, and then in November 1851 to St Augustine's College, a school for Anglican missionaries in Canterbury, founded in 1848. Here he was known as Kalli, and in November 1853 he was baptised under the name Erasmus Augustine Kallihirua, with Captain Ommanney and a daughter of Sir John Franklin among his sponsors. He attended classes daily and made good progress in studying English.

In 1852–3 he helped in the preparation of a 'Greenland-Eskimo Vocabulary, for the Use of the Arctic Expeditions, Published by Order of the Lords Commissioners of the Admiralty'. The introductory notice signed by Captain John Washington RN says (pp.vi–vii):

At the Midsummer vacation, in 1852, Kalli-hirua passed some days with me, and we went partly over the Vocabulary. I found him intelligent, speaking English very fairly, docile and imitative; his great pleasure appearing to be a pencil and paper, with which he drew animals and ships. At the Christmas holidays we revised more of the Vocabulary, but not having leisure to finish it before his return to Canterbury, the Warden of St. Augustine's, the Rev. Henry Bailey, with the assistance of Dr. Rost, Professor of Sanscrit at that College, very kindly undertook to complete it, so that every word has now been revised from the lips of a native.

According to Carl Petersen,[4] Kallihirua 'assisted with preparing an Eskimo dictionary which was to be used by the Belcher Expedition.' However, the words in the vocabulary, with some possible exceptions, are in West Greenlandic, not Kallihirua's North Greenlandic (confirmed by Michael Fortescue, personal communication). It was prepared by two Danish experts on West Greenlandic, P. L. W. B. Platou and K. D. Nøsted, and modelled on John Washington's Labrador Eskimo and English vocabulary published by the Admiralty in 1850.

In Canterbury Kallihirua did not appreciate the English climate – just as most Europeans, then and since, do not appreciate the Arctic climate. A surviving note in his own hand reads as follows (Bugge 1965: 171; Murray 1856: 30):

I am very glad to tell, How do you do, Sir? I been England long time none very well. Very bad weather. I know very well, very bad cough. I very sorry, very bad weather, dreadful. Country very difference. Another day cold. Another day wet, I miserable.
　　Another summer come. Very glad. Great many trees. Many wood. Summer beautiful, country Canterbury.

When Kallihirua expressed a wish to see his relatives again, and to undertake missionary work among them, he was sent in the autumn of 1855 to St John's, Newfoundland, to complete a short course of instruction before being sent to Labrador. However, he fell sick and died in St John's on 14 June 1856.

This story and its cultural and historical contexts are made vivid and meaningful by the combination of images and documentary evidence. Without its caption the image from Prichard would not be recognisable as a portrait of an Inuk. The image with this caption then suggests that European stereotypes of Inuit appearance were less pervasive than one might suppose. The identification provided by Norris confirms that the engraving was based on a photograph, no doubt taken in Canterbury between Kallihirua's arrival there in November 1851 and 1 June 1855, the date of Norris's preface to the fourth edition of Prichard. The note by Norris in turn leads to the evidence on Kallihirua's biography found by Bugge at St Augustine's College. The picture of Kallihirua with the cap of his HMS *Assistance* uniform can then be dated to 1851, before he went

Fig.2. Engraving of Kallihirua published in *Missionen i Nordpolarlandene* (1869; see note 1).

to Canterbury, and related directly to his reception and service aboard that ship. Since he was from Greenland, some of the important sources are in Danish. Other sources are in British naval and missionary records. Obviously, further research would yield more information on Kallihirua and the contexts of the portraits of him, and may yet uncover the actual photographs that lie behind the two engravings.[5]

Photographs and other depictions are evidence of both the culture and history of those who produced them and the culture and history of those who appear in them, as well as on the historical circumstances they share. Photographs (and engravings based directly on photographs) are usually less distorted and biased representations of ethnographic and historical reality than are drawings and paintings done directly from the life. Yet paintings may nevertheless be more indicative of psychological reality, and here a fine oil portrait of Kallihirua, full-face and profile, by an unknown artist, in the National Maritime Museum, Greenwich, speaks quite directly to the modern observer.[6] But every image, and the presentation of every image, exhibits some bias, subtle or obvious. To elucidate these biases and stereotypes, it is useful to consider the contexts of the image. Who is represented? Why, when, where and by whom was the photograph taken? How was the subject posed and dressed or re-dressed? Why was the image preserved and diffused, rather than lost or hidden? Not all these questions regarding the images of Kallihirua can as yet be answered, but as this conference demonstrated, the relevant contexts for historical photographs may be illuminated by discussions among specialists with diverse interests, backgrounds and languages.

## Notes

1. Aage Bugge, 'Kallihirua: Polareskimoen i Canterbury' (Kallihirua: A Polar Eskimo in Canterbury), *Grønland* 13 (5): 161–75, 1965, and 'Polareskimoen i Canterbury: Supplerende Oplysninger vedr. Kallihirua' (A Polar Eskimo in Canterbury: Supplemental Information about Kallihirua), *Grønland* 14 (1): 17–22, 1966. The Danish history of Arctic missions is *Missionen i Nordpolarlandene*, Kjøbenhavn, Foreningen til gudelige Smaaskrifters Udbredelse, 1869. No author or editor for this last is mentioned in the work itself; the title page says it is translated from German. The probable original, of which we have not yet located a copy, is *Die Mission in der Polarländern* (*Missions-Bilder*, vol.5), Calw and Stuttgart, J. F. Steinkopf, 1867, 119 pp., woodcuts. The only copy of Murray 1856 we have located is in the National Library of Canada (reproduced as CIHM/ICMH Microfiche 38903). A second, undated edition (from the same publisher) in the Cambridge University Library was brought to our attention by Ann (Savours) Shirley.

2. Carl Petersen, *Erindringer fra Polarlandene optegnede af Carl Petersen, Tolk ved Pennys og Kanes Nordexpeditioner 1850–1855*, udgivne af Lauritz B. Deichmann (Memories from the Polar Regions written by Carl Petersen, interpreter on Penny's and Kane's Northern Expeditions, 1850–1855, edited by Lauritz B. Deichmann), Kjøbenhavn: P. G. Philipsens Forlag, 1857, pp.35–6; quoted in Bugge 1966: 18.

3. Knud Rasmussen, *Myter og Sagn fra Grønland, III: Kap York-Distriktet og Nordgrønland* (Myths and Traditions from Greenland, III: The Cape York District and North Greenland), Kjøbenhavn: Gyldendalske Boghandel Nordisk Forlag, 1925, pp.138–9.

4. Carl Petersen, *Den sidste Franklin-Expedition med 'Fox,' Capt. M'Clintock, ved Carl Petersen, Tolk ved Penny, Kanes og M'Clintocks Expeditioner* (The last Franklin Expedition with the *Fox* Captain McClintock, by Carl Petersen, interpreter on Penny's, Kane's and McClintock's Expeditions), Kjøbenhavn: Fr. Wøldikes Forlagsboghandel, 1860, pp.86–7; quoted in Bugge 1966: 20.

5. There is a brief account of Kallihirua by Clive Holland in the *Dictionary of Canadian Biography*, 8, pp.447–8, Toronto, Buffalo and London: University of Toronto Press.

6. Reproduced on pp.340–41 of 'Early Eskimo Visitors to Britain' by Ann Savours, *Geographical Magazine*, 36 (6): 336–43, 1963.

Nicholas Whitman

# Technology and Vision:
# Factors Shaping Nineteenth-Century
# Arctic Photography

A photograph is the product of a combination of diverse elements. The process itself has a strong influence on the look of the photograph. Different types of cameras, film and papers all leave their signature. In addition to the technical influence, there is the person behind the camera. Photographers have different capabilities and different standards of excellence. The photographer has an agenda: an idea to communicate. Every photographer has an 'eye', a way of composing, a personal visual code. This essay examines four photographers who ventured into the Arctic for different reasons but whose work only becomes more interesting as time passes.

Nineteenth-century New Bedford, Massachusetts, was a seafaring centre in the United States. Whaling was the principal reason for this activity, but shipping and trade also contributed to the vitality of the port. Even while the fleet hunted whales around the globe, New Bedford remained home base. When the western Arctic yielded up the bowhead whale in the latter half of the nineteenth century, New Bedford's fleet concentrated on this area. New Bedford-owned vessels sailed from Honolulu and San Francisco, not returning home for decades in some cases. Coincidentally with the push farther and farther north for whales, the medium of photography was being refined.

Introduced in 1839 by Louis Jacques Mandé Daguerre with his process, the daguerreotype, photography fired people's imaginations on both sides of the Atlantic. However, the daguerreotype could only yield consistent results in a controlled studio environment under the direction of a trained professional. Portraiture was its principal use. The daguerreotype process dominated photography during the 1840s but other systems were emerging. In England Fox Talbot devised a process based on a paper negative, the calotype. As with its rival the daguerreotype, it was not practical for field work. The calotype process was slow, inconsistent and produced a very soft image. Business interests attempting to capitalise on the process enforced expensive, restrictive licensing, making the process all but inaccessible. However, from each step in the development of the medium came elements which, when combined, brought it closer to a process that could function efficiently in the field. Daguerre had shown the magic of a sharp image. Talbot had devised a way of producing multiple copies from a single negative. It was now Frederick Scott Archer's turn to contribute to the development of practical field photography by devising a light sensitive emulsion which when coated onto a clear base of glass created a sharp negative. Light-sensitive paper was also devised so the negative could be printed. This reconfiguration of systems converged in the 1850s. The limited field work now possible is exemplified by the Englishman Roger Fenton's views of the Crimean War in 1855. In the United States the Civil War (1861–65) was widely documented by the same method.

Thus, twenty years after its introduction, photography was finally able to take to the field. With the end of the Civil War in 1865, hardened field photographers moved on to photograph the grandeur of the western frontier. Timothy O'Sullivan, William Henry Jackson, and Carlton Watkins were three of the finest photographers of this group. Painters also dealt with the same subject matter. The grandiosity of the land seemed to demand equally grandiose paintings in suitably heavy, ornate, gilded frames. New Bedford painter Albert Bierstadt was a premier artist among this group. While most of America looked west for natural drama, another of New Bedford's successful painters looked north. That painter was William Bradford.

Born in 1823 and raised in Fairhaven, just across the Acushnet River from New Bedford, Bradford grew into adulthood as the port reached its zenith. Despite his well-intentioned parents' attempts to steer him toward the practical pursuits of business or farming, Bradford remained true to his vocation of sketching and painting. As a result, he was able to support himself through his realistic oil paintings of whale ships.

Beginning in 1861, Bradford made summer trips along the cost of Labrador in search of subject matter. In 1869 he chartered the steam bark *Panther* and sailed among the ice floes off Greenland. To ensure success Bradford collaborated with two Boston professional photographers, John Dunmore and George Critcherson. Wet plate was the process they employed. Whereas the war and frontier photographers used a specially equipped wagon to haul their heavy glass plates and serve as the necessary portable dark room, Bradford's travelling darkroom was a ship. Nevertheless, film speed was very slow by contemporary standards, and some exposures were measured in minutes rather than in the fractions of a second currently required. This is a serious deficiency when subjects move or, as in the case of the *Panther*, when the shooting platform itself is unstable. Slow film speeds meant that every negative was made from a tripod-mounted camera. The wet-plate process required that the negative be freshly coated just before use because it had maximum sensitivity when wet. Firstly, a view was composed on the camera's ground glass; secondly, the photographer went to his dark room and prepared a plate; and finally he exposed the plate in the waiting camera. Shooting from a ship in motion at moving icebergs meant that, by the time the camera was set up and the photographer had returned from the dark room with his plate, the scene could be totally different. Thus, it took a conscious team effort to make things work, with Bradford deciding on the compositions while Dunmore and Critcherson handled the cameras and plates. Slow emulsion speeds for the printing paper also meant that enlargements were not possible. If you wanted an 11 × 14 in (28 × 36 cm) print, you had

Fig.2. William Bradford, John Dunmore, George Critcherson, 1869. *Arctic Regions #32.* 'The Glacier as seen forcing itself down over the land and onto the waters of the fjord.'

to coat a sheet of glass that size. Cameras were often custom-made and Bradford's team used several. Negative sizes were not standardised as they are today. Yet another factor affecting the final look of prints from wet-plate negatives is the blankness of the sky. These negatives were hypersensitive to blue light and as a result skies were grossly over-exposed; conversely, red subjects appear too dark.

For all their limitations the team did achieve excellent technical results. With regard to his subject matter Bradford concentrated on two areas: first, he produced a travel log with views of landmarks, ruins, natives and his ship; second, he made many views of dramatic icebergs and the faces of glaciers as they met the sea.

In 1873 his *Arctic Regions* was published in England under the patronage of Queen Victoria. This elephant folio volume is substantial, with its cover of tooled maroon leather and ornate lettering. Accompanying a narrative of the voyage are 125 original photographs each individually mounted in place. Protected by the closed book from light and airborne contaminates, the prints survive to this day in excellent condition. Photographs from the voyage were also sold individually, often in fancy frames. In addition, Bradford used the photographs as the basis for dramatic Arctic paintings. The photographs became a sketch pad for grand compositions.

By the 1880s the hunt for the bowhead whale had taken most of New Bedford's fleet to the shallow seas around Alaska. Unlike open water whaling for sperm whales, bowhead whaling brought the ships close to shore. As whales became scarce whale men pushed further north and east, taking greater risks in the ever dangerous ice. Ships took to overwintering in the Arctic, allowing themselves to be frozen in to get an early start on the next year's season.

The native people along coastal Alaska were greatly affected by the presence of the American whalemen. On the plus side Eskimos worked for the whalers, helping with the hunt and supplying fresh meat for the crews. In exchange they acquired useful items such as metal tools, guns and cloth. There were, however, many abuses, both intentional and unintentional. The bowhead whales, a native staple, became scarce, as did walrus. At Point Hope and other locations starvation resulted. Alcohol and the disruption of traditional family and village systems also brought upheaval, turmoil and grief.

To maintain order and to help mariners in distress, the federal government sent Revenue Cutters to the area. The USRC *Bear* was one of these vessels. She patrolled from 1886 to 1924, and on her 1888 voyage there was a photographer of great skill and sensitivity on board. His name and assignment are unknown. However, through his work it is possible to see that he was systematically documenting all significant buildings and emplacements. He photographed the natives as he found them. He focused on their homes, villages, graves, boats and faces. The whalemen are secondary – rarely evident in this series. The views, mostly stark and desolate, are among the earliest glimpses of the settlements along the

Fig.3. Unknown
photographer aboard
USRC *Bear*, 1887.
'Starved to death near
Cape Thompson,
Alaska.'

Fig.4. Unknown
photographer aboard
USRC *Bear*, 1887.
'Natives and kayaks at
Saint Michaels,
Alaska.'

north-west coast of Alaska. Made just a few years after what Ernest S. Burch has determined to be the end of the traditional period of native life, these photographs give us one fleeting glimpse of the way life had been for centuries and would never be again.

Above all else this series shows the plight that had befallen the native people. The photographs would be convincing evidence of the need for the assistance the Revenue Service helped provide. The photographs could have been used to help justify the Service's mission. Possibly it was hoped that by showing these photographs the need for food caches could be established until natural sources could be replenished. They may have been instrumental in the effort to end the abuse. Much is unknown about this series but we do know it is a clear and systematic document with a sympathetic point of view.

We also know that this anonymous photographer was using dry plates in his camera. Dry-plates were a significant improvement over the wet-plate system. Introduced in the 1880s, they were mass-produced and sold in light-tight boxes, ready for use. Thus it was no longer necessary to set up a darkroom in the field, and plates could be exposed and stored until they were convenient to process. Of course, these were still glass negatives and subject to the disadvantages of glass: specifically weight and fragility. Dry-plates came in standard sizes and equipment likewise became standardised. This photographer used a camera which took a 5 × 8 in (13 × 18 cm) plate which was a good choice for the long horizons of the landscape. The camera was mounted on a tripod, which limits mobility but encourages careful composition. The emulsion speed was still slower than modern emulsions.

Albumen prints were made by contact printing from glass negatives of both the wet- and dry-plate variety. The negative and paper were placed emulsion-to-emulsion in a spring-loaded frame and exposed in sunlight. The paper was then fixed and washed in water. Albumen paper, so named for the egg-white binder within which the light-sensitive silver salts were incorporated, accounts for the majority of nineteenth-century photographs. The paper was a standard, widely available product in the 1880s. This series of prints was mounted on standard photo-finisher's cards. The cards were inscribed with the location of the view. Unfortunately albumen prints are subject to degradation from light, airborne contaminates and improper initial processing, and as objects these photographs were rather crudely made. They have faded, the blacks are soft, and the whites have become so degraded that much highlight information is lost. Nevertheless, so much evidence remains, and so much more hinted at, that one is irresistibly drawn in to peer into the fog and see back through the years.

In 1886 Herbert Aldrich was a twenty-five-year-old reporter for New Bedford's *Evening Standard*. That year his doctor diagnosed him with tuberculosis and informed him he had a year to live. Aldrich took his note book and camera to the western Arctic to spend his final days recording the activities of the whaling fleet. During the summer of 1887 he observed and recorded whaling on several different vessels and was a guest on eight different ships. In the relatively confined area of whaling grounds the ships worked in close proximity to each other. Thus Aldrich was able to photograph a variety of whaleships. As a professional news-gatherer, he was systematic about recording each step of the whaling operation, including taking views of the less glamorous steps of processing the whale. In addition to his journalistic professionalism, Aldrich augmented his glass plates with one of the latest advances in photography: a portable camera.

Aldrich himself described his kit: 'Being provided with a Scoville detective camera, 700 films, and 250 Carbutt plates, I was prepared for all emergencies, and embraced many.' Aldrich processed his film and made prints while still on board ship so he knew he had succeeded. The camera Aldrich used was small, light and portable by nineteenth-century standards. By contemporary standards the camera was a handful. That it was a 'detective camera' simply meant that it was not shaped like a conventional camera. The camera was contained in an unobtrusive box with a hole for the lens and a built-in viewfinder. It could be hand-held. The rig dispensed with the need for a tripod and with the ritual of setting up the camera and going under the focusing cloth to compose the upside-down view on the ground glass. Not only was this simpler but it allowed photography of subjects who were unaware – a 'detective camera'. Of course, for those advantages there were trade-offs. The viewfinder was approximate, thus compositions were less exact. Camera shake and the resultant image degradation were likely unless the scene was well lighted and the operator was careful. The negative was 4 × 5 in (10 × 13 cm). He made prints by contact so they too measured 4 × 5 in. These were mounted on cards, and he created a numbered series. The best of this series was mounted on custom-printed captioned mounts. He evidently attempted to sell these. It is not known in what quantity he succeeded, but many individual, Aldrich card-mounted photographs are found in public and private collections in the United States.

Mostly Aldrich photographed while on board ship but this did not deter him from photographing the many natives who were visitors to the vessels. He described the difficulty of photographing native people and how he accomplished it:

I wanted very much to have a couple pose, that I might photograph them but he declined, saying that I would take his picture and carry it off to another land; then he would have to die and go with it. I meekly accepted his reasoning, which left no room for argument, seated myself on the carpenter's bench, and soon had three fine pictures of him. As he did not understand the mystery connected with the 'click' of my camera, and was unconscious of being photographed, I hope he will not be called upon to follow the picture.

Taking advantage of his portable camera,

BELOW
Fig.5. Black smoke lofts up from the try works as bar *Helen Mar* renders oil from the blubber of a bowhead whale off the northwest coast of Alaska. (Photographer: Herbert Aldrich, 1887)

BOTTOM
Fig.6. The headbone of a bowhead, which has been hoisted aboard a whaling craft *Lucretia*. Two men look on from the cutting stage. Aldrich is either in the whale boat or on the ice photographing. (Photographer: Herbert Aldrich, 1887)

Aldrich was able to break free from his tripod and thus compose views from new angles. To illustrate 'trying out' – rendering the blubber into oil and baleen into processed whalebone – he photographed onto the deck from aloft. Views of 'cutting in' the bowhead whale are made from a whale boat and from the ice looking back at the ship. His views of whale boats hunting were made from high in the rigging of the whale ship. To help compensate for the camera being hand-held, Aldrich used higher shutter speeds which helped to stop motion. For the first time we see men naturally working, rather than posed artificially. The motion of boats and ships is frozen, waves have definition and the black, oily smoke from a ship 'trying out' is sharply rendered. It is easy to take all this for granted because this is the look of modern photography. As distinct from Bradford's images for instance, we count on the camera to stop action so we can consider ethereal subjects such as waves or smoke, but in 1887 this was all uncharted territory. Aldrich appreciated what his equipment was capable of and he exploited it to full advantage.

In the 1880s Aldrich published an account of his experiences in the book, *Arctic Alaska and Siberia, or, Eight Months with the Arctic Whalemen*. Reproductions of several of his photographs are included as illustrations. Herbert Aldrich's trip to the Arctic seems to have been a tonic for what ailed him: rather than dying in the year he lived until the age of eighty-seven.

The fourth and final photographer I present was neither an artist nor reporter nor professional photographer. He was the captain of the whaling schooner *Era*. During the first decade of the twentieth century, as the whaling industry was dying, Comer brought the *Era* to Hudson Bay on several cruises. He would overwinter there and in the spring take several whales, but by this time whales were quite scarce, so to augment his trip Comer traded with the Inuit for the furs of musk-ox, bear, seal, fox and wolf. But Comer's interest in the Inuit went well beyond trade; he was genuinely concerned for the welfare of a people he admired. His trade goods (guns and ammunition, cloth, pots and tools) helped the Inuit people survive. Comer and his ship were an agent of change but he had a sense of history and change, and did many innovative things to make a record of it. Though not formally schooled, he was an enthusiastic anthropologist and trusted field-man for several organisations. For instance, on behalf of the American Museum of Natural History he made sound recordings, recorded oral history, took plaster casts of faces and hands, collected artefacts and made photographs.

Comer principally worked with a $4 \times 5$ in ($10 \times 13$ cm) dry-plate field camera. While he perhaps lagged behind in his use of glass plates fifteen years after the introduction of roll film, it should be noted that glass plates with improved higher-speed emulsions were popular well into the 1920s and beyond. As it has turned out, the supports for all the early flexible-base films have proven at best dimensionally unstable and at worst highly flammable. Properly processed and stored glass negatives are very durable. Thus, for whatever reason, Comer's use of glass-based negatives was fortuitous.

But Comer was not oblivious to technical innovation. He used flash powder to light and photograph dark interiors such as his view of a group of Eskimos in the *Era*'s cabin. In a diary entry for 1 February 1904 he describes a misadventure in flash lighting: 'I took two flashlight pictures but have not developed the plates yet. The first flashlight I probably did not fix right as it came near taking the roof of the cabin off – at least the report sounded loud enough to have done so.'

Comer's interior views were a significant accomplishment. Working in the tight, dark quarters of the ship or snow houses was a technical challenge. But it is his intimacy with the people he photographed at which one can only marvel. In contrast to the ruination that is illustrated in the *Bear* series, through Comer's lens we see the Inuit hunting, building snow houses and, most remarkably, carrying on their family life in their homes (fig.8). Even the spiritually significant shaman's bound rituals are recorded (fig.7). In addition to photographing the Inuit in their own environs, Comer set up a simple studio aboard the *Era*, using a sail as a backdrop, and then posing and making full-length portraits of individuals and small groups. While he appears to be interested in the subject's clothes he also noted the subject's names.

Whereas Bradford, Aldrich and the *Bear* photographer travelled widely and incessantly, Comer, his ship buried in snow, had the long Arctic winter to tinker with photography. There are other differences as well. His photography and other documentation are concentrated in a smaller geographical area and extend over several years. Not only did Comer process his plates aboard ship he also used the new, faster-speed gelatin/silver paper to make prints in his shipboard darkroom. He did experience technical problems including camera shake and poor focusing. Negative and print processing was often sloppy. The new gelatin/silver papers had much greater sensitivity than albumen-coated paper but did require a darkroom for processing. This is

similar to the system used today for black and white photographs. Comer pasted his $4 \times 5$ in ($10 \times 13$ cm) contact prints on mounts. He assigned series numbers which exceed 200, indicating the production of at least that many different images. As with Aldrich, multiple copies were made and distributed.

In the work of these four photographers equipment, process and point of view all figure largely in the resulting photographs. Each group of photographs has a look and feel that is unique. While it is often the case that rather ordinary photographs become meaningful as time passes, one cannot help but find that these photographers anticipated change. Their hard-won successes, made in a difficult environment, with an early technology, stand as primary documents of a rapidly changing Arctic.

Douglas Wamsley and William Barr

# Early Photographers of the Canadian Arctic and Greenland

Fig.1. Daguerreotype of Sir John Franklin prior to his departure for the Arctic, taken by John Beard, May 1845.

## Introduction

This paper examines all the expeditions that are believed to have attempted photography in the Canadian Arctic and Greenland, from the Franklin Expedition in 1845 to the British Arctic Expedition of 1875–6, in terms of their equipment, their problems and their degree of success. During this period Arctic expeditions were sufficiently innovative to utilise the latest available technology, and in many cases successful results were achieved, particularly in Greenland, under difficult circumstances. The results of these early efforts at photography in the Canadian Arctic and Greenland provide an extremely valuable record of the exploration vessels, their crews and equipment, and of Greenlanders and Greenland settlements.

## Sir John Franklin's last expedition

Photography is generally considered to have been born in 1839. In that year the perfecting of the first practical process of photography, the daguerreotype, was publicised by Louis Jacques Mandé Daguerre (Gilbert 1980). The first expedition to the polar regions to include photographic equipment was the ill-fated last expedition of Sir John Franklin, which left England at the height of the popularity of the daguerreotype. Before the departure of HMS *Erebus* and *Terror* from Greenhithe in May 1845 Richard Beard, a popular London photographer, was commissioned to supply the expedition with a complete daguerreotype apparatus for use in the Arctic regions (*Illustrated London News* 1851).

Ironically, the only known images to have been produced by the Beard apparatus are the portraits of Sir John Franklin and his officers taken on HMS *Erebus* at the request of Lady Franklin prior to

their departure. Fig. 1 shows the daguerreotype of Franklin taken by Beard. The Franklin Expedition perished in the Canadian Arctic and it is not known if the apparatus was used, and no photographic plates or equipment have ever been located.

## Sir John Richardson's search expedition, 1847–9

As anxiety over the fate of the Franklin Expedition began to mount, the British government dispatched a series of expeditions in the hope of rescuing Franklin and his crews. In 1848 an overland expedition led by Sir John Richardson descended the Mackenzie river and, travelling by boat, searched the mainland coast from the Mackenzie delta east to the mouth of the Coppermine. Among other things, the expedition was provided with a photographic apparatus by the famous photographer William Henry Fox Talbot (Richardson 1847–8; Levere 1993).

At the time Daguerre announced his process Talbot was experimenting with a different one called the 'calotype' process (Gilbert 1980). In the case of the Talbot calotype process, paper sensitized with silver nitrate and common salt was exposed to light in a camera, thus producing a paper 'negative'. By placing the 'negative' in contact with another piece of similarly treated paper, any number of positive prints could be obtained. The calotype process offered distinct advantages over daguerreotypes for travel photography because the sensitized paper could be chemically treated up to days or weeks prior to exposure.

Although a Talbot calotype apparatus was included in a written list prepared by Richardson of articles required for his searching expedition (Richardson 1847–8), he makes no mention of it

in his published account of the expedition (Richardson 1851). The added weight of the photographic apparatus may have been deemed excessive, and it may never have left England.

## The Kane expedition

In 1853 Dr Elisha Kent Kane, who had served as surgeon on a previous expedition in search of Sir John Franklin in 1850–51, led his own expedition in search of the Franklin Expedition in the area north of Smith Sound, between Greenland and Ellesmere Island. A daguerreotype apparatus was procured for the expedition (Kane 1856).

Kane selected his friend Amos Bonsall to accompany the expedition and instructed Bonsall to take lessons in producing daguerreotypes. Relatively soon after the expedition's return, on the occasion of Kane's funeral in 1857, Bonsall informed a reporter that it was his belief that his main duty was expected to be the taking of daguerreotypes of Arctic scenery, but that the instrument had not worked (Corner 1972). In his memoirs published years later in 1902, however, Bonsall reported that at the time of the expedition's return from the Arctic the results of his photographic work were left on a sled on the ice which was carried away and lost (Bonsall 1902: 43). Bonsall termed it an 'irreparable loss', which suggested some limited degree of success.

A published letter written by Dr Isaac Israel Hayes, surgeon of the expedition, on 20 July 1853 confirmed that Bonsall did have some success with the photographic equipment while in Greenland. The letter states that while the ships were at Proven, Greenland, on their way northward, Amos Bonsall had the first opportunity to test the daguerreotype equipment (*The Times* 1853). Hayes wrote:

A number of fine pictures have been taken, representing the geological and picturesque character of the country. The difficulties apprehended in the working of the chymicals have been overcome, and Mr Bousalt [sic] confidently thinks that he will be able to take pictures with a great deal of decency, even in the highest latitudes we may reach.

Kane makes at least one reference to the use of the apparatus in his narrative of the expedition. On 31 January 1854 he noted that two attempts were made to photograph the returning sun while at the expedition's winter quarters high in the Arctic. The camera was used indoors to avoid the effects of the cold (Kane 1856, vol.1: 155). How frequently, if at all, the camera was again used is uncertain. But part way through the second winter, in February 1855, Kane had reached the same conclusion as Bonsall (or at least

as Bonsall expressed it in the interview in 1857), namely that the results of their photographic efforts were wholly unsatisfactory. Kane had to settle for using the daguerreotype plates as mirrors to reflect sunlight into his ship, the *Advance* (Kane 1856, vol.2: 46).

Although no definite conclusion can be drawn from the few sketchy details available from the published accounts, and notwithstanding Bonsall's expectations while in Proven, it is quite possible that the low temperatures adversely affected the use of the chemicals and the chemical processes involved in taking daguerreotypes while the expedition was in its winter quarters. Kane's attempt on 31 January 1854 would suggest as much.

## The Belcher expedition

On 24 April 1852 one of the most ambitious of the British search expeditions, consisting of five ships under the overall command of Captain Sir Edward Belcher, was preparing to leave England for the Arctic. While the ships were lying at Greenhithe, Mr Watkins from Mr Beard's photographic establishment took photographic portraits of Belcher and eight other officers on board HMS *Assistance* (*Illustrated London News* 1852a). In addition, the Admiralty had ordered that a calotype apparatus be taken on the expedition; its construction was supervised by Mr William Edward Kilburn, who specialised in both daguerreotypes and calotypes. Dr William Domville, surgeon on board HMS *Resolute*, was responsible for the calotype apparatus (*Illustrated London News* 1852b).

*En route* to its search area the squadron called at Disko on the west coast of Greenland on 5 June to obtain supplies (Belcher 1855). While at Disko Dr Domville noted in his private journal that he unsuccessfully attempted to obtain a photograph of some of the Greenlanders with his calotype equipment; Domville stated that the subjects would not remain motionless for the lengthy exposure time required (Domville 1852–3: 33).

Domville appears to have had greater success with more co-operative subjects, however. The photographic holdings of the National Maritime Museum in Greenwich, London, include two calotypes identified as being by Surgeon Wm. J. Domville of HMS *Resolute*. One depicts an officer seated on a rock (fig.2) and the other a group of three ships anchored in a bay, which is probably in Greenland, rather than in any of the harbours visited by the squadron in what is now the Canadian Arctic (R. G. Todd, personal communication, September 1995). It seems very probable that these photographs were taken by

Domville in the summer of 1852, and thus are of great importance as being probably the earliest known surviving photographs from anywhere in the Arctic. After the above-quoted note about his attempts at photographing Greenlanders, there is no further reference to photography in Domville's journal which, in terms of a continuous account, ends in November 1852.

After pushing north across Melville Bay to Cape York and the North Water, the squadron headed west through Lancaster Sound in the Canadian Arctic to a rendezvous at Beechey Island. Here HMS *North Star* (Commander William Pullen) took up winter quarters and remained as a depot. The other four ships separated into groups of two and continued the search in other parts of the Canadian Arctic. These four ships were later abandoned and their crews returned by sledge to the *North Star* at Beechey Island.

No further references to the calotype apparatus occur in the expedition accounts until August 1854 at Beechey Island. The journal entry of Captain Leopold McClintock for 1 August 1854 reads 'I am practicing with a calotype but am not very successful' (McClintock 1852–4). It seems probable that the calotype apparatus had been transferred from *Resolute* to *North Star* before the two ships went their separate ways in the summer of 1852, and that it had been lying unused on board *North Star* for the intervening two years.

McClintock had retreated by sledge (after abandoning his ship, HMS *Intrepid*) to Beechey Island, arriving at the *North Star* on 28 May 1854. There, a captain without a ship, he no doubt found the time weighing rather heavily and, one must surmise, stumbled on the calotype apparatus and tried his hand at photography, probably with advice and assistance from Dr Domville.

After his first less-than-successful attempt McClintock persevered; by 8 August he reported, 'made considerable progress on the use of the calotype' (ibid), and with practice he became quite proficient; thus on 12 August he noted, 'Got some good calotype impressions of Beechey Island' (ibid). On the 21 August he even tried his hand at portraits, noting that he 'succeeded tolerably well with some calotype portraits' (ibid). McClintock's photographic activity on this date was confirmed by George Ford, carpenter on board HMS *Investigator*, who had sledged to Beechey Island with his shipmates. Ford recorded in his journal on 21 August that 'Capn. McClintock after dinner taking likenesses on deck with a calotype' (Ford 1850–54).

There is no information available as to whether

any of McClintock's portraits have survived, but two photographs now in the possession of one of the authors (Wamsley) are almost certainly two of the landscapes that McClintock photographed. Fig.3 shows HMS *North Star* lying offshore in the ice of Erebus Bay, as seen from behind Northumberland House on Beechey Island. From various lines of evidence provided in the photograph, one can demonstrate that it was almost certainly taken at or on the date on which McClintock reported getting 'some good calotype impressions of Beechey Island' (McClintock 1852–4). Clearly identifiable is the depot or storehouse built by Commander Pullen, named Northumberland House. Work has already begun on cutting a channel in the ice to free the ship, using ice saws and explosives. By 12 August the ship was daily being warped to the end of the section which had just been cut; this appears to be precisely the situation portrayed in the calotype. The channel was completed right out to open

TOP
Fig.2. Calotype of one of the officers of HMS *Resolute*, taken by William Domville, probably in West Greenland, June 1852.

ABOVE
Fig.3. Calotype of HMS *North Star*, Erebus and Terror Bay, from Beechey Island, August 1854, taken by Captain F. Leopold McClintock. Northumberland House is in the foreground.

water on 20 August and *North Star* gained the open water the following day (ibid).

The other surviving calotype shows Beechey Island as seen from the *North Star*. Unfortunately it is not nearly as clear as fig.3. Northumberland House and the surrounding structures, etc. can be distinguished, although not in any detail.

Despite the fact that McClintock's instruction in photography was probably confined to what Domville was able to teach him, he must be congratulated on the quality of fig.3 in particular. As some of the earliest-known photographs from the Canadian Arctic, these two examples of his work are of very special significance.

### Captain Inglefield's photographs, 1854

A further twenty original glass negatives probably dating to 1854 or possibly 1853 of scenes and people in Greenland are held by the National Maritime Museum. They derive from Captain Edward Inglefield's two voyages to Beechey Island in HMS *Phoenix* in 1853 and 1854 to resupply and to help evacuate the Belcher expedition. In that they are glass negatives, the photographer must have been using the 'wet-plate' or 'wet collodion' process, an improvement over the calotype process in terms of print quality.

The wet collodion process used a chemically treated glass plate for the negative rather than paper as in the calotype process. The glass plate was covered with a tough, transparent membrane of fast-drying chemicals called collodion. The process was aptly termed the 'wet-plate' process because the plate had to be exposed within fifteen

minutes after being dipped, before the solution dried on the plate and reduced its sensitivity to light.

The collection from Inglefield's expeditions was discovered in 1994 during a major move at one of the National Maritime Museum's outstations (R. G. Todd, personal communication 1995); they were in an unlabelled box but on one of the negatives (depicting a Greenland settlement) the information 'Holsteinbourg. E. A. Inglefield 1854' had been scratched in the emulsion. Two of the buildings shown on this photograph (fig.4) – the church and the manse – are still standing, thus confirming this identification (Robert G. Williamson, personal communication October 1995). The collection includes portraits of ship's officers and crew members, portraits and group shots of Greenlanders, and the view of Holsteinsborg already mentioned. Unfortunately, since Inglefield's ships called at the various Greenland settlements, it is practically impossible to identify the portraits and group shots of Greenlanders positively. If these photographs were all taken on the *Phoenix*'s outward voyage, they must postdate the two photographs by Domville but predate the two McClintock photographs from Beechey Island.

### The McClintock expedition, 1857–9

Later, in 1857, McClintock led his own expedition to the Arctic in an attempt to determine the fate of the Franklin Expedition; sponsored by Lady (Jane) Franklin, the expedition sailed from Aberdeen aboard the steam-yacht *Fox*. McClintock

Fig.4. Wet-plate image of Sisimiut (Holsteinsborg), spring 1854, by a photographer from HMS *Phoenix*, possibly Captain E. A. Inglefield.

ensured that a camera and the various necessary chemicals and equipment went with this expedition. Dr David Walker, the expedition's surgeon and naturalist, was also the official photographer (McClintock 1859: 8).

On 5 March 1858, as the ship drifted with the ice in Baffin Bay, McClintock noted that Walker took a photograph of the ship 'by the albumen process on glass; the temperature at the time was well below zero' (McClintock 1859: 91). The view of the *Fox* shown in fig. 5 is almost certainly that photograph. By his remark McClintock identifies the process being used as the wet collodion process.

No photographs taken by Walker appear in McClintock's account of the expedition (McClintock 1859). Nonetheless, his recognition of photography's potential value, no doubt based on his earlier first-hand experience on Beechey Island, mark McClintock as being a noteworthy player in the history of Arctic photography.

**The Hayes polar expedition of 1860**
Within a year of the return of McClintock's expedition to Britain, another expedition was bound for the Arctic, one which, using a process similar to that used by Dr Walker (i.e. the wet collodion process), would produce the first multiple photographic prints from the Arctic regions. Its leader was Dr Isaac Israel Hayes, who had served under Dr Elisha Kent Kane on Kane's 1853–5 expedition. Hayes succeeded in purchasing a schooner, which he renamed *United States* (Hayes 1867), and in obtaining scientific instruments from various academies for the purpose of exploring the Smith Sound route and searching for the fabled 'Open Polar Sea'. Since Hayes could not afford to recruit a professional photographer, the responsibility for photography was undertaken by Hayes himself.

Having sailed from Boston, the *United States* reached Upernavik on the west coast of Greenland on 12 August 1860. Four days out of Upernavik, in iceberg-infested waters, Hayes reported his first attempt at photography (Hayes 1867: 45–6). The expedition pushed north to Port Foulke, on the Greenland shore of Smith Sound; this became the expedition's winter quarters and the starting point in the spring of 1861 for a sledge trip during which Hayes claimed to reach a new 'farthest north', from which he sighted the 'Open Polar Sea'. Returning from this trip in June 1861 (Hayes 1867), he took the earliest surviving photograph from the expedition; it shows the icebound schooner in Port Foulke.

Hayes methodically took scientific observations and photographs in the vicinity of Port

ABOVE
Fig.5. Wet-plate image of McClintock's ship, *Fox*, in Baffin Bay, March 1858, taken by Dr David Walker.

LEFT
Fig.6. One image of a stereo-pair of 'The Esquimaux hunters Marcius and Jacob, Port Foulke, June 1861,' taken by I.I. Hayes.

Foulke. In mid-August Hayes reached Godhavn where he noted that he had succeeded in 'completing [his] series of photographic views' (Hayes 1867: 445).

From June 1861 to the end of the expedition Hayes took at least eighty-two photographs (Russack 1975). These include views of the ship, topographic features, native Greenlanders and Greenland settlements. Given that he was an untrained amateur labouring under adverse conditions, the fact that he achieved so many successful photographs was nothing less than amazing.

Hayes's photographs were published as both paper and glass 'stereoviews' by the photography firm of T. C. Roche (Russack 1975). Although no actual photographs were used to illustrate his book, Hayes's published account of the expedition reports that a full-page engraving (of which there are six) entitled 'Tyndall Glacier, Whale Sound' is drawn from a photograph by Dr Hayes and that the engravings of the tail-pieces were made from sketches and photographs taken by Dr

Hayes (Hayes 1867). Fortunately, although rare, numbers of Hayes's stereoviews have survived (see fig.6). Hayes did succeed in amassing the first extensive photographic record of an Arctic expedition. With this expedition the use of photography as a means of documenting people, places and events in the Arctic had come into its own.

### Dr Hinrik Johannes Rink, 1860–65

It should be noted that the Hayes photographs are not the only surviving photographs of Greenland and Greenlanders from the early 1860s. Another series of photographs of Greenlanders, Greenland dwellings and landscapes were taken in Godthåb and Sukkertoppen between 1860 and 1865. These photographs, of which approximately sixty are known to survive, were taken by Dr Hinrik Johannes Rink, who lived in Julianehåb from 1853 to 1857 and Sukkertoppen from 1857 to 1868. They are currently in the collection of the Arctic Institute, Danish Polar Center, Copenhagen (Henriette Berg, personal communication May 1996). Fig. 7 is one of these photographs. It appears to have been produced from a series of individual photographs taken by Rink in 1862–4 in the districts of Sukkertoppen and Godthåb and is unique in that each individual is identified.

### William Bradford's pleasure cruise

In 1869 the artist, William Bradford, organised an expedition to the Arctic for an artistic purpose. For the expedition he invited two professional photographers, John Dunmore and George Critcherson, from J. W. Black's Studio in Boston.

The photographers succeeded in exposing 300 to 400 glass-plate negatives (Dunmore 1869). Bradford published an elaborate account of the voyage entitled *The Arctic Regions* (Bradford 1873), of which 350 copies were printed by subscription. In large format, this work includes 135 photographs by Dunmore and Critcherson. It is the first published work to include photographs of the Arctic. The Bradford expedition aptly demonstrated not only that photography could succeed in the Arctic regions but that it could provide valuable images that could not otherwise be recorded and that those images could be made available in multiple copies.

### The *Polaris* expedition, 1871–3

In 1871 Charles Francis Hall on board USS *Polaris* led an expedition to the Arctic in an attempt to reach the North Pole. Among the equipment at his disposal, cameras are listed by the chief scientist, Dr Emil Bessels, in his account of the

expedition (Bessels 1879). However, none of the illustrations in the official account of the expedition (Davis 1876) are photographs or even engravings based on photographs, but rather wood engravings based on sketches made in the field. This is scarcely surprising since half of the expedition personnel drifted with the ice from Kane Basin almost to the Strait of Belle Isle and were lucky to escape with their lives; photographic plates would have been the last thing on their minds as they abandoned ship. The remainder of the ship's complement (including Bessels) retreated south by boat, and again probably did not take any photographic plates with them. In an official report to the President of the United States regarding the expedition it was reported that there was a partial failure in the area of photography because of the lack of 'suitable opportunities' or to 'some insurmountable impediment at the time' (Robeson 1873: 291).

### The advent of dry-plate photography

By the mid-1870s photographic equipment was becoming standard on exploring expeditions. This was due in large part to the introduction of the 'dry-plate' process. The use of dry plates, or photographic plates which were sensitised with chemicals months before use and exposed in a dry state, made the handling of plates and the taking of exposures much easier than with wet-plates.

### The Second German Arctic Expedition, 1869–70

During the Second German Arctic Expedition of 1869–70 the *Germania* and *Hansa* (Captain Carl Koldewey and Captain Paul Hegemann, respectively) made an attempt on the Pole by trying to push north along the east Greenland coast. During this attempt *Hansa*'s mate, Herr Hildebrandt, was taking photos, both of groups on deck and of the ship from the ice (Koldewey 1874). Some of the scenes which Hildebrandt tried to capture were probably quite dramatic, including the ship nipped in the ice. After drifting south with the East Greenland Current, beset in the ice, *Hansa* was crushed and sank on 22 October; her crew established a camp on the ice, then made their escape to the southern settlements of west Greenland by sledge and boat. Unfortunately, as noted by Koldewey, none of Hildebrandt's photographs survived this ordeal (Koldewey 1874: 91).

### Sir Allen Young's two expeditions

In June 1875 Sir Allen Young conducted an ambitious private trip in the steamer *Pandora*, for

the purpose of visiting Greenland, the magnetic north pole and navigating the Northwest Passage (Young 1876). Young enlisted George R. de Wilde as artist and photographer for the expedition, and succeeded in publishing photographs of the expedition (Young 1876).

On his return Young privately published an account of the expedition, entitled *Cruise of the 'Pandora'* (Young 1876). Although modest in comparison to *The Arctic Regions* by Bradford, it included twelve tipped-in photographs taken by de Wilde, including five taken at Beechey Island (see fig.8). The photographs are of very good quality, although not of the same calibre as Dunmore's from Bradford's expedition. Although Young's geographical achievements were not significant, he did succeed in publishing the second book to contain Arctic photographs.

Young made a second voyage to the Arctic in *Pandora* in 1876. The photographer for this trip was William Grant. Young's published work regarding the expedition entitled *The Two Voyages of the 'Pandora'* makes several references to Grant's photographic activity, at Holsteinsborg (Sisimiut) on 31 July (Young 1879) and Godhavn (Qeqertarsuaq) on 31 July (Young 1879). His book, however, uses engravings for illustrations. It should be noted that William Grant was an active photographer in the Arctic in the 1870s, serving as photographer on board *Willem Barents* in 1878 and 1879.

**The British polar expedition of 1875–6**
By 1872 the British government was persuaded to sponsor another expedition to the Arctic on the scale of the Franklin Expedition. Sir George Strong Nares was appointed commander of the expedition, which consisted of the ships HMS *Alert* and HMS *Discovery*. Through Nares' persistent efforts at procuring the photographic equipment and publishing albums of the views, together with the efforts of the photographers in obtaining the views, a remarkable and useful photographic record of the expedition was obtained.

Nares requested that each of the ships of the expedition be supplied with photographic apparatus (Nares 1875–6: 22). George White, Junior Engineer of the *Alert*, and Thomas Mitchell, Assistant Paymaster of the *Discovery*, were selected as the photographers and were assisted by Colour-Sergeant William Wood of the Royal Marines (Markham 1876).

The expedition sailed from England on 29 May 1875 and proceeded to Godhavn where it stopped for supplies. Here, Markham noted that the photographers 'got to work with the photography, and obtained seven excellent negatives'

(Markham 1876: 332). The ships proceeded north through Smith Sound and Kane Basin during which time the photographers continued their efforts. HMS *Discovery* proceeded as far as Lady Franklin Bay, on north-eastern Ellesmere Island, where it established its winter quarters. HMS *Alert* proceeded farther north through Robeson Channel to Floeberg Beach, the most northerly point then reached by any ship (Cooke and Holland 1978: 240). Throughout the northward trip the photographers methodically photographed topographic features, in accordance with their instructions.

In April 1876 the dash for the Pole was attempted from Cape Joseph Henry at the northern tip of Ellesmere Island (Cooke and Holland 1978: 240). Although achieving a farthest north, the party suffered from scurvy and was forced to return to the ship. Other sledge journeys were carried out to explore the area near the ships. Two of these sledging parties each carried 26 lb (9.8 kg) of photographic equipment (Bell 1972). The photographers on both ships were remarkably successful, but the effects of scurvy on the expedition caused Nares to return home to England in August 1876.

The photographers succeeded in taking 121 exposures, and Nares was pleased to inform the Admiralty that 107 negatives were 'good enough to print from and would form an excellent Photographic history of the late Arctic Expedition' (Nares 1875–7: 15). Fig.9 shows an exposure taken by Thomas Mitchell of HMS *Discovery* and some of the crew. Nares personally handled the arrangements for publishing a limited number of photograph albums.

The photographs taken by the Nares expedition completely demonstrated the utility of photography for documentary purposes. Only a handful of the photographs taken by White and Mitchell capture images of the natives of Greenland and therefore provide a limited documentary record of these people at this time. However, as a means of documenting the geography of Smith Sound through Robeson Channel, the Nares expedition photographs fully demonstrated the use of photographs as a means to capture images effectively. With the very successful use of photography on this expedition Arctic photography may be said to have come of age. Thereafter, it became an almost standard activity of nearly all Arctic expeditions.

**Conclusions**
The authors hope that this review of the first few decades of the use of photography in the Canadian Arctic and Greenland will be found to

Fig.8. Wet-plate image of *Pandora*, stopped by ice in Peel Sound, 1 September 1975, taken by George De Wilde.

Fig.9. Dry-plate image of party remaining on board HMS *Discovery*, Discovery Harbour, during spring sledging season, 1876.

be fairly comprehensive. The main intent was to identify those pioneer efforts and to demonstrate that Arctic travellers adopted photography as a means of recording events and landscapes soon after the medium was discovered, and despite the inherent difficulties associated with the Arctic climate. Furthermore, as successive advances were introduced, these were readily adopted by Arctic photographers. Inevitably, certain initiatives in the Arctic may have been overlooked. We would appreciate hearing from any readers who can identify such omissions.

Pamela Stern

# The History of Canadian Arctic Photography:
# Issues of Territorial and Cultural Sovereignty

Though most Canadians have never ventured to the Arctic, the north, as both a place and an idea, is well embedded in the national psyche of Canada. It represents adventure, grandeur, glory and opportunities for riches. One contemporary Canadian social commentator describes his nation as 'a country of parkas and toques, mukluks and moccasins; toboggans, snowmobiles and komatiks . . .' and goes on to assert that the 'igloo is [the] one indigenous piece of architecture' (Berton 1987: 100). This said, Berton still marvels at the attempts of southern Canadians to claim an Arctic heritage, and thus forces us to consider why this might be the case. It is more than simply exaggerating the importance of winter on the lives of ordinary Canadians. The Arctic *is* Canada's frontier, still sparsely settled and unconquered four centuries after Martin Frobisher mistook iron ore for gold and became side-tracked in his quest for the Northwest Passage. In those 400 years southerners have fantasised about the fortunes to be made in the north from commercial shipping, mineral extraction (including oil and gas), whales and furs. But, for the most part, Canadians showed scant interest in the Arctic region prior to the turn of the century when a growing sense of nationhood forced it to consolidate its borders (Jenness 1964; Zaslow 1981).

The southern (primarily European) public's love affair with the Arctic began long before Canada became a nation, and grew out of both the successes and failures of those who sought the region's elusive riches. The tales of these adventurers captured the imagination of a sedentary public. Stories, however, were not the only things the travellers brought home. From the earliest days of Arctic exploration nearly all expeditions engaged naturalists to make collections and artists to document the lands and cultures encountered. Images and objects of curiosity provided tangible evidence of unknown regions and, more importantly, linked the possessor to the exotic locale. Having something to hold, to look at repeatedly, gave the armchair traveller a sense of ownership of not just the object but also of the place from whence the object came. The development of photographic technology in the mid-nineteenth century and its improvements in the late nineteenth century permitted more and more people to hold, examine and possess a piece of the Arctic.

The earliest-known efforts at photography in the Canadian Arctic were made in 1853 and 1854 by Amos Bonsall, a midshipman aboard the *Advance* during the Second Grinnell Expedition, and by Leopold McClintock, captain of the *Intrepid*. McClintock recorded making some calotype portraits and images of Beechey Island (off the south-west coast of Devon Island) in his diary for August 1854 (cited in W. Barr 1990). Upon being hired by Captain Elisha Kent Kane, Bonsall took lessons in daguerreotyping. The Second Grinnell Expedition was plagued by numerous disasters culminating in the forced abandonment of the *Advance* in May 1855. There is little information about the subject of Bonsall's photographs and all seem to have been lost when the ship was abandoned. In his own memoir of the voyage nearly half a century later, Bonsall (1902: 43), the last surviving member of the Second Grinnell Expedition, referred to this as an 'irreparable loss, and one that to this day I have never ceased to regret'. Time seems to have altered Bonsall's memory, however. At the time of Kane's death in 1857 Bonsall had reported that his efforts at daguerreotyping had been largely

Life in contemporary Copper Inuit communities, while clearly changed by contact with outsiders, still bears many similarities to pre-contact culture. Much of the material culture is new, but the activities, postures and even facial expressions have remained the same.

Fig.1. Mary Okheena and daughter Carol cooking near Holman, 1987; see also figs 6 and 7. (Photographer: John Paskievich)

unsuccessful (cited in Corner 1972: 292). Captain Kane, who had also attempted a few daguerreo-types, referred to them as 'useless' except as 'mir-rors to transfer the sun-rays into the cabin' (Kane 1856, vol.2: 46).

While Amos Bonsall and Leopold McClintock were experimenting with two of the earliest methods of photography, technical improve-ments in the medium along with commercial fac-tors led to a far wider use of photography to document expeditions to every part of the globe. It was during McClintock's next voyage, the suc-cessful Franklin search expedition of 1857–9 aboard the *Fox*, that photographs were made using the improved technology: wet collodion glass plates. These were made by the ship's physician and naturalist, Dr David Walker. Most early photographers were scientists, physicians, artists or other individuals of letters (Seiberling 1986: 3), and this was also true for the Arctic pho-tographers. It was the officers and gentlemen rather than the common sailors who had the leisure to pursue photography as well as access to the new technology.

The wet-plate technology was also employed by a small group of Hudson's Bay Company employees posted in the James Bay area in the 1860s. These included James L. Cotter, Charles Horetzky, William Bell Maloch, George Simpson McTavish and Bernard Rogan Ross (Ross 1990: 94). The journals kept by Arctic fur traders often referred to their intense isolation and inactivity, and it is likely that photography provided one respite from boredom.

During the same period the American painter William Bradford employed professional photog-raphers to sail with him along the Labrador coast aboard the *Panther*. The photographs which resulted from that voyage served as 'sketches' for a number of Bradford's oil paintings.

Although dry glass-plate technology first became commercially available in 1858, it did not come into widespread use until the 1880s. It was, however, tried in the Arctic during George Strong Nares's unsuccessful attempt to reach the North Pole in 1875/6 (Ross 1990: 94). The dry-plate method of photography was a significant improvement over the wet-plate technology. The older method required that the glass plates be coated with light sensitive chemicals just prior to exposure and developed immediately afterwards. Dry plates were commercially prepared and could be developed at the photographer's leisure. As a consequence expedition photography took on a new importance.

It was during the 1880s that Arctic photogra-phy began in earnest. In 1884 and 1885 geologist Robert Bell sailed north with Lieutenant Andrew R. Gordon, first on the *Neptune* and then aboard the *Alert*. The goal of these voyages was to prove (or disprove) the feasibility of shipping grain from a proposed port on Hudson Bay. Bell made many photographs of ice, landforms and people and went to considerable efforts to publicise these Canadian explorations through newspaper fea-tures and slide lectures (Minotto, et al. 1977c: 3).

Gordon made a third voyage without Bell in 1886 and concluded that ice conditions in Hudson Strait and Bay were not compatible with commercial navigation. Others, with greater opti-mism, disagreed, and a fourth expedition aboard the *Diana* was organised in 1887. Commander of the voyage, Dr William Wakeham, was deter-mined 'to keep if possible a complete photo-

RIGHT
Fig.2. Copper Inuit woman fishing *c.*1916. Canadian Arctic Expedition. (Photographer: G. H. Wilkins)

FAR RIGHT
Fig.3. Delma Klengenberg fishing near Holman, spring 1983. (Photographer: Richard G. Condon)

graphic log of ice conditions' to support his conclusions, 'as such a record must be of more value and less open to criticism than any amount of written description' (Minotto, et al. 1977b: 3). To this end Graham Drinkwater was engaged to document the ice conditions, while Bell and Albert Peter Low, also a geologist, were chosen to explore and photograph the coasts of Hudson Strait. Wakeham's assessment did not differ significantly from that of Gordon. This did not satisfy the proponents of commercial shipping, but Wakeham did accomplish one thing important to the emerging nation of Canada: in the presence of both Scottish whalers and Inuit, Wakeham claimed Baffin Island for Canada. The flag-planting ceremony, a mere eleven years after Canada's confederation, was photographed for posterity by Drinkwater (Minotto, et al. 1977d: 6).

Sovereignty over the Arctic islands began to concern Canada by the turn of the century (Zaslow 1971). Although Great Britain had transferred title for the Arctic archipelago to Canada by Order of Council in 1880, Canada had no way in which to enforce this action. Norwegian explorer Otto Sverdrup claimed Ellesmere Island and several smaller islands for Norway. American whalers dominated Herschel Island and the Beaufort Sea, while both American and Scottish whalers were present in Hudson Bay and Davis Strait. Several Americans were attempting to reach the North Pole and the Norwegian Roald Amundsen was navigating the Northwest Passage. Furthermore, Canada had ceded considerable territory to the United States as a result of the Alaska/Canada boundary dispute. According to Zaslow (1981: 62), these threats to Canada's 'national identity and northern patrimony' led the country to pursue its northern sovereignty claims. Robert Bell, who had risen to the post of Acting Director of the Geological Survey of Canada, initiated an ambitious attempt to assert Canadian control over the Arctic islands. The resulting voyage of the *Neptune* in 1903/4 and that of the *Arctic* in 1904/5 were especially notable for the prodigious photographic work of the participants.

The *Neptune* Expedition of 1903/4, commanded by Albert P. Low, had the explicit aim of asserting Canadian sovereignty over Hudson Bay and the eastern Arctic. Low was accompanied by Northwest Mounted Police Major (later Superintendent) John Douglas Moodie and forty-one others including a number of scientists. The *Neptune* anchored and spent the winter at Fullerton Harbour in north-western Hudson Bay, and a police post and customs station were established ashore. This was also the wintering

location of the American whaling ship *Era*, captained by George P. Comer. The choice of Fullerton Harbour was no coincidence (Low 1906: 20), a fact not lost on Comer (Ross 1976, 1984a).

Comer had been whaling in Hudson Bay since 1893, but the whaling era was drawing to a close. Trade in skins, particularly musk-ox, but also fox, wolverine, wolf and bear had become an important addition to the whaler's cargo. Comer, himself, supplemented his income by collecting data and ethnological specimens for Franz Boas and the American Museum of Natural History. In this capacity Comer made hundreds of photographs of the Inuit of Hudson Bay (Ross 1990).

It is likely that Comer held ambivalent feelings about the presence of the Canadians at Fullerton Harbour. Entries from his diary note that the well-supplied crew of the *Neptune* fostered morale problems among his own shoddily attired crew. The *Neptune* also competed with the *Era* for Inuit labour and supplies of fresh meat. Comer was particularly resentful of the regulation imposed by Major Moodie. On the other

TOP
Fig.4. Fish drying at summer camp, *c.*1916. Canadian Arctic Expedition.

ABOVE
Fig.5. Fish drying at summer camp near Holman, 1988. (Photographer: Richard G. Condon)

hand, Comer made use of the medical services provided by the *Neptune*'s doctor, Lorris Elijah Borden, and social visits between the two ships were common (Ross 1984a). A shared interest in photography often brought the two groups together. In addition to Comer and Low, photographs were made by Moodie, Borden and the official expedition photographer, George F. Caldwell.[1] They shared equipment, subjects and tips regarding processing.

This photographic collaboration was repeated during the winter of 1905/6 when the vessel *Arctic* replaced the *Neptune* at Fullerton Harbour. The photographers that season, in addition to Comer, included Moodie, his wife Geraldine, Captain Joseph-Elzéar Bernier and an official expedition photographer, Frank Douglas MacKean.

The voyages of the *Neptune* and the *Arctic* were instrumental in establishing Canada's claim on the Hudson Bay and the Arctic archipelago, and the photographic work was not inconsequential to that effort. Low, in particular, seemed to understand this. His well-distributed account of the voyage, entitled *The Cruise of the Neptune* (Low 1906), was illustrated with his photographs from that expedition, greatly enhancing its popular appeal (Ross 1990: 100; Zaslow 1971: 264). Low, a supporter of Arctic development, also spoke at the Canadian Club[2] of Ottawa and other forums about Canada's Arctic prospects (Burant, this volume). Bernier made three more voyages between 1906 and 1911 covering virtually the entire Arctic island chain and ultimately 'taking possession for the Dominion of Canada of the whole Arctic Archipelago' (cited in Cook 1980: 3) and becoming a Canadian folk hero. His book (Bernier 1909) was also illustrated with photographs documenting his Arctic travels. The Moodies sent proof sets of their photographs to Royal Northwest Mounted Police headquarters, to the Department of Marine and Fisheries, and to Prime Minister Wilfred Laurier.

Another photographer was active in Hudson Bay between 1901 and 1904. A. A. Chesterfield, a Hudson's Bay Company trader at Great Whale River, amassed an impressive photographic collection. But unlike the Comer and Low materials, these remained unknown until they were stumbled upon in a faculty office at Queen's University in Kingston, Ontario, in 1974 (James 1985: ix–xii). The Chesterfield photographs are very different from those by Comer and Low. The latter often photographed their human subjects in snow houses, while the former did most of his photography at the trading post and mission. Chesterfield's pictures also present little

material evidence of acculturation. Low's and Comer's are replete with it.

Sovereignty was apparently still at issue in 1912 when anthropologist Vilhjalmur Stefansson sought support for what was to be a three-year investigation of Victoria Island and the Coronation Gulf region. Although Stefansson, who had previously visited the region in 1911, had received backing for his endeavours from American sources, the Canadian government decided to fund the expedition in order to forestall any American claims on its territory (Jenness 1964: 26). The resulting Canadian Arctic Expedition (1913–18) produced an unparalleled body of photographs of Copper Inuit credited to Stefansson, G. H. Wilkins and Diamond Jenness.

Most, if not all, of the early Arctic photographers gave little thought to how the native subjects of their photographs might use or interpret the images made of them, their homes and their territories. The slow, painstaking process and bulky equipment of early photography clearly required the co-operation of subjects, and Ross (1990: 100) argues that at least for Low and Comer there is no evidence that the Inuit made efforts to escape the camera's lens. But we must consider, too, that Inuit norms of polite behaviour may have deterred them from refusing even the most absurd requests made by powerful and economically important outsiders. Upon their return to the south, in addition to Low, Comer, Bernier, Wilkins, Stefansson and many others gave slide lectures detailing their exploits in the frozen frontier and thereby brought the Arctic to the public. Zaslow (1971: 277; 1981: 65) credits Stefansson, in particular, with generating both public and government interest in the Arctic. The photographs and slides provided the viewer with a vicarious sense of being there 'as a participant (albeit passive) in a new experience' (Davis 1981: 2). According to Brody (1987: xi), photographs do 'not carry information, so much as effortless proximity, a denial of distance'. I believe that the public showings of slides especially, were crucial in generating popular interest in, and a public sense of ownership of, the Arctic. Interestingly, Comer noted in his diary that Superintendent Moodie used the same technique to woo the Inuit to Canada:

Major Moodie gave an exhibition of lantern slides this evening. It had the appearance to me as though he wished to impress the natives on the power and greatness of Canada (Ross 1984a: 169).

That the arrival of explorers, missionaries, traders, whalers and police completely changed Inuit cultures is an understatement of the high-

LEFT
Fig.6. Kitiqisiq
cooking, 1916.
Canadian Arctic
Expedition.
(Photographer:
Diamond Jenness)

BELOW LEFT
Fig.7. Agnes Nigiyok
cooking outside her
home in Holman,
1987. (Photographer:
John Paskievich)

est magnitude. By the end of the Canadian Arctic Expedition the trickle of outsiders into the Canadian Arctic had become a flood. Advances in photographic technology, including the development of smaller cameras and flexible roll film, served to encourage northern photography by both outsiders and natives. There was an exponential increase in the number of photographs made in the Canadian Arctic. Many of these remain in private collections.

Regardless of the intents of the early photographers or the purposes to which the images were originally put, the existence today of historic photographs permits Arctic peoples to repossess their histories and to reassert sovereignty over their cultures. Ross (1990) has documented several examples of this, and in the remainder of this paper I would like to discuss historic photographs in the context of the central Canadian Arctic community of Holman.

Holman is located on the west coast of Victoria Island at the mouth of Prince Albert Sound. Most of the approximately 400 residents are descended from the two northernmost groups of Copper

Inuit and several families from the Mackenzie Delta region. The community was established in 1939 as a mission and trading post, but it had few permanent residents prior to the 1960s. Although Holman remains smaller than most Canadian Arctic communities, it has followed a similar course of development. The economy is a mixed one of wage labour, subsistence hunting and trapping, arts and crafts production and social assistance. People live in government-subsidised houses heated by oil furnaces. Sports, especially ice hockey, are an important aspect of community life. People increasingly look to the south to satisfy their entertainment and recreational needs. Television is ubiquitous, and holidays in Yellowknife or Edmonton are becoming common. English is the primary language spoken by most residents under the age of forty-five and the only language spoken by those under the age of thirty.[3] Nonetheless, Holman is very much an *Inuit* community.

The Copper Inuit who settled in Holman were among the last groups of Inuit to come into regular contact with people from outside the region. Consequently, the photographs made by the Canadian Arctic Expedition show little evidence of acculturation. Much of the social change that resulted from contact occurred within the memories of Holman's oldest residents.

Beginning in 1985, the late anthropologist Richard Condon began a project to identify and document historic photographs made in and around the Holman region. He visited archives in Canada and the United States, tracked down former missionaries, retired traders and others known to have visited the Holman area, and pestered Holman residents to dust off long-forgotten family albums. Through these efforts he assembled a collection of photographs taken between 1911 and 1966. With the assistance of Holman-resident Julia Ogina, Condon used the photographs to interview elders about a variety of topics.[4] What began as a simple photograph identification project turned into something much larger and ultimately resulted in the recently published book, *The Northern Copper Inuit* (Condon 1996). The book combines historical and archaeological reconstruction, photographs, and reminiscences of elders to provide a personal history of and by the people of Holman. Condon came to see the project as a form of repatriation of cultural materials (Condon and Ogina, 1990).

Condon used the photographs as mnemonic devices to trigger dormant memories of elders about the past, but they became much more. It appears that viewing historic photographs and clothing specimens may have triggered a sort of cultural revitalisation in Holman (Driscoll-Engelstad 1995). The initial reaction to viewing historic photographs of the Holman region is to note how much Copper Inuit culture has been transformed first by culture contact and then by sedentary community life. Upon a more careful examination, however, evidence of cultural continuity is also apparent. The recognition of this is vitally important to aboriginal cultures often under assault from a variety of sources. Thus, while historic photographs are of interest to academic and other researchers, their greatest value may lie in their utility to the subjects and their descendants.

## Notes

1. According to the National Photography Collection (1979: 79), the choice of Caldwell as expedition photographer was somewhat controversial. No photographs attributed to him are known to exist.

2. The Canadian Clubs formed around the turn of the century in nearly every Canadian city. The purpose of the clubs was (and still is) 'the encouragement of the study of history, literature and resources of Canada, the recognition of native worth and talent, and the fostering of a patriotic Canadian sentiment' (Merrifield 1993: 3).

3. In this respect Holman differs from Inuit communities farther to the east where Inuktitut continues to be the first language taught to children.

4. The photographs themselves generated a great deal of interest and it reached the point where elders who had not yet been interviewed would call out to Julia and ask her when she would come by with the pictures (Richard Condon, personal communication 1989).

Dorothy Harley Eber

# Peter Pitseolak
# and the Photographic Template

Peter Pitseolak, who was born in south Baffin Island in 1902 and died there in 1973, was the Canadian Arctic's first native documentary photographer. He is famous today because he took photographs, but with the help of his photographs he has also created remarkable drawings and watercolours, towards which, at least on one occasion, there has been some ambivalence. To briefly sum up his photographic career, he acquired a camera in 1942 or 1943 and began to photograph for his own delight. Both Pitseolak and his wife Aggeok taught themselves to develop and print, and their earliest pictures were developed in hunting igloos out on the land and then printed back in Cape Dorset where Peter Pitseolak worked for the fur traders[1] and had a small wooden house. Aggeok has left a rather moving description of how their photographs were taken and developed:

When Peter Pitseolak wasn't working we would go out camping for a while. When he was out hunting he would put the camera on top of the igloo until the film was all used up [in order not to subject it to temperature changes]. It was in a case and he used caribou skins to wrap it up. He would put the dog traces over it so it wouldn't blow away. Only after he finished the film he would take the camera inside and take out the film. The igloo didn't appear to be an igloo because we had a canvas tent inside it which made a difference to the temperature. We would develop on top of the sleeping platform with the three-battery flashlight and after we did the washing we would keep the negatives overnight in a warm place on top of the box [near the *kudluk*] We would use two *kudluks* and plenty of oil which made a good temperature. An igloo with a lining was good enough even though it was made out of snow.[2]

In 1946 Peter Pitseolak stopped working for the traders and established what was to be his last camp out on the land at Keatuk, close to Cape Dorset. Here he continued photographing and caught scenes of camp life and visitors to his camp, and after tuberculosis made it difficult for him to move around, people posed for him in his hut and he took many portraits. He caught the life and times of the people of his day. After his death in 1973 the Canadian department of the Secretary of State bought his negatives and some original prints from his estate and placed them on permanent deposit at the Notman Photographic Archives, one of Canada's great photographic resources, at the McCord Museum of Canadian History in Montreal. In the years since Peter Pitseolak's death his reputation has grown and there have been several exhibitions of his work in the north and the south. One exhibition made a two-year tour of Arctic schools with the photographs laminated on folding screens narrow enough to go through the doorways of the smallest Arctic aircraft.

Since Peter Pitseolak's actual photographs and the inventive matter in which he and Aggeok taught themselves to develop and print have received considerable coverage,[3] this paper discusses a less studied aspect of his photography – its relation to his drawings and watercolours and the graphic work he did for the print programme of the Cape Dorset West Baffin Eskimo Cooperative.

Many here will be aware of the importance of the art programmes which the Canadian government began to introduce widely in the Canadian Arctic in the 1950s and 1960s, the years when the Inuit moved from the camps to the settlements.

They were essentially 'make-work' programmes, designed to give displaced people something to do and a way to earn income at the moment when, as Inuit sometimes say, 'We began to live with money'. These art programmes were successful beyond the dreams of even the most optimistic bureaucrats – they resulted in an outpouring of remarkable sculpture and, most important to this discussion, the emergence of the Eskimo print. It has been said that today there is not an art gallery in the Western world without an Inuit print. The pioneering work was done in Cape Dorset and there is a particularly luminous galaxy of Cape Dorset print artists whose names are widely known, inside and outside Canada – Kenojuak, Pitseolak, Ashoona, Parr, Pudlo, Lucy and a few others. Peter Pitseolak's name is not usually included in this list of artists of the first rank and, considering the charm and elegance of some of his work, one sometimes wonders why. It seems that he may have learned too much from his camera.

From the start of his artistic career Peter Pitseolak was well aware of the advantages and usefulness of the template. So of course was Vermeer, one of the many old masters who used the light box. Peter Pitseolak's earliest works on paper were watercolour drawings he made for the second Lord Tweedsmuir, who, as a young man in 1939 while his father was Governor General of Canada, worked as a trader in Cape Dorset with the Hudson's Bay Company. Lord Tweedsmuir gave Peter Pitseolak his watercolours, and arranged to have his mother send him more. In 1939–40 Peter Pitseolak created a remarkable series of pictures that show the centrality of the fur traders to Inuit life of the time.

For Tweedsmuir beside his sled he made a template from a photograph of a trader he found in the December 1934 and September 1935 issues of *The Beaver*, then the magazine of the Hudson's Bay Company. Other watercolours in the series also show influence from photographs in these issues. Later, after he got his camera, he would make his own templates, regularly setting up shots to be photographed.

How did Peter Pitseolak arrive at the idea of the template? Was it an independent original idea? Possibly, but not necessarily. When, sometime after Peter Pitseolak's death, I visited Lake Harbour where the people have long been well known for ivory carving and incised tusks, a man called Isaccie Ikidulak showed me a photograph of his grandmother and two other women taken by the Reverend Archibald Fleming, later Bishop of the Arctic, who lived in Lake Harbour and photographed there during two two-year periods

between 1909 and 1915 (see Geller, this volume). The photograph was inscribed on the back and signed by the bishop with his Inuit name. The three figures were heavily outlined as if used to draw figures on an ivory tusk, a technique that Peter Pitseolak, who was a noted ivory carver, employed to advantage, as is demonstrated by tusks preserved in the Prince of Wales Northern Heritage Centre, Yellowknife, in the collection of the Winnipeg Art Gallery, and elsewhere. One does not know if or when the Fleming photograph was actually put to use as a template but it is possible the concept may already have been known on the south Baffin coast at the time. Peter Pitseolak created the Tweedsmuir watercolours. Besides Fleming, many others who had close contact with the Inuit, photographed on south Baffin Island in the early days. These include Robert Flaherty in 1913/14, Rear Admiral D. MacMillan in 1922/3 and Dewey Soper, the naturalist and explorer who worked in the eastern Arctic between 1923 and 1931 and actually lived for a time in Lake Harbour. He created many watercolours from black and white photographs.[4] The early Tweedsmuir watercolours, now in the possession of the Canadian Museum of Civilization in Ottawa, are the earliest Inuit watercolours. They predate the appearance of the first Eskimo prints by just under twenty years.

The techniques for the Eskimo print were of course introduced by that vital figure in the history of Inuit art, James Houston, who first went to Cape Dorset in 1951. The print-making experiments began about 1957 but at least four years before this Peter Pitseolak had already completed another remarkable series of watercolour drawings. These tell the story of Taktillitak, a drama as well known in Cape Dorset as Robin Hood, according to James Houston. They were acquired by Houston himself and in the early 1980s were presented to the Canadian Museum of Civilization by his former wife Alma Houston, who was with him during the Cape Dorset years. In a telephone interview on 9 March 1981 James Houston told me that he believed he received Peter Pitseolak's watercolours in 1952 or perhaps 1953. 'It's about 30 years ago,' he said, 'so my memory may not always be clear.' At the time, Houston said, he was greatly interested in the story – he later illustrated and published a children's book with the Taktillitak story as its theme. 'Many people came and related the story to me,' he remembered. 'Many had spoken of it to me.' Peter Pitseolak did, too, but, Houston says, 'Peter Pitseolak went one step further; he went on and drew a series of pictures.'

While hunting for seabirds, so the story goes,

Fig.1. Peter Pitseolak with his favourite 122 camera which took postcard-sized pictures. He always referred to his cameras not by the manufacturer's name or the lens opening but by the film he used. Taken by his wife Aggeok, who became an accomplished developer and printer of negatives, probably with a Brownie 'box', c.1946–7.

Taktillitak was carried away on an ice floe to a very small island where he ran out of food. He built his own grave and lay down to die. After dreaming of seals, he got up again and killed a seal with a club. He killed more seals and made a sealskin float. He paddled to the shore. He walked over the land and reached Taseeujakjuk camp. The camp was in mourning with his clothes laid out on the ground. His friends were so happy to see him they cried.

To execute these watercolours, Peter Pitseolak

created a very remarkable series of photographic templates indeed. He had campers at Keatuk camp act out the story and photographed it scene by scene. We see the old-style Inuit grave with rocks around the body, the *avataq* (or seal) float and the weeping friends. He made a bow and arrow so that he could photograph the actor pretending to use it.

There are many negatives relating to this story in the Peter Pitseolak Collection. In Cape Dorset there are people who remember that acting out the story was hard work. Ashevak Ezekiel, Peter Pitseolak's stepson, recalls that the actors sometimes began to lose interest in their roles. He told me:

Sometimes when Peter Pitseolak wanted to take pictures I had to be in them. Ahalona! I definitely used to get tired of it. Sometimes it would go on for a long time and we had to do it just right. But there were no arguments between Peter Pitseolak and the people – people didn't want to say 'no' because Peter Pitseolak was quick to have a hot temper.

His mother Aggeok said, 'I could tell when Ashevak was lazy to be in the pictures but he always said "yes" even when he didn't want to – he would have been scared to say "no" to his stepfather.'[5] Peter Pitseolak was not always an easy genius to live with.

Ashevak Ezekiel told me that Peter Pitseolak made his photographs after Houston told him to make a story of something he could draw – and Houston agreed that he probably said something of the sort. In our interview he said, 'At that time we didn't know where we were going or what we were doing. But some people did draw and in time we cast a wider net.' He was frank about his reaction to the Taktillitak drawings when he got them. 'I never valued them because he'd been so influenced by the south.' In many ways, he noted, Peter Pitseolak was 'a very advanced sort of person,' but, 'rightly or wrongly, he interested me less than about everybody else in the arts – everybody else was working from a one-dimensional perspective.' Peter Pitseolak had no lessons in how to represent three-dimensional space on a flat surface, but with the help of photography he worked out his own rules.

How did Peter Pitseolak use his photographic aids? His widow Aggeok told me he sometimes had them beside him as he drew and he sometimes traced directly on the paper. He also apparently made use of stock figures cut out from cardboard since these figures appear, as the photographic templates do, in many drawings in different clothes and situations. We gain some insight into his working methods from Aggeok's description of how he went about making an ivory tusk, dated 1967, in the Winnipeg Art Gallery.

Peter Pitseolak thought it much better if he took a picture of what he was going to make on an ivory tusk. Then he would trace a small figure directly from the picture. First of all he polished the ivory and after this was finished he drew on the tusk with a carbon paper between the tusk and the picture.[6]

Carbon paper would have been readily available at the Hudson's Bay Company post.

For this particular tusk he photographed the back views of women in the traditional *amauti*. On another tusk which turned up recently in an

Inuit art gallery the back views appear but the lowest figure shows a woman bending over a barrel of fish. It is in polychrome. It hasn't been established what Peter Pitseolak used for colour. The same template has also been used for drawings on paper. Another sequence set up for the camera shows traditional seal hunting at the seal hole. Aggeok would explain that such pictures were taken 'to show how for the future'. Of some images of Peter Pitseolak tending his fox traps, Aggeok said, 'That's Peter Pitseolak showing how.'

It's worthy of a footnote that another artist spotted template potential in Peter Pitseolak's photographs. Many have admired his portraits and around 1976 an Ontario artist John B. Boyle took a couple of templates from an image of Peter Pitseolak's daughter Kooyoo breastfeeding her baby with her husband Kovianaktilliak beside her. One of them appears in a lithograph by Boyle. He sent a copy to Kooyoo and she was delighted (she thought she might knit the artist something – I don't think she ever did but it is the thought that counts).

Templates helped Peter Pitseolak accomplish what was most important to him. They helped him to make Inuit life 'real' – that was his expression – to render true-to-life representations of the Inuit world. This was his aim both in his photography and in his graphic work. Although initially he may have primarily had his grandchildren in mind, it was always his intention to leave a record. In this, his photographs succeed magnificently. The Canadian Arctic has had

LEFT
Fig.4. In 1952–3 Peter Pitseolak had campers at his Keatuk camp act out the story of Taktillitak, which he photographed scene by scene. He used the photographs to help create a series of watercolour drawings depicting the tale.

LEFT
Fig.5. In his Taktillitak watercolours Peter Pitseolak painted pictures to show how Taktillitak, while hunting for seabirds, drifted on an ice floe to a very small island where he ran out of food. This picture, for which he used the template, shows him building his own grave and preparing to lay down to die.

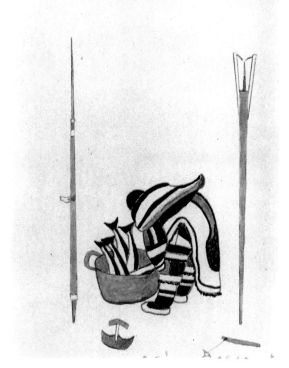

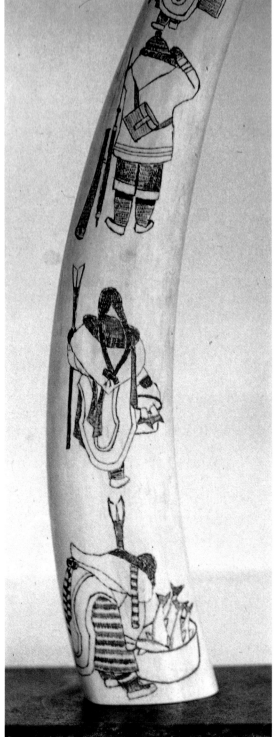

marvellous photographers. Some of the earliest Canadian photographs were taken in the north. But Peter Pitseolak's family photographs provide a special perspective. School children told Aggeok that they saw from the pictures 'how it really was'. Some are currently being put on a CD-ROM for use in the schools. There are some magnificent images among the Peter Pitseolak photographs – but just as important perhaps are the 'snapshot' pictures which suggest the rela-

tions between people and give us the sense of a warm living community. The photographs provide an insider's view of the last days of the camp system and are filled with detail, probably unobtainable to an outside camera. Peter Pitseolak wanted to bring the camera's veracity to his art work, and in his drawings he used his templates to show the Inuit and their various techniques and practices in as 'real' a manner as possible.

After the print-making programme got under

way in Cape Dorset, Peter Pitseolak regularly contributed drawings. They are always interesting and they constitute an important resource for scholars. He told the old Inuit stories and legends, usually fully annotating them, and documented the old style of life with an emphasis on the material culture – the equipment, clothing and habitation. A few drawings were turned into prints, though Peter Pitseolak commented once that those selecting the drawings for the yearly print collections did not favour 'the real'. In fact, his drawings often did not adapt well to the stonecuts and stencils the Co-op produced. Sometimes his Inuit legends went on for six pages. And the drawings that used the photographic templates directly were only a few inches in size.

While the Co-op did not make great use of Peter Pitseolak's drawings during his lifetime, after his death it released some large lithographs rendered after his drawings by apprentice craftsmen in a newly established lithography workshop. And the Co-op prepared a remarkable series of small-scale lithographs from drawings which Peter Pitseolak created towards the end of his life and which made great use of his templates. These employ brilliant colours and seem to me to be some of Peter Pitseolak's most effective works but they have not as yet been released.

To my mind Peter Pitseolak is the super-realist among Eskimo artists. I like the term magic realist. He will always be numbered as one of the great artists of the north – because he took photographs.

Figs 9 and 10. Peter Pitseolak liked to render his art work in vivid colours. His skill in depicting detail with the aid of his templates is seen at its height in the small-scale drawings he made towards the end of his life. Many of these have been turned into lithographs, but are as yet unreleased. He can be called the 'magic realist' among Inuit artists.

**Notes**

1. At various times for both the Baffin Trading Company and the Hudson's Bay Company.

2. Eber, Dorothy Harley, 'Peter Pitseolak: A History for Seekooseelak', in *Peter Pitseolak (1902–1973): Inuit Historian of Seekooseelak*, edited by David Bellman, McCord Museum of Canadian History, Montreal, 1980, p.14. A *kudluk* is a lamp.

3. Pitseolak, Peter and Eber, Dorothy Harley, *People from Our Side*, Hurtig Publishers, Edmonton, 1975, Indiana University Press, Bloomington, 1978, McGill-Queen's University Press, Montreal, 1993; Eber, Dorothy Harley, 'How it Really Was', *Natural History* (February 1977) pp.70–75; *Peter Pitseolak (1902–1973): Inuit Historian of Seekooseelak; Photographs and Drawings from Cape Dorset, Baffin Island* edited by David Bellman, McCord Museum, Montreal 1980.

4. See his illustrations in *My Life Among the Eskimos: the Baffinland Journals of Bernhard Adolph Hantzsch 1909–1911*, translated and edited by L. H. Neatby, Institute for Northern Studies, University of Saskatchewan. Saskatoon, 1977.

5. Eber in Bellman, op.cit. (n.2), p.20.

6. Eber in Bellman, op.cit. (n.2), p.25.

Peter Geller

# Pictures of the Arctic Night: Archibald Lang Fleming and the Representation of Canadian Inuit

Some of the main contributors to the popular image of Canadian Inuit, in North America and Great Britain, were the missionary institutions involved in the Canadian north. The Anglican Church, as the unofficial 'established' church in the north, benefiting from formal and informal ties with the officers and servants of the Hudson's Bay Company and the members of the Canadian government's northern administration, played a major role in the Arctic in the first half of the twentieth century. During this period Archibald Lang Fleming (1883–1953), first Anglican Bishop of the Arctic, was a key figure in the history of the construction of 'Eskimo' images.

As a missionary in the field, and then as the chief spiritual leader and head administrator of the Anglican Church of Canada's Arctic mission, a position he held from 1927 to 1948, Fleming helped set the terms of the Anglican Church's approach to ministering to the Inuit. Through his ongoing fund-raising efforts, which relied heavily on photographic means of communication, he both publicised and justified the Church's northern work. Travelling extensively to points both north and south in Canada, and with regular visits to Great Britain and the United States, Fleming spoke and wrote about the Canadian 'Eskimo', the 'Arctic wilds' and the role and place of the Church in the north.[1] As a prolific photographer as well as collector of Eskimo pictures, Fleming presented these visual messages to his audiences as an integral part of his depiction of the Inuit. In this respect, Archibald Lang Fleming provides an intriguing case study of the way in which one important institution, the Anglican Church, envisioned the Inuit, and the means by which these views were disseminated to the North American and British public.

## Into the Twilight: the life and writings of Archibald the Arctic

According to his own reconstruction of the past, Fleming's Arctic interest was initially sparked in the winter of 1894 by his sister's story of her encounter with an Eskimo who had been brought on a whaler from Baffin Land to Dundee, Scotland. Steeped in exotic tales of missionary adventure, the eleven-year-old Fleming found himself 'transported from the sweltering heat of African grass huts to the frozen realms of Arctic night with shimmering aurora borealis and houses built of snow!'[2] As the young Fleming pursued the trade of ship's engineer with a prominent Scottish firm, he continued to hold on to his boyhood visions. In the fall of 1908, after answering an appeal in a missionary paper for men to preach the gospel to the 'poor Eskimos' of Ungava,[3] Fleming found himself studying theology at Toronto's Wycliffe College. The following year he set out for Lake Harbour, Baffin Island. There, with the already experienced missionary Revd J. W. Bilby, he spent the next two years learning the native language, living and travelling among the Inuit, and establishing a mission.[4]

After a year's furlough in Toronto, during which Fleming was ordained (and also married to Helen Grace Gillespie, his wife until her death in 1941), he again set out for the Arctic in the summer of 1913. After two years at Lake Harbour Fleming was forced to curtail his Arctic travels due to ill health. He made a return trip to Baffin Land in the summer of 1920 to take stock of the 'spiritual well-being' of the natives, but, declared 'unfit for active service', he settled into the less physically strenuous duties as rector in Saint John, New Brunswick.[5]

# I WANT TO GO TO SCHOOL!

Fig.1. 'I Want To Go To School!', from *the Arctic Mission*, 1932.

Throughout the 1920s, however, Fleming retained an interest in the Anglican Church's work in the Arctic. With the assumption of responsibility for the maintenance of Canadian missions by the Missionary Society of the Church of England in Canada (MSCC), a result of the withdrawal of the London-based Church Missionary Society from Canada in 1921, the Arctic sphere came under new consideration.[6] In the fall of 1927 Fleming accepted the newly created position of Archdeacon of the Arctic, taking on the spiritual, administrative and financial responsibilities of the newly reorganised Church of England in Canada's missions to aboriginal people and non-natives in the northern parts of the Dominion.[7]

As he embarked on this new phase in his career as a northern missionary, Fleming's *Dwellers in Arctic Night* appeared.[8] Published in England and Canada in 1928 by the Society for the Propagation of the Gospel in Foreign Parts and the Missionary Society of the Church of England in Canada, this book provides a particularly timely view of the development of Fleming's thought. Using his earlier personal experiences in

the Arctic as a starting point, *Dwellers in Arctic Night* presented a combined report on Inuit culture and heroic missionary adventure, in the process situating the 'Eskimo' as an object of social analysis and spiritual need.

Originally to be entitled 'Children of the Twilight', Fleming consented to change the book's name when he learned of the similarity with anthropologist Diamond Jenness's soon-to-be released popular ethnography of the Copper Inuit, *The People of the Twilight*.[9] The original title, however, was more in keeping with Fleming's characterisation of the Inuit. For Fleming, the Eskimo were clearly situated in a position of dependency, 'children' who required the protection and guidance of the missionary. This involved positioning the Inuit within a progressive evolutionary understanding of cultural development; in Fleming's words the Eskimo were 'a race of men who take us back thousands of years to the Stone Age ... living the simple nomadic life of our forefathers'.[10]

An integral component of Fleming's portrayal of the Inuit as 'primitive children of the snow' involved the projection of a correspondence

ESKIMO MOTHER AND CHILD.

*Plate 1.*

# DWELLERS IN ARCTIC NIGHT

by
ARCHIBALD LANG FLEMING,
*Archdeacon of the Arctic.*

ILLUSTRATED.

MISSIONARY SOCIETY OF THE CHURCH OF ENGLAND
IN CANADA,

Church House, 604 Jarvis Street,
Toronto 5, Ont., Canada.

1928.

Fig.2. 'Eskimo Mother and Child' and title page, from *Dwellers in Arctic Night*, 1928.

between the physical aspects of the environment and their cultural adaptations. In this 'bleak and barren land, where hard cruel winter reigns for nine months out of every twelve,' Fleming reasoned, 'it is therefore only natural that these people should have retained simple, primitive views of life.'[11] Just as the cultural development of the Inuit was seen to be tied to the bleak and barren nature of the 'arctic wastes', so too was the undeveloped nature of their religious and spiritual life.[12] This correspondence between the physical conditions of the Arctic and the inner life of the Inuit was encapsulated in the motif of 'twilight'. The Inuit, as 'children of the twilight', were placed in a transitional position, in the semi-darkness between the spiritual wilderness of the Arctic night and the guiding light of Christ's way.[13]

Fleming would continue to refine this theme throughout his career. In 1941 he titled his yearly review of his journeys through his diocese *Twilight*; the publication's cover, a Fleming photograph, further established the pamphlet's theme. Taken as he travelled by motor boat between Aklavik and Fort McPherson, this image portrayed the midnight sun poised between the vastness of the Arctic sky and the expanse of the

Peel River. Yet Fleming was more than the unseen observer of the landscape. He was an active interpreter of the environment, and his text worked to frame the narrative of his episcopal visitation in the following terms:

Arctic Canada is a land of strange contradictions. This is true regarding the country, the climate conditions . . . and the people. For weeks around mid-summer and mid-winter it is the land of twilight – in summer because the sun never sets, in winter because the sun does not rise above the horizon . . .

But Arctic Canada is a land of twilight in other senses as well because it is at the transitional period between primitive pagan simplicity on the one hand and highly organized civilization on the other.[14]

Accompanying these words were Fleming's pictures. Photographs of the polar ice pack and the Arctic coastline gave way to images of the exterior and interior of All Saints' Cathedral, Aklavik, vividly illustrating the strides made in this Land of Twilight during Bishop Fleming's tenure.

## Out of the Twilight: seeing the north transformed

Fleming's use of the motif and imagery of Twilight carried with it another level of meaning, tied in to his role as international spokesman for the Arctic Missions. As well as displaying photographs in his books and pamphlets and in the *Arctic News* (the annual Arctic Mission newsletter), Fleming presented lectures illustrated by lantern slides (and sometimes films), all intended to bring the 'Eskimo' and the north out of the twilight of Canadian and British consciousness and into the glaring lights of public perception. As the headline to a newspaper report of one of Fleming's illustrated lectures put it, 'Archdeacon Fleming Brings New Light To Bear on Eskimo and Indian'.[15]

In shedding light on the Arctic night, Fleming was not content to rely solely on his skills as a speaker and writer. He was particularly aware of and adept at making an appeal to the visual sensibilities of his audiences. As an author and a high profile lecturer, he incorporated techniques of missionary communication that were already established by the early decades of this century.[16] Fleming's formation as an authoritative commentator on the Inuit was conditioned by the attempt to represent his northern knowledge in visual, as well as written, form.

As early as 1913, returning from his first two years in the field, the recently ordained Reverend Fleming gave an illustrated lecture to a Toronto audience on 'The Eskimo of Baffin Land'. Fleming made effective use of the lantern slides at his disposal; more than entertaining illustrations, they functioned to reinforce and give added weight to his spoken argument. Pictures of arrow and spear heads were shown as Fleming discussed the abilities of 'primitive man . . . to subsist on the natural resources of the country', while slides of sealskin tents, kayaks, and snow huts followed his verbal descriptions of the yearly rounds of a life that changed with the seasons.[17] Images of the people themselves (presumably portraits) were thrown on the screen as Fleming provided detailed information on physiognomy, situating the Eskimo as an object of study and highlighting their physical 'otherness' as a race apart. Fleming was caught up in the common – but waning – anthropological pursuit of assigning fixed racial origins. As he later stated, drawing on the assumption of the 'objective' nature of photographic meaning: 'Even a layman with no scientific training looking at photographs of Eskimo can recognise the Mongolian high cheekbones, sleek black hair and peculiar epicanthic fold of the eyelid, while sometimes the eyes are oblique.'[18] In attempting to understand and make explainable his sojourn among the Inuit of Baffin Land, Fleming turned to the categories of anthropological knowledge, employing photographs as

scientific evidence for the classification of racial 'types'.[19]

Given this early interest in incorporating visual images in his northern work, it is not surprising to find Fleming further developing their use as Archdeacon and later Bishop of the Arctic. Preaching and speaking in England for three months in the winter and spring of 1928, his

CHILDREN OF THE ARCTIC.

Fig.3. 'Children of the Arctic', from *Dwellers in Arctic Night*, 1928.

repertoire included a choice of three subjects: a lecture on 'The People of the Polar North'; a lantern slide-show, 'Life and Travel Amongst the Eskimo'; and 'Our Canadian Eskimo', a talk accompanied by motion pictures.

As Fleming recognised, a lantern slide lecture, like a well-titled and edited film, could present his version of the Eskimo and the Arctic mission experience with or without his presence.[20] 'Across the Canadian Arctic, Baffin Land', designed for British audiences in 1930, served as an introduction to and appeal for the reorganised Arctic Missions, with Fleming at its helm. Any committed church worker, armed with the set of forty-one slides, the prepared lecture notes, and a copy of *Dwellers in Arctic Night*, could present this authoritative picture story.[21] Following the establishment of place – a map of Canada set the scene as the first slide – this missionary picture show proceeded imaginatively to transport its audience northward with photographs of the schooner *Lorna Doone* (which took Fleming north in 1909) and the Hudson's Bay Company's *Bayrupert* (wrecked on a reef off the Labrador coast in 1927). In representing the tenuous supply and communication lines, these pictures showed, in the words of the accompanying lecture, 'the hardships endured by the missionaries in the early days'. Views of icebergs and an unnamed ship making its way through the ice pack further signified the 'dangers and difficulties' in going north. Once in the Arctic, viewers were exposed to a variety of subjects which formed the core of the show. Pictures highlighting the missionary presence (the mission building at Lake Harbour, for example) were interspersed with slides illustrating the material culture (particularly clothing and kayaks) and way of life of the Inuit (seal hunting, igloo building and fox trapping).

Another category of image, that of the portrait and group shot, portrayed the 'Eskimo' as the subject of missionary desire. Yet how was it possible, through photographic representation, to convey the life of the spirit? How could one portray the goals and successes of the missionary programme – the hoped for and imagined end to primitive ways – while drawing upon the power and resonance, as Fleming recognised, of the photographic image? Through juxtaposition of image and text (both spoken and written), and presenting contrasting images together, the lantern slide shows and publications worked towards building a visual language of the transition from darkness to light. This was in part accomplished through the photographs' apparent ability to render visible not only facial features but underlying feelings and beliefs.

One of the first studies of the Eskimo in *Dwellers in Arctic Night* was a portrait of an unidentified man, captioned 'An Unevangelized Eskimo'. Similarly, in the lantern slide show 'Across the Canadian Arctic' the commentary for a slide entitled 'An Unevangelized Eskimo from Baffin Land' proclaimed: 'You have only to look at this face to realise that the light of the Gospel had not yet penetrated into the heart and mind.' This portrait was immediately followed by that of Sow-ne-ah-lo, an influential leader who, although strongly opposed to Christianity, before dying apparently instructed the young men of his village to 'learn the commands of God and the words of Jesus, and believe'. The presenter of the lantern slide show was referred to the appropriate passage in *Dwellers in Arctic Night*, where she would also find the portrait of an unidentified 'Native Christian Leader'.[22] These pictures framed their subjects according to the conventions of portrait photography, composing head and shoulder shots in three-quarters view; at the same time, these faces were meant to reflect subtly the inner qualities implied by their respective captions and lantern slide lecture commentary. Native faces and bodies, captured on film, could

AN UNEVANGELIZED ESKIMO.

not only function as contributions to and evidence of 'scientific knowledge' but were also believed to convey the unseen matters of the heart and mind.

A further example of the visual contrast between the unevangelised and the converted appeared the year following the publication of *Dwellers in Arctic Night* in the inaugural issue of the annual illustrated newsletter of the Diocese of the Arctic.[23] Two photographs on the back page of this first issue, placed side by side, evoked a vivid visual argument for the possibilities of missionary success. On the left a young woman, seated with a three- or four-year-old child on her lap, stood for the unredeemed native: 'Eskimo Mother and Child, Perry River. These are pagans.' Beside this image the studio portrait of 'Eskimo Boys, Sam (the taller) and Ben', cheerfully sporting their Lakefield Preparatory School uniforms, testified to the civilising possibilities when children were released from the supposedly 'negative' influences of Inuit culture.[24]

In this classic example of the photographic representation of native 'improvement', the imagined Eskimo is transformed.[25] Initially approached by John Ell Oudlanak, a prominent Inuit leader of Southampton Island, to have his son educated 'outside', Fleming decided to embark on this educational 'experiment'. Fleming's views were bluntly stated to O. S. Finnie, director of the Canadian Northwest Territories and Yukon Branch: 'Only let me say that the idea is not to educate these boys and send

FAR LEFT
Fig.6. 'Sow-ne-ah-lo',
from *Dwellers in
Arctic Night*, 1928.

LEFT
Fig.5. 'A Native
Christian Leader',
from *Dwellers in
Arctic Night*, 1928.

BELOW
Fig.7. 'Eskimo
Mother and Child'
and 'Ben and Sam',
from *Fellowship of the
Arctic*, 1929.

\*　　\*　　\*　　\*

**Eskimo Mother and Child, Perry River.
These are pagans.**

**Eskimo Boys, Sam (the taller) and Ben**

\*　　\*　　\*　　\*

them back to the simple primitive Eskimo life, but to send them back for all practical purposes as white men.'[26] In reducing the complex life stories of Samuel Pudlutt and Benjamin Oudlanak into simplified two-dimensional images of the 'civilising' process, 'Sam and Ben' came to represent an assimilationist ideal of religion and education united in a project of cultural reformation.

Although captured as 'white men' for a fleet-ing moment, the experiences of the two nine-year-old boys boarding at Lakefield School did not live up to the hoped-for transformation. After attaining a level of literacy in the classroom and learning sports on the playing field, the two boys returned to the eastern Arctic, having spent much of the second half of their school year ill, the victims of a lack of immunity to influenza, pneumonia, measles and tonsillitis.[27] As Fleming himself acknowledged, the physical dangers of

Some of the Brownies (Junior Girl Guides) at Aklavik, N.W.T. It has been found that the training developed by the Girl Guides, Brownies, Boy Scouts and Cubs is of great value in teaching the native children the meaning of co-operation. Under normal circumstances the Indians and Eskimo are individualists.

Fig.8. 'Some of the Brownies at Aklavik, N.W.T.', from *Arctic Advance*, 1943.

such an 'experiment' were great. Yet overriding this concern was the hoped-for elevation of the native. It was this belief that justified the continued 'need' for Eskimo and Indian residential schools in the north; that saw as necessary and desirable the separation of the younger generation from their 'pagan' parents. The desired goal was encapsulated in the image of aboriginal boys and girls in the uniforms of 'civilisation', dutifully displaying themselves as dark-skinned 'white men' to the camera's gaze.

As Fleming formulated the Church's social policies in the north during his early years as administrator of the Arctic Missions, schools loomed large in his mind as instruments of Christian advancement. In Fleming's understanding the Eskimo were 'simply an undeveloped race' who, given the advantages of the white man's education, would be able to advance and reach their potential. The *Arctic Mission* newsletter continued to trade on the hoped-for transformative effects of 'Christian education'. As the caption beside the picture of a little wide-eyed Inuk boy in the newsletter of the Fellowship of the Arctic pleaded, 'I Want To Go School.'[28]

As Anglican-run institutions sprang up in the Northwest Territories and Yukon under Fleming's regime, the opportunities for visual

propaganda increased proportionally. Throughout the 1930s and 1940s Fleming's yearly pamphlets on his episcopal visitations situated the Inuit within the successful movement from primitivism to civilisation. Churches and schools and hospitals (built and run by Anglicans, of course) dot the landscape, while Eskimos begin the journey towards the establishment of 'an indigenous Church in Arctic Canada'.[29] The captioned pictures in these annual illustrated pamphlets can be read as photo-essays which constructed their own visual argument for continued Anglican involvement in social services for the Inuit. Inside the pamphlets' pages the northerners pictured, both native and white, are invariably connected to the various incarnations of the Anglican Church and its good works.

Fleming's review of his 1943 trips to the western Arctic and Hudson Bay included a photograph of a group of young smiling girls at Aklavik, sporting Brownies' tunics and caps, caught in an informal pose by the bishop's camera.[30] The accompanying caption is particularly emphatic in its appeal for a new order in the north, modelled on the imperial ideal:

It has been found that the training developed by the Girl Guides, Brownies, Boy Scouts and Cubs is of great value in teaching the native children the meaning of co-operation. Under normal circumstances the Indians and Eskimos are individualists.

This caption displays a curious expression of ethnographic understanding; more importantly, perhaps, it confirmed the belief in the transformative abilities of discipline and training, positioning these techniques of power as a major and continuing factor in the Anglican programme. In *Twilight*, Fleming's visual and written report of his episcopal visitation of 1941, Canon Shepard (principal of the residential school at Aklavik) traded his robes, as pictured a few pages before, for the stetson, cravat and breeches of the Scout Master. Shepard leads a troupe of uniformed aboriginal Boy Scouts, Girl Guides and Brownies on, one presumes, a trek towards 'civilisation', imagined in the terms of empire and Christianity.[31]

At the same time, such pictures demonstrate the continued use of photographic means of representation to highlight (and make visible) an idea of native northerners. As portrayed in Fleming's illustrated lectures and publications, Inuit were integrated into a vision of the north as part of the Canadian Dominion and the British Empire, members of settled communities that were centred around the services of Church (and, to a much lesser extent, commerce and state). But the Arctic was still a Twilight Land, where 'pagans' continued to co-exist with the converted.[32] And so the work of reaching the 'true nomads either on the coast or over the wide open spaces of the Arctic prairies' continued, while audiences in southern Canada, the United States and Great Britain followed and (hopefully) supported this great missionary adventure.[33]

In his devotion to bringing the Inuit into the Christian fold, Fleming both recognised and capitalised on the power of photographic representation as a potent and accessible medium of communication. These Eskimo pictures received a wide distribution throughout the North Atlantic world, both in Fleming's own publications and lectures, and through the publicity he secured as Archibald the Arctic, head of the Arctic Missions.[34] These images, however, remain problematic, disturbing reminders of an ideology of cultural dominance that underlay the humane goals of 'educating' and 'civilising' and 'Christianising' the native. In the selectivity of their presentation such photographs mask the failure of Church and state attempts at native education, for example, as well as submerging the specific historical circumstances behind the individual images. Picturing northern native peoples as sites of transformation, Fleming presented the Eskimo as moving from a state of primitive paganism to that of Christian civilisation, refashioning the Inuit for the consumption of audiences throughout North America and Britain.

## Notes

I wish to acknowledge the Social Sciences and Humanities Research Council of Canada and Carleton University for supporting this research, and the Canadian Department of Foreign Affairs and International Trade and the organisers and sponsors of the 'Imagining the Arctic' conference for the opportunity to present my findings to such a knowledgeable and enthusiastic audience. The staff of the Anglican Church of Canada General Synod Archives provided invaluable assistance in locating and accessing relevant materials; thanks are also due to Rob Barrow of the Manitoba Museum for his photographic expertise.

1. See *Fellowship of the Arctic* (1929), 4. In his last message in *The Arctic News* (1949) Fleming wrote: 'I have given the best years of my life to this work – as missionary in Baffin Land, as Archdeacon of the Arctic and as Bishop of the Arctic – in order to try and build up our first Canadians who dwell in the lonely wilds of Arctic Canada.'

2. Archibald Lang Fleming, *Archibald the Arctic* (London: Hodder and Stoughton, 1957), 17–18; see also Fleming, 'A message from the Bishop,' *The Arctic News* (1947), 4, for another version of this pivotal experience.

3. See typescript of George Holmes (Bishop of Moosonee), letter to the editor, *The Life of Faith* (23 May 1906), included in Anglican Church of Canada General Synod Archives (hereafter GSA), A. L. Fleming Papers, M70–1, Series 3-A, file 1, John T. Griffin to Editor, *The Life of Faith* (1947).

4. Fleming, *Archibald the Arctic*, 40–135.

5. Ibid., 137–220; and correspondence in GSA, M70–1, Series 3-A, file 1.

6. An exception to this withdrawal of British support was the maintenance of two northern missions by the Bible Churchman's Missionary Society (London) from 1925 until 1950.

7. GSA, M70–1, Series 3-A, file 1, 'Copies of letters about the proposed re-organization of the Church's work in the Arctic', 26 October 1926 to 20 December 1926; see also MSCC *Current News* Bulletin No.2 (1927), highlighting the newly created Fellowship of the Arctic.

8. Archibald Lang Fleming, *Dwellers in Arctic Night* (Westminster and Toronto: Society for the Propagation of the Gospel in Foreign Parts and the Missionary Society of the Church of England in Canada, 1928).

9. Diamond Jenness, *The People of the Twilight* (New York: The Macmillan Co., 1928). On the change in title see GSA, M70–1, O. S. Finnie to Fleming, 27 March 1928 and Fleming, *Dwellers in Arctic Night*, viii.

10. Fleming, *Dwellers in Arctic Night*, 3–4.

11. Ibid., 35; and 24–5.

12. See ibid., 34–8, 55, 80–88; and Fleming, *Archibald the Arctic*, 154: 'The soul of the Eskimo reflects the free moods of hostile nature – silent like the stillness of the frozen sea at one time, then restless and hilarious like the rushing spring floods at another.'

13. For example Fleming, *Dwellers in Arctic Night*, 72. This story of the Eskimo's emergence from darkness and 'groping after the Light of life' was subsequently retold in

other publications. In a 1934 survey of Anglican missions in Canada, issued as study material for Church members, the subheadings of the section on the Eskimo indicated the spiritual 'progress' being made, using the terms popularised by Fleming. See H. Walsh, ed. *Stewards of a Goodly Heritage: A Survey of the Church's Mission Fields in Canada* (n.p.: Joint Committee on Summer Schools and Institutes of the Church of England in Canada, 1934), 30–49.

14. Archibald Lang Fleming, *Twilight* (n.p., 1941), 2.

15. *Quebec Chronicle Telegram* (28 February 1929).

16. See Jennifer S. H. Brown, 'Mission Indian progress and dependency: ambiguous images from Canadian Methodist lantern slides,' *Arctic Anthropology* 18, No.2 (1981), 17–27, for an insightful analysis of earlier missionary efforts using visual communication.

17. A. L. Fleming, 'The Eskimo of Baffin Land,' 15 February 1913, in GSA, M70–1, Series 7-A, file 14.

18. Fleming, *Dwellers in Arctic Night*, 7.

19. On the relationship between anthropological thought and the constructions of photographic meaning see the essays in Elizabeth Edwards, ed., *Anthropology and Photography, 1860–1920* (New Haven and London: Yale University Press, 1992); on the adoption of anthropological concepts by missionaries see Charles R. Taber, *The World Is Too Much with Us: 'Culture' in Modern Protestant Missions* (Macon, Georgia: Mercer University Press, 1991).

20. GSA, M70–1, Series 3-B, file 6, Fleming to Revd G. P. Whately (SPG), 8 April 1929, on film showings without Fleming in attendance; Miss E. Blackstone, Honorary Secretary of the Arctic Mission Fund in England was praised by Fleming as she 'has at her own expense purchased a most excellent electric lantern and gives delightful illustrated talks on the Arctic'. *The Arctic News* (1933), 4.

21. GSA, M70–1, Series 7-A, Item 2, 'Across the Canadian Arctic, Baffin Land', lecture notes on lantern slide show given 5 February 1930 (South Osset Church).

22. Fleming, *Dwellers in Arctic Night*, plate 7, facing page 15; plate 31, facing page 111; and plate 46, facing page 166; on Sow-ne-ah-lo see 103–10.

23. See *The Fellowship of the Arctic* (1929), 4. Produced out of the Diocese of the Arctic office (located at Church House, Toronto), this publication (which was renamed *The Arctic News*) was distributed in Canada and Great Britain to supporters and members of the Fellowship of the Arctic.

24. It is worth noting that this photograph of Sam and Ben was chosen over that of a more sombre-looking one taken during the same studio sitting (GSA, P8495, Diocese of the Arctic Photograph Collection, item 101; caption on back of photograph; 'Ben and Sam brought out by A.L.F. to Lakefield School for one year as a try out. The experiment was not repeated.')

25. Note that Fleming tried, unsuccessfully, to obtain photographs 'of the two boys in native clothing' (see GSA, M70–1, Series 3-B, file 13, Ralph Parsons (District Manager, HBC) to Fleming, 18 June 1928). In this juxtaposition of photographs one can also discern an echo of the late nineteenth-century image of the vanishing primitive; see, for example, the promotional postcards of the Carlisle Indian School (Pennsylvania), discussed in Brian W. Dippie, 'Representing the Other: the North American Indian,' in Edwards, *Anthropology and Photography*, 136.

26. GSA, M70–1, Series 3-B, file 13, Fleming to O. S. Finnie, 22 November 1928.

27. "Eskimo boys" romance finds tragic sequel in return to arctic: Archdeacon's experiment fails not in proof of intelligence but in physical adaptability', *Toronto Star* (26 June 1929), clipping in GSA, M70–1, Series 4-B, Box 6.

28. GSA, M70–1, Series 3-B, file 13, Fleming to O. S. Finnie, 22 November 1928; Ralph Parsons (District Manager, HBC) to Fleming, 18 June 1928; *The Arctic Mission* (1932), 2. Fleming worked closely with the Indian and Eskimo Residential School Commission of the MSCC, recruiting staff, raising funds and formulating policy (see GSA, M70–1, Series 3-B, file 17).

29. Fleming, *Twilight*, 14.

30. Archibald Lang Fleming, *Arctic Advance* (n.p., 1943), 13.

31. Fleming, *Twilight*, 7; 13. See also the photograph by D. B. Marsh in *The Arctic News* (Spring 1946), 1, in which a Union Jack and waving parade of Aklavik Scouts, Cubs, Brownies and Guides march right out of the picture's frame.

32. See, for example, the 'Pagan Eskimo Family of Victoria Island' on the cover of the brochure appealing for members and gifts for the Fellowship of the Arctic, enclosed in Archibald Lang Fleming, *Sentinels of the North* (n.p., 1939).

33. Fleming, *Twilight*, 12.

34. For a sense of the publicity garnered by 'The Flying Bishop' in the British and Canadian press see GSA, M70–1, Series 4-A, Scrapbooks, 1933–4 and 1938 and Series 4-B, clippings, 1926–9.

Zebedee Nungak and Stephen Hendrie

# Contemporary Inuit Photography in Nunavik: Two Decades of Documentary, Photojournalistic and Corporate Photography at Makivik Corporation

Development, with a capital 'D', and the Quebec question have both played a part in the evolution of contemporary Inuit photography in the northern Quebec region known as Nunavik. Development in the sense that the massive hydro-electric project announced in 1970 by then premier Robert Bourassa sparked a vivid reaction from the aboriginal groups (Inuit and Cree) who have lived in the northern Quebec region for thousands of years. Meanwhile, the Quebec question – its desire to be a sovereign country – has also had the effect of making the Inuit of Nunavik exceptionally well attuned to the political activities and overtures coming from Quebec City and Ottawa.

These outside influences sparked the Inuit into action in the early 1970s (fig.1) to assert their rights to their land, and not to be literally bulldozed off it by the construction crews tearing up the tundra. It was a political awakening the southern governments were unprepared for.

The Inuit mobilised and formed the Northern Quebec Inuit Association (NQIA) in 1972 to protest the proposed development that was taking place in the James Bay territory. Led by young Inuit leaders such as Charlie Watt and Zebedee Nungak – names now very familiar to people across Canada – the NQIA soon started publishing a monthly magazine, called *Taqralik*, in May 1974 (fig.2). Legend has it that Charlie Watt telephoned William Tagoona who had just started working for the federal government in Yellowknife. Tagoona was enticed to come to Kuujjuaq (formerly Fort Chimo) and start the magazine. He stayed with it a year, and then went to work for the CBC Northern Service, where he continues to broadcast a daily current affairs radio programme. He was followed in the editor's shoes by Moses Nowkawalk of Inukjuak, and soon after by Alec Gordon, who stayed as editor for several years. Alec Gordon now works alongside William Tagoona in Kuujjuaq at the CBC.

With a monthly magazine, the Northern Quebec Inuit Association published regular editions featuring photographs of the meetings they held in various northern communities. Out of necessity, then, Inuit developed techniques of photojournalism in order to communicate the activities of the NQIA to Inuit living in the northern communities, and to people who had taken an interest and had begun to subscribe to the magazine from outside the region.

Events in many cases determined the style of photography used to illustrate stories. During meetings of the Northern Quebec Inuit Association, much like the current meetings of Makivik Corporation, though on a smaller scale, *Taqralik* photographers snapped images spontaneously during the sessions, which usually lasted for a week. Typically, what emerged from the meetings were several rolls of photographs featuring Inuit speaking at microphones, often very animated, in heated exchanges. Following the thread of discussions, photographers (who also wrote the stories) were prompted to interrupt their note-taking on important occasions in order to snap an important image, hoping later to match it to the story.

At the closure of these lengthy meetings, a group photograph would be taken. For the photographer, this would always be a challenge. The end of a meeting was always unpredictable. It could end as scheduled at 5:00 pm, just as it could easily be past midnight. In any case, the photographer would have to be ready. The delegates tended to be exhausted at the end of a long meet-

Fig.1. NQIA group
photograph, Quaqtaq,
1976. (Photographer:
Alec Gordon)

ing, and impatient to leave. The photographer had to act rapidly in order to get all the delegates into place for the group shot. If there was time, this might be done beforehand, outside, where lighting conditions would permit a fast shutter speed. Otherwise, the photograph was usually taken inside the gymnasium where the meeting was held, after tables and chairs had been cleared allowing the entire group to fit in the picture.

In recent years, when Zebedee Nungak has been the First Vice-President and now President of the Corporation, his assistance has made the group photograph an animated event. He has developed a dance-like technique which guarantees a spontaneous outburst of laughter from the delegates. Once he achieves this effect, he returns to his spot in the middle of the group and the photograph is snapped. This is done a few times, and the results are always excellent.

*Taqralik* metamorphosed over the years, depending on the funding levels it was accorded by Makivik Corporation. During one two-year period from 1978 to 1980 the publication transformed itself into an independent monthly newspaper called *Atuaqniq*. Still funded mostly by

Makivik, it began to run advertisements and sought financial support from other northern organisations. William Tagoona and Alec Gordon were the core writers, augmented by Michael McGoldrick, a stalwart soldier for the Inuit cause, bitten like many southerners are with the northern bug. *Atuaqniq*, starkly black and white in its presentation, published biting editorials, frothing letters to the editor, and vividly illustrative front cover photographs, often spreading across the entire top fold beneath the masthead. In the last issue, dated June 1980, the staff wrote that they had to decide whether to take holidays (as they had not taken any for two years) or keep the paper going. They took holidays!

*Atuaqniq* folded, and an independent publication has been sorely missed, but a slim mimeographed version of *Makivik News* took up the slack at that point for a year or so before *Taqralik* was revived in a much thicker version. Under the editorship of Harry Hill it published for several years as a monthly, until June 1986, at which time the name changed again back to *Makivik News*, when it was issued on an occasional basis (sometimes monthly, sometimes bi-monthly, sometimes quarterly). Charlie Patsauq, who had earned his photographic stripes working on *Taqralik* in its heyday, kept on with *Makivik News* as the publication shifted locations from Kuujjuaq to Montreal to Inukjuak. He was joined for three years from 1988 to 1991 by Emanuel Lowi, who had a penchant for Leica cameras. The two excelled in producing vibrant images, developing their own black and white prints in a small darkroom in Inukjuak. Charlie Patsauq produced *Makivik News* on his own for a few months, and was joined by Stephen Hendrie in June 1991. Tragically, Charlie Patsauq passed away in January 1992, in a fire. Bob Mesher, who had worked as a summer student, was hired full time in September 1993 and rose to the position of editor of *Makivik News* in June 1995.

During the years leading up to the signing of the James Bay Agreement, from 1973 to 1975, many photographs were published of the field trips that were undertaken by the Inuit negotiators. Some of these featured images of the arrival of the NQIA directors being met by members of the community at the airstrip (there were few airport facilities in those days). They are telling photographs in that they illustrate the paucity of installations in the communities before the Agreement was signed. In this sense, the early photographs taken during the NQIA years are also of a documentary style, especially seen from the perspective of 1996.

Perhaps the most political photographs taken by the *Taqralik* staff occurred on 11 November 1975 during the signing ceremony of the James Bay Agreement. In Quebec City, between 11:30 pm and midnight, representatives from all of the seven parties to the Agreement, and the signatories (there were eleven Inuit signatories), staff members, officials, and media gathered to witness an historic event in Canadian history (fig.3).

The black and white images which emerged from the ceremony are now part of the collective psyche in Nunavik. The images of Charlie Watt, flanked by Zebedee Nungak on one side, and Quebec Premier Robert Bourassa a few seats away, and Cree Grand Chief Billy Diamond still further, are etched into the memories of many. Seeing the photographs brings back various memories for people who view them, whether they were participants or beneficiaries of the process. Yet many of the photographs are simple depictions of young men signing a large telephone-book sized document. Knowing the political implications of the signature is what forces the viewer to look more closely at each detail of the photographs. We peer into the eyes of the people and try to guess what they may have been think-

ing. We look at their hands as they sign, their fingers holding down the paper firmly, and at other details, such as the period clothing and hairstyles.

In the contemporary political discourse maintained by Makivik's President, Zebedee Nungak, those signatures inked on the white paper by the eleven Inuit men were the first time Inuit had signed with informed consent on an issue of such fundamental importance to them: their land (fig.4). Doctoral papers have been written on the relationship of the land to the Inuit, and rightly so. It is beyond this essay to get into the depth of that relationship, but suffice it to say that it is an intrinsic link between person and terra firma. Thus, when Zebedee Nungak expresses the injustices done to his people by the historic transfers of land in 1670, 1870 and 1912, of the Nunavik territory from one political jurisdiction to another, he does so with considerable passion and conviction. There are no archival photographs we have discovered that illustrate these historic strokes of the pen, but there were no Inuit in sight at these ancient signing ceremonies, nor were Inuit ever consulted about the land transfers.

TOP
Fig.2. *Taqralik* covers. (Photographer: Harry Hill)

ABOVE
Fig.3. James Bay and Northern Quebec Agreement signing ceremony 11 November 1975.

Fig.4. Zebedee Nungak signing James Bay and Northern Quebec Agreement, 11 November 1975.

The land issue settled on 11 November 1975 with the signing of the James Bay Agreement was something the Quebec government was obliged to attend to once it had obtained the 'Ungava' territory as a result of the 1912 Boundaries Extension Act. Satisfying the condition became imperative for the government only when Inuit and Cree took them to court as the bulldozers scarred the land, ripped up trees and carved new roads into the 'Nouveau Québec' soil. The thought of the heavy equipment being forced to remain idle, as a result of the interlocutory injunction granted to the Inuit and Cree on 15 November 1973 by Quebec judge Albert Malouf, also contributed to the urgency to settle the outstanding land issue.

So it was the pressure of 'Development' and the political elements that concentrated minds in the early seventies in Quebec and produced Canada's first modern land claims agreement: the James Bay and Northern Quebec Agreement. It granted the Inuit party $90 million in compensation over a period of twenty years (the final payment being in December 1996), specific title to certain lands in the Nunavik region, and exclusive hunting, fishing and trapping rights over the whole territory. It also gave the Inuit new institutions, such as the Kativik Regional Government (to administer the new municipalities), the Kativik School Board, and Hunting Fishing and Trapping Committees to oversee wildlife management in the region.

The Agreement also provided for the creation of an Inuit-owned economic development corporation. This was to become Makivik Corporation. Makivik, which means 'advancement' in

Inuktitut, had the mandate to manage the compensation funds, implement the James Bay Agreement for the Inuit, and represent the Inuit politically. Makivik took on many of the tasks initiated by the Northern Quebec Inuit Association (NQIA), which folded its activities in 1978.

Makivik was officially created on 23 June 1978 by a special act of the National Assembly in Quebec City. It maintained the publication of the magazine begun by NQIA. There was no lapse in publishing despite the change in organisations.

With the creation of the new corporation, and the infusion of funds to develop the region, a new brand of photography began to emerge, that of corporate photography. Makivik would soon have an Annual Report to produce. The activities of the fledgling corporation were photographed by staff of Makivik's Communications Department. At the outset, Makivik's activities consisted of implementing the James Bay Agreement (not an obvious process considering it was the first such Agreement), investing the compensation funds and creating regional businesses.

The sort of corporate photography which emerged over the years was a continuation of the political photographs taken during the period leading up to the signing of the Agreement, and the documentary style of photographs taken during meetings. It was decidedly not the brand of 'corporate photography' to be found in glossy stock photographic catalogues, replete with hired actors posing in artificial business environments with saccharine smiles. Rather, it depicted real people engaging in real social, political and economic activities, in the act of developing their region. Thus Makivik's corporate photography retained a spontaneous look to it.

The exceptions to this were the portrait photographs of the members of the Executive and Board of Directors. The Annual Reports required a series of posed portrait photographs which were taken with great care by the Information Department staff working for Makivik over the years. Charlie Patsauq was one of the notable photographers who photographed the Executive and Board members. He studied photography at Dawson College in Montreal. He used a 4 × 5 camera for the portrait-photographs of the executives one year to produce tack-sharp images, which were published as full-page colour photographs.

As Makivik's subsidiary companies grew, so did the collection of images about them. The main subsidiary companies have always been in the aviation industry. As a result, many images of small twin-otter, HS-748, float airplanes, and now a Dash-8 aircraft, are in the Makivik photograph archives. These are augmented by an increasing number of jet aircraft which are flown by First Air, a subsidiary Makivik purchased in September 1990. Again, the photographs involving the aviation activities are done in a spontaneous manner, using the actual flight crews and depicting real-life situations. The most frequent images that are published feature a mixture of passengers and flight crew in on-board or on-the-ground situations (fig.5).

Capturing images of Makivik's fisheries activities has been more difficult over the years because of the fact that our staff would have to spend three months out on a factory freezer trawler in order to obtain photographs of the fishing crew in action on the shrimp boats. Makivik's subsidiary company, Seaku Fisheries, manages an offshore shrimp licence, which is fished by a ship called the *Aqviq*, owned by Faerocan. Over the ten years this company has been in existence, over 100 Inuit have trained to work on the factory freezer trawler. We have resorted to loaning camera equipment to the Inuit crew members in order to obtain photographs of their activities. Also, Seaku's General Manager, Marc Allard, has taken excellent photographs of the *Aqviq* in port at St John's, Newfoundland (fig.6).

Aside from the corporate aspect of Makivik's activities, it continues to devote considerable time to address political issues. At times, photographing these events harkens back to the era of the signing of the James Bay and Northern Quebec Agreement, especially in the case of the Quebec sovereignty issue.

Accommodating Quebec within the Canadian federation has been at the top of the political agenda ever since the formation of the Dominion of Canada in 1867. The contemporary brand of Quebec nationalism was unleashed in the 1960s in what is known as the 'Quiet Revolution'. It was a time when the powers of Church and state were separated, and the visceral issues affecting French Canadians living in Quebec erupted, requiring considerable redress. Many legitimate concerns needed attention, the fundamental issues of power and language being among them. Before pools of capital were created for Quebec entrepreneurs, the face and language of business in Quebec was English. The majority francophone population were far from being masters in their own house, and, like any group in a similar situation, they demonstrated their political dissatisfaction. Though many grievances have been settled over time, and the power structure among business, political, and cultural circles has shifted to francophones, Quebec nationalism persists.

ABOVE
Fig.5. First Air cargo handler, Dorval Airport. (Photographer: Stephen Hendrie)

LEFT
Fig.6. *Aqviq* Offshore factory freezer trawler operated by Faerocan for Seaku Fisheries Inc. (Photographer: Marc Allard)

The effects on the Canadian federation have been felt ever since and are known the world over, as Quebec has held two referendums in its struggle to separate from Canada and create a new country for itself.

For the Inuit of Nunavik, the political activity in the south of its region has meant considerable time spent in the process of communicating the issues involved in the Quebec separatism movement. While Quebecers have voted in two referendums (20 May 1980 and 30 October 1995), Inuit have voted in four. They have held an Inuit-only referendum prior to the Quebec vote on both occasions (14 May 1980 and 26 October 1995). This added voting activity has meant additional political activity on behalf of the Makivik leadership (fig.7).

The political photographs that accompany this process are indicative of the determination that

ABOVE
Fig.7. Press
conference 27 October
1995, Montreal.
Commenting on
results of Inuit
referendum held 26
October 1995.
(Photographer: Bob
Mesher)

RIGHT
Fig.8. FM radio:
Zebedee Nungak at
Ivujivik Radio
Station, 22 October
1995, talking about
Quebec sovereignty.
(Photographer:
Stephen Hendrie)

and begin a broadcast which could last up to four hours. The start of the programme consisted of communicating the Inuit position on Quebec sovereignty, and usually included a summary, in Inuktitut, of the reasons why separatists wanted to create a new country. After the position had been laid out, the phone lines would be opened up, and Zebedee would take calls from listeners for about an hour to an hour and a half, depending on the size of the community. Callers tended to be very supportive of the position the Inuit leadership had taken, and confirmed the sense that the leaders were heading in the right direction. In turn, the leadership came away from this process with a renewed sense of vigour in stating the Inuit opposition to the sovereignty project.

The photograph of Zebedee Nungak (fig.8) speaking at the FM-radio station was taken in Ivujivik on Saturday, 21 October 1995. The following Friday he was in Montreal inside a crowded hotel conference room to face a room of media, some local, some national and others from the international press. There, he delivered the result of the Inuit vote in their referendum held the day before. Ninety-five per cent of Inuit voted 'No' to Quebec sovereignty in their own referendum. Journalists stood intently to hear the results. 'We say "No" and in doing so it is clear, it is resounding. It thunders across the 55th parallel, and along the Arctic Coast from Kuujjuraapik to Killiniq', Nungak stated shortly into the press conference.

Bob Mesher, who is the editor of *Makivik News*, snapped photographs of this press conference as Zebedee Nungak spoke, and then turned the microphone over to Rosemarie Kuptana, the President of the Inuit Tapirisat of Canada. She underlined the support of the Inuit from other parts of Canada for the Inuit in Nunavik.

The pair were together four days later in Ottawa to comment on the much closer results of the Quebec-wide 30 October referendum. In that campaign the federalist 'No' camp won by a narrow margin of 50.6 per cent to the 49.4 per cent captured by the sovereignists who voted 'Yes'. This time the setting was the Charles Lynch Press Theater in the Canadian parliament buildings. With a backdrop of the nations' flags, the Inuit message was tempered with the knowledge that such a close result did not settle the issue, and that another constitutional round would surely emerge, and soon.

That it did. The same day, while returning to Montreal, news of the resignation of Quebec Premier Jacques Parizeau could be heard on the radio. It became immediately clear that with the onset of winter political shuffling would take

Inuit will be the ones who decide their future in Canada. The political process Inuit engaged in leading up to the October 1995 Quebec referendum can be dated back to their initial press conference on 8 December 1994, held in a Montreal hotel. At that time Inuit declared their firm opposition to the sovereignty project and continued to speak out against it since that time.

At academic and business forums the Inuit message was repeated on several occasions in southern Canada during the winter, spring and summer of 1995. Meanwhile, in the north the message was communicated by FM radio in the Nunavik communities, and by northern television across the Arctic regions. The Makivik leaders travelled to all but one of the fourteen Nunavik communities to deliver the political message in the weeks leading up to the Inuit referendum, held on 26 October 1995, four days prior to the Quebec vote.

Upon arrival in each community, Makivik President Zebedee Nungak, the spokesperson on this issue, would go to the local FM-radio station

place in Quebec City and Ottawa to set the stage for another act in the Canadian political process.

For Inuit, it was a matter of waiting for a few months, while the dust settled, before returning to the debate. It was done in the course of a luncheon speech to the Rotary Club of Toronto. They had wanted Zebedee Nungak to speak before the 30 October referendum, but remained keenly interested following the close result. On 23 February 1996 the Makivik President delivered a speech to the 200 guests which instilled a strong sense that the history of 'strokes of pen' was just that: history. 'That can never be done again without our consent,' he stressed, stabbing his finger emphatically in the air to underline his point.

Again, the photographs which came back from the lab complemented the steely determination of the speech. They would be used to illustrate the political message in a column run in *Makivik News* called 'Constitutionally Speaking', a summary of the political developments regarding the Quebec issue and how it affects Inuit.

The images would take their place alongside other political photographs collected over the past twenty years (fig.9). Inuit have been active in the Canadian political process, on this same issue, in all previous rounds. At constitutional conferences in Ottawa and across the country, the dates and months and years can no longer be easily remembered. We have to refer back to the printed page for an accurate dating of images where a photograph caption is missing from a negative.

The Canadian political process is one in which Inuit from Nunavik have excelled at participating. Charlie Watt, founding member of the Northern Quebec Inuit Association and one of the main architects of the James Bay Agreement, is now a Canadian Senator, after having served as President of Makivik Corporation for many years. Another former president, Mary Simon, is now Canada's Ambassador to the Arctic. Images of these leaders are part of Makivik's photographic history, and by extension, part of Nunavik's.

In the space of twenty-five years a rich photographic record of contemporary events has been kept by Makivik Corporation and its predecessor, the Northern Quebec Inuit Association. These images testify to one of the most vibrant political processes in Canada. The small percentage of images which have been published are a fraction of the wealth in imagery that exists in Makivik's collection.

Fuelled by the large-scale and intrusive development of the James Bay hydro-electric project,

Fig.9. Winnie Cookie of Kuujjuaraapik testifies at hearings on Great Whale Hydro Project, Inukjuak, July 1991. (Photographer: Charlie Patsauq)

as well as the constant political threat of Quebec separatism, Inuit have told their story using contemporary photographic techniques. The style of photography has been one of verisimilitude and spontaneity rather than one of controlled studio imagery and artifice. The trials and tribulations of failing, as well as the joys of victory, shine through the images. In their thousands the photographs are a quarter-century snapshot of the Inuit of Nunavik.

Jim Burant

# Using Photography to Assert Canadian Sovereignty in the Arctic: The A. P. Low Expedition of 1903–4 aboard the CGS *Neptune*

In 1903 a government expedition aboard the chartered whaling ship *Neptune* was sent to winter in Hudson Bay and to patrol the northern waters of the Arctic, in order to assert Canadian sovereignty and solidify claims to the Arctic islands. To ensure that the world could be shown substantial evidence of Canada's sovereignty over the archipelago, the expedition was accompanied by an official photographer. Photographs would play an integral role in the expedition's activities, as well as contributing towards shaping Canadian society's ideas and attitudes to the Arctic islands. This expedition was a result of the decision of the British government to turn over its claim to the Arctic archipelago to Canada in 1880.[1] Since that date several Canadian government forays had been made into the Arctic regions, both overland and by ship. In almost every case photography had been used to document the work of such expeditions as well as the inhabitants of the vast region for which Canada had become responsible.

The Canadian government had been an important supporter of the concept of using photography to record the salient features of its geography, its human endeavours and its inhabitants, employing it as early as the 1858 Canadian government expedition to western Canada.[2] The Geological Survey of Canada (GSC) had begun to use photography as early as 1860, the first date from which there are surviving collodion negatives.[3] Although Robert Bell, director of the Survey, could assert as late as 1901 that 'photographs are taken to illustrate the geology, scenery, the character of streams etc.',[4] many GSC staff were also taking photographs of the native communities and individuals encountered during their annual field trips. George Mercer Dawson,

a GSC field officer, who began using photography in the field in 1876, has been called 'one of the pioneers in obtaining accurate information about the North American Indians'.[5] The Survey did not yet have a separate photographic unit in the mid-1870s, but had already incorporated reproductions of photographs into their annual reports.

The GSC had extended its survey activities into the sub-Arctic and Arctic regions in the 1870s and 1880s, with extensive surveys being carried out by such men as R. G. McConnell, J. B. Tyrrell, George Dawson, Robert Bell, and Albert P. Low, whose seven-year odyssey of exploring and mapping Rupert's Land and Labrador began in 1892.[6] Low followed the Eastmain, Kaniapiskau and Koksoak rivers to Fort Chimo, Ungava Bay, in 1893, and then explored the Hamilton and Northwest Rivers in Labrador in 1894. In 1897 he would survey the south shore of Hudson Strait, and in 1898 the east coast of Hudson Bay.[7] Low usually took photographs during these expeditions, and he was considered an excellent photographer (fig.2).

Although there were other overland surveys of the sub-Arctic during this era, none of them touched upon the Arctic islands. Only in 1884 did the Canadian government begin to correct this oversight, with the despatch of the first of three annual expeditions to investigate the navigability of Hudson Bay and Strait, on board the SS *Neptune* in 1884 and 1885, and the SS *Alert* in 1886,[8] all under the command of RN Lieutenant Andrew N. Gordon. In 1884 and 1885 GSC officer Robert Bell was the expedition's 'geologist, taxidermist, photographer, and medical officer'[9] and had as a result taken a number of photographs as part of his survey work, including views of

natives he had encountered in Hudson Strait
(fig.3),[10] in order to obtain anthropological and
ethnological data he considered essential to the
scientific study of the region. Prior to the second
expedition, Bell also corresponded with Dr Franz
Boas, who had in 1883–4 been on southern Baffin
Island, studying native life there. Boas was seeking a paid position with the GSC to continue his
studies, but the GSC was only willing to offer to
transport him to Baffin Island and back, and Boas
decided not to go.[11] Although a second photographer, W. W. Fox, a reporter for the Toronto
*Star*, was on board the *Neptune* in 1884 as well,
none of his photographs have ever come to light.

The three Gordon expeditions concluded that
the navigation season was too short to encourage
a Hudson's Bay route for Western grain.[12] But in
1896 the new government of Sir Wilfrid Laurier
was under renewed pressure to find a northern
route to the markets of Europe, and another expedition to investigate the navigability of Hudson
Bay and Strait, under the command of William
Wakeham, on board the SS *Diana*, cruised the
area from July to October 1897.[13] Its findings
were similar to Gordon's, although the Wakeham
report would extend the shipping season by two
weeks. Wakeham made a specific point of
demanding a staff photographer, noting: 'My
own idea has always been to keep if possible a
complete photographic log of ice conditions as
such a record must be of more value and less open
to criticism than any amount of written descrip-

tion.'[14] As a result, 241 photographs were taken
by Graham Drinkwater, including ice conditions
(89), Inuit individuals and families (46), the crew
of the ship in everyday activities (38), and, most
importantly, ceremonies where Canadian sovereignty was asserted, such as at Kekerton Harbour
in Cumberland Sound on 17 August 1897.[15]
Wakeham proclaimed Canada's authority over
Baffin Island in particular, and the rest of the
Arctic islands in general, in this ceremony, in the
first overt step to establish Canadian rights in the
Arctic islands.[16] As in 1884 and 1885, Robert Bell
of the GSC was on board *Diana*, but on this occasion he landed on southern Baffin Island to
explore and survey the coast eastwards and to
journey into the interior, and he documented
native life in a series of photographs (fig.6).[17] Low
was also on board *Diana* until 18 July when he
and his field crew were dropped off at Douglas
Harbour to survey the southern coast of Hudson
Strait. Like Bell, Low also documented his journey in a series of fifty photographs.

Canada's timid exploratory surveys were
barely adequate in the face of international disputes which could have taken place over the
possession of the Arctic islands. American,
English and Scottish whalers had been operating
in Arctic waters since the 1820s, and in many
areas had hunted the stock virtually to extinc-
tion.[18] They also introduced disease (one group,
the Sadlermuit of Southampton Island, had been
virtually wiped out by measles in 1900) and worse

to the native populations; and conducted a lively and sometimes unfair trade in skins and ivory, to the disadvantage of the Hudson's Bay Company.[19] At the same time, explorers like Peary, Amundsen, and Sverdrup also focused international attention upon the seemingly open Arctic shores. Robert Peary's highly publicised attempts to reach the North Pole in 1898, 1905 and 1909 brought the

ABOVE
Fig.5. 'Group of
Esquimaux, Blacklead
Island [N.W.T.]
Aug. 19, 1897.'
(Photographer:
Graham Drinkwater)

RIGHT
Fig.6. 'Group of
Eskimo at Fort
Chimo [P.Q.] 1897.'
(Photographer: Albert
P. Low)

attention of the American public to the Arctic, while Otto Sverdrup's sober, scientific and methodical explorations of the islands to the west of Ellesmere Island from 1898 to 1902 preceded his efforts to have first Sweden, and after 1905 Norway, claim these territories for themselves. Finally, Roald Amundsen's attempt to sail the Northwest Passage showed the lack of control exercised by Canadians in these waters.[20] Events surrounding the Yukon Gold Rush in 1897–8,[21] and subsequent disputes about the location of the Alaska Boundary, were to show that the United States was a formidable opponent in territorial disputes.

Over the winter of 1902–3 planning for a Canadian government expedition to the Arctic began, which would assert Canadian sovereignty by means of proclamations and by the enforcement of Canadian customs laws and which would also assess the potential of the Canadian north in terms of natural and human resources. A large volume of correspondence between the Ministries of the Interior and Marine and Fisheries, the Royal North West Mounted Police, and the Geological Survey exists, which showed the problems arising out of such planning. No one wanted to pay for the expedition, and everyone wanted their own men to command it; there was a desire to distract attention from the voyage's true aims, because it was feared that other nations would challenge Canadian sovereignty prior to its proclamation, and there were questions as to the powers to be delegated to the RNWMP officers in their as yet unlocated police station.[22] Once some of these problems had been resolved, planning proceeded quickly.

A Newfoundland sealing vessel, the steamship *Neptune*, was acquired for the expedition's use, and Albert Low, the veteran GSC officer, was instructed to outfit her for a two-year cruise in Arctic waters.[23] The Department of Marine and Fisheries was ostensibly in charge of the project, with the declared intention being 'to cover the cost of the extension of the coast service and surveys on the northern coast of Canada'. Various official orders were received by Low from the Deputy Minister of the Interior, from Robert Bell, and from W. L. Magee, Clerk of the Privy Council.[24] Finally, Major John Moodie and four constables of the RNWMP were posted to the expedition, with orders to establish a permanent police post somewhere on the north-west coast of Hudson Bay.[25]

The *Neptune* set sail from Halifax on 23 August 1903, with a scientific team consisting of Albert Low, commander and geologist;[26] Lorris E. Borden, MD, surgeon and botanist;[27] G. B. Faribault MD, assistant-surgeon;[28] Andrew Halkett, naturalist;[29] C. F. King, topographer and meteorologist, also from the GSC;[30] and George F. Caldwell, photographer. There were also the RNWMP detachment; the ship's captain, Robert S. Bartlett, an experienced Arctic sailor; and a crew of twenty-nine. The ship sailed up the coast of Labrador to Nachvak and then to Port Burwell, where a native interpreter, Ford, was hired. The cruise continued on to Blacklead Island, Cumberland Gulf, where a Scottish whaling station and an Anglican mission were headquartered. Here, as at other whaling stations visited on Baffin Island, Major Moodie explained his intention to enforce Canadian government customs regulations. From Baffin Island the expedition then passed through Hudson Strait first to Winchester Inlet, and then to Fullerton Harbour in the north-west corner of Hudson Bay, where the American whaler *Era* of New Bedford, commanded by Captain George Comer, was also wintering. By mid-October the police quarters had been erected, with the assistance of crew members from the *Era*.[31] As winter set in, two groups of Inuit settled in near the two ships, the expedition employing the Kenipitu (Qairnirmiut) tribe, consisting of about twelve able-bodied men and their families, while the American whalers employed the Aivillik tribe, with about twice as many members.

After a winter passed with a routine of weekly dances, short exploratory trips, sports on the ice, but marred by the death of Dr Faribault and a crew member, the *Neptune* resumed its cruise on 18 July 1904. Returning through Hudson Strait to Port Burwell, it met the supply ship *Erik*, exchanged supplies, invalided several men home and left behind the disenchanted Major Moodie, who would return to Ottawa to stir up controversy. The *Neptune* meanwhile sailed north to Smith Sound and Davis Strait, and along the coasts of Greenland and Ellesmere Island, where on 11 August a proclamation of sovereignty was made, a cairn built, a Canadian flag raised and photographs taken. Jones and Lancaster Sounds were explored before the expedition landed at Beechey Island to conduct another formal ceremony of possession. Here a metal canister containing messages from the Norwegian Magnetic Pole Expedition of Roald Amundsen and dating from August 1903 was found near the cenotaph marking the Franklin Expedition's final wintering spot, and retained for transmission to the Swedish-Norwegian government.

From North Somerset, where another formal ceremony of possession took place, the expedition proceeded to Bylot Island, and then to Ponds

Inlet, where they met several Scottish whalers. Finally, by early September 1904 the *Neptune* was back at Cumberland Gulf, where supplies were landed to relieve the Inuit camped there, who had suffered due to a season of poor weather and bad hunting. The ship then sailed south to Port Burwell, returned through Hudson Strait to Cape Fullerton, and then sailed back east through the Strait. Along the way, the native pilot was dropped at Wakeham Bay, where his family and friends came out to greet him. Low took this opportunity to photograph members of the Okomingmiut tribe, their kayaks and umiaks.[32] The *Neptune* sailed into Port Burwell on 1 October 1904, only an hour before the *Arctic*, commanded by Captain Joseph Bernier and carrying Major Moodie and his wife Geraldine, arrived from the south. Bernier carried a letter from the Canadian government recalling the *Neptune* from northern waters, the news of which was received by the crew with relief. The expedition arrived at Halifax on 12 October 1904, having been gone for fifteen months, and having covered more than 16,000 km of Arctic waters. Over 3,200 km of coastal surveys had been completed, additional geological, meteorological, and natural history information had been gained, and Canadian sovereignty had been widely proclaimed.[33]

The work of the expedition has been well documented, with the results published in a number of places: House of Commons Sessional Paper Number 28, Part IV, of 1905, contains the 'Report of Superintendent J. D. Moodie On Service in Hudson Bay (Per SS Neptune, 1903–04)', including his recommendations for controlling the whalers, collecting customs, taking care of the natives, making patrols, and setting up posts;[34] Sessional Paper Number 22, 1905, 'Report of the Deputy Minister of Marine and Fisheries', contains Andrew Halkett's report upon animal life in the north;[35] and Sessional Paper Number 21, Appendix Number 12, was entitled 'Preliminary Report On the Dominion Government Expedition' and reported on the travels of the *Neptune* in northern waters.[36] Low produced two documents: the first was a section of the Geological Survey of Canada's *Annual Report for 1904*[37] on the geology and natural history of Hudson Bay and the Arctic archipelago; as GSC Reports were widely read by prospective mining investors and people interested in developing the country, this report would have stimulated further interest in developing the north. The second was his book, *Report on the Dominion Government Expedition to Hudson Bay and the Arctic Islands On Board The D.G.S. Neptune*

1903–1904, popularly known as *The Cruise of the Neptune*.[38] This book gave Canadians the first clear idea of their northern territories. Besides containing an account of the *Neptune*'s journey, there was a historical summary of Arctic exploration; a description of the Arctic islands; an account of the Inuit population, manners, customs, religion and other subjects which Morris Zaslow has noted as expressing 'the nation's concern with conserving the region's wildlife for the original inhabitants, and protecting the Eskimos from the inroads of diseases and changed ways of life introduced by the white man';[39] a description of the geology of the region; a discussion of the whaling industry in Hudson Bay and the northern waters; and, finally, an account of, and favourable comment upon, the proposed Hudson Bay route for shipping grain. Low included sixty-three photographs of various places, people and objects in the northern territories in the book, which added immensely to his clearly written text and created a superb picture of the Canadian north for a public which had heretofore been almost wholly ignorant of such matters. Zaslow has stated that Low's 'descriptions of the people, both native and white, and of the conditions in the region, were realistic and frank'.[40] In addition to his reports, Low also began to publicise the north and its advantages in public addresses, such as that made before the Canadian Club in Ottawa on 22 December 1904.[41]

The inclusion of an official photographer on the *Neptune* expedition demonstrated the importance and usefulness of the camera as a device for gathering information about the country. Parliamentary Sessional Papers contain detailed accounts for all of the items bought for the journey. R. F. Smith of Montreal supplied all of the photographic material to be used, including lenses, plate holders, special tripods, a panorama Kodak, a cartridge Kodak, Goesz lens No. 3 and volute, a wide-angle Zeiss lens and shutter, and printing paper, film, plates, and other photographic supplies, total cost being $666.70.[42] Who used this equipment is another matter. George Caldwell, the official photographer, seems not to have taken any of the photographs which survive from the expedition, nor does anyone mention his taking photographs in the extensive published and unpublished accounts of the expedition.[43] Little is known of him; he may have been from the Survey Branch of the Department of the Interior, although this is not certain.[44]

Newspaper stories later suggested that he lacked any knowledge of photography and was in fact a prospector with considerable practical but little scientific knowledge.[45] He was probably not a photographer, although he would take photographic equipment with him on another government expedition to the north in 1905.

Besides Caldwell, there were at least three men on board the *Neptune* with practical knowledge of photography: Albert Low, who had carried and used photographic equipment on previous GSC surveys; John Moodie, whose photographs are to be found in RCMP files; and Lorris Borden, whose diaries mention his own picture-taking efforts.[46] In addition to the expedition equipment, Moodie would send for additional photographic equipment to R. F. Smith from Cumberland Sound in the fall of 1903,[47] implying that he already had some.

The photographic legacy of the A. P. Low Expedition of 1903–4 is quite extensive and has been painstakingly reconstructed thanks to a unique numbering system devised by Low, which include a number and the inscription 'APL 1903–04' in the lower left-hand corner of each picture he took. Although the highest number located is 156, only 139 still exist in GSC collections or in albums from private collections as either prints or negatives or both.[48] Additional photographs by Major Moodie and Dr Borden also exist, although the exact number is not known.[49] Moodie seems to have taken an extensive number, as a letter from the Topley studio to NWMP Comptroller Fred White implied.[50] Topley refers to a set of prints made from Moodie's negatives, which may correspond to the twenty-two photographs taken at Fullerton during the winter and spring of 1903 still in RCMP files, of which copy negatives are in the NA. More research into this aspect of the photographic legacy still needs to be done.

Borden's diary mentions the expedition's photographic efforts on several occasions. On 14 November he commented on a dance held on board *Neptune*, and noted that 'a flash light was taken of the natives which seemed to startle them very much'.[51] In this regard, one should note that there exist two photographs, one by Low and one by Moodie, which were taken during the Christmas eve dance on board *Neptune*, each from a slightly separate angle, but obviously using the same flash powder explosion (figs 7–8). On 28 and 30 November 1903 he discusses patients suffering from psoriasis, and his and Low's efforts to take photographs, which they successfully developed two days later (fig.9).[52] Borden also mentions taking pictures on the ice during the expedition's cruise in July and August 1904.

A fourth photographer is associated with the *Neptune* expedition. This was George Comer, whose diary of the *Era*'s journey to the north

TOP
Fig.7. 'Group of Eskimos and Crew Members on board the "Neptune" at Fullerton, N.W.T., Christmas, 1903.' (Photographer: John D. Moodie)

ABOVE
Fig.8. 'Dance on board C.G.S. "Neptune", December 24, 1903.' (Photographer: Albert P. Low)

Fig.9. 'An Eskimo –
only one case of
psoriasis seen by Dr
Borden, 28 November
1903.' (Photographer:
Albert P. Low)

between 1903 and 1905, as mentioned, has been edited and published. Comer was a fascinating and complex man. Not only an experienced polar mariner, sealer and whaler, he was also an amateur ornithologist and mammalogist, and took an active interest in Inuit life and customs. On this voyage he had been commissioned to obtain a full ethnographic collection for the Museum für Völkerkunde in Berlin, and to secure clothing, charms and amulets from the Sadlermuit, plaster casts of heads, hands and feet, song recordings (for which he brought a graphophone), and notes of Inuit customs for the American Museum of Natural History in New York. He also compiled population figures for the principal Inuit groups, including details such as names, heights and weights of both sexes.[53] It is clear from Comer's diary that he and Low often took photographs together (fig.10), that they sought each other's advice on photographic techniques, and that they printed their photographs in Low's makeshift darkroom on board *Neptune*. In fact, Low's numerous photographs of the Inuit may have been inspired by George Comer's commission for the American Museum. Comer's diary entry for 16 February 1904 notes:

Today got several of the women to tattoo their faces with paint, as the tattooing on their faces will not take and show in a photograph. In this way I got five very good pictures showing as many different tribes – the Iwilic, the Netchilic, the Kenepetu, the Ponds Bay, and Southampton styles. Commander Low and Major Moodie also took pictures of the same. The commander came over this evening and gave me some good instruction in developing the plates.[54]

Several of Low's photographs from this session survive, and are among the most beautiful and impressive taken during the whole period (fig.1). It must have been an interesting scene – three different photographers waiting their turn to take photographs of these Inuit women, while outside the temperature hovered at 34° below zero.

Comer's diary also contains an entry on 1 February 1904, noting the problems of flash photography in the north:

This evening had the graphophone out and the cabin full of natives. I took two flashlight pictures but have not developed the plates yet. The first flashlight I probably did not fix right as it came near taking the roof of the cabin off – at least the report sounded loud enough to have done so.

The fraternisation between whalers and natives was frowned on by Major Moodie – Low would later take photographs of Comer and his crew, with Comer proudly seating on his lap the child whom he had had by an Inuit woman, Niviatsilaq, also known as Shoofly Comer (fig.11). But although Moodie fumed, he could do nothing but cause resentment on the part of the Americans.[55]

The photographic documentation taken by Low and Moodie on this expedition gives the observer a clear and precise picture of the assertion of sovereignty made by the Canadian government in 1903–4, as well as of the native populations which they encountered at Fullerton and at other locations during their voyages in the eastern Arctic. The momentous events of the journey are recorded for posterity, as well as the customs, practices and costumes of individual Inuit from several tribes. Some absences are notable – Low and his compatriots were unable to take photographs of native rituals and dances, as Comer would, because they had not gained the Inuit's trust, while the proclamation ceremony held by Major Moodie for the Inuit at Fullerton on 14 November 1903 (which raised Comer's ire about Moodie's 'paternalism') is not recorded. In spite of this, the photographic legacy extensively documents the first concerted Canadian government effort to claim the north, and demonstrates clearly the ongoing government commitment to using photography to maintain and to enhance its influence in the north. Succeeding Canadian expeditions and employees would continue to use photography to document events, activities and inhabitants, about which others will write and have written. For the period from 1880 to 1905, however, one can see the development of photography as an initially tenuous but increasingly important aspect of Canadian government activity in the Arctic.

## Notes

1. W. F. King, *Report upon the Title of Canada to the Islands North of the Mainland of Canada* (Ottawa: Government Printing Bureau, 1905), page B.

2. See Huyda, Richard, *Camera in the Interior* (Toronto: Coach House Press, 1980). H. L. Hime took photographs during this expedition, which are now preserved at the National Archives of Canada (hereafter NA).

3. Morris Zaslow, *Reading the Rocks* (Ottawa: Energy, Mines and Resources Canada; and Toronto: Macmillan & Co., 1975), p.69, describes photographs taken by James Richardson on the north coast of the St Lawrence river between Mingan and the Straits of Belle Isle. Zaslow's history of the Geological Survey of Canada is filled with important information about the use of photography, but he does not deal with it as a separate phenomenon.

4. Robert Bell, *Geological Survey of Canada Annual Report* (1901), Vol.14, Canada: Parliamentary Papers, p.14A.

5. Ralph Greenhill and Andrew Birrell, *Canadian Photography 1839–1920* (Toronto: Coach House Press, 1979), p.113. For a detailed examination of Dawson's early work on British Columbia, refer to Douglas Cole and Bradley Lockner, eds, *The Journals of George M. Dawson: British Columbia, 1875–78* (Vancouver, BC: University of British Columbia Press, 1989), particularly Vol.II, p.551 ff., which lists all of Dawson's photographs of British Columbia in this period.

6. Zaslow, op.cit., pp.158–9. McConnell carried out an extensive 6,400 km journey from the BC coast across the Rocky Mountains to the Arctic ocean and back in 1887–8, while in 1893 Tyrrell crossed the Barren Grounds via the Dubawnt River to Chesterfield Inlet, and surveyed the west coast of Hudson Bay, which he wrote about in *Across the Sub-Arctics of Canada* (Toronto, 1894).

7. Zaslow, op.cit., pp.167–8.

8. Claude Minotto, Mary Psutka, Jim Burant and Joy Williams 'To photograph the Arctic frontier: Part III', *The Archivist* (Ottawa: National Archives of Canada), Vol.4, No.4 (July–August 1977), pp.1–5.

9. Zaslow, op.cit., p.171.

10. Such natives are now referred to as Inuit, although the then contemporary term in use was Eskimo. The Bell, Low, Drinkwater and other GSC photographs are usually to be found in the NA, Geological Survey of Canada photo collections, including photo accs 1969–120, 1970–088, 1974–424, and others. There are also several private collections containing prints.

11. Douglas Cole and Ludger Müller-Wille, 'Franz Boas' Expedition to Baffin Island, 1883–1884', *Études/Inuit/ Studies*, Vol.8, No.1 (1984), pp.37–63, with a note about the 1885 correspondence on p.60.

12. Morris Zaslow, *The Opening of the Canadian North, 1870–1914* (Toronto: McClelland and Stewart Limited, 1971), p.255.

13. Ibid., p.259.

14. NA, Department of Marine and Fisheries, RG 42, Vol.338, File 13205, letter from William Wakeham to Frances Gourdeau, 8 April 1897.

15. National Archives of Canada, Wakeham Expedition Album, Photo Acc. no.1975–235.

16. Zaslow, op.cit. n.12, p.260.

17. The Wakeham expedition is discussed in greater detail in Minotto, Burant, Psutka and Williams, 'To Photograph the Arctic Frontier: Part I', *The Archivist*, Vol.4, No.5 (July–August 1977), pp.3–6. The Robert Bell collection at the NA (Photo acc. 1963–058) contains 23 glass negatives and 36 paper negatives, as well as 25 prints. No effort has yet been made to find out if further photographs exist in GSC collections, but a cursory glance has revealed none.

18. For an excellent account of whaling in general in the nineteenth century, see W. Gillies Ross, *Arctic Whalers, Icy Seas: Narratives of the Davis Strait Whale Fishery* (Toronto: Irwin Publishing, 1985).

19. Mary Psutka, *Wakeham Expedition To Hudson Strait & Cumberland Sound, 1897* (Ottawa: National Archives of Canada manuscript report, 1976), p.6; A. P. Low, *The Cruise of the Neptune, 1903–4* (Ottawa: Government Printing Bureau, 1906), pp.137–8, 271, 277–8. See also National Archives of Canada, Geological Survey of Canada Papers, RG 45, Vol. 107, pp.395–6: letter from Robert Bell, Acting Director of the GSC, to Clifford Sifton, Minister of the Interior, 1 December 1902.

20. Zaslow, op.cit. n.12, p.260.

21. Zaslow, op.cit. n.12, p.106.

22. NA, Royal Canadian Mounted Police Papers, RG 18 A1, Vol.236–05, Part I. Letter from Colonel Fred White, Comptroller of the NWMP to Superintendent J. D. Moodie of 5 August 1903.

23. NA, RG 45, Volume 108, p.157.

24. Orders in Council had been passed by the Privy Council and approved by the Governor-General on 13 August 1903, which appointed Low to the command of the expedition, and gave him judicial authority in the north. He was also provided with copies of important documents, including the Fisheries Articles of the Convention of 1818, so that the rights and privileges of American fishermen would be known. See NA, RCMP Papers, RG 18 A1, Vol. 259, File 650–03.

25. NA, RCMP Papers, RG 18 A1, Vol.293, File 236–05, Part II.

26. Canada, *Civil Service List*, 1903, p.28.

27. Borden's personal papers, including his diary of the expedition, are now at the National Archives of Canada. See NA, Manuscript Division, MG 30, B 46.

28. NA, RCMP Papers, RG 18 A1, Vol.280, File 683–04, entitled 'The Death of Dr. G. B. Faribault on Hudson's Bay Expedition', contains further information on Faribault.

29. Canada, *Civil Service List*, 1903, p.162.

30. *Ottawa City Directory for 1903* (Toronto: Might Directories Co.), p.327.

31. Low, *Cruise of the Neptune*, op.cit., pp.26–7. See also W. Gillies Ross, ed., *An Arctic Whaling Diary: The Journal of Captain George Comer in Hudson Bay 1903–1905* (Toronto: University of Toronto Press, 1984), which includes Comer's own concerns about the depletion of the fishery and the fate of the natives of the region.

32. Low, *The Cruise of the Neptune*, op.cit., p.134.

33. Canada, Sessional Papers, 1905, Vol.9, Paper No.21, Appendix No.12, pp.20–21.

34. Canada, Sessional Papers, 1905, Vol.12, Paper No.28, Part IV.

35. Canada, Sessional Papers, 1905, Vol.9, Paper No.22, Fisheries, Report of the Deputy Minister, pp.xlvii–xlviii; Hudson Bay Expedition.

36. Canada, Sessional Papers, 1905, Vol.9, Paper No.21, Appendix No.12, 'Preliminary Report On the Dominion Government Expedition In the SS Neptune To Hudson Bay and Northward'.

37. Geological Survey of Canada, *Annual Report for 1904* (Ottawa: The King's Printer, 1906).

38. Albert Peter Low, *Report on the Dominion Government Expedition to Hudson Bay and the Arctic Islands On Board The D.G.S. Neptune 1903–1904* (Ottawa: Government Printing Bureau, 1906).

39. Zaslow, op.cit. n.3, p.174.

40. Ibid.

41. *The Canadian Annual Review for 1904* (Toronto, 1905), pp.154–6.

42. Canada, Sessional Papers, 1905, Number 1, Auditor-General's Report: Cost of Extension of the Coast Service and Surveys of the Northern Coast of Canada. Steamer 'Neptune' – $103,412.11, page P.42. Detailed costs for each item were one 6½ × 8½ Zeiss lens, cost $256; three plate holders, $7.50; two special tripods, $14; panorama kodak, $20; one series V lens No.2, $28; one 5 × 7 cartridge kodack [sic], Goesz lens No.3 and volute, $108; one wide-angle, Zeiss lens and shutter, $ 33.50; and printing paper, film, plates, and other photo supplies, $666.70.

43. There may be some photographs by Caldwell in the Department of Fisheries, now the Department of Fisheries and Oceans, in Ottawa, but there are none in the National Archives.

44. This supposition is based on the memorandum of 5 August 1903, probably circulated by the Department of the Interior, Minister's Office, which stated that a photographer from the Survey Branch of the Department of the Interior would accompany the expedition. NA, RCMP Papers, RG 18 A1, Vol.293, File 236–05, Part II.

45. Toronto *Mail and Empire*, 27 August 1904.

46. NA, Manuscript Division, Lorris Borden Papers, MG 30 B 46 Vol.1. Diary entries for 19 and 20 October 1903 (pp.38–9), 30 November 1903 (pp.63–4), and 21 July 1904 (unpaginated) all relate to his work in photography.

47. NA, RCMP Papers, RG 18 A1, Vol.293, File 236–05, Part II.

48. The author has compiled a full list of these 139 photographs, which is available to anyone who would like a copy. Many negatives are missing, probably due to the accident which took place during a departmental move in April 1913, when a drawer full of GSC negatives was dropped in transit.

49. Although 36 photographs were in the Borden Papers in NA, some of them carried Low identification numbers.

50. RCMP Papers, RG 18 A1, Vol.293, File 236–05, Part II. Letter of 18 October 1904.

51. NA, Manuscript Division, Lorris Borden Papers, op.cit., p.58.

52. NA, Manuscript Division, Lorris Borden Papers, op.cit., pp.63–4.

53. W. Gillies Ross, 'George Comer, Franz Boas, and the American Museum of Natural History', *Études/Inuit/Studies*, Vol.8, No.1 (1984), pp.145–64.

54. Ross, op.cit.

55. Ross, op.cit., contains several passages where Captain George Comer pours out his resentment at Moodie's heavy-handedness towards the natives.

Donny White

# In Search of Geraldine Moodie:
# A Project in Progress

Fig.1. A self-portrait
of Geraldine Moodie
in her Battleford
Studio, c.1895.

The search for pioneer photographer, Geraldine Moodie, began over fifteen years ago while I was working with a series of frontier photographs in a small museum in western Canada. Intrigued not only by the images but also by the photographer, whose markings simply read, 'G. Moodie, Maple Creek', I began my search. Upon discovering that Moodie was female, I became fascinated and determined to discover as much as possible about this woman who practised photography on the Canadian Prairies during the late Victorian period. Little did I know that I was charting new territory and that Geraldine's photography was held in private and institutional holdings spread across two continents. Nor did I realise that this woman, who made a major contribution to Canadian history through her frontier photography, was virtually unknown.

My early efforts in documenting the elusive Geraldine were sporadic due to time and financial restraints, and the knowledge that the information was as scattered as her photographs and piecing it together would be like working on a giant jigsaw puzzle. However, in 1993 I intensified my search and embarked upon a project to create an inventory of Moodie's work in institutional and private holdings, as well as produce an illustrated history of the best of her work.

Drawing upon the archival sources investigated to date, the intention of this paper is to provide an overview of Geraldine Moodie's career as a photographer, highlighting those years spent in the eastern Arctic, and to demonstrate the importance of her photography to today's scholars. In order to appreciate this photographic legacy it is also necessary to know and understand the remarkable woman behind the camera and the trials she faced, virtually alone in her profession, in a male-dominated society on the Canadian frontier during the late Victorian/early Edwardian period.

Geraldine Moodie was born in Toronto, 31 October 1854, the third child of Agnes Dunbar Moodie and Charles Thomas Fitzgibbon. Her grandfather, Colonel James Fitzgibbon, was a military hero of the War of 1812, and her maternal grandmother, Susanna Strickland Moodie, was a well-known Upper Canada writer.[1] It is through the numerous letters of Susanna Moodie to her sister, Catherine Parr Traill, that we are provided with a glimpse of Geraldine's personality during her early years.

Losing her father at an early age, Geraldine's formative years were spent in close proximity to her mother's family and she was greatly influenced by them. As a girl she assisted with the task of 'painting the illustrations', prepared by her mother, for Catherine Parr Traill's book *Canadian Wildflowers*.[2] The work on this publication and subsequent projects instilled in Geraldine a lifelong passion for the documentation and illustration of Canadian plant life. Geraldine was educated in Ottawa and travelled to England in 1877 for an extended visit to her great-aunt, Sarah Gwillym. It was here she met John Douglas Moodie, a distant relative, and married him at Telford, Surrey, on 8 June 1878.[3]

In 1879 the Moodies returned to Canada with their first-born. Following a brief stay with Geraldine's mother at Lakefield, Ontario, they decided to try their hand at farming in the Canadian West, and settled on a homestead north of Brandon, Manitoba.[4] During their time in Manitoba Geraldine pursued her interest in plant life, preparing a number of watercolours of wildflowers which she exhibited, along with her mother's work, at the 1886 Colonial and Indian

TOP
Fig.2. Cree Indians following a Sun Dance celebration in Battleford district, June 1895.

ABOVE
Fig.3. Branding scene on a cattle ranch east of Maple Creek, District of Assiniboia, N.W.T. c.1897.

Exhibition in London.[5] The Moodies' attempt at farming, however, proved futile, and they returned to Ottawa where in 1885, the year of the Northwest Rebellion, J. D. received a commission with the Northwest Mounted Police.[6]

From Ottawa the Moodies embarked upon a thirty-two year adventure that, notwithstanding hardship, sacrifice and pain, would take them to almost every major Northwest Mounted Police Post in western Canada and into the Hudson Bay district of the eastern Arctic. Following a number of postings in the Northwest from 1886 to 1891, the Moodies arrived in Battleford, the former territorial capital, where they remained for five years.[7] In the years preceding Battleford five additional children were born.

It was during her years in Battleford that Geraldine began to photograph in earnest, as evidenced by the establishment of a photographic studio in 1895.[8] Exactly when she began experimenting with the camera is uncertain as few records exist regarding the general details of her

life. It is assumed, however, that the rigours of raising six children on the frontier and the constant movement from post to post made it impossible for her to pursue her photography with any seriousness, until the posting in Battleford.

In a rare letter, dated 8 May 1895, Geraldine discussed her work in Battleford with her great-aunt, Catherine Parr Traill, providing us with a personal perspective of her photography.

> I have not seen much of the Indians this spring. I have several promises to come and sit for their pictures when I get my new studio and fixtures finished. I had so much demand for my small pictures I have [got a] large camera and have built myself a little model studio to work in. It is very fascinating work and I can make enough to pay expenses and something over when I fill all the orders I have . . . Some of the views about Battleford are very pretty and will make lovely pictures. There are some pretty bits about twenty miles out . . . scenes of some of the fights during the Rebellion of 1890 [sic] which I think will interest people in the East.[9]

The subject matter of Geraldine's photographs during this time includes the usual portraiture work, the Northwest Mounted Police and their activities and the native community. In June of 1895 she witnessed a native Sun Dance ceremony and captured some of the rituals and celebrants on film.[10] Although prior to the Sun Dance she was fairly meticulous in signing her photographs, following the ceremony, she appeared to realise their historic importance and began to copyright specific images.[11]

In 1896 the Moodies were once again on the move, this time south to the ranching frontier of the Cypress Hills at Maple Creek. Difficult as it must have been to leave her new studio, coupled with the recent death of her fourteen-year-old son George in a riding accident, Geraldine soon established herself in Maple Creek. Shortly after her arrival, the *Medicine Hat News* reported that Mrs Moodie was not only building a photographic studio in Maple Creek but intended to open a branch in Medicine Hat.[12] Fascinated with her new surroundings, Geraldine soon set about documenting the unique lifestyle of the ranching culture, as well as the activities of the Northwest Mounted Police and the customary portraiture work that included a number of interesting studies of children.

In August 1897, at the time of the Klondike Gold Rush, Inspector Moodie was ordered north to explore and map an overland route from Edmonton to the Yukon.[13] Geraldine, however, remained in Maple Creek and, with the help of a domestic, she continued to operate her studio and commute sixty miles by rail to Medicine Hat on a regular basis for special sittings – no small feat for a married woman alone on the frontier with five children.

During her years in Maple Creek Geraldine also began to photograph and hand-colour some of the unique plant life of the prairie, such as the prickly pear cactus. Three of these images she copyrighted, copies of which today rest in the British Library, with two hand-coloured examples found at the Thomas Fisher Rare Book Library at the University of Toronto.[14]

The years following Inspector Moodie's return from the Yukon in 1899 are full of turmoil and upheaval. Unfortunately, documentation during this period is even more fragmented and it is only through J. D.'s movements that we catch an occasional glimpse of Geraldine. Upon his return Inspector Moodie, confident of a posting in the Yukon, sold his property, including Geraldine's studio, and moved his family, with the exception of the older children who remained in Maple Creek, to Lakefield, Ontario, to await word of his posting. The Commissioner, not pleased with Moodie's presumption, placed him back west, leaving Geraldine in Lakefield to await word of a more permanent posting.[15] Geraldine's activities in the years after her arrival in Lakefield remain obscure but, judging from the number of photographs of wildflowers that exist, it can safely be inferred that she continued her documentation of plant life.

Obviously discontented with his placement at Cardston, an outpost of Fort Macleod, Inspector Moodie requested leave to volunteer in the South African War. Initially, the Commissioner was negative to the proposal but changed his opinion following some rather firm but diplomatic correspondence from Geraldine.[16] The origin of Geraldine's influence and obvious favour with the upper administration of the Northwest Mounted Police remains mysterious; however, it worked to her advantage on this occasion and would again in the years to come. In 1901, following his South African service, J. D. returned briefly to Fort Macleod, Alberta, and the following year was placed in command of the Moosomin sub-district in Eastern Assiniboia in the province of present-day Saskatchewan.[17] Although Geraldine returned west with her husband, it is not known if she practised her photography as no signed photographs appear to exist from this period.

In 1903 J. D. was promoted to Superintendent of the Northwest Mounted Police, given powers of Acting Commissioner and assigned the task of establishing Canadian authority over the coast and islands of the Hudson Bay and eastern Arctic

regions. On 22 August of that year J. D., with five of his men, joined the government expedition under the command of A. P. Low and sailed north from Halifax aboard the vessel *Neptune* (see Burant in this volume), which was equipped for patrolling and exploring the northern waters.[18] Although J. D. requested permission from the Comptroller of the Northwest Mounted Police to have his wife and son Alex join him, it was not until the following September that Geraldine and her son sailed north aboard the steamer *Arctic*.[19] This ship, with Captain Joseph Bernier at the helm, was to relieve the vessel *Neptune* and continue to enforce Canadian sovereignty over the northern region.

With the arrival of Geraldine, Alex and additional members of the Mounted Police force, the small barracks, established the year before at Fullerton on the coast east of Southampton Island, had to be expanded. Geraldine lived aboard the ship until her new residence, dubbed 'Le Chateau' by the men of the *Arctic*, was

Fig.4. Cree girl and boy believed to be taken in the Maple Creek studio, c.1898.

complete.[20] In the meantime she set about famil-
iarising herself with her new surroundings and
establishing a rapport with the Inuit whalers and
their families, who would become the primary
focus of her photography over the next year.
Geraldine also became acquainted with Captain
George Comer of the American whaling
schooner, *Era*, which rested nearby during the
winter months.

One can only marvel at the courage it took for
Geraldine to leave her friends and family and follow her husband into the northern frontier so far
from her perception of civilisation. Although her
life in the Canadian Northwest had been far different from the upper middle-class environment
to which she had been accustomed, it could
hardly have prepared her for the harsh realities
and isolation of the north. However, as Geraldine
was endowed with the spirit of adventure, I
strongly suspect it was she who pressured her
husband to seek permission for her presence in
the north.

The first winter at Fullerton must have been
a novel but lonely one for Geraldine. Captain
Comer's diary provides a wonderful account of
the daily routine and activities of the small community. According to the diary, the men aboard
the *Era*, the Inuit families who travelled with the
whaling ships, and the crew of the *Arctic* entertained themselves with dances, concerts and
lantern slide presentations; however, seldom is
mention made of Geraldine's participation in
these activities. I suspect that being the only non-

Inuit woman, and the wife of the Commander of
the Royal Northwest Mounted Police, made it
difficult for Geraldine to involve herself beyond
the confines considered acceptable for a woman
of her rank and station. Even though prevailing
social conventions were less rigidly adhered to in
the north, J. D., who had a reputation for being
overbearing and officious, would expect
Geraldine to maintain her distance.[21] But
Geraldine, who was not easily intimidated, knew
how to handle her husband and before long was
doing what she did best, photography.

Undaunted by the fact that the Department
of Marine and Fisheries had engaged Frank
Douglas MacKean as official artist/photographer
to accompany the *Arctic*, Geraldine, upon her
arrival at Fullerton in 1904, commenced photographing the Inuit people with an enthusiasm and
professionalism not exhibited by Mr MacKean.[22]
Although Captain Comer had been collecting
data, artefacts and images of the Inuit people for
several years for institutions such as the American
Museum of Natural History, the arrival of the
*Neptune* at Fullerton in 1903 saw an increased
interest in photographing the Inuit lifestyle by
members of the Canadian expedition.[23] Both
Commander A. P. Low and J. D. Moodie took
photographs during this first year. However, the
significance of Geraldine's arrival is twofold; first,
she is almost certainly the first woman to photograph in a professional manner (having owned
and operated three studios previous to this, she
had a different perspective than her male

colleagues); second, she was able to devote herself full-time to the subject at hand.

Judging from her portraiture work, the Inuit were at ease and comfortable with Geraldine, especially the women and children, who appear in many of her images. She photographed a number of the Inuit women posed alone or in groups wearing their beaded inner parkas or *attigis*. One notable portrait shows a favourite, whom she called Susie, wearing a beaded parka that the Moodies commissioned for the Governor-General's wife, Lady Grey.[24] Geraldine included a number of these portraits in a souvenir album she prepared as a gift for Captain Bernier following the winter at Fullerton.[25]

The seriousness with which Geraldine approached her work is evident not only in the wonderful portraits she produced of the Inuit people but also in the meticulous manner in which she carefully identified each of her subjects as best she could, according to the native spelling. She was also very conscious of inscribing her signature and copyrighting the better images.[26]

So serious did the Moodies consider her work, that in a 2 February 1905 letter from J. D. to the Department of Marine and Fisheries he dismissed the abilities of MacKean and recommended that Geraldine replace him as official photographer.[27] Later that year J. D., in an attempt to impress the authorities, forwarded several sets of photographs taken by both the Moodies to Comptroller White, to the Prime Minister Sir Wilfrid Laurier, and to the Deputy Minister of Marine and Fisheries, instructing 'that any prints taken from these be used only for Government purposes, as the negatives may be valuable to me in the future'.[28]

The fact that both the Moodies were photographing would create a problem for researchers and scholars in later years. As Geraldine did not always sign her work, confusion exists over some northern images held at the Royal Canadian Mounted Police Headquarters in Ottawa, which could be attributed to either J. D. or Geraldine. The confusion is further exemplified in the letter from J. D. to Comptroller White. When referring to the enclosed photographs he states, 'The most interesting pictures amongst those sent herewith will be those of the natives taken by Mrs Moodie'.[29] Although this might lead us to attribute all of the unsigned Inuit portraits in the Royal Canadian Mounted Police collection to Geraldine, an entry in Captain Comer's diary on 16 February 1904 would challenge this assumption. 'Today got several of the women to tattoo their faces with paint, as the tattooing on their faces will not take and show in

Fig.6. Shenuckshoo, Ivalik Chief and Whaler, Fullerton Harbor, *c.*1905.

a photograph. In this way I got five very good pictures showing as many different tribes ... Commander Low and Major Moodie also took pictures of the same.'[30]

Although Captain Comer mentions the exchange of information, equipment and plates among the men taking photographs during these years, I have found no evidence to suggest that Geraldine was included. Therefore, I suspect her work was largely conducted independently of the others, with the exception of her husband. As an experienced professional, she was probably not concerned with this exclusion, confident as she was of her abilities and being somewhat protective of her images.

Regardless of the confusion over some images, Geraldine photographed extensively in the year following her arrival in 1904, as is evident from the number of signed photographs found in collections across Canada and England. In addition to the fine Inuit portraits, she produced a number of images documenting the Inuit at work and aboard ship, the Royal Northwest Mounted Police and their barracks, as well as photographs of the steamer *Arctic* and various geographic locations along the coastline of the Ungava Peninsula, the Hudson Strait and the district adjacent to Fullerton.

The Moodies returned to eastern Canada in the fall of 1905.[31] The following year was spent with her mother at Lakefield where Geraldine continued her photography of Canadian wildflowers, probably motivated by the reprinting in

Fig.7. Inuit woman with the whaling name of Susie posed with a child. Susie is wearing a beaded parka believed to have been made for Lady Grey, wife of the Governor-General of Canada, *c.*1905.

nearby Hudson's Bay Company Post.[34] The documentation of the daily routine at Fort Churchill deviates somewhat from her earlier work at Fullerton when she concentrated more on portraiture work. Although Geraldine continues to sign and even date some of her images, she no longer appears to consider them of enough significance to copyright.

During these years in the north Geraldine also focused on documenting the wildflowers of the region. The surviving plates from her northern plant life study are at the Thomas Fisher Rare Book Library, University of Toronto.

The difficulty in transporting glass plates leads us to reflect upon the type of camera Geraldine utilised while in the north. Unfortunately, the only specific reference discovered is to a panoramic model that J. D. ordered in 1905 from Topley's Studio in Ottawa.[35] This would account for the number of panoramic images from this period that carry his signature. In respect to Geraldine, we can only speculate, although, judging from a statement in her letter to R. B. Thomson of the University of Toronto in 1937, it is obvious she considered the equipment used at Churchill as inadequate, stating: 'I put in a very lonely three years climbing over rocks and hills to procure the plants, and then photographing them with anything but professional appliances.'[36]

Geraldine may have tried to remedy the situation, as records show that early in 1908 she placed an order for photographic goods from Topley's in Ottawa, expecting it to arrive that summer. However, the difficulty in relaying messages and the rigours of transporting goods into the north became all too evident when Geraldine's order failed to arrive. Although she made inquiries concerning her order again in January of 1909, with instructions to contact the Comptroller of the Royal Northwest Mounted Police for advice as to the quickest method of dispatching the goods, Topley's did not receive her letter until March and claimed it would take two weeks to fill. The Comptroller suggested sending part of the order by cross-country patrol from Norway House to Churchill and part by the Hudson Bay supply boat leaving Montreal in late June.[37] The contents of the order are unknown and whether Geraldine received it in time to be of any assistance is doubtful, as she bid the Hudson Bay district a final farewell in late September of that year, arriving in North Sydney, Nova Scotia, on 4 October 1909.[38]

Unlike the press coverage and fanfare that marked J. D.'s return a few months later, the only reference to Geraldine's arrival is a short telegram from Comptroller White, welcoming her back to

1906 of a new, revised edition of the *Studies of Plant Life in Canada*, originally published in 1885 by her great-aunt Catherine Parr Traill and illustrated by her mother Agnes Chamberlin. In the preface to the book Mrs Chamberlin acknowledges 'the valuable assistance given her by her daughter, Mrs Geraldine Moodie, in photographing the paintings from which the plates used in the present edition were taken'.[32]

In August 1906 Superintendent Moodie, with a small party of men, returned north aboard the SS *Adventure* to establish a Royal Northwest Mounted Police post at Fort Churchill.[33] Geraldine accompanied J. D. to Churchill where she remained for the next three years, during which time she continued her photography. The official report of the Royal Northwest Mounted Police in 1907 includes a number of Geraldine's images recording the daily activities of the Inuit, the Royal Northwest Mounted Police and the

civilisation.[39] While the press and others were heaping accolades on J. D., with no mention of his wife who spent four of the six arduous years at his side, Geraldine was waiting patiently at her daughter's home in Maple Creek for word of their next posting.

The years following the Moodies' return from the Hudson Bay district were as tumultuous as those preceding their northern sojourn. Geraldine, now fifty-six years of age, continued to photograph, but in a more sporadic and spontaneous fashion, as J. D. was shifted from post to post over the next few years.

In August 1910, when J. D. was ordered to escort His Excellency, Lord Grey, the Governor General of Canada, across country from Manitoba to Hudson Bay, Geraldine photographed the send-off.[40] Unable to accompany her husband, she joined him later in Ottawa, where she learned they were to be temporarily posted to Maple Creek. One would think the Moodies would be pleased to be posted in the west, near their family; however, this appears not to have been the case, as Comptroller White remarked in a letter to Commissioner Perry: 'I gathered from him, as also from Mrs Moodie that their desire is to be stationed in the North, as far away as possible from civilization, Athabasca preferred.'[41]

The posting to Athabasca was not forthcoming, and from Maple Creek the Moodies were stationed in Regina. In 1911 J. D. organised and led a contingent of Royal Northwest Mounted Police overseas to participate in the Coronation of George V.[42] Geraldine took a number of fine photographs documenting the preparation of this event. Although she undoubtedly took other photographs during her year in Regina, apart from a self-portrait no signed copies appear to have survived. As other people were photographing at the depot, it is difficult to attribute additional images to Geraldine, apart from those held by the family and the Royal Northwest Mounted Police Museum in Regina, Saskatchewan.

In 1912 the Moodies' wish to return north was granted, this time to Dawson in the Yukon Territory, where they remained for three years.[43] Unlike the relative isolation of the eastern Arctic, the Yukon was more settled and entertaining for Geraldine, who soon found herself immersed in Dawson society. Among her peers were Laura Berton, mother of Canada's celebrated journalist, Pierre Berton, and Martha Munger Black, wife of George Black, Commissioner of the Yukon.

Although Geraldine photographed in the Yukon, the only signed copy discovered to date that is credited to these years is a portrait of

Fig.8. Inuit in summer camp near Churchill, *c*.1907.

better images with her initials. In 1930, at the age of seventy-six, Geraldine began to photograph another series of prairie plantlife, a continuation of her work begun three decades earlier. Over the ensuing four years she photographed a number of specimens, placing the photographs into albums and carefully labelling each image.[45]

In 1936 the Moodies moved to Duncan BC to live with their eldest daughter, Melville, and her extended family, returning to Alberta eight years later. Geraldine Moodie died on 4 October 1945 at the home of her granddaughter, the Countess of Egmont, near Midnapore, Alberta, ending a lifetime of adventure that few women of her time could ever imagine.[46]

Geraldine Moodie's passing was noted with little more than the usual obituary in the local newspapers. However, this remarkable woman, who witnessed and documented traditional plains life, the passing of the open range ranching frontier and the turn-of-the-century Inuit culture of the eastern Arctic, would not remain forgotten. Geraldine may not have left a chronicle of her life, full of personal reflections and musings, but she did leave a remarkable visual legacy, spanning half a century, that has in recent years begun to be appreciated and recognised by researchers, scholars and students of women's studies. As we learn more about her photography, the search for Geraldine Moodie, the woman behind the lens, continues. As fragments of information are discovered and we try to piece them together, the best glimpse into the soul and creative spirit of this woman is still to be found in her photography.

Fig.9. Martha Munger Black (left) posed in Inuit parka, Dawson, Yukon, c.1912.

Martha Munger Black dressed in a native costume. This wonderful portrait was taken in a studio-like setting which would lead us to believe that other images may yet be uncovered. In addition to the signed copy, a number of Yukon photographs taken by Geraldine disappeared from a family album several years ago, with only the captions remaining underneath where the photographs had been placed.

Upon completion of her husband's service in the Yukon, Geraldine returned to the family ranch near Maple Creek, where she remained until J. D.'s retirement from the force in 1917.[44] Eventually the Moodies moved to Maple Creek where J. D. held the position of police magistrate for a number of years.

Following their move to Maple Creek, Geraldine pursued her two passions, gardening and photography. In a makeshift darkroom in her home she continued to develop photographs of family, friends and ranch scenes, signing the

### Notes

1. Ruvigny and Raineval 1906, p.86. Following the death of Charles Thomas Fitzgibbon in 1865, Agnes Dunbar Moodie married Lt. Col. Brown Chamberlin on 14 June 1870. Susanna Moodie is best known for her book, *Roughing It in the Bush*, first published in 1852.

2. Ballstadt, Hopkins & Peterman 1985, pp.198, 282.

3. Ruvigny and Raineval 1906, p.86. When referring to John Douglas Moodie in this paper, I have chosen, on occasion, to refer to him by his initials, J. D., a pattern established by his family and others who knew him over the years.

4. Ballstadt, Hopkins & Peterman 1985, p.265. The Dominion Lands Act of 1872 provided a quarter section of Dominion land (160 acres) free to settlers, in return for certain improvements to the property. Following proof of these improvements, the settler could apply for title to the homestead.

5. Agnes Dunbar (Moodie) Chamberlin Collection 1886–1937, Geraldine Moodie to R. B. Thomson, 19 November 1934.

6. RCMP Records, Group 18, Vol.3439, File 0–66.

7. RCMP Records, Group 18, Vol.51, File 287–91.

8. *Saskatchewan Herald* 1895, p.1.

9. Moodie 1895.

10. *Saskatchewan Herald* 1895, p.1.

11. It appears that a total of fifteen Battleford images were copyrighted. The National Archives of Canada holds copies of all fifteen in their copyright collection (1966–94), whereas thirteen of these images are held by the Museum of Mankind, Department of Ethnography, British Museum, and one rests with the British Library.

12. *Medicine Hat News* 1897, p.1.

13. Herchmer 1897.

14. In 1934 Geraldine donated to the University of Toronto all of her watercolours that were exhibited at the 1886 Colonial Exhibition, as well as several photograph albums containing approximately six hundred photographs of Canadian wildflowers that she documented from the turn of the century until the mid-1930s.

15. RCMP Records, Group 18, Vol.169, File 298–99.

16. Ibid., Vol.176, File 720–99.

17. Sessional Papers No.20 1903, Northwest Mounted Police Report, Inspector J. O. Wilson, Appendix G, p.76.

18. Ross 1984a, pp.252–4.

19. RCMP Records, Vol.281, File 716, part 1, J. D. Moodie to Comptroller White, 9 December 1903, p.6. It should be noted that by an Order-in-Council on 24 June 1904 the official name of the Northwest Mounted Police was changed to Royal Northwest Mounted Police and on 1 February 1920 to the Royal Canadian Mounted Police.

20. Ross 1984a, p.147.

21. Ibid., pp.104, 106, 119, 149.

22. *Archivist* 1978.

23. Ross 1984a, p.186.

24. Eber 1994, p.20, and interview with Joan Eldridge, great-granddaughter of Geraldine Moodie, Victoria, BC, October 1994.

25. The album is part of the Bernier collection held by the Musée du Collège de Lévis in Quebec.

26. The most complete collection of her northern work rests in the Museum of Mankind Department of Ethnography, British Museum, with smaller but significant collections at the Royal Canadian Mounted Police Museum (Regina, Saskatchewan), the Royal Canadian Mounted Police Headquarters and the National Archives in Ottawa, as well as the Musée du Collège de Lévis, in Lévis, Quebec.

27 *Archivist* 1978, p.3.

28 RCMP Records Group 18, Vol.302, File 750–05, J. D. Moodie to Comptroller White, 14 July 1905.

29. Ibid.

30. Ross 1984, p.95.

31. Perry 1907, p.5.

32. Traill 1906, preface.

33. Perry 1907, p.5.

34. Perry 1908, photographs.

35. RCMP Records, Group 18, Vol.302, File 750–05, J. D. Moodie to Comptroller White, 14 July 1905.

36. Agnes Dunbar (Moodie) Chamberlin Collection, 1886–1937, Geraldine Moodie to R. B. Thomson, 4 March 1937.

37. RCMP Records, Group 18, Vol.370, File 164–09.

38. RCMP Records, Group 18, Vol.380, File 617–09, Comptroller White to J. Lyons, Intercolonial Railway, 4 October 1909.

39. RCMP Records Group 18, Vol.380, File 617–09. Comptroller White to Geraldine Moodie, 4 October 1909.

40. Sessional Papers 1911, Royal Canadian Mounted Police Report, Commissioner, A. B. Perry, p.23.

41. RCMP Records, Group 18, Vol.3439, File 0–66, Comptroller White to A. B. Perry, 22 September 1910.

42. RCMP Records Group 18, Vol.3439, File 0–66.

43. Ibid.

44. RCMP Records Group 18, Vol.3494, File 0–66.

45. These albums are part of the collection of photographic materials donated to the University of Toronto in 1934.

46. *Calgary Herald*, 5 October 1945.

Fig.1. Portrait, in
Flaherty's style, of an
unidentified Inuk.

J. C. H. King

# The Photographic Album of C. M. Cato: The Eastern Arctic *c.*1909–14

Photographs make real images, and at the same time hide reality behind partial fragments of a dissolving past. Their meaning is further confused because of the ability to spread and shuffle these artefacts into evolving visual archives of albums for instance, and series of copy prints. While the process of construction of pre-photographic visual archives is well known, that for photographic archives is not well described. Collections of prints and drawings from voyages, for instance, or from princely or private collectors can be explained and re-assembled using voyage narratives, the careers of artists, and the engraving and printing history of illustrated publications. Little or no literature exists concerning the later but equivalent construction of photo-archives. Some, of course, of these accumulations are explicitly similar to archives of drawings and prints from named artists: the work of Robert Flaherty, or George Comer in the Arctic,[1] grew out of professional interests, and to a greater or lesser extent are documented with captioned explanations, diaries and other archival materials. Other accumulations do not have this structured context, thus prohibiting the simple elaboration of sources and meanings. In the Arctic early twentieth-century photography served many purposes: much of it was designed for the focused dissemination of information for propaganda purposes. Missionaries, such as Archibald Fleming, and Canadian government photographers such as A. P. Low, created manipulated images with conscious intentions (for instance, Fleming 1934).

## The Hudson's Bay Company's pictorial archives

A rather separate archival form is that of the personal, private collection, put together, as in the case of the album here, with non-specific and non-propaganda purposes in mind. Again these groups are, more often than not, composite juxtapositions of images which may have come from a wide variety of sources: from friends or colleagues present together on the same occasions, as well as prints bought in from professional photographers. An album may, of course, contain numerous images of events in which the album compiler has no direct experience. And for each image the most important person is the photographer, the often anonymous person, unseen but ever present. This paper looks at the personal journal, and the associated photograph album, of an officer, C. M. Cato, on the Hudson's Bay Company supply ship, the SS *Pelican*, during the period *c.*1909–14.[2]

The archives of the company, extending back three hundred years, include visual materials from the eighteenth-century onwards. Amongst these are, from the middle of the century, photographic archives, apparently made privately as personal records but seemingly seldom acquired contemporaneously by the company archives. From the beginning of the twentieth century the company began to accumulate a substantial official photographic archive, for use particularly in advertising and marketing. This numbered 100,000 images when transferred to the Provincial Archives of Manitoba in 1987.[3] Most of this photographic record seems to date, however, primarily to the period after 1920 and the foundation of the company periodical *The Beaver*, now a historical journal. Crucial in the development of the photographic record was the combining of the post of magazine editor and publicity director in 1933 (Geller 1993: 168). Cato's album therefore dates to a period at which

there was little or no official company photography, and in this characteristic is a nineteenth- rather than twentieth-century record.

### The eastern Arctic 1903–14

This period in the eastern Canadian Arctic was pivotal for a number of reasons. From a governmental point of view photography was a tool used to assist in the delineation of sovereignty in the face of American and Scandinavian exploration, and American mining and whaling. The Hudson's Bay Company's preoccupations were rather different. Throughout its history the company struggled to maintain a monopoly, or near-monopoly of the Canadian fur trade. Competition in the period preceding the First World War was increasing particularly in the Arctic, both from metropolitan firms such as Revillon Frères, and from whalers, who with the decline of whaling turned to trade in other commodities such as fox fur. Related to this was the depletion of fur resources in the sub-Arctic: the animals were being over-trapped. An area was said to be 'beavered out' when those fur bearers had been exterminated. One solution to this problem was the construction of additional posts in the high Arctic to create a new source of fox pelts. This both in part avoided the competition, at least from individual traders, and also gave access to untouched animal populations (Ray 1984: 347–9). While near-monopoly conditions were broken by the advent of war in 1914, these developments ushered in an era of influence in

the high Arctic for the company, which lasted for the best part of half a century, until the Second World War and the development of a permanent federal presence in the north during the 1940s. A first nation's view, that of Alootook Ipellie, suggests both that this new trade provided 'a king's ransom in furs and pelts' and, in time of hardship, a reliable source of credit to Inuit (Ipellie 1992: 43–4).

### The 1909 supply voyage of the *Pelican*

The 1909 Hudson's Bay Company voyage of the *Pelican*,[4] under the aegis of Ralph Parsons, is important for the establishment of the new post of Wolstenholme, at Eric Cove on the north-west point of Ungava Peninsula. This was named for Sir John Wolstenholme, an outfitter of Henry Hudson, who called Cape Wolstenholme after him in 1610. It was the first Arctic post established for the trade in white fox pelts, initiating a land-based fur trade at the end of the period of Arctic whaling. The trade in fox was well established by the beginning of the century, but it took the HBC a decade to make the decisions necessary to establish Arctic posts. The construction commenced on 14 August 1909, and by 18 September was well advanced, as indicated by one of the few captioned photographs: 'Worstenholme 18th Sept 1909'. The expedition carpenter John Ford, and Fred Groves and Mark Mucko, were left behind to complete the task. Ralph Parsons the Hudson's Bay Company man behind the expansion to the high Arctic was a significant photographer: Cato mentions that on 22 July the *Pelican* took on board Parsons' possessions for transfer to the new post. Parsons established both Wolstenholme and in 1911, also on the *Pelican*, the trading post at Lake Harbour, in the same year as Julian Bilby (1871–1932) and Archibald Fleming (1883–1953) founded their mission near the Robert Kinnes mica-mining depot. An evocative account of the place and period was provided by the country-born Anauta Ford Blackmore, whose husband W. R. Ford was drowned with C. G. T. Shepherd at Wolstenholme in 1913 (Washburne and Anauta 1940). Initially, the post was quite unsuccessful: it took Parsons two years to persuade Inuit to trade with him (Anderson 1939: 43; Copland 1985: 5). But thereafter he spread the trade in white fox fur to eighteen other posts through the Arctic. He had no love for Wolstenholme, saying that 'This place should have been called "Windholme" or something worse. Great Place for a lunatic asylum, that sort of thing would *pay*.' (Newman 1991: 184–5.)

## Cato's journal from the 1909 voyage

With the album is a journal, consisting of a series of log entries for the voyage entitled 'voyage of Auxilary Barque "Pelican" of London, to Montreal, Labrador and Hudsons Bay . . .' (Cato 1909). While this is not signed, the last entry for 3 January 1910 is initialled 'CMC', for C. M. Cato, the second officer on that voyage. Cato also served as mate or chief officer on subsequent supply voyages, including that of the *Nascopie* in 1912.[5] Little is yet known of Cato, except for his addresses, which indicate that he lived in Poplar and Stepney, in east London. The journal is a seemingly simple straightforward document, detailing in prosaic language the progress of the voyage, weather and relationships with fellow officers. It was not intended as an official document, since it contains mention of a row with a colleague, for which both were disciplined, as well as reflective thoughts on the life of a sailor:

Tonight at tea we were all discussing the merits & demerits of a seafaring career and we unanimously decided that going to sea was a mere existance [sic] & nothing more & the man that went to sea for pleasure was an adjective [abject?] fool & we all decided to buy a nice little farm somewhere & settle down & go to sea no more, but when that time will come for some of us I cant say I would like to do the settling down now & so would the rest of us but we want the chance. I suppose all sailors get this fit at times as I have heard the same old story so often. (f.5)

ABOVE
Fig.3. R. Parsons' 'Kyak Race' – 'The Return & winner'.

LEFT
Fig.4. Inuk in elaborate *amauti* with child, posing in front of a tent, probably at Chesterfield Inlet, 1912, on the maiden voyage of the *Nascopie*, with Robert Flaherty in attendance.

Perhaps the journal was intended for Cato's mother, with whom he lived for part of this time, or a sweetheart. In this it is unusual, since most of the surviving fur trade records are official documents from posts.

The seven-month voyage followed a well-established pattern. Beginning in London in May, the *Pelican* took four weeks to reach Cartwright, Labrador, on 14 June, arriving at Rigolet on 22 June. After off-loading cargo, they sailed to Montreal, anchoring there on 3 July. After visiting Quebec City (15 July), they then proceeded back up the Labrador coast, sailing north-east to reach Hudson Strait on 7 August, and Cape Wolstenholme on 12 August. The landing of the materials for the new settlement began with a twelve hour-stint the following day, Friday the 13th. The following day they were lost for an hour in the fog, and stranded on a sandbank, but by the third day the off-loading seems to have been completed since Cato 'took the gun & went for a walk over the hills & shot several loons [diver birds]' (f.32). On 23 August they left for Manitoba, arriving at Churchill for the period 11–26 September. On the return journey they stopped at Fort Chimo between 20 and 29 October, before going on to St John's and then back to London.

The diary is important as much for what it leaves out, as for what it details. The core of the narrative describes the weather, and schedules of port arrivals and cargo movements. Central to this is an early appreciation of the importance of ice, suggesting that this may have been Cato's first Arctic voyage. On 8 June he records early, and perhaps fanciful, impressions:

[We] turned round to have another go at the ice, at 4 oclock we came up with it once more & started to push our way through. This ship will smash up a piece of ice that would sink an ordinary ship, They dont bother to get out of the way of a piece of ice unless it is bigger than a house. We smashed into lumps of ice this morning which were quite 40 feet thick & the ship simply cut a channel for herself through them. By eight oclock this morning we were through the pack & in clear water on the West side of it, with only a few scattered bergs about, & the coast of Labrador, all ringed & snow covered in sight.

After the recording of first impressions, descriptive appreciation of ice is omitted from the narrative, although ice conditions are emphasised, particularly when on 8 August 'our propeller got caught & had every blade but one stripped off, so we will have to finish our journey with one blade' (f.30). To add to this difficulty, the rudder was lost on 24 August, and the replacement rudder smashed on 26 September. The voyage was further complicated by the rescuing of the *Paradox*, a steam ketch from Ipswich, with a crew of walrus hunters. She had been 'badly nipped by the ice, & was in a sinking condition, but the skipper of her would not abandon', when she was first sighted in Hudson Strait on 8 August (f.30). The following day she was abandoned and

Our mate & skipper went on board & took possession of her as a derelict, as it was a fine day

& smooth sea we hove her alongside, & took all the cargo out of her that was of any value, & when we had nearly emptied her we found she leaked less, so we set to work & patched her up, & then took her in tow to try & reach Wolstenholme with her. (f.31)

Much of the rest of the journal details the trials and tribulations of the *Paradox*: the on-loading and off-loading of cargo, although whose cargo and why is not clear; the dragging of the ketch's anchor, the breaking of the tow rope, the finding of the boat, the refloating of her; and the shipping of the crew out of Hudson Bay on the *Adventure* on 16 September. Apart from the enormous amount of extra work demanded of the crew, Cato's reasons for recording the travails of the *Paradox* are not clear, but it may be that her seizure as a derelict had financial implications both for Cato and for other members of the crew.

Cato recorded minimal interest in the people he encountered. These can be simply characterised as Labrador settlers, French-Canadians and Inuit; and of all three groups he had little or nothing to say. On 17 June Cato mentioned the settlers:

We met two schooners bound North. They were crowded with men women & children fishermen who were bound to the fishing grounds along the coast for the summer. We told them how far it was possible to get, but they went on to see for themselves. I cant imagine a harder life than these fishermen lead. They come up here as soon as the ice begins to break up & live in huts in the different small harbours along the coast. They depend on the small trading vessels for supplies of food & etc, & very often when anything happens to prevent the vessels getting up the coast, they are on the verge of starvation. This afternoon we had a boat alongside of us, one of the men wanted to know if we had a doctor on board, as his little girl had a bad cold & was very ill. So the skipper mixed him up some medicine for her, & he went away quite satisfied. (ff.14–15)

Quebec and French Canada are mentioned as briefly and in passing only. In Montreal on 6 July he noted:

In the evening I went ashore & had a look round, but an Englishman might as well be in a French city as I see no difference in Montreal, all the names over the shops & the advertisements about town are in French, & French is spoken almost everywhere. (f.22)

The natives, like the other peoples encountered on the voyage, are not individualised, and mentioned only in passing, in this case on an occasion when a group, having assisted the *Pelican*, lost their boat in Ungava Bay on 27 October:

We have had four Eskimos on board all day to Pilot us across the bar, & their boats has been moored alongside. At 6 p.m. it carried away both the mooring ropes & drifted shore. There was too much sea running to go after it in one of the ships boats . . . 28 October At Ungava . . . the decks were like glass. About eleven o'clock we saw the lifeboat belonging to the Huskies high & dry & after dinner we went ashore & examined her & found she had only started a couple of planks, as she had driven behind a small island, which sheltered her from the force of the sea. We fixed her up, & left the four men belonging to her ashore to float her off at high water . . . (ff.50–51)

Two points emerge. First, the main social division is between the crew of the ship and the others, and not, for instance, between native and non-native. It is not a division between the British and the non-British, but between crew and non-crew. If intra-group solidarity had been a concern, the writer would presumably have mentioned the crew of the *Paradox* and their no-doubt conflicting feelings about both being rescued and losing their vessel at the same time. Significantly, however, the only reference to Inuit assistance to the *Pelican* is that made above, when pilots were taken on board to provide the traders with vital navigational assistance.

Finally, perhaps the other important aspect of Cato's narrative is his attitude to the environment and natural history. As mentioned, Cato seems to have developed an early respect for navigating through ice, and the narrative is almost exclusively to do with wind and water in their broadest senses. One other point emerges, relating to animals and anthropomorphism, Cato does not mention animals – there is nothing about seals, walrus, caribou or whales, and perhaps particularly little about foxes and fox fur, although the voyage was designed to carry fur. While the on- and off-loading of cargo is mentioned at frequent intervals, fur is only mentioned once, in relationship to the on-loading of fur bales in Churchill on 25 September. Instead, there are brief snatches of narrative relating to birds, through which the writer seeks both to incorporate the wild and, at the same time, in hunting, to give it a recreational value at odds with the sentimentalising attitudes expressed elsewhere. So, for instance, on the voyage out a pigeon came on board and was turned into a pet, until it flew away and was killed by gulls. Later a snipe-like bird came on board and took up residence with the ship's domesticated fowls. And on other occasions, twice in August, Cato went hunting for loons.

## The album

The crew would have been able to take film back to Montreal or London for development, whereas Hudson's Bay Company clerks would have to wait at least a year to receive their processed and printed films. Cato's album is, however, a composite creation and, while the majority of pictures may be by Cato, it definitely includes images by other people. The inclusions of numerous representations of the *Nascopie*, which began supplying the Hudson's Bay Company in 1911, and photographs of Inuit from Keewatin suggest a great variety of occasions and sources. In this it contrasts vividly with the log and journal. One is a linear narrative from a single voyage, the other a spread of images, a personal composite record, from different voyages and photographers, perhaps both commercial and amateur. One of the difficulties involved in this is that the concept of ownership, creation or copyright in photographs was rather undeveloped, and indeed has remained

TOP
Fig.5. Naturalistic portrait of a native girl, holding and perhaps nursing a baby.

ABOVE
Fig.6. The Moravian supply and trading vessel *Harmony* in an unidentified Labrador harbour.

TOP
Fig.7. Line of
uncomfortable-looking
children, one holding
a telescope.

ABOVE
Fig.8. A series of at
least five snow
houses, with ice
windows, in spring.

so until recently. Because of the apparent mechanical simplicity involved in taking photographs – the release of the shutter – the identity of the photographer, particularly of amateur images, is in a sense irrelevant.[6] In the case of Cato's album, at the moment only a few pointers as to the identity and authorship of the prints can be found. This process is made more difficult because, while many of the images come from the 1909 supply voyage, others come from later visits to the Bay; and few prints are captioned. One of the images (82) shows a Keewatin woman with a superb beaded *amauti* (woman's parka). This is almost identical to a photograph said to have been taken by Robert Flaherty. The two exposures must have been made within a few seconds of each other. The Flaherty print is documented to Chesterfield Inlet in August–September 1912 off the *Nascopie* (Danzker 1979: 49,87). Both Flaherty and Cato were on board, so one might surmise that they were taking photographs together at the same time. Another speculative possibility is that the album includes photographs printed from negatives made by Flaherty. Both images, of the back of the *amauti*, could possibly have been taken by Flaherty, and some of the other intimate portaits of natives (13,14, 97–9, for instance) could also be by him. But there is no evidence for this apart from the superficial resemblance of composition. Another series of photographs seems to be by Ralph Parsons.[7] These include a series of four images of a kayak race, two images of a '1 mile dash' and two of a 'candy scramble' for children; unusually all of these are captioned.

Another approach to an album of this kind is to place it in the context of the two different groups of photographers: those who came and went on the supply ships, and those who remained through the years as company employees. Much of the twentieth-century photographic record of the Hudson's Bay Company seems to derive from supply ships' photographers, people who, like Cato, served as officers and travelled repeatedly to the Arctic. During the 1930s and 1940s both amateur and professional photographers travelled on supply ships, and made records both for their own purposes and for the company. This practice continued until very recently, for instance with the photographs of Charles Gimpel in the 1950s and 1960s (Tippett 1994). Photographers based on the supply ships were privileged for a number of reasons. Perhaps especially important is that the arrival of the ships was a time of excitement and entertainment, including kayak races, a moment when numerous Inuit would be on hand both to assist the unloading and to trade. Because of the importance of the moment it is reasonable to speculate that these transient photographers had an immediate intimacy with natives, no doubt dressed in their best summer clothing for the occasion, that was not neccessarily available to photographers who might stay longer in the community.

Perhaps the most interesting contrast is that between Cato's album and the log of the 1909 supply voyage. Whereas the written account is technical, the photographic record is personal and personalised, emphasising the familiar – the ship's crew and the sea – and contrasting these images with those of the 'other', of the exotic: natives and the occasional animal. It is also, in this respect, entirely different to what is the best published fur trader's *oeuvre*, the pictures of the professional photographer A. A. Chesterfield of 1901–4 (James 1985). C. M. Cato, with his log, and his own and other people's images, provides perhaps the earliest, if ambiguous, account of the Hudson's Bay Company trading for fox in the high Arctic. While authorship and meanings remain unclear, it is only by the gradual unravelling of the circumstances of creation that explanations can be assigned to these familiar constructions.

### Notes

1. As detailed by R. J. Christopher, this volume, and Ross 1984a.

2. Acquired at auction from Phillips, London, 1994, at the suggestion of Michael Graham-Stewart.

3. The information is taken from a mimeographed informational folder dated June 1989 (Beattie 1989). The total number of photographs was put at 175,000 images.

4. The *Pelican*, 289 tons, was said to be famous – a former British man-of-war and sister ship to the still better-known SS *Condor*. The vessel was purchased from the Admiralty by Hudson's Bay Company in 1901 to replace SS *Erik*. From 1901 to 1916 it was used to supply Arctic posts and transport fur. A Cleveland Smith commanded the ship at this time (1909–14) and is referred to by Cato. The *Pelican* was sold for breaking up in 1921.

5. The *Nascopie* is a more famous ship, working as a supply vessel in the eastern Arctic from 1911 until her demise in 1947 at Cape Dorset. The inclusion of the boat in photographs in the album is the best evidence that the photographs are a composite group, taken on a series of different voyages and at different times.

6. This problem, as, for instance, with Stefansson's proprietary assumption of the rights to the photographs from the Canadian Arctic Expedition, is dealt with elsewhere in this volume by Woodward.

7. Letter of 20.9.96 from Judith Hudson Beattie, Hudson's Bay Company Archives.

Inge Kleivan

# The Greenlandic Photographer
# John Møller

One of the earliest and most valued photographers in Greenland was John Møller (1867–1935), a Greenlander who lived in Nuuk in West Greenland. His photographs were once found in many private homes in Greenland, and copies of portraits and group photographs are still being made for Greenlandic families. John Møller's photographs are known from numerous publications. They were often used to give a visual impression of contemporary Greenland: during the last decades, however, their great historical importance has been recognised and they now illustrate Greenlandic society before modernisation started in the middle of the twentieth century. Selections of John Møller's photographs have been exhibited on several occasions both in Greenland and Denmark (Kleivan 1958; 1996).

A collection of about 3000 of John Møller's photographs are kept at the National Museum and Archives of Greenland in Nuuk. In 1954–5 they were sent to the Royal Library in Copenhagen for restoration, and about 2000 copies of the photographs were then included in the collections of the Royal Library. Elsewhere, the Arctic Institute at the Danish Polar Centre in Copenhagen keeps a small collection of John Møller's photographs. Attempts to establish dates, locations and motives for the photographs have been made in Copenhagen and Nuuk. Some dates are still incomplete and the information in the three archives is not always the same.

## Early photographers in Greenland
Several expeditions and Danish officials photographed in Greenland in the second part of the nineteenth century and at the beginning of the twentieth century. The earliest photographs surviving appear to have been taken in 1854 in Sisimiut (Holstensborg) on an expedition led by Edward Inglefield (see Wamsley and Barr, this volume). The earliest photographers included the Governor of South Greenland, H. Rink (1819–93). The best-known result of his activity as a photographer is a photo-collage with portraits of forty-one Greenlanders from Nuuk and Maniitsoq (Sukkertoppen) districts photographed in the years 1862–3. Lars Møller, father of John Møller, was one of them. The collage was included as an original photograph in Rink's collection of Eskimo legends and stories published in Danish (Rink 1866). A few photographs from 1866 signed 'L. M.' suggest that Lars Møller was the very first Greenlandic photographer.

## West Greenland in the middle of the nineteenth century
The Danish-Norwegian colonisation in Greenland started in the Nuuk area in 1721. The mission and trading station was moved to Nuuk, 'the foreland', in 1728 and called Godthåb, 'the good hope'. Nuuk became the administrative centre of South Greenland. In 1870 the number of inhabitants of Nuuk and the nearby Moravian mission station Nyherrnhut was 259; the number of inhabitants of West Greenland was 9,825, 2.4 per cent of whom were Europeans, nearly all of them Danes. Some important events took place in the decades before John Møller was born in Nuuk in 1867. Since the start of the colonial era the authorities had primarily been interested in the exchange of goods and in converting the Greenlanders to Christianity. In about 1840 visions of a Greenlandic community that resembled European society led to the beginning of a new policy. A college of education where the students were educated as catechists and teachers

Fig.1. Lars and Louise Møller, Nuuk 1917.

Fig.2. John Møller,
Nuuk c.1890.
(Photographer:
unknown)

started in Nuuk in 1845. In 1857 the first local
councils were established, and in the same year
two small printing presses arrived. The governor's printing office published both official information and entertaining reading material. One
press was used by the Moravian missionary
Samuel Kleinschmidt (1814–86), who from 1858
published educational and religious books.

In 1861 Rink started the publication of a free
journal or rather magazine, *Atuagagdliutit*,
'Something to read'. It included many translated
articles and stories, but Greenlanders from various localities also contributed with articles telling
about their own experiences and local events. It
contained colour illustrations, mostly lithographs
based on pictures in Danish magazines. Over the
years *Atuagagdliutit* has played an important role
in forming a common Greenlandic identity.
Another important publication was a collection of
Greenlandic legends, *Kaladlit okalluktualliait –
Grønlandske folkesagn*, published in four small
bilingual volumes (1859–63) and illustrated with
woodcuts by Greenlandic artists, primarily Aron
(1822–69), a hunter who lived in the small settlement Kangeq not far from Nuuk. From this
time the West Greenlandic population became
used to reading pictures.

## John Møller, photographer, printer, interpreter, writer, hunter and politician

John Møller's parents, Lars and Louise Møller,
(fig.1) both came from families that included some
Danish and Norwegian ancestors, and several
members of their families had been employed by
the Royal Greenlandic Trade Department. There
was a tendency to intermarriage between such
families. They had a regular income even if it
was a very modest one, and they were more
influenced by Danish culture than the majority
of their countrymen. But there was no doubt
at all about their ethnic identity: John Møller
and his parents were Greenlanders and had
Greenlandic as their mother tongue. The great
majority of Greenlanders were baptised with foreign names but they were pronounced in
Greenlandic; John Møller, for instance, was
called *Ujuut* (John) whereas his father was always
called *Aqqaluk* ('a girl's little brother').

Both Lars Møller and his son worked at the
printing office throughout their lives. After having been an apprentice in Nuuk, John Møller
finished his apprenticeship in Copenhagen. It was
here he learnt to photograph. During the eighteen months he spent in Denmark (1887–9) he
lived in a small institution for Greenlandic
apprentices, *Grønlænderhjemmet*, 'The Home of
the Greenlanders'. It was Rink's idea that young

Greenlanders who were being trained in
Denmark, mostly as artisans, were to learn
sufficient Danish language and culture to gain the
respect of their countrymen and to be able to represent them in an appropriate way in meetings
with foreigners. But at the same time they were
not to be spoilt during their stay abroad but to
remain Greenlanders in terms of their life expectations. John Møller became a successful member of this Greenlandic elite.

The photograph of John Møller as a young
man (fig.2) appears to have been taken not long
after his return to Nuuk in 1889. He is dressed
in a striped cotton anorak. The white handker-
chief in his breast pocket shows that he is familiar with this European fashion. Inside the anorak
he is wearing a coat of bird skin. The preferred
skins for such coats were made from eiderducks;
only the soft down was used, the rougher feath-
ers being pulled out (Birket-Smith 1924: 176).
The hood and sleeves are bordered with black
skin, preferably made from dogs.

John Møller was one of the few bilingual
Greenlanders at that time and he was employed
as an interpreter and secretary by the successive
governors of South Greenland when they made
their tours of inspection during the summer
(1889–1913). That meant that he had an opportunity to travel and photograph outside Nuuk
district. The great majority of his photographs
are, however, from his home town. John Møller
made other important contributions to Green-

Fig.3. Children in Nuuk, photographed c.1890. John Møller's younger brother, Stephen Møller, is standing to the right.

landic society. He was a politician, a member of the local council of Nuuk district from 1901 and also a member of the first Provincial Council of South Greenland, 1911–16. John Møller translated a few articles from Danish into Greenlandic, but it was of far greater importance that he wrote a number of articles himself. He dealt with subjects as diverse as the misuse of tobacco and Greenlandic orthography, but he wrote primarily about hunting. He was very interested in hunting and was also an active hunter.

## The photographic studio in Nuuk

When John Møller returned to Nuuk he was employed at the printing office. During the first years he only photographed out of doors during the summer but, when the office was rebuilt a few years later, a photographic studio, *Godthaabs photographiske Anstalt – Nûngme tarassugkanik ássilialiorfik*, was established (Møller 1961). The first photographs were included in *Atuagagdliutit* at the beginning of the 1890s. Among them was an outdoor photograph by John Møller of a woman dressed in a beautifully decorated *amaat*, the special coat worn by women carrying babies, with a small child looking over her shoulder. The caption in Greenlandic and Danish said that the photograph was an experiment. For many years, however, the quality of photographs reproduced in *Atuagagdliutit* was not satisfactory. But the establishment of the photographic studio in Nuuk proved to be a great success in another

respect. People now got an opportunity to have their picture taken for their own use and pleasure. At the studio people were photographed in front of a wall covered with white cotton. When in 1922 the printing office needed more space, the photographic studio was closed down but Møller bought the two cameras. He continued as a private photographer after he had retired in 1927 at the age of sixty.

Møller took some of his very first pictures of the members of Fridtjof Nansen's expedition, who in 1888 were the first to cross Greenland's ice cap. Over the years many Danes took the opportunity of having a professional photographer among them to have their picture taken at the studio, in their homes or in the open air. They might want to communicate the message to their family and friends at home that, even though they lived in the far north, their standard of living was not inferior to that in Denmark. They dressed up in their finest European clothes and had their well-furnished homes photographed. There is even a photograph of young Danes ready to play croquet. Or they might want to show those at home how interesting and exotic their surroundings were by being photographed dressed in Greenlandic costumes or together with Greenlanders. Or they were photographed ready to go hunting or skiing. A young girl had herself photographed while she was kayaking wearing a hat! Møller's photographs of the 'others' meant photographs of Europeans, and these photographs

OPPOSITE ABOVE
Fig.4. Stephen and
Hansine Møller,
Nuuk 1906.

OPPOSITE BELOW
Fig.5. Christmas party
in the home of
Andreas and Kirsten
Hoegh, Nuuk c.1924.

were taken at their own request. They were not shown outside the country as ethnographical evidence of exotic people. The great majority of Møller's photographs are of Greenlanders, but whether people were Danes or Greenlanders they nearly always look very solemn. They were no doubt instructed to stand still and not to move, and for most of them it was an unusual situation to be photographed. If one did not know, it would be hard to guess that the photographer was a Greenlander.

## Photographs of the photographer's own family

John Møller's younger brother Stephen Møller (1882–1909) appears in several of his early photographs of children in Nuuk, c.1890 (fig.3). The photographer has arranged his subjects into two lines of standing children and three boys sitting on the ground in the front, a way of arranging a group he had no doubt learnt from other photographs. Stephen is standing against the wall to the right. Most of the boys wear their hair cut in a fringe, whereas the girls are wearing their hair in a top knot with most of their head covered by a head scarf. When the top knot is not visible it is probably coming down the back of the girl's head. Since Møller's photographs are taken over many years they reflect cultural changes and it is possible to follow the development of dress and hairstyle. Even if he did not take photographs for ethnographical reasons, Møller's photographs are used for that purpose.

Stephen Møller also worked in the printing house and was sent to Copenhagen for further education (1904–5), but he suffered from tuberculosis and died at the age of twenty-seven in Nuuk. In the history of Greenland Stephen Møller is remembered for two reasons: he was one of the founders of a progressive lay Christian movement, Peqatigiinniat, and he made the drawings for the first illustrated Greenlandic spelling book published in 1910. On first impression the photograph (fig.4) of Stephen Møller with his wife Hansine, née Lynge (1886–1941), seems to have been taken in a painter's studio. There is a painting on an easel, other paintings are hanging on the wall – all of them landscapes – and Stephen Møller is sitting with his sketch book in his lap. It appears, however, from the background that the portrait must have been taken in the photographic studio. The chair with arm rests is also too fine to be part of the equipment of a painter's studio.

Stephen Møller is dressed in a European suit, white shirt and waistcoat. He has made sure that his watch chain is visible. There is no doubt that

he has brought his clothing with him from Denmark, and that he only used it on special occasions. His skin boots, kamiks, look quite new though kamiks were usually also worn by Danes in Greenland. His wife's outfit also looks quite new; it is probably her wedding dress. Her collar of beads is very small. Small coloured glass beads were imported at the end of the nineteenth century, and during the twentieth century the dimension of the collar of glass beads on the national costume grew considerably. Hansine Møller is wearing white kamiks of depilated seal skin to the knees with a border of tiny bits of coloured skin. Her long skin stockings include a piece of white cotton with crocheted insertions between the kamik and the fur border of the stocking. She was among the first Greenlandic women who did not wear her hair in a top knot. Instead she has plaits arranged rather high on her head. The young couple were married on 19 August 1906, and Stephen Møller died on 11 March 1909; the photograph was probably taken at the beginning of this period.

John Møller also photographed his father, Lars Møller (1842–1926), and his mother Louise, née Rasmussen (1847–1928), several times (fig.1). Lars Møller was the best known Greenlander of his time both within Greenland and outside it, due to his work as a printer, editor and illustrator of Atuagagdliutit. Lars Møller started to work at the newly established printing office when he was fifteen years old. A few years later he accompanied Rink to Copenhagen where he spent the winter of 1861–2 and learnt more about the art of printing. Like his sons, he only visited Denmark once. In 1873 he took over from the first editor of Atuagagdliutit, Rasmus Berthelsen, a Greenlandic teacher at the college of education (see fig.6). Lars Møller did not retire as head of the printing house and editor of Atuagagdliutit until 1922 when he was eighty years old. Lars Møller was decorated twice, in 1892 and 1917. The photograph may have been taken on the last occasion. There is a photograph showing Louise Møller wearing her hair in a top knot as late as 1913 (Kleivan 1958: 305). Four years later she seems to have changed her hairdo: she is still using a head scarf but has arranged it in such a way that it covers the top of her head. She is wearing dark long boots of depilated sealskin decorated with a knee piece.

At the request of various Danes, Møller photographed the interiors of their homes but unfortunately there are very few photographs of Greenlandic homes, not even one of his own. He took, however, several photographs of the home of his eldest daughter Kirsten (1896–1969) who was married to a Greenlandic minister, Andreas Høegh (1892–1978). It looks like a Danish home but it was an exception. Other Greenlanders did not have that much room or furniture. As a child, Kirsten Høegh had been given special lessons together with the children of the Danish rural Dean of Greenland, and both she and her husband were bilingual, having spent some time in Denmark.

As a guest in his daughter's home, Møller photographed a Christmas party in about 1924 (fig. 5). It illustrates that Møller did not only take formal portraits. The Christmas tree is a traditional Greenlandic one made from twigs of juniper placed in holes in an imported pole. All the participants are Greenlanders. The hostess, Kirsten Høegh, is situated in the middle in front of the Christmas tree. She is smiling, which is quite exceptional in Møller's photographs. Andreas Høegh is standing second from the left. All the men and the boys are dressed in light-coloured or white-cotton anoraks that had become fashionable for special occasions instead of black anoraks. As far as one can see, they are using *kamiks*. Kirsten Høegh is wearing a dress like the small girls, except one who is dressed in her national costume like the other grown-up women. The girls are wearing short, white *kamiks*, whereas the boys are wearing black *kamiks*. It is possible that both Kirsten Høegh and the girls wore their national costume when they went to church but later on changed into fine European dresses for the evening. Kirsten Høegh was one of the first Greenlandic women to wear European dresses, but there exist later photographs showing her dressed in her national costume for special occasions.

Jørgen Chemnitz (1890–1956), manager of a settlement, later interpreter and member of South Greenland's Provincial Council, and his wife Kathrine, née Josefsen (1894–1978), are standing to the left. Kathrine Chemnitz was one of the founders of the first Association of Housewives in Greenland in 1948. She represented Greenlandic women (half the population of Greenland!) in the big Greenland Commission that in 1950 laid down guidelines for the modernisation of Greenland.

### The College of Education

Another Greenlandic family that played an important role in Greenlandic society is the Berthelsen family. Rasmus Berthelsen (1827–1901) was a central figure in the second part of the nineteenth century. In the photograph reproduced here (fig.6) he is sitting next to his third wife Louise, née Poulsen (1842–1907), surrounded by stand-

ing family members. The little boy in a sailor's jacket standing between his grandparents is obviously tired of waiting for the photograph to be taken. The beautiful young girl in the middle is their daughter Ane Sophie. Berthelsen spent

Fig.6. Rasmus and Louise Berthelsen; the young girl in the middle is their daughter Ane Sophie, later married to Gustav Olsen, Nuuk c.1897.

head scarves and have their hair arranged in a top knot. In contrast to the other articles of clothing, the caps and scarves were not home-made.

Rasmus and Louise Berthelsen's daughter Ane Sophie (1882–1951) married Gustav Olsen (1878–1950) when he finished the normal six-year course of studies at the teachers' training college in 1900. After working as a catechist, he was ordained into the ministry of the Church of Greenland to become the first missionary among the Inughuit (the Polar Eskimos) when a Danish association *Den grønlandske Kirkesag* established a mission station at Cape York in 1909. The family visited Nuuk in 1921–2 where they were photographed wearing their Inughuit dress (fig.7). After that Gustav Olsen worked as a minister in various towns in West Greenland until he retired in 1936.

Gustav Olsen is sitting on a stone with their youngest child but one, while Ane Sophie is standing by his side with their youngest child in an *amaat*. Inughuit women used to wear a loose hood in connection with an *amaat*, and it may be that she is holding such a hood with her left hand. She no longer has a West Greenlandic top knot. It is not clear from the photograph whether she has gathered her hair in the double roll at the nape of the neck used by Inughuit women or in a European way. Like their father, the two sons to the right wear trousers made of polar bear skin and *kamiks* of depilated sealskin up to their knees. The coats of the two boys are made of caribou skin, whereas the other coats appear to be fox skin; on all the coats the hood opening is bordered with a fox tail. A small flap is visible on the bottom of Ane Sophie's coat and that of her two daughters. Like their mother, the daughters are wearing the characteristic long boots of the Inughuit made of depilated sealskin. The long stockings, probably made of caribou skin (Holtved 1967: 56), have a border of polar bear skin, whereas the short trousers of fox skin are hardly visible. The family has chosen not to wear mittens.

There is no snow and it is unthinkable that they used these warm skin clothes at that time of the year during their stay in Nuuk. There might have been two reasons for being photographed in this way. It was nice for the family itself to own and to present other members of the family and friends with a copy of a portrait of themselves in Inughuit dress. But it was also a very interesting image to show to Christians both in Greenland and in Denmark who supported the mission among the Inughuit. Olsen wrote a small book (1912) illustrated with photographs for West Greenlandic children to make them acquainted

some years in Denmark (1843–7), finished his studies at the newly established College of Education in Nuuk and spent his whole life working as a teacher at the same institution. At the same time he was a head catechist and the first editor of *Atuagagdliutit*, and he helped Rink to translate Greenlandic legends into Danish. He has also written the most popular Greenlandic hymn, mainly used at Christmas, *Guuterput* ('Our God').

Berthelsen is wearing a Danish decoration that he received in 1897. The photograph may have been taken on that occasion or somewhat later, but before Ane Sophie married in 1900. Like Lars Møller (fig.1), Berthelsen is wearing a black anorak used on special occasions but in contrast to him he is wearing long sealskin trousers tucked into his short *kamiks*. Two of the boys are wearing flat woollen caps with a big tassel in the middle; in other photographs Berthelsen wears a similar cap. The women, except one, are wearing

historian Daniel Thorleifsen expresses it in this way in his preface to a jubilee publication: 'There were the selfless catechists who taught as best they could despite the worst possible remuneration and living conditions. Others played important roles as poets, composers, writers, teachers, administrators or politicians' (Thorleifsen 1995: 7) – or as ministers. One of the teachers who had a strong influence on the students for about half a century was Jonathan Petersen (fig.8). He attended the College of Education himself (1897–1903) and was the first Greenlander to be trained as an organ player in Denmark (1910–11). He wrote songs and hymns, and composed and edited several songbooks and collections of melodies, which have been widely used both in the school and elsewhere. Petersen was very interested in the Greenlandic language and published a dictionary (1951) under the modest title *ordbogêraq*, 'the small dictionary'. It is still valuable as a book of reference. Petersen was the organist at the church of Nuuk and taught music and Greenlandic at the College of Education from 1905 to 1946; he even continued after he had retired, working till 1952.

Jonathan Petersen is photographed with his second wife Bolette (1896–1986), fifteen years younger than him, who is sitting looking at their small daughter who has just been baptised. The photograph dates from 1913. Petersen is looking very grave and staring directly at the photogra-

with and interested in the Inughuit children, their distant countrymen.

Graduates from the College of Education, *Ilinniarfissuaq*, in Nuuk have played a very important role in the development of Greenlandic society over more than 150 years. The Greenlandic

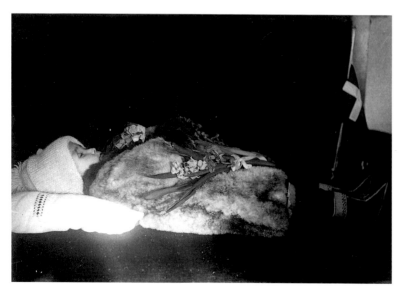

TOP
Fig.9. Little dead child, Nuuk *c.*1925 (?).

ABOVE
Fig.10. A little boy in a kayak is imitating how an able kayaker uses his double-bladed paddle, Nuuk *c.*1910 (?).

pher but one hand is resting on the chair behind his young wife. He is wearing a wing collar with his black anorak and under it a pullover. Many years after this photograph was taken Bolette Petersen became one of the founders of the first Association of Housewives in Nuuk in 1948. She has drawn up her sleeve to make sure that her knitted woollen wristlets decorated with glass beads are visible. Similar wristlets are seen in the photograph of Hansine Møller (fig.4). In contrast to Hansine, who used white *kamiks* to the knees, Bolette is wearing long boots. They are not only decorated with a knee piece like Louise Møller's boots (fig.1) but also with a strip down the front of the leg. The decoration consists of two narrow white stripes with coloured skin mosaic in between. The colour of the boots may have been red. The little child is dressed in a white christening robe.

### Photographs of dead children

The custom of photographing dead members of the family, especially children, was once wide-spread in Europe, and a small number of photographs of dead children (fig.9) feature in John Møller's collection. Parents might want a picture of their child as it looked when they had to part with it. That it was the very last, maybe even the only photograph of the child, made it especially valued. The dead child in the photograph is wearing a warm knitted pixie cap and has fine small *kamiks* on his feet. The body is covered by a blanket made of soft warm eiderdown skin and, like the children in similar photographs, he is probably dressed in his very best clothes. Flowers from a flowerpot are placed on the little boy's chest. The child is resting on a pillow with a fine white pillow case decorated with crocheted insertions. The little flag is at half-mast.

The few photographs Møller has taken of dead children are not dated, but they may have been taken in the 1920s. He would have been asked to take these photographs in private homes. In his book on the health situation in Greenland Alfred Bertelsen, who was for many years a doctor in Greenland and took many photographs himself, includes a portrait of a dying six-month-old child. It has the following caption:

The child died the day after it was photographed. Since I sometimes have heard complaints from Greenlanders that photographers according to their opinion have shown an undue interest in photographing them in 'interesting' situations, I would like to inform that the picture above was taken by request of the mother, especially to serve as a remembrance for the father who at that time was away from home (Bertelsen 1943: 47 translated by I. K.).

The photograph in question was taken in Nuuk in 1924 by Kristoffer Lynge (1894–1967), the Greenlander who successfully succeeded Lars Møller as head of the printing office and editor of *Atuagagdliutit*.

Photographs of dead children were not hidden away but displayed. In the early 1960s I saw a framed amateur photograph of a little dead child placed on a chest of drawers in a Greenlandic home in Aappilattoq in South Greenland.

### Photographs of kayakers

Møller took a number of photographs of kayakers both on sea and on land when they were preparing to set out or after they had returned with seals. He also photographed boys practising in kayaks in a small shallow lake in Nuuk, and a little boy in his kayak placed on the ground (fig.10). In many cases boys with fathers who could not use a kayak, primarily men who were employed by the Church or by the Royal Greenlandic Trade Company, did not learn to use a kayak. John Møller got a kayak when he was fifteen years old, but he does not seem to have started kayaking again when he returned from Copenhagen at the age of twenty-one. Throughout his life, however, he spoke up for preserving the tradition of using kayaks. In an article about the utilisation of living resources included in Nuuk's bicentenary publication, he presented statistics showing the dramatic decline in the amount of blubber from seals and white whales sold to the Royal Greenlandic Trade Company in Nuuk during the 1920s and the corresponding growth in cod fishing. The lack of skin prevented many from getting a kayak. Møller concluded his article by urging men who were able to keep a kayak not to give up 'the kayak which is an unequalled craft for hunting' (Møller 1928: 124).

It is difficult to date the photograph of the little boy in a kayak exactly (fig.10), but it may have been taken *c*.1910. The boy may only be three years old. It happened that children that young got their own kayak. Little boys were, of course, accompanied by their father or another experienced kayaker at sea. In this photograph the boy is practising how to use the double-bladed paddle on safe ground. Boys' kayaks were not provided with hunting implements until they were skilled kayakers.

## Posed photographs

Most of Møller's photographs were organised in some way or other. Maybe at the request of a Dane, Møller arranged a few photographs in his studio to illustrate certain aspects of traditional Greenlandic culture. In one of them two boys are sitting on the floor in a trial of strength, pulling hooks with their arms. They are stripped to the waist and are wearing sealskin trousers. In another photograph the well-known story-teller Jakob Eugenius (1863–1934) has been photographed just as he is describing how he threw his harpoon with his right hand and used his paddle with the other to make sure that he did not lose his balance in the kayak. This was not a case of reconstructing former events since such activities still took place in Nuuk outside the studio.

The majority of Møller's group photographs are outdoor shots. Among the group subjects are children of the Nuuk district at their confirmation, students at the College of Education and women who trained to become midwives, a job where they had to be prepared to offer other kinds of medical help as well at the many more or less isolated settlements. Other subjects for group photographs included the Provincial Council of South Greenland, the Royal Greenlandic Trade Company's employees, sailors, etc.

Besides photographing people, John Møller photographed buildings (some both during construction and after), small settlements, towns, monuments in Nuuk, ships and landscapes. In so doing, he created a photographic archive of South Greenland.

## Concluding remarks

John Møller differed from other early photographers in Greenland by working as a photographer throughout his adult life and by using a studio. He drew strength from the fact that he was a Greenlander and belonged to a respected family. He was well known to people and so did not see them as objects. As a rule it was people themselves who asked Møller to take their photographs. They decided if, when and where they wanted their photograph taken, and they decided whom they wanted to be photographed with and what they were going to wear. People had these rights because they paid. Families with limited means are not represented to the same extent. John Møller, however, did not try to document the poverty that existed. He did not live in a metropolis with anonymous citizens but in a society where everyone knew everyone else. Therefore he did not intrude on people to record and display their misery. However, the photographs reflect the ethnic and social structure of the Greenlandic society of his time. There are Danish officials, managers of settlements and sailors, and there are Greenlanders who continued their education and training in Denmark as well as those who were only educated and trained in Greenland. There are Greenlandic hunters, servants and unskilled workers. In contrast to foreign photographers, Møller did not have an ethnographical intent when he worked as a documentary photographer.

Some of the people that John Møller photographed are alive today but the Greenlandic society reflected in his photographs is in most respects very different from contemporary Greenlandic society. The cultural identity of Greenland today is to a certain extent drawn from these photographs of well-dressed people in Greenlandic costumes including skilful kayakers. They are an important link to the past – John Møller's photographs make modern Greenlanders feel proud of their ancestors.

Ann Christine Eek

# The Roald Amundsen Photographs of the Netsilik People, 1903–5

## The explorer

Roald Amundsen (1872–1928) was one of the greatest polar explorers. A Norwegian, he dedicated his life to this pursuit, which ended with his unresolved disappearance while on a rescue expedition close to the North Pole. He is best known for his conquest of the South Pole, which brought him international recognition in 1910–12. However, he first came to public attention by being the first to sail through the Northwest Passage, in 1903–6, on the *Gjøa*. This established him as an outstanding Arctic explorer. Significant photographs of the Netsilik survive from the *Gjøa*'s voyage ninety years ago. Some, at least, are believed to have been taken by Amundsen, although there seems to be more information about the conditions under which they were taken than about how they were finally used.

Amundsen's book *The North West Passage*, published in Kristiania in 1907 and in London in 1908, reveals his dreams and deep desires as a young boy growing up in a world full of tales of exploration and heroism. Filled with overwhelming admiration for the Norwegian Fridtjof Nansen, gloriously celebrated while returning from the successful Greenland Expedition in 1889, he had a secret wish to succeed in what was then regarded as one of the greatest challenges: 'If *you* could make the North West Passage!' He was supposed to study medicine, but when his widowed mother died a few years later he put all his energy into becoming an Arctic explorer, knowing that the man 'who conquered the North West Passage would undoubtedly receive a hero's welcome' (Barr 1993).

He studied to become a sea captain, and when he later took part in the Belgian Antarctic Expedition in 1897–9, a plan matured in his mind: 'I proposed to combine the dream of my boy-hood as to the North West Passage with an aim, in itself with far greater scientific importance, *that of locating the present situation of the Magnetic North Pole.*' (Amundsen 1908:5.) He also learnt from Fridtjof Nansen that exploration by that time had to be combined with scientific work to attract the serious interest of sponsors.

After long preparations, including raising funds, buying the small ship *Gjøa* and furnishing the expedition with supplies for five years, the ship left Kristiania (Oslo) in June 1903. Three months later *Gjøa* reached 'virgin waters' west of the peninsula Boothia Felix, north of Hudson Bay. When Amundsen discovered a natural harbour on King William Island, he immediately chose it for winter quarters as it also satisfied scientific requirements for magnetic observations. In September 1903 they anchored *Gjøa* in the small bay on the south-east coast of the island and settled down to start the observations which lasted nineteen months. The place, which they later found out was called Ogchoktu by the local Inuit tribes, was named Gjøahavn. Today it has been renamed Gjoa Haven.

## The collector

On 14 October 1905, when *Gjøa* had sailed through the Northwest Passage, Amundsen wrote a letter from King Point, in the north-west corner of British North America (Canada), to Professor Yngvar Nielsen at the Ethnographic Museum of the University of Oslo. He explained that, although the 'Eskimo tribes' he had met on King William Island in 1903–5 had utterly primitive living conditions, he had become close friends with one particular group, the Netsilik.

Fig.1. Netsilik woman Onaller with her son on her back.

He had found that their tools and equipment bore no trace of 'civilisation', and by trading scissors, needles, knives (even arms and ammunition) for their objects, he had thus assembled a complete collection of tents, sledges, kayaks and a lot of other items. His letter concluded humbly: 'We also have a lot of interesting Eskimo photographs. I hope this complete collection from the – I dare say – least known of Eskimos alive today may be of interest.' The letter was filed at the Ethnographic Museum as no.11 in 1906. The collection of items was deposited at the Ethnographic Museum in the fall of 1906, and became the property of the museum after the Norwegian state in 1907 had covered the outstanding amount for the whole expedition (Gjessing and Krekling-Johannessen 1957). It is, however, not known when and how the photographs became part of the collections.

Although explorers in this area, like the John Franklin expedition in 1847–8 and others, had been in contact with local groups of Inuit people, very few knew about the existence of these tribes as none of the expeditions had brought back any information about them. According to Dr Tom G. Svensson of the Ethnographic Museum of Oslo, the 900 objects Amundsen brought back to Norway constitute the largest and probably the most important collection of Netsilik objects. He also considers that the objects, together with the meticulous and well-informed descriptions of the lives of the Netsilik people in his book, make an essential contribution to the understanding of Inuit history and culture of this area (Svensson, personal communication, February 1996). This unique material is one of the most interesting collections in our museum and parts of it were first exhibited in 1907.

**More or less unknown photographs**

In 1987 the Englishman Roland Huntford wrote an excellent book based on a collection of Amundsen's lantern slides which had been found the year before quite by chance. This collection of slides, made from negatives which are to be found in different archives all over south-east Norway, is considered to give a complete impression of the Amundsen photographs. It should, however, be seen as an expression of Amundsen's need to publicise himself as an explorer. Of the Netsilik photographs, only the one of the group in front of the ship (fig.2) seems to have been used for slide shows. Quite probably Amundsen later in life thought that it was not this part of his work which had given him the glory of a national hero and worldwide respect, even though it is indeed his ethnographic studies and collection of artefacts which has proved to be of lasting value (Huntford 1987).

In Norway there exists a large number of photographs from Amundsen's *Gjøa* and other expeditions in the form of original negatives on glass plates and nitrate film, lantern slides, contact prints, prints and reproductions, the collection at the Norwegian Polar Institute being the largest. The total number, however, is not known as the material in the different institutions has not yet been completely registered or investigated. Nor is there a complete survey of the Amundsen photographs.

Planning an exhibition about Amundsen and the *Gjøa* expedition at the Ethnographic Museum in 1989, equally the 150th Anniversary of Photography, I suggested we present a selection of the Amundsen photographs in our care. Most of them were not very well known as they had been stored away for many years.

The work in connection with the presentation did not, however, include a complete inventory; I cleaned and examined about 100 original glass plates, mainly 5 × 7 in (13 × 18 cm), made duplicate negatives of them and reproduced the thirty-two contact prints filed in our library. Many photographs were in very bad shape but I managed to put together an exhibition that was later shown in several places in Scandinavia. Due to unsatisfactory captions it is difficult to verify the exact number of images depicting the Netsilik, but of at least thirty-two Netsilik photographs exhibited there are several that have probably never been shown anywhere else before.

## Who was the photographer?
The photographs are attributed to Roald Amundsen as leader of the expedition. In his book, though, Amundsen from the start explicitly named the second-in-command of the ship, the Danish lieutenant Godfred Hansen, as 'navigator, astronomer, geologist and photographer' (Amundsen 1908). As there were two Hansens on board, the Dane was usually called the lieutenant. Huntford claims that most of the crew took photographs when there was a need for it (Huntford 1987). As a consequence the quality of the photographs varies considerably. The image of Amundsen studying the map of Gjøahavn in his cabin (fig.4) reveals, though, together with many others, a conscious composition made by a trained eye, probably belonging to Lieutenant Hansen. Although he has even been described as 'a dedicated amateur photographer' (ibid.),

Lieutenant Hansen seems never to have mentioned anything about himself being the photographer, not even in his own 'Gjøa Expedition' published in Copenhagen in 1912, nor in the Danish Bibliographical Dictionary where one can

find a biography of the lieutenant, who in 1937 was appointed Rear Admiral of the Royal Danish Fleet.

## Primitive conditions
There is no information about the photographic equipment used, but from the use of glass plates there must obviously have been at least two cameras, one with ordinary lenses, the other with the possibility of stereo-photography, as there exist

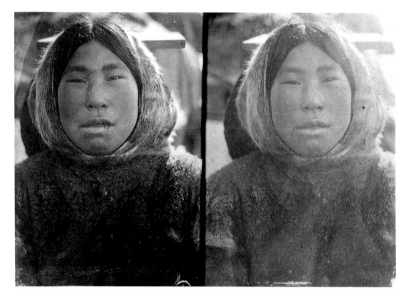

Fig.5. One of
Lieutenant Hansen's
images – the Netsilik
woman Kabloka, on
board *Gjøa*. The
contact print of one
of the stereo-
photographs suggests
the variable quality of
the negatives.

RIGHT
Fig.6. The Netsilik
medicine man
Kagoptinner, 'The
Gray-haired', in the
snow hut of his son
Poieta.

both kinds of plates. In his book Amundsen published a photograph of the lieutenant at work
photographing the woman Kabloka, and, of the
pictures that were actually taken on that occasion,
at least two of them are stereo-photographs in our
collection. As the quality of the simultaneous
exposures of the stereo-photographs differs considerably (fig.5), I chose only to present the best
images. Photo-historians might not approve of
such procedures, but it is important to present
photographs that are pleasant to look at so that
the viewer will concentrate on each image and
thus better understand its visual message.

The collection of glass plates clearly shows
signs of having been processed under primitive
conditions. Amundsen tells how Lieutenant
Hansen in the summer of 1904

took advantage of the most favorable period to
hurry on the development of his photographic
plates. Now he had a plentiful supply of fresh
water, previously so scarce, and by damming and
diverting, he arranged quite a dam in one of the
watercourses, and in this artificial rinsing-place he
splashed and washed to his heart's content.
(Amundsen 1908)

While preparing the ship for departure in the
summer of 1905,

the cabin could no longer be used as a dark room;
but as it was absolutely necessary for the Lieutenant
to have a dark room, the problem was eagerly
discussed . . . Lieutenant Hansen finished it at
length by using as a dark room one not originally
intended for that purpose – I need not particularise
further – 'necessity is the mother of invention'.
(ibid.)

The primitive darkroom conditions did, however,
harm the negatives quite badly, as time has
revealed damage due probably to bad chemicals,
unsatisfactory processing, washing and storing.
Some plates were broken, others were so severely
bleached that one could not see any details. But
with the aid of multi-contrast film and filters it
was possible to develop almost hidden images.

## A documentation not planned for

Amundsen had apparently not planned any photographic documentation of the people of the
Arctic as he and his crew had not expected to
meet any people at all in what they considered to
be quite barren surroundings. During their two
years on King William Island they did, however,
encounter several tribes of native people. When
the crew of the *Gjøa* met them for the first time,
after some weeks on the island in October 1903,
their feelings were quite mixed as they had been
told that indigenous people of northern Canada
could be quite aggressive.

To demonstrate they did not fear these 'arctic
barbarians', Amundsen and two members of the
crew marched with military precision with rifles
in their hands to meet the Inuit people, who came
towards them 'talking excitedly, pointing with
their hands, laughing and gesticulating' (ibid.),
showing no sign of hostility. Amundsen shouted
what he thought to be greetings in their language
while two other members of the crew stood smiling at the scene in safety on board the ship.
Suddenly, the men coming closer started shout-
ing 'Manik-tu-mi' several times, greeting him in
a very friendly way. He was surprised to find the
men of what appeared later to be the Ogluli
tribe (one of the five tribes he later found out
were living in the King William Island area)

much more handsome than the people he had met earlier on Greenland, and when they went down to the ship together he 'could hear the clicking of the camera of the Lieutenant, again and again, and he really did not feel dignified like a commander' (ibid.).

Amundsen did not meet the group of Netsilik people until March 1904. This was on an excursion with one of the crew members to put up depots for later expeditions. The Netsilik actually lived at the centre of the Boothia Isthmus but in the winter they used to cross the frozen strait to King William Island to hunt for seal, the name Netsilik meaning 'Seal people'. Suddenly meeting a group of men on their way to hunt and greeting them with 'Manik-tu-mi', they were immediately accepted and were invited to their camp, a group of sixteen snow huts, which was the largest camp Amundsen ever saw.

## The ethnographer

The Netsilik at once gave the impression of being even cleaner and better dressed than the Ogluli people Amundsen first encountered, and soon his reserved attitude turned into deep admiration. While most of the other members of the crew were busy with magnetic observations or ship maintenance, Amundsen spent a lot of time making excursions with the Netsilik, during which he became more acquainted with them and their way of life. The family of the medicine man Kagoptinner, 'The Gray-haired', took very good care of him and invited him to sleep in their snow hut. With one of the sons, Amundsen traded a complete suit made of reindeer- and sealskin with underwear and all, for spear-heads and sewing needles.

Another Netsilik called Ugpi, or 'The Owl', became a close friend and was a great help to the members of the expedition. Amundsen described him: 'There was something serious, almost dreamy, about him, and he was quite free from that very annoying and wearisome custom common to other Eskimo of always making fun of others.' (Ibid.) The Inuit people were masters in building comfortable huts of snow or even ice, but during the summer the native people had to use tents, which were 'no triumph of art. Most of them are made of reindeer and seal skins sewn together. The best seal catchers have theirs made entirely of seal skin . . . seal skin is more precious than reindeer skin.' (Ibid.)

Amundsen also met *angaqoks*, shamans, but felt doubtful as to whether they had any extraordinary powers. He did not delve into whatever faith the Netsilik had, and remarked of their beliefs:

Fig.7. Portrait of Ugpi, 'The Owl', with bow and arrow.

If these people had any belief in a higher being they at any rate concealed it very jealously. They imagine a life after death; at any rate good men are assigned an abode in the moon, the bad in the earth; the stars are destined for those who had something of both in their nature . . . Evidently they loved life, but on the other hand they had not the slightest fear of death. (Ibid.)

Amundsen had understood that 'going native' was not done among Arctic explorers, but he had studied the example of Dr John Rae, a man from the Orkney Islands who with very small means had worked and lived quite successfully with the Inuit in the Canadian Arctic (Huntford 1987; Bunyan *et al* 1993). Amundsen gradually learned that everything the Netsilik and other native people did had a reason and by studying their way of living, working and travelling he began to understand the secret of surviving in the Arctic, knowledge he needed if he were to succeed in his own work.

Although Amundsen and his crew had the ship as a place to return to, and security against famine, they learnt to build snow huts, to hunt for reindeer and seal and to fish in the native way. Amundsen wrote:

We were suddenly brought face to face here with a people from the Stone Age: we were abruptly carried back several thousand years in the advance of human progress, to people who as yet knew no other method of procuring fire than by rubbing two pieces of wood together, and who with great difficulty managed to get their food just luke-warm, over the seal-oil flame, on a stone slab, while we cooked our food in a moment with our modern cooking apparatus . . . However we should be

RIGHT
Fig.8. A family
outside their tent in
the summer.

BELOW
Fig.9. Netselik boys
shooting with bow
and arrow.

wrong, if from the weapons, implements, and domestic appliances of these people, we were to argue that they were of low intelligence. (Amundsen 1908)

Amundsen was, however, shocked at the way the Netsilik, whom he admired for many reasons, treated their women. They did not offer him their wives for the night, like the Ogluli had done, but he was offered the daughter of one family in marriage. He noted: 'The women marry simply because they are given away by the parents, and the man marries the woman to procure another domestic animal. Such is the wife's position, neither more nor less.' (Ibid.) But his admiration for

the hard-working women is revealed in his descriptions of female skills such as needlework, and how the women chewed various kinds of skin to prepare it for sewing everything from underwear to kayaks: 'I can now understand why the Eskimo rub noses instead of kissing. The mouth, besides being a very good talking apparatus, serves a variety of purposes; it is the Eskimo's universal tool.' (Ibid.) The respect for these women is also expressed through several magnificent portraits, such as the one of the Netsilik woman Onaller with her son (fig.1) a beautiful-looking woman who was said to have a nagging tongue.

## How the photographs were used and received

Amundsen was no different from other explorers of his time in his use of the new media – photography – as a means of recording his explorations. He, too, took photographic equipment on his expeditions, to document his own work as well as to photograph people and other phenomena encountered. The photographs were later used as illustrations for books, magazines and slide-shows, which became a necessity for most explorers to support themselves, as well as for raising funds for new expeditions (Barr 1993). As Amundsen was never financially very well off, the lecture-tours were all the more important. During a six-month tour in the United States Amundsen gave 160 lectures, which was an exhausting experience.

The photographs were taken under most trying and primitive conditions, and yet in spite of the small number they bring the viewer very close to the people photographed. Apparently, Amundsen did not show the photographs to the Netsilik, as there is no evidence of their reactions. They had no understanding of pictures whatsoever:

... their favorite diversion when they visited us on the vessel was to look at the illustrated books. At first they generally set the pictures upside down, but with our assistance they soon got used to the proper way of looking at them. Now, as luck would have it, we had hardly anything else but pictures of the Boer war, and of these we had a large supply. It was death and killing and fire and slaughter, not very pleasant even to us, and the Eskimo impression of 'civilisation' derived from these pictures can hardly have been happy and alluring. (Amundsen 1908)

There is no information, either, of the public reaction to the Netsilik photographs at the time of publication. It is probable that most people primarily considered them to be very exotic and exciting, and the 'Gjøa Exhibition' of 1907 and similar displays of Arctic cultures at the Ethnographic Museum have always had a very strong appeal for the public. People seeing these photographs today are often amazed at the straightforwardness, simplicity and dignity of the people photographed.

There were conflicts, though: there were people who were opposed to being photographed, but the reason behind the peculiar image of three persons in a hut hiding their faces (fig.10) remains unexplained. Perhaps the photographer went too far, or perhaps these persons were new visitors who did not have the same confidence in Amundsen and his crew as did the Netsilik. By living as close to the Netsilik as Amundsen did, he gained their confidence, and the person who photographed them could probably do what he pleased as the people trusted Amundsen. While photographing people so ignorant of mass media, one has to tread very carefully and be very cautious about what one does, as they are not aware of what the photographer can do with these pictures afterwards, or what information, or preju-

dice, accompanies the images. There is more than enough evidence of visitors who have not understood the social code of native people in general and of Inuit people in particular. By not winning their confidence, they manage to do nothing but add to the vulgar and stereotyped image of native people as 'savages'.

## Bringing the Netsilik photographs 'back home'

In his book Amundsen expressed his concern for the future of the Netsilik, the people he studied so carefully, and his desire to learn from them how to survive in the Arctic. 'My sincerest wish for our friends the Nechilli Eskimo is, that civilisation may *never* reach them.' (Amundsen 1908.) After he had used the photographs of his friends for his publications it seems that the photographs, as well as his friends, fell into oblivion. The next expedition to visit them was led by the Dane Knud Rasmussen in 1923: in 1925 a trading station was established and the first missionary came. After the Second World War the Inuit people with their nomadic way of life began to

Fig.10. People in snow hut hiding their faces from the photographer.

settle down permanently in Gjoa Haven. Of the 900 people of Gjoa Haven today, five groups of Inuit constitute 90 per cent of the total population with the Netsilik being the largest group.

The anthropologist Dr Tom G. Svensson of the Ethnographic Museum of Oslo has specialised in native art in the northern Fourth World, particularly that of the Sami and Inuit. He visited Gjoa Haven in September 1993 to study the work of the Netsilik soapstone-carvers, of which Judas Ullulaq is said to be the most talented. Svensson also hoped to establish contacts for cultural exchanges between our museum and the community of Gjoa Haven.

In the Hamlet Office at Gjoa Haven Svensson found some reproductions of photographs from the Amundsen book hanging on the walls. Although some of the images were already known to the people of Gjoa Haven, their reactions were very strong when he presented a selection of newly printed large-size photographs as a gift to the community, and later showed them to schoolchildren, students and other people. The elderly people especially, found great pleasure in these pictures. They sat down on the floor to study the photographs for a long time, silently puzzling over who the people in the pictures might be. It is rumoured that Amundsen and his crew not only left needles and scissors behind in Gjoahavn but also pregnant women.

Dr Svensson was overwhelmed by the reactions, and for him these photographs became 'a kind of door-opener' to this small community. He also suggested that Amundsen's photographs should be used for studying the local Inuit history and culture, and upon his return to Norway our museum made an additional gift of thirty-eight prints to the local school. According to an article in a local newspaper in January 1994, the principal of the elementary school, Ms Clugston, reported that the photographs, which showed things that were in ordinary use at that time but unknown today, had had an unexpected effect on the children: 'The kids were so enthusiastic. Ordinarily they're not talkers. They were poring over the pictures and chatting.' (Brown 1994.)

Today, when modernity is a constituent part of Netsilik life, with aeroplanes, television and the internet, Amundsen's photographs seem finally to 'bring old *Gjøa* back to life'. Little boys no longer run around with their little bows and arrows to shoot at small birds, 'to be able later on to pursue and kill bigger game in hot chase' (Amundsen 1908). Today they use motorbikes and snow-mobiles. In the same way that the soapstone carvers of Gjoa Haven use sculpture to bring back the histories and myths that might otherwise have been lost on the way to a modern society (Svensson 1995), one can hope that Amundsen's photographs will be a way for its people to rediscover their own history and cultural background.

## Appendix: Procedures for making duplicate negatives from old glass plates of uneven quality, high or low contrast and/or with faded images

Old negatives on glass or other forms of support are usually very difficult to print on modern photographic papers. By changing the contrast, it is however possible to adapt the negatives to modern materials. Agfa Gevaert has manufactured an ortochromatic sheetfilm for graphic production, Gevarex GO 230 P, which has proved to be quite useful in obtaining duplicate negatives or negatives for reproductions. The contrast can be changed by the use of filters, yellow for high contrast and blue for low, but the film can also be used without filters at all. I have used Kodak Wratten filters, Yellow and Cyan or Blue, from grade CC 05 to CC 50.

The size of the sheetfilm used was 4 × 5 in (10 × 13 cm), and this had to be cut a little bit on one side as it is not originally manufactured for use in ordinary film cassettes. The film speed was set at 25 ASA. To make duplicates of glass-plate negatives, I reproduced the original glass plate by putting it on top of a light-table under the camera. After having processed the sheetfilm on which now appeared a positive image, it was contact-printed on the same kind of film (emulsion to emulsion), to produce a duplicate negative. The contrast of the negative was controlled by putting the filter either on the camera or between the light source and the film.

The same film was also used for making reproductions of original prints of different quality. For both duplicates and reproductions the film was developed, in reduced red light, according to what contrast was desired. To obtain a high contrast, Agfa Neutol paper developer was used with a 1 + 10 solution at +20 °C (68 °F) for 2 minutes, then put into water for a few seconds before fixing, washing and additional treatment required to make negatives of archival standard. To obtain a low contrast, Agfa Rodinal film developer was used with a 1 + 25 solution at +20 °C (68 °F) for 6 minutes, then treated the same way.

William W. Fitzhugh

# The Alaska Photographs of Edward W. Nelson, 1877–81

The photographs taken by Edward W. Nelson in Alaska between 1879 and 1881 are among the first obtained from western Alaska and are the first to document the native peoples of the Bering and Chukchi Seas region. Although earlier images of its native peoples are known, for instance, the Choris watercolours of 1816–17, Whymper's (1869) and Dall's (1870) sketches from the Yukon-Kuskokwim delta, and Alphonse Pinart's photographs from the Kodiak-Unalaska region in 1871, Nelson's photographs are the most important primary resource on visual anthropology from a time when Alaska was a little-known region in its earliest phase of Western contact.

Whalers had been plying the waters of the Bering and Chukchi Seas since 1848 and were actively engaged with the peoples of the Bering Strait and north-west Alaska. Some of Nelson's photographs were taken among these Inupiat and the Siberian Yupik and Chukchi. But the majority are from the shallow whale-free coasts of the Bering Sea, Nunivak Island, Norton Sound, and the lower reaches of the Yukon and Kuskokwim Rivers, where European contact was still very limited. Russian posts had been established at Kolmakovsky on the middle Kuskokwim in 1841 and at St Michael at the mouth of the Yukon in 1842, and Zagoskin had explored the lower Yukon for two years during 1842–4 (Zagoskin 1967). But even after three decades of gradually intensifying Russian trade that acquainted Yupik Eskimos and Ingalik Indian groups with Western goods and ways, the majority of native people in western Alaska not living directly on the Yukon or Kuskokwim had still to meet their first white man when Nelson arrived at St Michael in 1877.

Nelson's travels produced written, material culture, and photographic records of a people still at the frontier of Western contact. His photographs are especially valuable for their naturalism and lack of artifice. The 'reality' he constructed was that of a descriptive naturalist. Because Nelson was trained neither in ethnology nor in photographic arts, areas that even by the 1870s showed the effects of Western bias and lacked systematic field recording methods until Franz Boas reformed American anthropology in the 1890s, the records Nelson accumulated are perhaps more systematic and objective than had this work been conducted by a contemporary ethnologist. Nelson shot pictures as snapshots from life rather than as composed documents (but see below) and documented them with extensive ethnographic notes. His *c.*126 images give as unvarnished a view of the lives of Yupik and Inupiat peoples of western Alaska and their neighbours in Chukotka as can be found for this early period of Anglo-American contact.

This paper summarises Nelson's activities and travels among the peoples 'about Bering Strait', as he titled his monograph (Nelson 1887, 1899), and presents a preliminary review of the methods and subjects of his photography, which have not previously been described. In fact, the existence of the full corpus of Nelson's photographs only became known as a result of research conducted by the author and Susan Kaplan while preparing the exhibition, *Inua: Spirit World of the Bering Sea Eskimo*. After the discovery of Nelson's original glass plates in the photographic archives of the Smithsonian Institution, many of these images were included in the exhibition and in related exhibits and publications (Fitzhugh and Kaplan 1982, 1983; Fitzhugh 1983, 1988a; Rowley 1988). These images have now been inventoried and are a valuable new addition to the

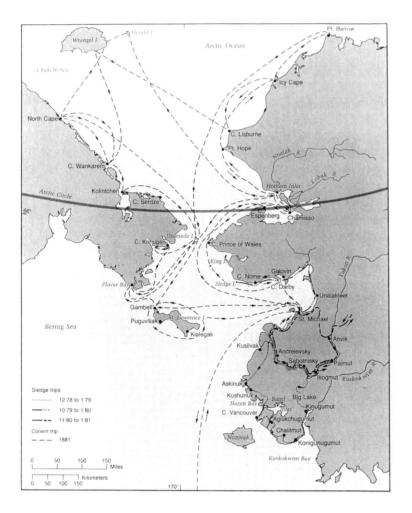

Fig.1. Travels of
Edward W. Nelson in
Alaska, 1877–1881.
Based for four years
in St Michael, Nelson
made photographs of
local Yupik people
and of Yupik, Inupiat,
Ingalik, Siberian
Yupik, and Chukchi
who came here to
trade in 1880–81.
Photographs were also
taken on his dog sled
trip up the Yukon in
the fall of 1880 and
on the *Corwin* cruise
in the summer of
1881. (Fitzhugh and
Kaplan 1982:Fig 4)

heritage of early Alaskan native life. They also
form an important source that contradicts the
claim of 'misrepresentation' that is frequently
levelled against Western observers, especially
those involved with visual media. Nelson's photography is not devoid of bias, but his selection
of subjects and style might be considered as a
'natural history' genre that presents the peoples
of western Alaska at an early stage of Western
contact with refreshing clarity.

## Nelson, the naturalist
Edward W. Nelson's four years' residence in
Alaska in 1877–81 resulted in monumental
achievements in the study of Alaskan natural history and ethnology. While serving as Weather
Observer for the US Signal Corps at St Michael
at the mouth of the Yukon River, he was able to
devote much of his time to making scientific
studies and assembling collections for the
Smithsonian Institution. Under the guidance of
the Smithsonian's Spencer F. Baird, who lobbied
for his appointment to the Signal Corps position
and who advanced funds and credits to purchase
collections and supplies, Nelson collected thousands of bird eggs, bird and mammal skins, fish,
plants, minerals, and insects, and more than ten

thousand ethnological objects, all with careful
documentation (Collins 1988; Fitzhugh 1983:
7–49). These collections and Nelson's detailed
observations of animal behaviour and native life
and customs (Nelson 1887, 1899) established the
foundation for systematic scientific knowledge of
western Alaska (fig.1).

Although he never held a permanent
Smithsonian appointment, Nelson went on to an
illustrious career as a pioneering naturalist of the
American Southwest and western Mexico
(Goldman 1935). In later life he became the
founding director of the US Biological Survey,
which was itself the predecessor of the US Fish
and Wildlife Service and of its recent short-lived
reincarnation, the US Biological Survey.

Nelson was never trained in anthropology but
nevertheless received acclaim for his ethnological
collecting among the Yupik, Inupiat, and
Athapaskan peoples of western Alaska (Lantis
1954). His magnificent series of artefacts, documented to village locations throughout much of
western Alaska; his Yupik dictionary and terminology listings; his carefully transcribed tales and
narratives; and his detailed and (for his day) relatively objective, ethnological observations have
all received meritorious citation. The one component of Nelson's ethnological collections that
has not been given close attention is his photographic work. While some of his photographs are
well known from their publication in 'The
Eskimo about Bering Strait' (Nelson 1899) and
in the *Inua* (Fitzhugh and Kaplan 1982) exhibition catalogue and the Nelson reprint (Fitzhugh
1983), others, including his illustrations for
Hooper's report of the *Corwin* cruise (Hooper
1883), are barely known. Still others have never
been published, and no attempt has yet been
made previously to analyse the corpus as a distinct collection.

On the other hand, Nelson's photography has
not been totally ignored. Thomas Sexton, an
Anchorage specialist in the history of Alaskan
photography, wrote a brief essay on Nelson's
photography (Sexton n.d.) and with Paula
Fleming's assistance assembled a preliminary
inventory of Nelson photographs from file prints
at the Smithsonian's National Anthropological
Archives. Sexton was primarily interested in the
photographic history and technology aspects of
Nelson's work. Several years ago an updated list
with some newly discovered photographs and
corrections to Sexton's list was prepared by
Alison Young.

My renewed interest in Nelson's photography
resulted from the discovery of Nelson's field journals which provide new information to identify

and contextualise the images. These diaries, which Susan Kaplan and I searched for at length at the time of the *Inua* project, appeared unexpectedly among the papers of Nelson's life-long friend, Edward Goldman, when his son, Luther J. Goldman, donated his father's papers to the Smithsonian Archives in 1992 (Cox 1993).[1]

## Early science in Alaska

Before delving into photographic matters it is useful to present Nelson's work in Alaska in the context of the Smithsonian's general programme of northern research (Fitzhugh and Selig 1981; Fitzhugh 1988a). When the Smithsonian was established in 1848, ethnology, archaeology and linguistics were central to its interests. It was therefore natural, with the appointment of Spencer F. Baird as Assistant Secretary in 1850, that these fields would be among those promoted as part of Baird's expansive plans for natural history collecting and documentation in western North America (Rivinus and Yousef 1992). In 1858 Baird sent Robert Kennicott, a young naturalist from Chicago, to begin a collecting programme in British North America. Assisted by the Hudson's Bay Company, whose factors provided help and logistic support (Collins 1946; Lindsay 1993), Kennicott made valuable collections of natural history and ethnological materials from Inuvialuit and Dene of the lower Mackenzie River between 1858 and 1862. Subsequently, local HBC factors B. R. Ross, Roderick MacFarlane and others contributed collections and scientific observations to the Smithsonian, and with Baird's encouragement sometimes published on these collections and on other Arctic matters in scientific journals.

In 1865 Kennicott accepted a position as Director of the Western Union Telegraph Survey, which was then engaged in charting a telegraph route down the Yukon and across the Bering Strait. Kennicott's 'Scientific Corps', composed of William H. Dall, Henry W. Elliott, Frederick Bischoff, Henry Bannister, Charles Pease, and J. T. Rothrock, had been selected because of their association with the Chicago Academy of Sciences, Baird and the Smithsonian. Although the project was terminated when a rival company successfully laid a trans-Atlantic cable in 1866, Kennicott's team was the first American group to gather scientific specimens and records from Russian America, which was still unknown to the English-speaking world. One of the members of the Telegraph Expedition, Charles H. Ryder, made the first photographs in Alaska (Sexton 1982; see below). After Kennicott's death in 1866, Dall assumed

direction of the Alaskan telegraph survey and coordinated communication with Baird. Dall's book, *Alaska and its Resources* (1870), was the first English-language description of Alaska and the first to include significant information on its native peoples, especially those of western Alaska. Dall's travels between 1865 and 1866 on the lower Yukon and along the Bering Sea coast, and on Nunivak Island and in the Aleutians in 1873–4, produced some of the earliest American documentation and ethnographic collections from these regions. His surveys prompted him to recommend that the Smithsonian conduct a more systematic ethnological survey of the cultures and natural history of western Alaska. This led in 1872 to the appointment of Lucien Turner as Weather Observer for the Signal Corps position at St Michael. However, in 1877 Baird decided that Nelson, a more energetic and experienced naturalist from Chicago, should replace Turner to conduct more extensive explorations.

Nelson reached St Michael in early summer of 1877 after a voyage from San Francisco. Shortly after Nelson's arrival, Turner departed to take up the Signal Corps post at Unalaska, where he continued to collect, but obtained few cultural materials. By this time Aleut people had been in contact with Russians for 150 years and with Americans since the 1840s. The French naturalist and linguist, Alphonse Pinart, had collected ethnological and linguistic data from the Aleutians in 1871. In addition to collecting skeletal and archaeological materials from Aleut burial caves, Pinart also took photographs of native peoples of the Shumagins and Kodiak Island (Dyson 1986: 72) and was the first to produce a photographic record of western Eskimo and Aleut people. Two years later, Dall travelled in these same regions and collected archaeological material, some from burial caves visited previously by Pinart (Dall 1875a and b, 1878, 1884; Pinart 1875).

## Beringian crossroads

Alaska in the 1870s and 1880s was a highly diverse social and cultural region. While Russian contacts had thoroughly transformed native cultures of the Aleutians and Kodiak, Russian influence north of the Aleutians, operating through isolated posts and itinerant Russian-American and creole traders, had had limited effect in changing the lives and cultures of this more remote region. Only in the Bering Strait and along the coast of Northwest Alaska was European ('American') influence strong as a result of the whaling enterprise. And in this region, after the purchase of Alaska from Russia

Fig.2. 'Portrait of an
Island Man' (SI-
6736). A Yupik, at St
Michael; probably
summer 1880, shortly
after Nelson received
his dry-plate camera
from Spencer S. Baird
in the mail.

in 1867, the US government, through the activities of its revenue cutters, first the *Corwin* and later the *Bear*, provided a modicum of official authority in an otherwise rough-and-tumble frontier. Interior Alaska, along the Yukon and Kuskokwim, was a real 'outback' governed by native groups and the self-motivated frontiersmen associated with a network of commercial companies. The Hudson's Bay Company had little sway in this region. Here, it was the Russian American Company and its post-1867 successor, the Alaska Commercial Company (Lee 1996), that held the majority of local Western control, backed up sporadically by the yearly visits of the revenue cutters, whose captains essentially 'governed' the region from Unalaska north to Barrow. North of St Michael, in 1877, there were no European shore establishments, and the only European actors were annual visitors in the form of whalers and the *Corwin*. Missionaries did not settle north of Unalaska until the late 1880s. Nevertheless, even by 1885 the social and cultural life of natives along the coast and interior of western Alaska had begun to change rapidly (fig.2).

It was into this rapidly changing multicultural world that the first scientific observers like Dall, Turner, Nelson and Pinart, and collectors like J. A. Jacobsen (in 1882–3) and the Earl of Lonsdale (in 1888–9), arrived. Culture, especially native religious views, had already changed drastically in the Russian-settled regions of south Alaska, where language and material culture were also greatly affected. North of Bristol Bay tradi-

tional culture still remained strong and largely intact, as was also the case in the whaling regions in Bering Strait and beyond. In the latter regions of north-western Alaska whaling contacts had introduced large amounts of Western material culture, but local economy, subsistence and social structure remained unaltered (fig.3). However, the depletion of whales and walrus by Europeans and the decline of caribou that followed the introduction of firearms among interior peoples had a pronounced impact on the residents of these regions. Only in the more isolated regions of the Yukon-Kuskokwim Delta and Bering Sea coast were cultures and environments still largely outside the European contact sphere (fig.4). Yet even here, the advance messengers of European contact known elsewhere – smallpox, tuberculosis and other infectious diseases – had wreaked havoc and had done so for decades (Arndt 1985; Dumond 1996).

Nelson's images provide a vivid panorama of this vast regional 'colloquy' of peoples – Ingalik/ Koyukon, Bering Sea Yupik, Aleut, Inupiat, Chukchi, Siberian Yupik, and various creole and European groups – that made up the population of this new American economic and political domain in 1877–81. His photographs and scientific notes document one of the most active frontiers in western North America.

### Pre-Nelson photography in Alaska
Although Nelson was the first to make photographic records of native peoples of western

Fig.3. 'Noatak Natives' (SI-3854). One of a stereo-pair of Inupiat men at a Hotham Inlet summer trading camp of 6–800 people visited by Nelson on 15–20 July 1881. The importance of European trade goods, seen in quilt-like calico parka and tobacco in the possession of a prominent leader/trader, is evident. Tobacco, once exclusively from the Siberian trade, was largely supplied by whalers in Bering Strait and Kotzebue in Nelson's day. (Hooper 1883:Pl./40)

Alaska and Chukotka, others preceded him in general photographic documentation in other regions. Of these, the most important is Charles H. Ryder (Sexton 1982; n.d.), who photographed in Siberia and Russian America for the Western Union Telegraph Company in his role as expedition photographer on board the *George Wright* in 1866. Ryder had a relatively minor role on this voyage, principally in supplying photographic images to be used by the expedition artists who were documenting the cable project. Fifteen wet-plate images attributed to Ryder are housed in the Bancroft Library's Scammon Collection, and others may exist bearing his stamp: 'Chas.

H. Ryder, W. U. Telegraph Company's Photographic Artist.' Most of these are shipboard shots of landscape and none provides significant information on native cultures.

In 1868 Eadweard Muybridge visited south-east Alaska military posts with an inspection party led by General Henry W. Halleck (Pierce 1977; Sexton n.d.: 4). Muybridge, a San Francisco photographer who was to become well known for his large-format images of Yosemite Valley and for his later studies of animal and human locomotion, produced *c*.36 images of south-east Alaska, mainly shipboard stereograph views using the wet-plate daguerreotype process.

Fig.4. 'Kolmakovski Men' (SI-6338). In the Yukon–Kuskokwim Delta the trading season was during winter when the marshy delta was a frozen highway rather than a barrier to movement. Five intent Yupik men visiting St Michael were photographed in 1880 wearing Yupik hoodless winter dress and suspiciously Russian-like hats.

Muybridge photographs are held in the Bancroft Library and at the National Anthropological Archives, Smithsonian Institution.

The third to precede Nelson in Alaskan photography was a brilliant nineteen-year-old French linguist and anthropologist named Alphonse Pinart whose visit to Alaska in 1871 was to investigate the theory that Alaska native peoples had originated in Siberia. Arriving by steamer in Unalaska, he secured a native *bidarka* (kayak) and paddled from there to Kodiak with his camera and plates stowed inside. Miraculously, his gear survived the rough, wet voyage, and he obtained a series of excellent stereographs of native subjects and villages (Dyson 1986: 72). He returned to Paris with an extremely important collection of artefacts which he published together with a number of his images (Pinart 1875). A set of Pinart photographs is held in the Bancroft Library. In this same year, 1871, Henry McIntyre, resident manager of the seal fishery, made a set of stereograph images of activities in the Pribilof Islands, including some views of Aleut workers (King 1994). Finally, during the Nelson period photography in south-east Alaska advanced with the work of Adolphus Hartmann and William Weinland on the inside passage in 1877 and William Henry Jackson at Fort Wrangel in 1879, being the first to produce photographic collections documenting native peoples in this region.

## Nelson sources and technique

When our reappraisal of the Nelson legacy began with analysis of his collections and archives for the *Inua* exhibition in 1980, we discovered that the Smithsonian Archives contained little 'Nelsoniana', except his letters to Baird and others. We now know why: Nelson had given his papers to Goldman rather than to the Smithsonian (Cox 1993). Nevertheless, by inhabiting the frigid cold room of the SI Photographic Services department, Susan Kaplan and Jane Walsh discovered and reassembled the scattered series of Nelson's original glass field negatives, many of which had never been previously printed or published. Later Kaplan and Walsh also found the original artefact plates reproduced in Nelson's Bureau of American Ethnology monograph, 'The Eskimo about Bering Strait', and we used these for the reprint edition of 1983. But we never found a complete inventory and description by Nelson of his photographic plates. Our current list, beginning with Sexton's inventory of National Anthropological Archives prints, has been assembled from Nelson's published plates and captions, and references to photographs being taken at various locations mentioned in his monographs, in the *Corwin* reports by Calvin Hooper, in John Muir's publications and papers, and in the Nelson diaries.

Establishing the chronology of Nelson's travels using the journals and the report of the *Corwin*

ABOVE
Fig.5. 'St Michael,
Island Man and
Family' (SI-6378).
Family portrait shows
a family with a variety
of traditional and
introduced materials
and styles. The
women wear
traditional materials
and the father a full
set of European-style
garments.

LEFT
Fig.6. 'Norton Sound
Family at Summer
Fish Camp' (SI-6916).
Here, at fish camp
with kayak rack,
drying fish, and
canvas tent a Yupik
family poses with the
elders wearing trade
cloth frocks.

cruise of 1881 (Hooper 1883; Muir 1917) has been important in identifying locations and subjects of his photography. Briefly, we may recount this itinerary. Nelson arrived in Alaska in the summer of 1877. During his first year he spent much of his time around St Michael gathering local natural history material and getting to know the native community. St Michael was a goldmine of cultural diversity, situated as it was near the boundary between Yupik, Inupiat and Indian territories. As it was the most important trading post in western Alaska and a transfer point to posts upriver on the Yukon, Nelson became familiar not only with local Yupik residents but also met a variety of other natives who travelled to St Michael to trade (fig.5). After break-up and throughout the summer, umiaks arrived bearing Yupiks from the Lower Kuskokwim, Nunivak and Bristol Bay; Yupiks from the lower Yukon villages also appeared, as did Ingalik and other

Indians from central Alaska; and Malemiut and other Inupiat groups arrived from Norton Sound, Seward Peninsula, Bering Strait, and Kotzebue. Even Chukchi and Siberian Eskimos occasionally appeared at St Michael to trade. Nelson bought ethnological materials from all these groups as well as from the local villages around St Michael. He also began learning Yupik and some Inupiat language.

In 1878 Nelson began travelling in the surrounding region, first by kayak with his native assistant Alexei (fig.6). Later, in 1879, in company with the Alaska Commercial Company trader, Charlie Petersen, Nelson made an arduous winter circuit through the lower Yukon-Kuskokwim Delta (Nelson 1882). This gruelling trip reaped great rewards in collections and ethnological data.

Nelson did not have a camera during these early years at St Michael. But, according to his journal, he received one 'in the mail', together with other scientific equipment and supplies from Baird when the *Corwin* arrived at St Michael on 21 June 1880. Nelson responded with thanks to Baird:

The photography outfit arrived in excellent condition by the Revenue Cutter *Richard Corwin* and I am very much pleased with it although I have been so pressed with work that I have not had opportunity to make use of it yet. However, the vessel leaves in a day or two and I shall set to work at once securing views, which, as you recommend, I shall leave for elaboration upon their arrival in Washington. (Journal, 7 July 1880.)

Nelson must have had some experience with photography, although to what extent is unknown. However, he seems to have had little trouble becoming familiar with the camera and, shortly after receiving it, produced 'quite a number of photographs of Chukchis who arrived at St Michael by umiak from East Cape, Siberia, accompanied by Diomede Islanders' (journal, 11 August 1880). In November Nelson made his first foray up the Yukon, travelling by dog sled and visiting the Lower Yukon Yupik villages and the Indian villages around the mouth of the Innoko at Anvik. On this trip he took the camera and made a number of images, and in the process discovered field photography to be both a technical and a social trial (fig.7). None of the Anvik photographs were published because Nelson felt his notes on the Ingalik were too undeveloped to publish and were tangential to Eskimo ethnology. His virtually complete manuscript on Ingalik ethnology was later annotated and published by VanStone (1978), unfortunately before we had found Nelson's photographs.

Following his return, Nelson continued the photographic documentation he had begun in St Michael that fall, securing shots of various native groups who came to trade at the post during the winter season. Many of these visitors were Yupiks from the interior of the Yukon-Kuskokwim Delta and Bering Sea coast who, because of the difficulties of summer travel in the tundra, conducted their fur trade with the post during the winter sledge season (fig.4). Yupik winter dress and snowy scenes identify this series.

Nelson had decided to quit his post and to return south to begin the task of publishing his

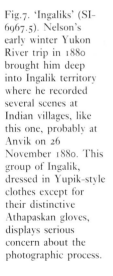

Fig.7. 'Ingaliks' (SI-6967.5). Nelson's early winter Yukon River trip in 1880 brought him deep into Ingalik territory where he recorded several scenes at Indian villages, like this one, probably at Anvik on 26 November 1880. This group of Ingalik, dressed in Yupik-style clothes except for their distinctive Athapaskan gloves, displays serious concern about the photographic process.

data in the fall of 1881. By this time he had contracted tuberculosis and his health was failing. He considered, but decided against, throwing in with some prospectors who had found interesting mineral deposits in the Nome area. However, at the last moment, he was asked to participate as Naturalist and Ethnological Observer in the 1881 cruise of the Revenue Cutter *Corwin*, under Captain Calvin Hooper's command. Nelson boarded the *Corwin* on 21 June and spent the next three months steaming about the Bering Strait and the Chukchi Sea coasts visiting many locations, more or less in the following order (fig.1): St Lawrence Island, Plover Bay, St Lawrence Bay, Big Diomede, East Cape, Diomede, Cape Chaplin, King Island, Cape Prince of Wales, Kotzebue, Hotham Inlet, Point Hope, Icy Cape, Barrow, Cape Wankarem and finally, in a historic dash, Herald and Wrangell Islands, where the *Corwin* team became the first Americans to reach these normally ice-bound locations, an illusory land that until then had been thought to be the southern fringe of a continent in the Arctic Ocean. During these travels they administered justice, tried to curtail the whisky trade, and searched for signs of DeLong's *Jeannette* expedition, missing since the previous year. During these travels Nelson was accompanied by John Muir, who frequently went with him on scientific forays ashore (Muir 1917).

On this trip Nelson met, collected from and photographed many other groups. His *Corwin*

series includes photographs of Inupiat groups from Bering Strait to Barrow; of Siberian Yupiks at St Lawrence Island, Plover Bay and East Cape; and Chukchi from St Lawrence Bay, Mechigmen Bay and other locations. On this cruise the camera became Nelson's chief scientific instrument. Hooper comments with amusement on the 'great diligence' Nelson displayed in always carrying his camera ashore on these ventures (figs 8, 9). But for the most part Nelson's images were of natives who posed while visiting on board ship (fig.10). These photographs included a series from the annual trade fair held in Hotham Inlet (fig.3). The *Corwin* series presents an interesting contrast to the St Michael and Yukon series owing to the greater acculturation of Bering Strait peoples and Northwest Alaskan Inupiat to Europeans through the whaling enterprise that had been underway there for thirty years.

Nelson's final shots in Alaska were from Unalaska, where he stopped for several days before sailing on to San Francisco (fig.11). Although a few record Aleut villages, most are landscapes. Shawn Dickson and her friends from Dutch Harbor have helped me identify geographic features in these shots. Some views record archeological sites that were destroyed by road construction in World War II.

In reviewing the entire series, there is little question as to the historical importance of the Nelson photographic corpus. Despite technical problems (see below), Nelson obtained about 126

Fig.8. 'Reindeer Chukchi Group near Cape North, Siberia' (SI-3844). Chukchi men and women appear relaxed and bear media smiles and ability (except for one) to hold a pose, in this *tour-de-force* image taken on 5 or 6 August 1881, showing little influence of European materials in men's herding costumes on the Siberian side of Bering Strait. (Hooper 1883:Pl./64)

ABOVE
Fig.9. 'Plover Bay
Tchukchi Tent
(Yaranga)' (SI-3861a)
and 'Plover Bay
Tchukchi Women'
(SI-3861b). This
image, taken as split
frame images on one
plate, shows Chukchi
women at camp in
posed and natural
groups (Nelson journal
14:14). This walrus-
hide tent scene was
published in Hooper
(1883: Pl./26) and
later as a retouched
print (Nelson 1899:
Pl.LXXXIII). The shot
of two women
appeared in the
*Corwin* report (Hooper
1883:Pl./36) and in
Nelson (1899:
Pl.LXXXIV) where it
was paired with a line
drawing of the same
image for clarity.

RIGHT
Fig.10. 'Indian Point,
Siberia (Cape
Tchaplin) Tchukchis
Trading' (SI-3851).
Part of stereo-pair
showing tonsured
Natives trading with
baleen and polar bear
hide aboard the
*Corwin.* (Hooper
1883:Pl./26)

images. Some of these are so dark or blurry as to
be unusable; but the majority, while not displaying the artistic talents exhibited by Pinart, convey a tremendous amount of documentary
evidence that ranges widely in subject matter and
geographic scope. Without predecessors, Nelson
had to pioneer his technique virtually single-
handedly, without tutoring, and often under the
most trying of physical conditions – in winter. It
is difficult for us to imagine these problems today
– and what it must have been like without a mental template of what a photographic product
should look like, especially for a person trained
in science, not in art or illustration.

A few comments are needed on technical
aspects, since these have a strong bearing on how
and what he photographed. We have not yet
identified the specific camera model used, but the
images indicate it was capable of taking both full-
size plates and stereographs with split images.
The latter were very popular in the late nineteenth century before the age of projection made
mass-audience viewing possible. They were also
valuable for scientific purposes where depth perception could be useful, and for developing
museum diorama displays. In addition, the split
images (e.g. fig.9) could be used to take two different images on one plate. The plates Nelson
used, gelatin dry-plate negatives, had only a few
years earlier replaced the wet-plate process that
required emulsion preparation, developing at
time of shooting and carrying bulky chemicals,

dark tent and temperature controls – an impos-
sibility in the field in Alaska. With dry plates,
Nelson could take a stock of unexposed plates
into the field and save exposed plates for development when he returned to St Michael. The
disadvantage was that the gelatin dry plate had a
slower film speed, so that without artificial light
Nelson could not photograph motion, interior
scenes or dim outdoors scenes. Some of his shots
spoiled or are so dark and blurry that he could

use them only after retouching or as templates for preparing pen-and-ink illustrations. Carrying a bulky camera, fragile glass plates and tripod introduced other obvious constraints, given Nelson's manner of travel. Nevertheless, he seems to have carried it at every opportunity after the fall of 1880 and even preserved important plates that broke after exposure in the field.

Nelson never complained of the physical difficulty of carrying the camera on sledge trips or overland, but frequently noted social problems in obtaining the desired images. Thus, while photographing Chukchi visitors at St Michael in the summer of 1880 he noted in his diary of 11 August: 'I made two trials to secure a copy of the tattooing [on] the Chukchi women [but] they became ill [when] I pointed the camera at them. After considerable arguing I secured my object.' (Journal, 11 August 1880; Nelson 1899: Pl.xi.) On St Lawrence Island, visiting villages in 1881 where the population had been devastated by starvation and disease in 1879, only with difficulty did he secure co-operation from the remaining living inhabitants, who 'showed dread of the camera', calling it 'bad medicine'. Hooper reports that, when high winds resulted in a failed attempt at exposure and Nelson came out from beneath the light cloth saying 'no good', one of the natives approached and asked if they 'would all die now'. At Cape Wankarem, Siberia, 'the people were quite jolly and thought it was great sport to be stood up and oogled at through the camera, but it was hard to make them keep quiet long enough to get a view.' (Neg.3858; Hooper 1883: 62.) But the potential evil power of an apparatus that produced inverted images on the glass focus plate was frequently unnerving. When Nelson asked if he could photograph a Chukchi reindeer herd, the Chukchi insisted he disassemble his camera completely, which he did; but, when Nelson refused to reveal the unexposed plate, they showed great anxiety that evil would befall their herd through its use (Hooper 1883: 76). He described photographing Point Hope people on the *Corwin*: 'I secured some good photographs of these natives on board, but when I took one of the chief [fig.12] alone I had considerable trouble in getting him to remain quiet, for he became extremely nervous when I covered my head in the cloth, and it was only when I told him that it would be bad for him if he moved that he (under the greater fear) remained quiet long enough to photograph.' When photographing a village scene at the Yupik village of Razboinsky on the lower Yukon, the adults all ran for cover into their sod houses when Nelson ducked beneath the cloth to shoot, leaving the children to fend with evil spirits for themselves. Only with great difficulty did Nelson convince them to return and remain still for the shot (neg.6371; Fitzhugh and Kaplan 1982: fig.118).

## Photographic series

A tally of Nelson's images by region and ethnic group reveals 126 existing plates as follows:

| | |
|---|---|
| St Michael Yupiks and post views | 44 |
| Lower Yukon Yupik villages (November 1880) | 11 |
| St Michael Indian visitors and Anvik | 10 |
| Siberia Yupik and Chukchi | 14 |
| North-west Alaskan Inupiat and King Island | 19 |
| Hotham Inlet Inupiat and trade fair | 10 |
| Unalaska (landscapes and two native village scenes) | 11 |
| Natural history shots (animals, ice cliffs) | 7 |

Subject matter analysis reveals a variety of purposes in Nelson's photographic strategy. Several types of views are so rare and so carefully staged that they may have been shot at Baird's request. In one example we find a view of two kayaks with the hunter in the foreground wearing a hunting visor and a gutskin *kamleika* in the act of casting a seal harpoon (fig.13). Nelson may have staged this photograph to use for publication or to construct a museum exhibit using collections he had obtained as props. The visor appears to be the same specimen as cat.no.176207 in the National Museum of Natural History collection (Fitzhugh and Kaplan 1982: fig.29). Sometime after it was collected this visor lost the engraved lateral ivory wings seen in Nelson's field photo.[2] From the background landscape we can discern the geography of St Michael. This photograph was later used to construct a diorama at the National Museum in the 1950s, using a *kamleika*, the Nelson visor, and what appears to be the same harpoon, line, and float board illustrated in the photograph (ibid.: fig.28). However, instead of using a Norton Sound kayak (of which Nelson collected several), the exhibit was constructed using his Nunivak kayak (Nelson 1899: Pl.79.2). The reason for this is familiar to museum curators who have worked with exhibit designers. Not only does it carry an illustration (a *palraiyuk* figure), it was shorter and could fit into a regular-sized wall case. Despite the inaccuracy, this exhibit has been a major attraction of the Smithsonian's Eskimo hall.

It is interesting to compare Nelson's photograph of the hunter with a shot taken by Edward Curtis in Nunivak Island in 1927 (Curtis 1907–1930: vol.20).[3] Curtis staged a virtually identical shot with a helmeted hunter in gutskin *kamleika* about to throw his harpoon. However, where Nelson's shot is from a distance, Curtis shot upclose from behind the hunter's shoulder, effectively engaging the viewer in the action. His purpose here was drama, not scientific documentation as in Nelson's shot. Curtis may have been inspired to make this shot by Nelson's published photograph.

Another photograph that may have been staged for possible museum display is a Malemiut family travelling by dog sled (Nelson 1899: Pl.LXXV). Activity shots such as these were hard to get using Nelson's bulky camera. For the same reason, successful shots of people working in bright snow conditions, like the Malemiut sledders or 'Setting fish trap through the ice on the Yukon near Ikogmut' (ibid.: Pl.LXXI), are rare.

Nelson took many views to record village scenes, architectural details of dwellings and *qas-*

git, and food storage racks; cemeteries and graves; and specific artefact types like sleds and kayaks. When the results were clear, these were used as photographic illustrations in his monograph; if too blurred or dark, they were reworked into line drawings. This was the origin of the pen-and-ink illustration 'Tomcod Fishing Through Sea Ice at St. Michael' (ibid.: fig.47), which was created using the overly contrasty photograph (Fitzhugh and Kaplan 1982: fig.82) as a model. Only one shot of ceremonial life exists ('Woman with ermine fillets . . .': Nelson 1899: fig.147); whether this is due to religious sensitivities or because these events took place indoors in winter, with too much motion and insufficient light, is not known.

By far the most common photographic rendition was the standard frontal upper body portrait, usually taken as a group shot, a posed arrangement that Nelson seems to have used to record clothing, physical features and general attitude. He took a few facial close-ups, other than to record Chukchi tattoo patterns, and these are often quite striking images. The purpose seems to have been straightforward. No attempt was made to arrange the group or to have people 'dress up' or act formal. People are seen in a variety of poses in whatever they happened to be wearing. There was no conscious manipulation to create a 'proper' image. Hence we see these people as they appeared in routine daily life, with new, dirty or worn fur garments, fancy clothes,

and everyday gear. Only the Ingalik Indians shot at St Michael stand out as paragons of sartorial splendour (fig.14). Nelson reported that Ingalik normally wore their finest clothing for their visits to the post. Those he photographed at Anvik were not so well attired.

Standard poses for physical anthropological documentation are not seen: i.e. front and side views of individuals; and there are no nude shots. This technique, later applied to many Inuit people of Canada and Greenland, never became a standard method for field anthropology in Alaska. Among the most effective of Nelson's shots were the group photographs of Inupiat taken aboard the *Corwin* in Bering Strait and Kotzebue (fig.15) and the somewhat evocative images of husband and wife or family scenes (fig.5; Fitzhugh and Kaplan 1982: fig.140). These and views of individuals and Indian pairs shot with their rifles were clearly composed for formal effect (ibid.: fig.286). Tattooing was common throughout western Alaska, and as we have seen, Nelson carefully photographed Chukchi tattoos (Nelson 1899: Pl.xi) and made sketches of tattoo patterns in his field notes and monograph. Generally, he did not take close-up portraits, instead shooting full-figure portraits, often in groups in their work settings, and as a result these images all have great anthropological, historical and humanistic value today. He took several shots of posts (Fitzhugh and Kaplan 1982: fig.3), his trader companions, his assistant Alexei (ibid.: fig.5) and, with con-

Fig.13. 'St Michael Man (Unaligmut) Casting a Seal Harpoon' (SI-3846). This shot, staged with a man dressed to represent a seal hunter in action, became the model for a National Museum of Natural History reconstruction erected in the 1950s, using the very same artefacts photographed here, except for the Norton Sound style kayak, which was replaced by a Nunivak kayak because it was several feet shorter and could fit into the case, and had a painting of a mythological beast on its side. (Nelson 1899:Pl.liii)

OPPOSITE ABOVE
Fig.14. 'Fort Yukon Tinneh, St Michael' (SI-6341a,b). Indians visiting St Michael during the summer brought out their fancy beaded clothes to wear at the post and were photographed in these and their more, by this time, 'traditional' European garments.

OPPOSITE BELOW
Fig.15. 'Cape Smith Eskimos' (SI-6394). This group of Inupiat create a wonderful assemblage illustrating the clothing and decorative styles of Northwest Alaska in 1881 (Hooper 1883:Pl./64). The central cluster of three adults and one child were used as the basis for a drawing published in Nelson (1899:Pl.XXVI).

summate modesty, only one shot of himself (Fitzhugh 1983:6).

Nelson did not have a plan for setting and background. He did not ask people to use props and did not have a 'studio' set. His photographs were taken wherever convenient and often have distracting backgrounds; building corners, upturned boats, tent corners, *Corwin* topsides and asymmetrical arrangements abound. Nelson was not a connoisseur or a visual stylist. His depths of field are disastrous. His habit was to erect his camera at a single station, like the grassy bank at the boat landing at St Michael, and use this location repeatedly for many shots, even at different times of the year. Comparison of backgrounds frequently holds clues as to where and when an uncaptioned image was shot; certain window frames and buildings can be recognised as being at St Michael, or Andraevsky, or Ikogmut (Russian Mission). A village scene at Andraevsky shows the native village and storehouses with a European log house present (Nelson 1899: Pl.LXXXI). Since we have never found a Nelson list of his plates, we have had to use these details and his journal to identify the locations and subjects in his unpublished images. Some of his images published in the *Corwin* report are not in the Smithsonian collection.

## Nelson photography as early systematic science

Nelson's photography needs to be evaluated in the context of his larger efforts in pioneering the establishment of systematic science and natural history in Alaska. Among all of the work conducted by naturalists Baird sent to Alaska, Nelson's accomplishments stand out as the most extensive and enduring. Dall, whose work for the Smithsonian began earlier and continued long after Nelson left Alaska to turn his attention to the Southwest, to Western Mexico and to wildlife administration, also made long-lasting contributions. But except for his general book and a work on masks and ritual objects (Dall 1870, 1884), Dall's accomplishments were topically more circumscribed, and his strongest scientific work was limited to the field of malacology. What can be said then about Nelson's photography in this larger 'Bairdian' context?

First, can we consider Nelson's photography to be 'systematic' in the same sense as his collections, documentation and published record? The answer has to be 'yes' considering the time period and conditions under which he worked. For one thing, Nelson did not receive a camera until the beginning of his final year of residence at St Michael, the summer of 1880. His journals indi-

cate that by then he had completed most of his collecting and observations on natural history and, with his increasing fluency in Eskimo language, had turned his attention nearly exclusively to ethnology. For the next year he carried his camera at all times and made photographs everywhere. As Captain Hooper noted, Nelson was virtually attached to his camera and seems to have considered it, together with his notebook, as a major tool of ethnographic documentation. Obviously, he experienced extreme limitations, both in the number of plates available and in opportunities for shooting. But his coverage, up the Yukon, around St Michael and throughout the *Corwin* cruise, included virtually all of the native groups and Westerners resident in the region. Throughout this period Nelson took only a few shots devoted strictly to natural history, for instance, the dramatic Ice Age giant beaver dams he found eroding from permafrost at Eschscholtz Bay in the summer of 1881 (Hooper 1883: plate facing p.80).

Comparing Nelson's work with his predecessors and contemporaries illustrates the systematic nature of his photography. Ryder, Muybridge, McIntyre, Jackson, Hartmann and Weinland shot mainly scenery and did not publish their work with scientific intent. Pinart, who did and whose main subject was native life, had a very restricted series, and his impact was lessened by its general lack of availability to scholars and the public, especially in North America. In considering the various subject series shot by Nelson, the technical difficulties in producing images, physical exertions of transport, and social difficulties confronting Nelson once he erected his tripod, one has to see this work as of major importance in his documentation of native life, in addition to his artefact collections and written ethnographic observations. It would be many years before a photographic survey of comparable scope would be compiled for this region of western Alaska explicitly for scientific purposes. In this sense, Nelson's photography needs to be considered together with his other ethnological accomplishments as 'systematic' and not as an opportunistic or casual enterprise. Even if one evaluates Nelson's 126 images from his final year by standards of later times, with smaller cameras and better film and emulsions, his work stands up well.

Comment might also be made on Nelson's use of his photographic data. The images were developed, in the field, at St Michael and on board the *Corwin*, but were only available as negatives at that point. The inclusion of many Nelson images, of geography and of native life and artefacts, in

Hooper's *Corwin* report (1883) illustrates their importance as conveyors of scientific documentation. The use of photography in scientific publications was not widespread at this time. Yet it is clear that Hooper, Nelson, Muir and others on this expedition valued this information, although it seems strikingly tangential to the section of the report prepared by the expedition's medical reporter and ethnologist, Irving Rosse (1883). It is fortunate for Alaskan anthropology that Nelson rather than Rosse (or even Turner or Murdoch) was Baird's man in St Michael.

A similar reliance on photography is found in Nelson's monograph of 1899, published many years after his return from Alaska. The causes for this delay – illness, prior commitments to publication of his natural history collections, and other fieldwork requirements – have been reported elsewhere (Fitzhugh 1983: 39–45). The book, recognised widely as a classic (Lantis 1954), makes extensive use of field photography, and utilised thirty-one of Nelson's plates, each of which is the basis for, or provides adjunct information about, some ethnological topic in the text. Comparing Nelson's journals with his monograph reveals the extent to which he drew upon both photographic and written records, and it is clear that many details of native life that are not found in his notes became part of the monograph only because of information taken from photographs. In fact, what distinguishes Nelson's report from other early monographs on Alaskan native culture is his use of photography to support descriptions of environmental, social and ideational aspects of culture. Absence of photography greatly weakens the anthropology of Murdoch's (1892) contemporary report from Point Barrow; the latter and even, to some extent, Franz Boas' pioneering report on the Central Eskimo (Boas 1888) and Turner's (1894) from northern Quebec, which are among our leading ethnologies of northern peoples, can all be faulted for lack of photographic illustration and overemphasis on material culture and de-personalised illustrations or sketches. By contrast, Nelson's monograph displays a broader and more balanced cultural presentation, and has a sense of history, cultural ecology and humanism that comes from its direct photographic representation of natives, seen as portraits and at work in their environment with their cultural surroundings. Today, one only wishes that he had recorded and published the names of his photographic subjects.

Finally, as a result of his extensive photography of people, Nelson gives us the opportunity to analyse and understand the social conditions of western Alaska in a way that could never be done by the use of his collections or writing alone, particularly with respect to Western influence and acculturation history.

## Conclusions

As can be seen from this rather cursory overview, Nelson's photography is a valuable source of ethnographic and historical data which should be seen both in its own right and as an important complement to his larger corpus of anthropological documentation. In the past these images have been known only for the supporting illustrative role they played in his Bering Sea monograph and in the evaluation of this work for the *Inua* exhibitions and the reprint edition of his book. However, it is now evident that a specific focus on Nelson's photography reveals it to have broader value for anthropological interpretation of early historic native life in western Alaska, for several reasons. First, with the discovery and inventory of the full set of Nelson plates, we now have a large body of work to deal with, *c.*126 images. More than half of these plates have never been published, and while some are of poor quality, they are nevertheless informative. Second, Nelson's field journals provide a direct link for most of these photographs in terms of actual field situations, social contexts at the site, and the artefact collections and field observations obtained. Third, the broad geographic spread of the photography enables one to investigate not only cultural variation over a huge area containing many environmental and cultural boundaries but also the history of external contact impacts on indigenous cultures in an extremely diverse region. While Aleuts had been exposed to Russian contact for 150 years, and Chukchi had been fighting Cossacks and Russians since the 1700s, some groups of Yupik people in the interior of the Yukon-Kuskokwim Delta in 1880 still remained outside the sphere of direct involvement with Europeans, even though they had experienced major indirect effects resulting from regional warfare, trade, disease and other phenomena. Even a superficial study of clothing materials and styles in Nelson's photographs reveals regional differences due to the effects of time lag in Western contact.

An important feature of the collection is its documentation of different levels of native–European contact and acculturation. The quizzical, reserved and sometimes even ethereal expressions and poses of some Yupiks of the Yukon-Kuskokwim interior (figs 2, 4, 5) contrast strongly with the cocky, boisterous and tough-looking Inupiats, whose clothing and ornamentation indicate greater familiarity with Europeans and greater availability of trade and trade goods (figs 3, 12, 15). Similar levels of contact are seen in the photographs of Ingalik visitors to St Michael whose highly decorative beaded garments and firearms indicate access to trade opportunities through the interior Hudson Bay supply system.

With specific reference to Bering Sea Yupik culture, Nelson's photography reveals interesting contrasts between the visual imagery of the people among whom he lived and travelled and the artefact collections he obtained. The prevalence of Western garment styles and materials shows that we should be careful not to overstate the case for Yupik cultural preservation and geographic isolation indicated by museum collection studies of Bering Sea Yupik technology and material culture (e.g. Fitzhugh 1988b, 1993). While people in this region appear to have retained much of their old 'palaeoeskimo' artistic and spiritual traditions during the nineteenth century, and were culturally distinct from their neighbours in many ways, Nelson's photographs and observations about trading contacts and travel reveal that Alaskan Yupik people were not isolated from events and cross-currents of the time, even though this was not detectable in all aspects of their material culture. We need to look carefully especially at photographic data of Yupik clothing as a gauge for the introduction of new ideas and materials in comparison to the more traditional, non-Western materials that dominate Nelson's and others' museum collections from this region.

A few other conclusions may be drawn. As has been recognised many times, the camera as an object creates a special dynamic between the photographer and his/her subject, and in Nelson's case revealed aspects of spiritual belief and behaviour that otherwise might not have been recorded, as in the case of the Chukchi tattoo and reindeer photographs. Nelson's difficulties in obtaining some shots clearly indicates the power of religious views about Europeans in general and the camera apparatus in particular. This may be seen in relation to another powerful piece of European technology: firearms.

Nelson's photographs recommence a new era of graphic representation of native life in western Alaska after a thirty-year hiatus in visual representation following a near-demise of expeditionary art that had flourished from the time of Cook until the heyday of Russian America in the 1840s. During that era artists like Webber, Choris, Tikhanov, Mikhailov and others dazzled the world with their vivid illustrations of Alaska natives. The decline of this tradition had as much to do with waning national exploration agendas as it did with the rise of science and photography, and the development of dry-plate technology necessary for portable photography in the north. Although Nelson was one of the first to use the camera as a scientific recording device, his work inevitably has come to have humanistic and artistic value as well. In the following decades few explorers and researchers went north without a camera. Unfortunately, few other Smithsonian naturalists in Alaska compiled a photographic record comparable to Nelson's; and those that attempted, like Murdoch at Point Barrow (to whom Nelson gave his camera on his departure in 1881), produced inferior results. In the end Nelson's work stands largely alone and unparalleled, but its effect on his successors is difficult to judge. In part this is because, apart from illustrating the *Corwin* report, his photographs were not published until fifteen years later in 1899 when his ethnographic monograph appeared, and so few saw or knew of his work.

Finally, as a genre of 'first photography', Nelson's images, unlike Edward Curtis' shots of Nunivak Islanders taken more than fifty years later, are unromantic and without artifice. They give us a clear and fairly unbiased view of different native peoples of western Alaska and Bering Strait as they existed in the early European contact era. As such, they are remarkable documents of historic and humanistic value. They provide an invaluable baseline for studies of traditional culture and are a rich and informative additional source in Nelson's remarkable corpus of ethnological documentation. They should be seen also as part of a developing tradition of imaging native life whose form and style was evolving through consciously created genres of scientific and artistic representation (drawing, engraving, painting) into the new and potentially more objective and informative genre of photography. Viewing native life from the vantage point of the naturalist more than the ethnologist, Nelson's photography provides both advantages and disadvantages for the recording and analysis of culture and history. But, because his purpose was documentation and not art, his photography provides a solid foundation for research into the early cultural life of western Alaska and the Beringian region.

### Acknowledgements
This paper was initially presented at a symposium, 'Visual Anthropology in the North', organised by Stephen Loring and Deanna Kingston of the Smithsonian's Arctic Studies Center for the 21st Annual Meeting of the Alaska Anthropological Association held in Juneau in 1994. The project evolved over the past several years with the assistance of Paula Fleming of the National Anthropological Archives, who helped locate elusive Nelson images; Bill Cox of the Smithsonian Archives, who prepared the Nelson-Goldman finding aid; Jeannette Smith, who transcribed the Nelson diaries – a difficult task given Nelson's cramped hand – and dug out the Nelson-Baird correspondence from the Smithsonian Archives; and Victoria Oliver, who helped

compile information from these documents. The work of Thomas Sexton and Robert King, both of Anchorage, helped with early photographic history and technology. Jane Walsh and Susan Kaplan deserve much credit for discovering the original 'lost' Nelson glass plates in the Smithsonian Photographic Archives, and get badges for courage since they lost blood in the process. Alison Young helped compile an early list of Nelson photographs during a University of Alaska internship at the NMNH. I also thank Jonathan King and Stephen Loring for editorial comments that have strengthened my early draft. Post-publication comment on this paper would be appreciated since a more extensive treatment of Nelson's photography will be included in the forthcoming edition of the Nelson field journals.

## Notes

1. These diaries have now been transcribed and are in final stages of editing for publication by Smithsonian Institution Press.

2. It is possible that Nelson removed these ivory wings himself, for the 176,000 series contains specimens that Nelson retained for some time in his own private collection before he donated them to the museum. Many of the finest Nelson pieces have this catalogue number range. Perforations used for mounting these wings are seen on the sides of the visor.

3. University of Washington Library Archive, neg. NA 1995 (Lowry 1994).

Chris Wooley and Karen Brewster

# More Than Just Black and White:
# Marvin Peter's Barrow Family Album

Most historic photograph collections from Alaska's North Slope consist of images which captivated non-resident photographers. Photographs of whaling camps, walrus butchering, reindeer herding, trading ships, sea ice travel and holiday celebrations abound in the photograph collections of explorers, teachers, missionaries, scientists and other itinerant photographers on the North Slope. Sea mammal hunts, skin boat travel, dancing, and skin clothing were (and still are) favourite subjects of North Slope visitors. Such photographs are valuable ethnographic records ostensibly taken either to satisfy a desire to document and understand Inupiat culture or to capture an exotic image for posterity.

The Marvin Peter collection contains many images of scenes which only a long-term resident could have witnessed: a marriage ceremony; a business meeting; girl scouts making their pledge; friends hanging out at the local lunch counter; a man sitting next to an infant in a high chair; Russian and American amphibious planes searching for a lost pilot; and dozens of portraits of friends and family. The crisp black and white photographs are candid views of Barrow life in the 1930s, 1940s and 1950s, and provide a window into an Inupiat community which was adapting to the economic and political forces of the twentieth century.

### Marvin Sagvan Peter (1911–62)
Marvin Peter was the son of Peter Takkak and Betsy Qaaqattak. Peter Takkak was a reindeer herder, but the family lived at Nuvuk (Point Barrow proper) about 7 miles (11 km) north of the modern town of Barrow. Marvin and his sisters Ida Numnik and Olive Kanayurak, and his younger brother John, grew up at Nuvuk. Marvin

went to school in Barrow until about the fourth grade.

Marvin was born into the post-commercial whaling era on the North Slope. In 1908 the bottom fell out of the baleen market, and the fur trade replaced commercial whaling as the vehicle whereby Inupiat people obtained flour, tea, tools, ammunition and other essential trade goods. The *qargi*, or community house, had fallen into disuse, Western-style houses were being built, and disease epidemics such as the 1918 flu outbreak were killing hundreds of people. In contrast to the Canadian Inuit photographer Peter Pitseolak (Eber, this volume), we can only speculate regarding Marvin Peter's photographic training.

Marvin had rheumatism when he was young. His sister, Ida, had worked at the Barrow Presbyterian Hospital for missionary Dr Henry Greist and his wife, nurse Mollie Greist. The Greists noticed that Marvin always sat on his legs and never walked nor stood up. Dr Greist asked to see Marvin, diagnosed him with 'inflammatory rheumatism' and offered to straighten his legs. A few years later, in 1928, Marvin accepted the Greists' offer and moved into the hospital for over a year of treatment. Dr Greist was also a photographer and may have taught Marvin photography during this time. The Greists soaked and massaged Marvin's legs and they eventually loosened up enough so he could get around on crutches.

Marvin developed his artistic talent during his primarily immobile childhood. Mrs Greist recalls:

He could make all kinds of tools for the hunters, bone needles, and steel needles for the women's sewing machines, dog harness, lashing sleds, making seal and fish nets, traps, repairing typewriters, making parts for lamps. Knitting was an art with him – crocheting – cutting quilt pieces for me perfectly – hooking rugs ... He could draw almost anything he looked at. He expertly skinned birds, ducks and geese, and blew eggs for my work of collecting for Ornithologists (M. Greist n.d.: 67).

Yet, Marvin was unhappy until his family moved from Nuvuk into Barrow. After the move he was able to support his sisters, younger brother, and a blind grandmother by making baleen baskets. He used a cane to get around town and needed crutches to go any distance out of Barrow. He couldn't participate in whaling because of his crippled legs, but he helped as much as possible with walrus and caribou hunting to obtain shares of meat. He also hunted ducks near Point Barrow, assisted by his younger brother, John Peter. As an adult, Marvin lived by himself, but always shared food with his sisters and other members of his extended family. According to his sister Ida, 'He was always working on something.'

## The Marvin Peter photograph collection

During a lull in the 1990 Alaska Eskimo Whaling Commission meeting in Barrow, Ida invited the staff of the Inupiat History, Language and Culture Commission (IHLC) to visit and look through her old photographs. We had been looking at pictures in Molly Lee's book about basketry, which prompted Ida to mention Marvin's old pictures. Like so many old photographs of relatives, the pictures themselves were bent and worn, but they were numerous, varied and unique.

A box of over 400 negatives was with the photographs, and several were negatives of the prints Ida had shown us. Some were in dated and labelled sleeves. Many were nitrate negatives that were deteriorating and were a safety concern because the film is flammable. Ida graciously donated the negatives to the North Slope Borough for conservation and restoration, in return for a copy of the prints. Following the advice of Susan Kaplan, Director of the Peary-MacMillan Arctic Museum in Brunswick, Maine, IHLC contracted historic photograph restorer David Mishkin to produce duplicate safety negatives and prints. Karen and other IHLC staff have analysed many of the prints and recorded more information about people and events Marvin preserved on film, a process which is ongoing.

A recent development has been the incorporation of the Marvin Peter photographs into Project Jukebox at the University of Alaska Fairbanks Oral History Office. Project Jukebox is an interactive multi-media computer system designed to preserve oral histories, digitised photographs, maps and texts. The user can view historic photographs while listening to an elder discuss the image. The Marvin Peter Photograph Album Jukebox combines the audio commentary of Barrow elder Rex Ahvakana with a selection of the photographs. This type of project preserves the photographs in a digital medium while providing easy public access to oral and visual history.

The photographs are rather ordinary, a quality which makes them historically valuable. During the early twentieth century many published photographs and movies of Inupiat people – like images of native people all over North America – were manipulated to cast the people into a publicly accepted mould. Ann Fienup Riordan (1990: 16) notes that Eskimos were inevitably stereotyped as 'happy, peaceful, hardworking, independent, and adaptable' survivors of the harsh natural environment, but the inevitable victims of Western civilisation. To some degree, photographs of North Slope Inupiat people by Edward Curtis (1907–30), Eva Richards (1949), Henry Greist (n.d.), and William Van Valin (1941) fit the mould of exotic images attempting to portray Arctic life to outsiders. This is not to denigrate the historic importance of their work but, rather, to contrast it with the more personal and domestic images of a resident photographer like Marvin Peter.

The Marvin Peter photographs are personal and convincing views of Barrow. They capture an insider's vision of community life. The collection has been called a Barrow family album. Marvin was an artist who lived in a small, relatively close-knit Inupiat community and he knew his subjects personally. His photographs are more than black and white images, they are an aperture into the community and a visual genealogy. There is nothing imaginary about them.

They reflect the larger community's values – family, friends, relatives and important milestones. The photographs of couples, children, church, and civic groups preserve images of Barrow families and civic groups from the pre-statehood and pre-oil pipeline era. The collection shows an Inupiat community adjusting to new socio-economic and political realities. Marvin Peter, an Inupiat artist, tapped the lifeblood of his community by preserving his vision of it.

## Marvin Peter's images of life in Barrow

Marvin was a talented baleen basket-maker and made money by selling his baskets to people on trading ships and through arts and craft shops.

He used the money to buy groceries and supplies for his family. A 1961 receipt from the Alaska Native Arts and Crafts Clearing House in Juneau, which was with the negatives, indicated that Marvin sold several small but numbered baskets for 12 dollars apiece.

Marvin later worked as a janitor and taught basketry and crafts at the Barrow school, and his students sold the baskets through a Co-op in Juneau. Pauline Burkher taught at the Barrow school between 1937 and 1943 and remembers Marvin as a good teacher who invented a basket-weave which the students could easily manage. According to the late Harry Brower Sr, of Barrow, 'We liked going to his class ... We could speak Eskimo in Marvin's class.' Native children in those days were normally forbidden to speak their own language in school. Harry recalled Marvin telling them traditions about Nuvuk that Marvin learned as a boy. Marvin's unique teaching style and outlook on life are remembered by his descendants. His grand-nephew, Danny Matumeak, recalls, 'Marvin taught me to look at things differently. I am proud to have learned from him.' Danny said Marvin taught him that quickly made baskets may sell, but 'patience brings in bigger money'.

During an interview to identify some of the photographs, an elder remarked that she recalled when Marvin took one of the photographs – a treasured four-generation portrait of her family. Most of the photographs date from the 1930s, 1940s and 1950s, and many are prized portraits of parents or grandparents of current North Slope residents. Many Barrow people have requested and received copies of the photographs. In some cases they are the only photographs some current Barrow residents have of their grandparents.

Historic images of Inupiat people are multi-dimensional. Photographs can be items of ethnographic study, art objects and family heirlooms all at the same time. Professional researchers can make an important contribution to native communities by working to continue the process of visual repatriation and by making collections accessible to the communities where the photographs were taken many years ago.

Although Marvin was unable to hunt and travel with his peers, he strengthened and preserved his ties to the community and to the land through his art and his camera, and captured elusive scenes from Barrow's recent past. Marvin Peter's photographs are a visual record of his intimate connection to the land and its people. His vision of his community stands in marked contrast to the more prevalent but relatively superficial early twentieth-century images of Inupiat people on Alaska's North Slope. Like a family album, these images will be treasured for generations.

## Acknowledgements

I would like to thank the North Slope Borough IHLC in Barrow for approving and supporting this project from its inception. Numerous Inupiat elders in Barrow and elsewhere have been gracious with their time and expertise in identifying people and events in the photographs. They are the experts of Arctic photography. Thanks are due to the University of Alaska Fairbanks Oral History Project for incorporating the photographs into Project Jukebox. Dr Susan Kaplan of Bowdin College in Brunswick, Maine, provided important initial preservation and duplication advice. David Mishkin of Portland, Maine, carefully and professionally duplicated the deteriorating negatives. Diane Brenner of the Anchorage Museum of History and Art, Ted Spencer of the Alaska Aviation Heritage Museum, Dr John Bockstoce, Mr Rex Ahvakana and Mrs Pauline Burkher have also helped. Most importantly, Ida Numnik of Barrow, Marvin's sister, donated the negatives to the North Slope Borough IHLC to be conserved for posterity. Her generosity benefits residents of the North Slope and beyond.

RIGHT
Fig.1. Marvin's uncle
Martin Sakip with
Henry Panigeo (R).

FAR RIGHT
Fig.2. Clara Mukpik
(L) with Edith
Panigeo Rowry (R),
kitchen workers at the
Barrow Presbyterian
Hospital.

BELOW
Fig.3. Barrow
wedding scene –
marriage of Edna
Nusungina to Bob
Rice, officiated by
Commissioner Hugh
Saltzman, with Joe
Panigeo looking on.

BELOW RIGHT
Fig.4. Marvin Peter
preparing baleen for
use in weaving a
baleen basket.

OPPOSITE, ABOVE LEFT
Fig.5. Clyde
'Takkaak' Numnik
(L); unidentified (C);
Forrest 'Manuluk'
Solomon.

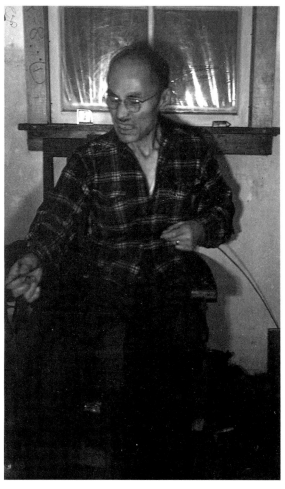

OPPOSITE, CENTRE
LEFT
Fig.7. Family scene in
Barrow, later 1940s.

OPPOSITE, BELOW
LEFT
Fig.9. Nellie
Sikayugak and Lizzie
Kingosak at the
summer post whaling
festival, Nalukataq.

OPPOSITE, ABOVE RIGHT
Fig.6. A very contented group preparing a meal at a
summer camping place.

OPPOSITE, CENTRE RIGHT
Fig.8. Ellen Kanayurak with her children.

OPPOSITE, BELOW RIGHT
Fig.10. A group of people on the boat *Pandora*, going
down the coast to the Will Rogers and Wiley Post crash
site at Walakpa for dedication of the memorial in the late
1940s. (Will Rogers, Cherokee humorist, and Wiley Post,
aviator, died in a plane crash near this campsite, 15
August 1935.)

Bill Hess

# The Gift

*At the time of writing Bill Hess was a photographer working with the North Slope Borough, Alaska, the native corporation responsible for northern Inupiat affairs. He published the Corporation's magazine* Uiñiq *single-handedly until 1997. In this essay he introduces a selection of his photographs with an account of Inupiat whaling.*

Dark clouds hung low over the ice as we swung our picks and chopped our way through the rugged pressure ridges. Ahead of us, even darker bands of 'watersky' materialised in the cloud cover, telling us the lead was opening beneath. Finally, we reached the ragged line separating the thick, sturdy shore-fast ice from a broad expanse of broken, slushy young ice. Shattered and tumbled about by the force of nature, this young ice had been reduced to rubble into which I did not want to place one foot. With one misstep, a man could slip beneath it and never be seen again.

Yet, Kunuk walked nimbly and confidently out into this broken rubble. Johnny, his eldest son, followed. I did too, taking care to place my feet in their prints. Soon, we could see the lead – a narrow channel of dark water separating the shore ice from the polar pack.

We retreated, then set up camp on safe ice near a series of ice-peaks about 15 ft (4.5 m) high. I noticed Kunuk, Jonathan Jr and Claybo standing atop these peaks, scanning the distant and slowly widening lead for whales. I climbed up to join them.

'We saw two whales already,' Claybo said. We watched for fifteen minutes, seeing nothing. Kunuk climbed down. I watched him drive off to the north on his red Ski-doo. Suddenly, a small black triangle pulled my vision back into the lead.

A v-shaped spray rose into the air, where it hung as the black, graceful curve of the whale's back rolled beneath. 'Bowhead!' I whispered excitedly. Claybo and Jonathan Jr laughed good-naturedly.

Soon, another bowhead came. Both lingered, out beyond the rubble ice. I looked at the whales and then the ice, stretching in all directions, rough and broken. What a tiny group of people we were, out here, alone in this great sea of ice! A shiver rippled across my spine, ran upwards through my skin and shook my shoulders.

The first whale lifted its flukes into the air, then dove beneath the surface. Soon, the second followed.

Kunuk returned. He had found a camping spot where we would relocate in the morning. He went into the tent, pulled out tools, parts and explosives and began making bombs. Randy Edwards, Kunuk's fourteen-year-old grandson by his daughter, Esther – now dead of breast cancer – and her husband, Danny, watched closely. Occasionally, Randy would ask a question and Kunuk would respond in his always quiet, calm voice. Outside the tent, Johnny, Claybo and Jonathan Jr carefully removed the kinks from the long rope which attached the harpoon to the fluorescent-pink, teardrop-shaped float. They then wrapped the rope around the float in neat coils.

Come morning, camp was struck quickly. Spirits were high, thoughts positive. Everyone seemed to feel good. This was just how I had always heard a crew should behave if it wanted to convince a bowhead it was worthy of its gift.

'A whale is coming,' announced Malik, 'I can feel it. Someone is going to catch a whale today; I'd say a little after noon.'

We fired up snow-machines and, towing the

Fig.1. Kunuknowruk, a decorated Vietnam war veteran, hunts geese offshore from Point Hope, June 1991.

skin boat and a number of sleds, drove off to the new campsite. I had expected it to be a place free of the rubble ice. I was wrong.

We took our picks and began to cut a trail through the rubble, which had firmed up a bit overnight. By the time we reached the campsite, I was hot, soaked in sweat. I knew if I did not get out of these wet clothes, I would soon be miserably cold. We had barely begun to pitch camp when a pod of belugas swam by. Minutes later, a bowhead broke the water just to the north of us, but the boat and weapons had not yet been made ready.

Soon, the tent was staked. Caribou skins covered the floor. Claybo tumbled into them and fell asleep.

Eli armed the big, brass shoulder gun, which resembles a hand-held canon, with one of the bombs Kunuk had made the night before. Kunuk laid the harpoon and bomb-load darting gun in place over the bow. The rope attaching the float to the harpoon was wrapped in a neat, flat coil on a platform just behind the harpoon. The hand-carved paddles were tucked into the thin ropes binding the bearded sealskins to the boat frame.

Before the umiak could be put into position, a whale came. Waving his arms frantically, Johnny signalled crew members still hauling gear through the rubble to kill their snow-machines. Hurriedly,

Kunuk and the available hunters grabbed the gunwales of the umiak, pushed it to the edge of the ice and shoved off. Randy stayed on shore and, overcome with excitement, lost his breakfast between two chunks of upturned ice.

We did not see the whale again.

Claybo ran out of the tent, irritated that he had slept through the first chase. 'I am not going to sleep again,' he vowed. 'No way! Not until we catch a whale!' I remembered previous seasons passing by with no whale at all. Claybo could become one sleepy hunter.

Suddenly another whale blew. Again, chase was given and again the whale vanished beneath the water.

I wanted to change into dry clothes, but what if a whale was struck while I was doing so? Surely, with three seasons of whale hunting behind me and not one struck whale, I could take at least ten minutes to change into dry clothing!

I entered the tent and removed my parka. I placed a manual Canon F-1 with an 80–200 mm zoom lens in one pocket and in the other, another with a 24 mm wide angle. I laid the parka just inside the tent flap. I sat down on the grub box, and pulled dry clothing from my duffel bag. I removed my boots, my socks and my warm outer garments. I was clad only in a t-shirt and my light-weight, inner pants. Suddenly, the tent flap

whipped open, revealing Johnny's flashing eyes. 'Whale!'

I jammed my feet back into my boots. I yanked my cameras from my parka.

In this state of near-undress, and with my untied boot strings flapping free, I slipped outside, crouching low. No more than five feet in front of the umiak, the triangular hump of the head of a bowhead glided silently through the water. Grasping his harpoon, Kunuk crouched behind of the bow. Eli was just behind him, shoulder gun in hand. The rest of the crew crouched low on the ice around the gunwales, ready to shove off. I had long been told how a bowhead gives itself to good-spirited crewmen – how this animal is so smart, grand and powerful that even the best crew could not kill one unless it first gave itself to them.

In spirit, largely because I had lived so much of my life in native America, and because I have a native American family, I had always accepted this concept. In intellect, I had reasoned that it was the hunter and crew with the most skill and stealth, those best able to work together, who would get the whale.

What I now saw inflated my spirit and rose beyond my intellect. The whale appeared to bow in front of the umiak. It looked and felt as though it were offering itself to Kunuk.

I was crouched on the left side of the umiak. The strike would be made on the right – out of my camera view. I scooted behind the boat to the backside of the windbreak. I heard the hollow, scratching sound of the umiak keel scraping over the ice and then the splash of the boat entering the water. I heard the blast of the bowhead's last exhaled breath. I popped my head over the wind-break. Only Kunuk, raising the harpoon, and Eli, bringing the shoulder gun into firing position, were in the umiak. Claybo stood directly between them and my lens. Kunuk, positioned for the strike, was beginning the motion to hurl the har-poon. I scooted just inches to the right, to where I could see at least a portion of Kunuk's torso beyond Claybo. I pulled the viewfinder to my eye. I saw nothing but a foggy, blurred image – my breath had iced over the viewfinder. Focusing by instinct, I began shooting, cranking my thumb as fast as it would go.

Kunuk thrust the harpoon into the whale, a bit behind the head. The darting gun fired its bomb into the animal, blowing the heavy, wooden shaft back over Kunuk's ducked head. Eli followed close behind with the shoulder gun. An explo-sion flashed out from the barrel. Eli was flung backwards in the boat by the recoil. The whale disappeared beneath the surface. Seconds crept by. Nobody moved. The shock of the two bombs going off in the whale reverberated through flesh, water and ice. Johnny and Jonas ran back across the ice with the float, unravelling the rope as they went. Malik sprinted close behind them. After several more tense seconds, the whale rose to the surface. It rolled onto its side, where it raised a flipper into the air. It had given itself to Kunuk and his crew.

'Thank God!' someone shouted. Suddenly, everyone was clasping hands, hugging, laughing, crying.

Tears burned my cheeks, making it hard to focus. Perhaps a few of my tears were for the death of this great animal. Yet, in its death I had witnessed something ancient and beautiful. I had just witnessed the gift of the whale.

Fig.6. Approaching a bowhead, Point Hope, May 1991.

OPPOSITE CENTRE
Fig.7. Malik, one of the most successful and respected harpooners on the North Slope, says goodbye to one of three grey whales which he befriended during the famous great grey whale rescue at Point Barrow, October 1988.

OPPOSITE BELOW
Fig.8. Members of a special unit of US National Guard Eskimo Scouts participate in war games at 50 degrees below zero, February 1989.

TOP
Fig.9. Each year around the Fourth of July, the village of Point Lay harvests a year's worth of beluga in a single hunt, July 1990.

LEFT
Fig.10. Pulling up an *ugruk*, or bearded seal, July 1989. In most cases, it takes between six and eight ugruk skins to cover an umiak, or skin boat.

ABOVE
Fig.11. The Junior prom, Point Hope, April 1991. The girls made their gowns in class.

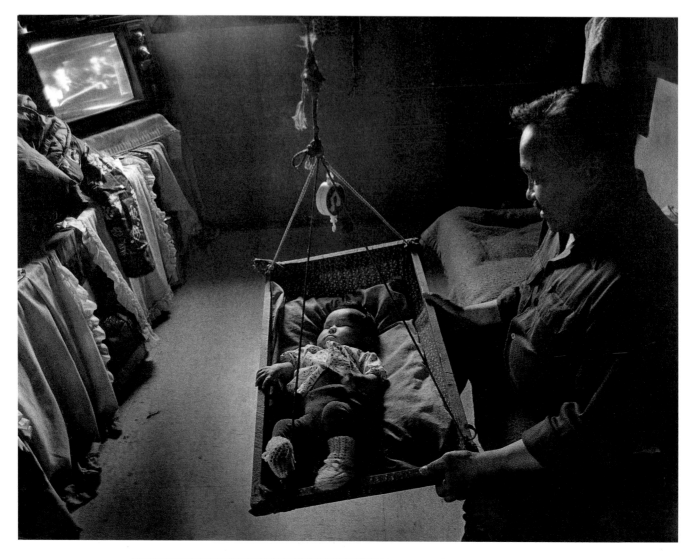

Fig.12. In the Iñupiat village of Ambler, located on the Kobuk River, a boy comes into the world between two story tellers, one traditional, and one not, July 1982 (or 1983).

RIGHT
Fig.13. Canada's Martha Flaherty and daughter in Greenland, July 1989.

FAR RIGHT
Fig.14. The late Patrick Attungana of Point Hope, a respected whaler and Elder, June 1991.

OPPOSITE
Fig.15. Each June, successful crews stage great whale feasts at which the gift of the whale is distributed throughout the community. The skins from successful boats are sewn into blankets from which celebrants are tossed high into the air. June 1989.

Eileen Norbert

# Charles Menadelook Photographs –
# A Family Collection

Alaska natives who document their lifestyle can provide much information and an intimate understanding of their own people. It is valuable because the record is from the perspective of their world view. One such person who documented the Inupiat lifestyle with photographs was my grandfather, Charles Menadelook, an Inupiat born in Wales, Alaska, in the late nineteenth century. He had the distinction of being one of the first Inupiat teachers in Alaska. Fortunately, he was also an avid photographer.

My great aunt, Teresa Soolook, said he had five large photograph albums with the negatives kept in cigar boxes. Many years after he died, my grandmother, Etta Soolook Menadelook, was sent to a tuberculosis sanatorium. Prior to this she had given the negatives to at least her three eldest children, my mother included. The ones my Uncle Roger inherited were sold after he contracted TB so that he could send money to his family. Another uncle, Charles Menadelook Jr, was also sent to a TB sanatorium where he asked my mother to send him some negatives. Unfortunately, he died there and the family lost those negatives. After my mother died, my eldest sister inherited mother's negatives and later gave them to me. It has become apparent how valuable they are.

For a man who began life somewhat tragically, Charles Menadelook went a long way. When he was a baby, his father Kakaduk was murdered with a harpoon while hunting on the ice. Kakaduk had been a very successful Inupiat trader.

My grandfather was a man of contrasts, a man who adapted well to his changing world. He lived by his traditional Inupiat values and customs but was also comfortable in three-piece suits and a different lifestyle. He was a superb Inupiat athlete and also took his piano to most of his teaching posts. He continued to hunt seals, walrus, waterfowl and other game. Even though he embraced Christianity, he and my grandmother were one of the last couples in Diomede to participate in formal spouse exchange. It is still a wonder how he reconciled Christian beliefs and Inupiat traditions, which were and are considered 'sinful'.

As a teacher, he was strict, disciplined and demanded excellence, characteristics he applied to himself. He also had a temper. My great aunt Anna Ahmasuk related how, after arguing with my grandmother, he would pound on the piano for an hour or so until he calmed down. Menadelook insisted that his sister Anna learn the piano. He also taught her how to speak English. Grandpa Menadelook had the vision to see that his world was changing and used education to help prepare his students to adapt.

Fortunately, he took photographs wherever he went, providing a visual record of life from 1910 to the early 1930s. He taught from Noatak down to Unalaska in the Aleutian Islands. Most of his teaching posts were in the villages on the Seward Peninsula – the Bering Strait region.

His photographs captured all aspects of Inupiat life and show the activities which were part of everyday life. They capture the values and the lifestyle that photographs of people posing do not. His photographs include co-operative hunting, fishing, trading, celebrations, women processing game, and family and friends.

Fourteen years ago I received a grant from the Alaska Historical Commission to gather and document historical photographs taken by native photographers from 1911 to the 1950s. Most of

LEFT
Fig.1. Traditional house in Gambell, Alaska, made of driftwood bottom, walrus hide roof. Seal meat or walrus meat is hanging on the racks – 1920s.

CENTRE
Fig.2. A successful hunt at Diomede. Please note how people work together – 1920s.

BELOW
Fig.3. A man spring hunting in Wales. He has traditional men's hunting clothes – 1920s.

the collection was my grandfather's – the rest, it turned out, were all from my family's collections. I then went to several villages and talked to elders. It was wonderful – this is where I received my education about my people. Schools do not teach these things in the Bering Strait region. Elders could and did talk for over an hour about one photograph. It brought much joy to the elders to see these photographs and talk about them. They were able to relate many details in the photographs which an outsider would not know or see. For example, informants were able to say exactly where a photograph was taken because of Inupiat place names. They were also able to identify where a person was by their style of clothing, or what time of year it was by the snow conditions and other weather signs and details in the photographs.

My grandfather would be very proud today and I feel very fortunate to be able to honour and acknowledge the valuable service he did by documenting, through his photographs, the continuity and change of Inupiat life.

I am currently pursuing funding to create an exhibition of this collection in Alaska, particularly in the villages of the Bering Strait region and for use in our schools. Inupiat are visually orientated – what a wonderful tool it would be for our children. I also plan, eventually, to do a book.

RIGHT
Fig.4. An umiak full of Diomede women on their way to pick greens – 1920s.

BELOW LEFT
Fig.5. Man from Wales with an umiak load of seals. Three seals were caught in a net between Wales and Shismaref – 1920s.

BELOW RIGHT
Fig.6. People in Shishmaref working together to build a new sod house or iglu. Note people are all wearing waterproof mukkluks. Sod houses in the background – 1920s.

LEFT
Fig.7. Four men in kayaks after a successful walrus hunt – 1920s.

CENTRE
Fig.8. Men working together after a successful hunt. All have traditional hunting clothes – 1920s.

BELOW
Fig.9. A woman cleaning out a seal. She will make it into a seal poke – a container which was used to store food. This was in Wales in the 1920s.

Nelson H. H. Graburn

# The Present as History: Photography and the Inuit, 1959–94[1]

Fig.1. Kananginak
Putuguk, 'The First
Tourist', Cape Dorset
1992.

## Introduction

This paper is about the photographs I have taken during field work in the Arctic spanning nearly forty years. This field research began with a summer in the Salluit (Sugluk, Quebec) area of the Hudson Strait in 1959 and another in Qimmirut and Iqaluit (Lake Harbour and Frobisher Bay, Northwest Territories) in 1960: this was followed by a year in Nouveau Québec (Ungava) in 1963–4 and another in the same area plus Kingait (Cape Dorset, NWT) in 1967–8, a trip through the central Arctic (i.e. Inuit communities of Keewatin and Franklin, NWT) in winter 1976 and through Nouveau Québec, Baffin Island, and Nuuk,

Greenland, in winter 1986, and lastly a short trip to Bethel and Nelson Island, Alaska, in autumn 1994.

My original intent was to focus on photography as part of the relationship between 'anthropologist and informant' in the Arctic. However, following the conference's emphasis on post-hoc interpretations of historical collections, I have rewritten the paper to reflect on my own ethnographic photography as a collection of more than 6,000 images[2] that are soon to 'become history' and on ethnographic situations that are illustrated by photographs taken at particular times and places. Heeding my original intent, I start by considering the touristic temptation to take photographs which confirm the visitor's initial and commonly shared stereotypes about the unique and timeless in Inuit life. The paper notes that both the Inuit and metropolitan outsiders construct stereotypes of self and other which constantly change in response to each other, and to the media penetration and globalisation of popular culture.

## The exotic image: photography as ethnography

In a recent print entitled 'The First Tourist' Kananginak Putuguk of Kingait, NWT (fig.1) sums up the Inuit stereotype of the intrusive white man. It shows a white man, inappropriately clothed, with aggressive camera, obviously active, directing a passive and puzzled-looking female Inuk, who is wearing traditional skin clothes (rarely used in the artist's adult lifetime), holding a stretched ringed sealskin, with the almost ubiquitous iconic prop, the *inuksuk* cairn of piled stones (Graburn 1987b). This stereotype may also be held by white people interested in the Arctic or may be applied to cross-cultural photography in general (cf. Sontag's 1977 contention that photography is an acquisitive, aggressive or violent act). The fact that this image was produced as a commercial print, for sale mostly to white enthusiasts of native arts, appeals to the humour, the self-deprecation or even to the guilt of those who fasten their gaze on contemporary Inuit as 'Other'. Coincidentally, it also demystifies or de-exoticises contemporary Inuit arts which for the most part consist of exotic images of traditional Inuit life and Arctic fauna, devoid of the very white presence which initiated, promoted and brought these arts to us in 'the South' (Graburn 1976b, 1978a, 1983).

This stereotype of the visiting photographer, fascinated by the opportunity to witness, capture and present to his reference group 'back home' such going-out-of-use items as igloos, skin clothing and dog sleds, is a tempting role for the tyro ethnographer, one which few have avoided. Most ethnographers are amateurs when it comes to photography, and their initial efforts are closer to those of 'ethnic tourists' (Smith 1977: 2; Graburn 1977: 26–7) than to professional visual ethnographers (Collier 1986). Both Chalfen (1987) and Cohen, Yeshayahu and Almagor (1992) point out that early in a journey a visitor photographs the first occasions when he or she encounters the prototypically distinctive or 'authentic' characteristics of the place or people. In my own early sojourns in the north and resultant publications such images were captured and

Fig.2. Dog sledding across rotten ice in the Hudson Bay, near Inujjuak, June 1968.

presented in the romantic spirit of 'I saw the real Eskimo too'. See, for instance, my 'Igloo camp near Qikirktaluk, Hudson Strait, with Jani Piluktuti and Qakangakjuk Oqituk preparing the dog sled, April 1964' (Graburn 1969: 30).

Photography can be taken as a metaphor for ethnography itself. Since the 1980s ethnography has been questioned and criticised as a characteristically colonial activity, forcing the 'objects', the less powerful people being observed, to provide facts and images for strangers from the metropolitan world who set the agenda for the interaction on the basis of their own intellectual foci and tastes (e.g. Clifford and Marcus 1986). Such images are, by being selective, relatively easy for the ethnographer to promulgate (fig.2). Not only does the visitor set the topical agenda, but he attempts to travel in time, using his photographic images to render the subject people as living in some timeless past (Fabian 1983), often called 'Hunting and Gathering' or the 'Stone Age' (e.g. 'Mosesie's dog team struggling through melted snow. Ivujivik, June 1964.' King 1987: 11).

## The real world

Belief in the isolation and apparent timelessness of native culture is only supportable by eliminating those aspects of native life which show evidence of trade and change or by not looking at native life too closely (for instance, in my photograph of Qujuk scraping tubular section of *ujjuk* bearded sealskin, Ivujivik, June 1964 [King 1987: 190], one's attention is brought to the semicircular *ulu* knife and the raw, wet sealskin, rather than to Qujuk's rubber boots or the Fort Garry coffee tins). Such photography tries to sustain the powerful but trivialising appeal of the 'unacculturated' native, either by carefully eliminating evidence of the modern 'present' as did Boas in

TOP
Fig.3. At home in her tent, Ikaujurapik making bannock in an enamel pan to cook over the metal *qullik* oil lamp beside her. Qimmirut, Baffin Island, July 1960.

ABOVE
Fig.4. The Kaitak family in their summer tent. Salluit, September 1959.

changes brought about by contact and trade, in order to implement programmes such as sedentarisation, schooling and health clinics. With little theoretical training (I was then working for my MA in Anthropology at McGill University) and practically no instructions from the NCRC, I attempted to be a 'vacuum cleaner' kind of ethnographer, recording and photographing 'everything', ingenious current adaptations as well as indigenous customs (Graburn 1963, 1969). For instance, in July 1959 I was fascinated that Papigatuk of Salluit used a hacksaw to cut nails from a brass pipe to repair his boat, knowing that brass would not rust – I photographed him, with the implication that making nails by hand was truly representative of a pre-modern culture.

I was also interested that the Inuit had imported musical instruments, first from the whalers and later from the Hudson's Bay Company (HBC) stores, and that their preferred dances were Scottish reels. I photographed such dances at the Catholic Mission in Salluit in 1959, and in 1960 I photographed Akudliksiq playing the accordion and her brother Jamesie playing the violin in their summer tent in Qimmirut. At the same time I was disappointed that the eastern Arctic Inuit no longer practised drum dancing, and was happy to witness, participate in and photograph community drum dancing in Qamanituak and Kangirksliniq when I first carried out field research in Keewatin in 1976.

I was also fascinated by the scenery, the ice and the midnight sun. I took many photographs of Inuit hunting and retrieving animals from ice floes; of the massive, winter, land-fast, sea ice sheets called *tuvak* with and without Inuit (see fig.2); of the midnight sun in summer; of the barely visible midday sun in winter; of sea mists and storms; and, of course, of the brilliant flowers which bloom in the short summer.

But most of my photographs, like those of the Inuit themselves (see below), portrayed Inuit individuals or families (fig.4). These were for the most part photographs neither of representative Inuit nor of notable ethnographic events, but of known, named people, taken as aids to my own memory or, as I was frequently requested, to send or give back to Inuit friends (see below). Indeed, like the photographs of scenery, only a tiny proportion have ever been published or used to illustrate slide lectures or museum exhibitions.

Because I am shy and very conscious of the professional ethics of anthropologists, I have always attempted to ask permission to take photographs of people beforehand, allowing for poses, unlike many more daring and maybe more successful photographers such as Fred

his own photography (Jacknis 1984) or by using captions which draw attention to the 'traditional' and away from the indexes of change (Graham-Brown 1988: 146). Such ideological 'airbrushing' parallels the nineteenth-century collecting activities of the field staff of the Smithsonian Institution, who tried to avoid evidence of trade goods in order to illustrate the then pervasive theory of cultural evolution (Graburn 1996b: 12–13).

When I first visited the Canadian north in 1959, traders had been living in the Hudson Strait region for nearly fifty years and Anglican missionaries had been visiting for sixty years. Although the Inuit lived in winter igloos and summer tents, everyday life inside them showed material changes which the Inuit welcomed (fig.3).

In 1959 and 1960 I worked as an ethnographer to make community studies for the Northern Coordination and Research Center (NCRC) of the Department of Northern Affairs (DNA). The Canadian government needed to understand

Bruemmer (Bruemmer 1993) and Charles Gimpel (Tippet 1994). However, the subjects of my photographs often seemed to want to 'put their best face forward', such as smoothing their hair, or they tried to do something which they hadn't been doing until I raised the camera, such as including their wife or holding their favourite dog (as did Aisaki Pallayak, embracing his wife Suzi and his favourite puppy in Salluit, June 1959, and Qimpirkpi holding his dog in Qimmirut, June 1960). Perhaps the Inuit were trying to 'play themselves' or even to look exotic for the visiting white man. But then sometimes the anthropologist (or *Apirku*, 'the questioner', as I was then known) tried to appear 'exotic' too, such as when I had Inuit photograph me with my own camera in a kayak at Kangirsujuak, July 1959, or eating raw seal meat out on the sea ice of Tuvaaluk, Diana Bay, in April 1968.

But not all scenes are of happy Inuit and there are no idyllic villages where jealousy, anger or loneliness never strike. Some orphan children appear to be unhappy most of the time, and few Inuit adults are happy all the time. Sometimes the going gets rough, and the ethnographer is often challenged as to how to leave out the rough spots and is certainly ethically forbidden from photographing and broadcasting the pain.[3] I, like other ethnographic photographers, usually felt few qualms about photographing children in distress but never did so for adults.

### Ethnography and cultural change

Although my first two Arctic research trips were to produce baseline community studies (Graburn 1963, 1964, 1969), when I returned my research inevitably involved the study and recording of change. One institution that was then getting established was formal education. In summer 1960 I witnessed and photographed the Inuit children attending their first school in the old Nursing Station in Qimmirut, with John Hughes as their teacher. I later photographed many classroom situations, for instance when my wife was a Federal Day School teacher in Puvirnituq, Quebec, in 1967–8.

Ever since 1959, when I found that what the Inuit of Salluit had to say about their soapstone sculpture was so different from anything the dealers and collectors 'down south' said, the study of the Canadian Inuit and other Fourth World arts became my major concern (Graburn 1967, 1976a and b). In 1967–8, briefly in 1972, again in 1976 (central Arctic) and 1986 (eastern Arctic and Greenland), and in 1994 (Alaska), I carried out research on these changing arts. This is not a particularly sensitive research topic,

though major artists often compete with one another and some men look down on the efforts of women sculptors. Most Inuit are proud of their art production, increasingly so as the subject matter usually portrayed – traditional ways of life – disappear into the distant past. They generally like to be photographed while producing the arts, e.g. Eli Sallualuk Qirnuajuak carving a used print block into a new sculpture, Puvirnituq, summer 1968 (King 1987: 30), or Sagiaktuk pulling a print from the inked stone block that he made from his wife Qakuluk's drawing, Kingait, NWT, 1986 (King 1987: 31).

Art production has been a very useful means of livelihood in times when the hunting or weather is bad, when jobs are scarce or for the infirm or elderly. Many formally untrained men and women such as Qirnuajuak Ashevak of Kingait, or Angusalluq of Qamanituak, NWT, have become world-famous artists, some say the best in Canada, and, what is equally important to them, they may make a good livelihood, occasionally over CAN$100,000 a year.

For many successful Inuit men carving performance has become the symbolic equivalent of hunting prowess (fig.5), demonstrating their ability to undertake a big job and support a large family with their own skill, strength and imagination, and often involving tackling the very hardest rocks (Graburn 1976a and b). But the 'proof of the pudding is in the eating': ultimately the white man and the market govern recognition and success; the crucial transaction is when the Inuk artist brings the new work to the buyer at the

Fig.5. Axangajuk Shaa, with his sculpture of a caribou's head. Kingait, May 1986.

Fig.6. Trick photo by Charlie Adamie, with his son appearing to look through a partly defrosted window behind his mother Elsie; a snapshot of the same two at an earlier age is mounted in the corner of the frame. Inujjuak, Que, June 1986.

store or Co-operative. I often photographed Inuit coming to the store or print shop to sell their sculptures or drawings, anxiously awaiting to learn the price paid to them, while other Inuit hung around, trying to glimpse or overhear the price paid in this competitive livelihood.

Since 1967 the majority of my photographs have concerned Inuit art and artists. Most have been images of art works, usually taken in the less than satisfactory lighting conditions of Co-op store rooms, white peoples' and Inuit houses, as well as in galleries and houses in the south. These images, which illustrate the artistic and regional diversity of Inuit art, as well as remarkable changes over time, also constitute by far the greater part of my published photographs (Graburn 1976a, 1978a, 1980, 1983, 1987a; Trafford 1968; and so on).[4] Images of artists at work or with their works of art have appeared less frequently (Graburn 1976b, Graburn and Lee 1989; King 1987; and in this chapter) though they are usually included in my slide lectures and to illustrate museum exhibitions.[5]

### Ethnography and photography: who is watching whom?

So far I have discussed my photographs of Inuit people, hardly contradicting the objectifying stereotype in Kananginak's tourist print. The Inuit have been portrayed in more than a century of publications as exotic people thriving where others feared to tread, and in recent decades (when their life has been drastically changed) as overflowing with natural artistic talent.

Ever since I have been visiting them, at least a few Inuit have been taking photographs too. Most famous is the renowned photographer and camp leader Peter Pitseolak, with whom I lived for three months in Kingait, NWT, in spring 1968. His book *People from Our Side*, published posthumously in 1975, consists of selections of his photographs and written local history, brought to fruition by Dorothy Eber (Pitseolak and Eber 1975). But he was an exception with regard to the range of subject matter and the seriousness of documentation. Inuit have always liked taking snapshots as long as they have been able to get camera and film.

Putulik Oqituk, the HBC clerk in Salluit when I arrived in 1959, had a box camera and took photographs. The problem was that the mail to send out the film for developing and get it back came and went only by ship once every three to nine months. When I sailed south in October, I took Putulik's films and got prints made, as I have done for a few other Inuit, and with permission I looked at the photographs and kept extra prints.

Inuit photographs were overwhelmingly snapshots of local people, especially children: close and distant family members, visitors in the village, children at play and at school, and people at the workplace, which could include the store or unloading big game from boats on the shoreline. Other subjects included the graves of long-departed kin, families moving tent sites, people getting married or being affectionate, and objects of humour such as someone wiping up after a dog peed inside the HBC store, children learning or pretending to smoke. In those days most such prints rarely survived long in nomadic and permissive Inuit igloo and tent households.

With the advent of regular air travel in the mid-1960s film could be flown in and out quickly, and a range of colour films became available. Inuit photography became more common and some started keeping albums or framed photographs (fig.6). In the past twenty-five years the relationship between Inuit and white outsiders underwent change. Inuit became much less shy or self-conscious about being photographed, and they often photographed white visitors; many Inuit quite naturally considered themselves the equals of *qallunaat* visitors not only in hunting, travelling and Arctic life, but also in photography, commercial art, and many other imported ways of life. Near the end of my stay with Peter Pitseolak he suggested that we should go outside to take photographs of each other: I took a photograph of him, then he proceeded to take a whole pack of Polaroid film of me!

Not only is photography no longer an exclusively *qallunaat* skill – a number of Inuit photographers attended the conference on which this volume is based – but Canadian Inuit, especially in the NWT have become, in wealth and lifestyle, on a par with many white families and often share their taste in popular culture too. Most Canadian Inuit now live in what the rest of the world considers large ranch-style homes,[6] often equipped with televisions and VCRs, mementos of travel 'outside (the north)' for work or vacations, and popular cultural and religious images.

Though their material culture may have changed and many say '*Inuit pivalliajut* (the Eskimos are progressing)' (Graburn 1974), in character, in family life and personal interaction, especially with children in the home, the Inuit have, thank goodness, *not* changed in the ways that really count (fig.7).

The speed of development and change is very uneven both between regions of the Arctic and in different decades. Many Inuit look to Greenland, *Kalaallit Nunaat*, an independent country of well-educated European-type Inuit, as a model for their future. And it is true that Greenland appears to be further 'ahead' (fig.8) and to have a high standard of living. It has passed the 'demographic hump' (children are born at about replacement rate) unlike other Arctic areas, but it also has AIDS and severe drinking problems.

'Reverse exoticism', taking photographs to show outsiders pictures of Inuit doing things that 'modern' Western man does but are not expected of Inuit, has a long history (Lee and Graburn 1986 plate 4 shows Inupiat Eskimos driving a motor car in Nome in 1906). It is a temptation these days, especially in Greenland. For instance, fig.9 shows a young Greenlander Jan Peterson ready to go windsurfing in the Davis Strait in winter, standing with ethnographer Valerie Chaussonnet. Similarly, the exhibition of a Canadian Inuit house interior with gas stove, TV and computer had some shock value in the British Museum exhibition *The Living Arctic* (1987).

## Conclusions: the personal and the historical

We have seen the power of photography to document and inform or even to deceive, but perhaps its greatest power is to cater to nostalgia in allowing a glimpse of others and even ourselves when the world was younger. Photographic collections such as mine have personal meanings for myself and for Inuit and whites in the north, but inevitably over time the personal meanings become collective and historical. Bringing together my two themes of photographs both as part of interpersonal relationships and as key his-

torical documents, we can better understand the necessity to avoid the temptations of either sustaining stereotypes, whereby the 'Other', the Inuit, merely confirm the external gaze, or of 'reverse exoticism', which mocks the changes in

TOP
Fig.7. Anthropologist Molly Lee playing with Lizzie and Ben, the children of Annie and Mark Putulik in whose house we stayed, and Qaunak, the little girl who inverted her eyelids on purpose. Salluit, May 1986.

ABOVE
Fig.8. Nuka Moeller and his friends celebrate a Bahai service in a member's home. March 1986.

LEFT
Fig.9. A young (Inuk) Greenlander Jan Peterson ready to go windsurfing in the Davis Strait in winter, standing with ethnographer Valerie Chaussonnet. Nuuk, Greenland, April 1986.

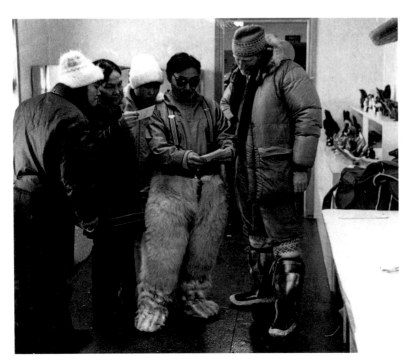

Fig.10. Kiurak Ashoona (wearing the polar bear pants) and friends in the sculpture shop at the West Baffin Eskimo Co-op look at prints that I had taken there nineteen years earlier. Kingait, May 1986.

Inuit culture, because, in the future when personal memories are gone, these one-time glimpses will be *the* historical record.

This article contributes to the literature about Arctic photography in three ways. Firstly, it presents a case study of a career that has engaged with photography in the north for almost forty years and it creates a basic typology of the kinds of occasions on which anthropologists take photographs in the field. Secondly, it considers the ethics of photographing in several kinds of situations. And, thirdly, it compares and contrasts the kinds of situations an anthropologist photographs with those chosen by the Inuit themselves.

I have always sent back prints of photographs I have taken of Inuit or, if I return to the same place, I carry copies with me to show and give back (fig.10). Actually, Inuit very frequently asked me to take their photographs and send them back the prints.[7] This presumably satisfies their personal need to see themselves as others see them or to monitor the impression they give to others. Some may be included in albums as a record of that historical moment. But over the years those moments have become history and many Inuit subjects are no longer alive. In 1986, when writing to each community council asking permission to carry out research again in seven communities which I had last visited from seventeen to twenty-three years before, I promised to bring with me photographs of Inuit or their deceased relatives. The people of Salluit, where I had lived in 1959 and visited in 1964 and 1968 (resulting in a community ethnography, Graburn 1969), requested that I also make (at their expense) and send

poster-sized portraits of some important long dead elders. I expected these to be hung in the new community hall, and I was surprised when they were all immediately sold at cost to their living relatives, first come first served. I also made a set of slides of my black and white photographs (from 1959 and a few later ones) and gave a slide lecture with them the night I arrived. I was asked to give the talk again and again, day after day, five times! And when I was asked to do it again for the sixth time to be filmed for the local Inuit TV studio (Taqramiut Nipingit), I fainted from exhaustion and had to be taken to the Nursing Station. I left the carousel of those slides at the TV studio for safe keeping and permanent community use but I do not know if they have been shown again or broadcast.

In every community I also gave a slide talk in Inuktitut about Inuit arts, showing each community the artists, the rock and the art styles of other communities (this was also broadcast on Greenland television). These talks were very popular; some Inuit asked me to send them copies of photographs of other artists and sometimes of their art work. Though I have personally given prints to hundreds of Inuit in all villages I have visited and the set of 'archival' slides and poster prints to the people of Salluit, one important issue for which I have no solution is the pressing contradiction between the Inuit's very real need to have access to the estimated hundreds of thousands of photographs taken by visitors to the north (including anthropologists) during the historic period, and the inherent difficulties in maintaining archives in these communities where photographs can be secure, not only for the immediate present but, even more importantly, for future generations.

If they are deposited in museums or archives in 'the south', they will be of little use to Inuit; most Inuit and nearly all whites would have great difficulty using them without intimate personal knowledge, even though they are basically documented. Inuit communities have personal knowledge of the contexts of photographs taken there, but few have archival repositories; regional cultural institutes such as Avataq and the Inuit Cultural Institute have archives but little personal knowledge. And after personal knowledge fades, historically situated images become just representative stereotypes from the past. This, perhaps, is the most pressing problem we have to address in the coming years.

### Notes

1. When it was first proposed that I submit a paper for this conference, the organisers suggested that I give a

paper on 'The Alaska Commercial Company (ACC) Collection' based on the fact that Molly Lee and I had recently completed research on the Hearst Museum's large nineteenth-century native Alaskan collection (Graburn, Lee and Rousselot 1996). However, the few photographs of the ACC activities in Alaska were already published in Molly Lee's history chapter. She had already decided to submit a paper on the Gladys Knight Harris collection of photographs of North Alaska. I therefore decided to write a paper about 'The Role of Photography in Relationship to Natives of the Eastern Arctic' based on my own experiences.

At the conference I was impressed by the focus on *historical* collections and their past and potential uses. In the discussion of Peter Pitseolak's photographic agenda I pointed out that he was aware that he was recording his present 'as history', to which Bill Sturtevant replied that in fifty years all our photographs will be used for historical research. My paper is thus the study of a collection with the photographer and some of the subjects still alive, to discover what went into the construction of the collection before it becomes history.

2. The collection includes the following sets of photographs: Salluit and Kangirqsujuak, Quebec (1959) – 11 black and white films and one of colour slides (all I could afford then!); Qimmirut and Iqaluit, NWT (1960) – 9 black and white and 1 colour; Kujjuak, Kangirqsuk, Quartak, Kangirqsujuak, Salluit, Ivujivik, Puvirnituq, Kujjuarapik, Quebec (1963–4) – 5 black and white and 17 colour; Kujjuarapik, Inujjuak, Puvirnituq, Salluit, and Ivujivik, Quebec, and Kingait, NWT (1967–8) – 28 black and white and 40 colour; Yellowknife, Kugluktuk, Ulusakvik, Qamanituak, Kangirqslinirk, Naujat, Arvviat, NWT (1976) – 12 black and white and 16 colour; Kujjuak, Salluit, Puvirnituq, Inujjuak, Sanikilluak, and Kujjuarapik, Quebec, and Kingait, Iqaluit, Pangnirtung, NWT, and Nuuk, Greenland – 28 black and white and 30 colour (some taken by accompanying anthropologists Molly Lee and Valerie Chaussonnet).

The black and white negatives from Salluit (1959) and Lake Harbour (1960) were returned to the Department of Northern Affairs, which paid for them, while I kept a print of each. Unfortunately, they cut each 35 mm strip into individual frames, and stored them, badly scratched, in brown paper envelopes with labels like Dogs, Domestic, Tents, mixing them unattributed with other anthropologists' films. I stored the other black and white negatives in glassine holders in ring binders, each film next to its proof sheet and typed catalogue sheet (with date, topic, place, etc.). Colour slides are kept in metal boxes, arranged by trip with their catalogue sheets in ring binders.

3. Ironically, when I was writing and later delivered a paper on Inuit child abuse (Graburn 1987a) observed during my field research in 1959–68, I was condemned publicly by non-Inuit colleagues for broadcasting negative aspects of Inuit behaviour when 'they and their public image have suffered enough already'. Yet, I was thanked by a number of Inuit for looking into an aspect of their more traditional child-rearing that they thought might throw some light on chronic outbreaks of abuse that had later occurred.

4. Publishing images of Inuit works of art is subject to Canada's copyright laws which prevent even the owner of any work of art from taking or publishing a photograph of it without specific permission from the artist or the artist's representative, unless the collector also bought the copyright (L. E. Harris 1994). For decades permission to reproduce a work of art was handled for Inuit of the NWT by the Ottawa-based Eskimo Art Council (for graphics) or

by the local artists' co-operative (for sculptures), and for Quebec Inuit both were handled by the Fédération des Co-operatives du Nouveau Québec (of Lévis and later Montréal). Licence to depict art works for non-profit or educational purposes was usually granted with no mandatory fee, save a copy of the book or journal, whereas use of the same images for purposes such as advertising, calendars, and even front covers or frontispieces warranted a hefty fee. By the late 1980s this function of the Eskimo Arts Council was judged too paternalistic and stopped (soon the council itself was disbanded); permission often had to be sought from the individual artist. Efforts to write directly or with local help to get permission for reproduction, even from artists whom I know and to whom I could write in Inuktitut syllabics was often time-consuming and frustrating, especially if I did not know their proper address (e.g. PO Box No.) or whether they were still alive. In one case, after months of correspondence, I successfully got permission from Henry Ivaluakjuk of Iqaluit to reproduce one of his paintings, but the publisher inserted a caption with the wrong artist's name and title (Graburn 1993a: 179)! I have not since published images of the work of living Inuit artists in works sold in Canada.

5. Enlargements of my photographs have appeared in some exhibitions, e.g. *Living Arctic* at the Museum of Mankind, 1987–9; at the UC Blackhawk Museum, 1991–4; and most extensively in 'Creating Tradition: The Art of the Canadian Inuit', which I curated in the Hearst Museum, UC Berkeley, 1992–3.

6. After I gave a slide lecture about the Canadian Inuit to an audience in Japan (1979), some people jokingly said that the Japanese should move to Canada as they could never hope to inhabit houses in Japan as spacious as those of the Inuit!

7. After returning from a research trip, I have all the accumulated film processed (I gave up sending rolls in the mail from the north after a few were lost). I then record and catalogue all the images, transferring field notes (usually written on the backs of cigarette packs; the Inuit were amused that I kept notes 'like them') into sets of captions (see note 2). I then get extra prints made, and send them whether requested or not, with letters to all the people portrayed in the northern communities. After our three-month trip through the eastern Arctic in 1986, Molly Lee remarked that it took us *longer* to process, catalogue and write captions for all the images, and to get extra prints made and write letters and send them and all the photographs (in this case well over 50 letters with nearly 300 prints!) and purchase requested items and send them too, than did the trip itself!

## Acknowledgements

I wish to thank many people for their help in writing this paper. Firstly, I must thank Dr Molly Lee who accompanied me on our 1986 research trip during which many of the photographs discussed were taken. She and Jonathan King and Henrietta Lidchi have sent me useful comments on earlier drafts. On 9 October 1996 I repeated the slide lecture for the Canadian Studies Program at UC Berkeley, and I thank Professor Tom Barnes, Dr Rita Ross, curator Roslyn Tunis, graduate students Cari Borja, Ayfer Bartu, Arthur Mason and particularly Naomi Leite and Lucien Taylor for their very incisive critiques.

Molly Lee

# With Broom and Camera: Gladys Knight Harris's Photographs of Inupiat Women, 1949

Fig.1. Mrs Paul Green contemplating the source of the evening meal. Kotzebue, 1949.

## Introduction

In her 1855 essay, 'Photography', Elizabeth Eastlake, with the straightforwardness characteristic of an age intoxicated by science, wrote that the newly invented camera could deliver up 'cheap, prompt, and correct facts to the public'. 'Photography', Lady Eastlake continued, 'is the sworn witness of everything presented to [its] view. What are [its] unerring records . . . but facts of the most sterling and stubborn kind?' (Quoted in Banta and Hinsley 1986: 39.) In contrast, a common preoccupation of photographic criticism of the late twentieth century is exposing the photograph as a total manipulation, as much or more so than any visual art form (e.g. Graham-Brown 1988; Lyman 1982).

In this paper I shall take a third position, arguing that, quite apart from manipulation, every photograph is an original document whose existence is as serendipitous as the chance encounter of the sewing machine, the umbrella and the dissecting table that was the Surrealists' call to arms. Using examples from Gladys Knight Harris's remarkable black-and-white photographs of Inupiat Eskimo women in the 1940s, I shall show, furthermore, that, despite their originality, photographs consist of three components by which they may be analysed fruitfully: time, space and personal happenstance.

## Gladys Knight Harris: personal happenstance, 1892–1946

Several factors in Gladys Knight Harris's biography show the compelling relationship between personal happenstance and visual imagery. As such, they had a direct bearing upon her trip to Alaska and the kinds of photographs she made there. Harris was born in 1892 in Gualala,

Mendocino County, California, where her father managed a lumber company. In those days Mendocino lumber was delivered to market by ship, and, as a child, Harris recalled listening to the sea captains' yarns about their voyages up the coast to Alaska, where they also took delivery of lumber. Later, she was to recall that these tales were the genesis of her curiosity about the north. According to Harris's son,[1] 'With Gladys, the magic word was always "go".' From the time he was a small boy he recalls his mother restlessly voicing her wish to visit Alaska (Harris 1996).

Gladys Knight Harris received her BA and MA in Home Economics in the early 1920s. As this training was perhaps the strongest force shaping her photography, it will be helpful to look briefly at the state of the home economics discipline at the time of her education to appreciate its influence on her photographer's eye.

The Home Economics Movement grew out of the profoundly didactic, mawkishly sentimental American culture of the late nineteenth century. Home-making was celebrated as an art of virtue and self-sacrifice, a position that effectively reinforced the walls of the home as the outer perimeter beyond which its female inmates dared not venture. In 1890 Bostonian Ellen Richards struck the first blow at the stronghold, advocating the need for household management courses in higher education. The Lake Placid Conferences of 1899–1909 standardised courses and pushed them beyond the level of cooking and sewing for the first time. By 1919, when Gladys Knight Harris entered college, World War I had again enlarged the scope of Domestic Science to include cultural and technical specialities. Now, recipients of an advanced degree could look forward to careers as diverse as dietetics, teaching,

home advising, public health and social service (Carver 1979: 3–25).

Harris chose teaching, but after marriage to a high school principal she settled into domesticity, only to have it interrupted eight years later by the death of her husband. In 1928, on the eve of the Great Depression, Harris, a widow with two young sons, returned to teaching Home Economics in high schools and community colleges around southern California (K. Harris 1996).

Fig.2. Mrs Rexford
sewing bags for
beluga meat storage.
Kotzebue, 1949.

Fig.3. Mrs Jessop
shee fishing.
Kotzebue, 1949.

In the early 1940s Gladys Knight Harris retired from teaching. Far from taking to her rocking chair, however, she embarked upon a second career. From her son, Knight, a trained photographer, she borrowed four cameras: a 4×5 Speed Graphic, a 2¼×2¼ Rolleiflex, a 35 mm Contax, and a Bell and Howell movie camera. With these in hand, Harris enrolled in a photography programme at the Frank Wiggins Trade School in Los Angeles. At Frank Wiggins she took the standard photography courses: portraiture, landscape, movie making and darkroom techniques (Harris 1996).

In 1946, after two years in the Wiggins photography programme, Harris acted on her long-cherished dream. Armed with her son's cameras, she took the wheel of his 1939 Oldsmobile and headed north. Her plan was to stay in Alaska long enough to document the landscape and the Eskimos' way of life for lectures and educational films (Harris 1996; Harris 1947–9).

### Time/space: Alaska in the late 1940s

The second and third components contributing to the uniqueness of Harris's photographs were the time and space in which she photographed. When her borrowed Oldsmobile was unloaded on the dock in Juneau, the Alaska confronting her was no longer the remote outpost of civilisation that she had dreamed of as a child and the one explorer Vilhjalmur Stefansson (1922; 1926) had popularised in the 1920s. World War II had changed all that. Between 1939 and 1949 Alaska's population had swollen from a sparse 74,000 to more than 112,000 inhabitants. Moreover, it had undergone a dramatic demographic shift. Whereas 60 per cent of the pre-war population had been scattered across the land in small villages, most newcomers were non-native immigrants from the Lower Forty-Eight (the continental United States), who congregated in the burgeoning cities of Anchorage and Fairbanks.

In the late 1940s, when Gladys Harris arrived, Alaska was experiencing a period of economic prosperity surpassing any other before or since. The war effort had wound down, but strategic defence construction from the escalating cold war had stepped in to take its place (Naske and Slotnik 1987: 123–31; Wooley and Martz 1995: 66–71). Thus, in the three years she spent in the territory Harris was able to fall back on her training as a home economist, supporting herself by working as a dietician at military bases in and around Anchorage, when she wasn't out in the bush on a photography junket. A cheerful and direct person, Harris got to know military pilots in the base dining rooms, and they ferried her north when they had space. In addition to hundreds of images from south central, south-east and the interior of Alaska, Harris managed to photograph in Nome, Teller, Unalakleet, Point Hope and Kotzebue.

But the accessible parts of Alaska were not the only ones affected by the War. By the time Harris came north, Inupiat Eskimo settlements were connected to the outside world by short wave radio and bush plane. Since 1944 Alaskan Eskimo men had patrolled their remote shorelines as members of the Territorial Guard, and with the intensification of the Cold War, the Arctic Coast, because of its proximity to the USSR, had come in for its share of defence construction. Village life still revolved around subsistence activities, but for the Inupiat particularly the 1940s were a watershed.

### The Gladys Knight Harris collection: the convergence of time, space and individual happenstance

With this brief summary of the three elements contributing to the uniqueness of Gladys Knight Harris's photographic images, let us turn to the collection itself. Deposited at the Southwest Museum, Los Angeles, with selected copies at the Rasmuson Library at the University of Alaska, Fairbanks, the Gladys Knight Harris collection consists of about 8,500 images in all, over 6,000 in black and white, more than 2,000 colour slides, 15 reels of motion picture film, and 75 colour transparencies. Approximately 25 per cent of the total images are from the Arctic, most of them from the village of Kotzebue, where Harris passed the spring and summer of 1949. A ramshackle town of about 300 people in those days, Kotzebue sits on the edge of the Arctic Ocean

just north of the Arctic Circle. Strung along the shore line were a post office and store, a school, hospital, church and a coffee shop (Smith 1977: 56–7), above which Harris rented a room during her stay.

Gladys Knight Harris's collection is unusual for its size, for the relatively under-represented period in which it was made, and for the female gender of its photographer and most of its subjects. Another remarkable feature is Harris's conscientious record-keeping. As a result of her training in photography she secured photographic release forms from each of her subjects, paying them a dollar per pose. The forms contain valuable documentation supplementing the rudimentary captions she included with her photographs.

Harris's images of women can be grouped into three main categories: subsistence activities, child-rearing and skin-sewing.

*Subsistence* In the five small notebooks she left,[2] Harris made detailed notes on some of the activities[3] she photographed. On 9 May 1949, for instance, she wrote:

I packed up my gadget bag, Speedgraphic and movie camera ... and walked along until I came to

piles of ice built up like ... igloos, only without a roof. Inside these ice circles, higher on the windy side, sat Eskimo women jigging for shee fish through a hole in the ice. The hole had been chopped by a sharp cutting blade, probably made from an old auto spring and fastened to a very heavy pole ...

Harris was able to photograph a number of women ice-fishing that day, among them Mrs Jessop (fig.3), Mildred Gallahorn and Clara

Fig.4. Frank Knapp and his son, Billy, have a reading lesson. Kotzebue, 1949.

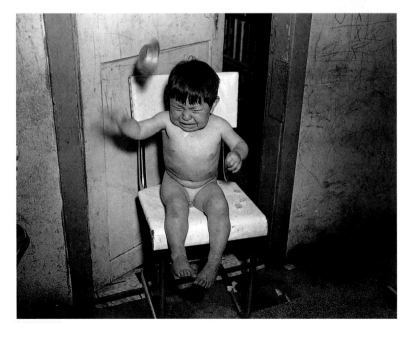

Forslund, with whom she became close friends during her stay in Kotzebue.

The compendium of Harris's photographs gives a vivid impression of the variety of household chores undertaken by the women of Kotzebue during the brief, bright Arctic summer. We see Belle Arey and Minnie Norton stripping whale intestines for making the so-called Eskimo raincoat. Another shows Mrs Henry tired but happy after a long day cutting up beluga whale. In another, Lola Kenworthy and her friends remove a beluga bladder. And in another Priscilla Hensley snacks on a piece of fresh seal meat. In a different scene Mrs Rexford (fig.2) has hauled her hand-operated sewing machine down to the beach to stitch up sacks for stockpiling beluga meat in a cold-storage pit. Notice that the machine is marked as one of a special type made especially for the Alaska market. On another day Lizzie Copproch – whose old-time chin tattoo caught Mrs Harris's interest – gathers driftwood. Finally, Harris captured Mrs Norton tanning a wolverine skin.

Despite the lighting difficulties, Harris managed a few interior shots of subsistence activities carried on at home. In fig.1 Mrs Paul Green contemplates the source of the the family's next meal beneath a line of drying diapers. In addition to human interest, such images are valuable as an index of trade goods available to a Kotzebue family in the late 1940s.

*Child-rearing* Nowhere is Harris's eye for the decisive moment more apparent than in her images of children. In one, Clara Forslund loads up baby Virginia Rexford into her mother Rhoda's parka for the trip home. In another, visiting Diomede Islander, Moses Milligrok, shows off baby Hannah clutching an ivory bracelet he hopes to sell. In others we see children at play and teenage girls participating vicariously in a dance (fig.6). And here (fig.4) Billy Knapp gets a reading lesson from his father Frank.

*Skin-sewing* As a home economist, Harris was predictably enthralled with the dexterity and imagination of Inupiat skin-sewers. She managed to capture on film many steps in the process including skinning out muskrats, choosing skins, hand-working muskrat parkas, and Esther Vestal modelling a finished squirrel coat. She also recorded Clara Forslund sewing the intricate Inupiat trim on a summer *kuspuk*.

## Analysis and conclusions

Where can we position Harris's work in the continuum between the photograph as objective reality at one end and as a metaphor for experience at the other? According to her son, her main purpose in making the trip to Alaska was to record the Inupiat Eskimos 'as they really were', and inasmuch as Harris, unlike Edward Curtis, for example, made no attempt to bracket out Western trade goods, she was true to her mission. On the other hand, though her home economics training weighed heavily in her choice of content, Harris focused on daily chores that contrasted dramatically with those of housewives in the Lower Forty-Eight, editing out those that resembled what she could see at home. Moreover, many of her images, though superficially candid, are obviously posed. For instance, no one who has been inside an Eskimo house would make the mistake of wearing a heavy fur parka designed for temperatures well below freezing for an inside activity such as sewing. It contrasts with a genuinely candid image Harris snapped at the Nome Skin Sewers' Co-operative, which shows women dressed as they really were for such pastimes.

Furthermore – and her notebooks bear this out – Harris's attention to photographic conventions such as cropping, lighting, and composition clearly reflect the thought, effort and training that went into them. As Barthes (1981: 19–24) argues, images succeed because of the co-presence of information and small, poignant details (which he calls the 'punctum'), such as the shininess of Esther Vestal's nylon stockings (perhaps her only pair) that can be seen in fig.10.

The recent strategy of unmasking as contrived images once thought to be factual (e.g. Becker 1978; Lutz and Collins 1993; Lyman 1982) represents the disillusionment of being thwarted yet again in the fruitless quest for objective reality, a quest that has informed Western aesthetics since the Renaissance. It is a paradigm that has outlived its usefulness. It is time to accept photographic contrivance as a given and move on to speculate about how it is that photographs signify to begin with (Barthes 1981). The approach I suggest – to use time, space and personal circumstances as a framework to shed light on a photographer's choice of shutter speed, camera angle and the like – may be over-simplified, but at least it furnishes a contextual basis on which to build. Consideration of the impact of these factors on Gladys Knight Harris's work transports her images of Inupiat Eskimo women from the 'there-then', as Edwards (1992a: 7) puts it, to the 'here-now'.

### Notes

1. I am grateful to Knight Harris for sharing his reminiscences of his mother with me.

2. Harris's notebooks are uneven in the amount of documentation they contain, both for her activities and photographs. They are a bricolage of recipes for Eskimo ice cream and toilet bowl disinfectant, a detailed life history of one Inupiat woman who befriended her, outrage at the treatment of sled dogs, and a few notes on Arctic characters such as Lt Colonel Marvin 'Muktuk' Marston, founder of the Alaska Territorial Guard, and long-time Kotzebue trader Archie Ferguson. In these notes Harris brought a wry, self-deprecating humour to her photographic tribulations: 'On way home today I fell in a big snow bank … I looked up and there … was a beautiful dog team. I shot a lot of film – with the cap on the lens. Dam [sic]!'

3. One activity Harris did not report was her skill as a hunter. According to Knight Harris, she had been a crack shot all her life and, as soon as the Inupiat men realised it, they began giving her the bow seat in their skin boats, where she polished off seals without ever missing a shot. Knight Harris says that after her return he found a 32 Special in the pocket of a parka she gave him to try on.

TOP
Fig.9. Clara Forslund prepares her toilette. Kotzebue, 1949.

ABOVE
Fig.10. Esther Vestal shows off her squirrel parka and nylon stockings. Kotzebue, 1949.

Kesler E. Woodward

## Persuasive Images:
## Photographs of Vilhjalmur Stefansson
## in the Stefansson Collection on
## Polar Exploration at Dartmouth College

The purpose of this paper is twofold – first, to make those interested in Arctic photography more aware of the research potential of the rich photographic holdings in the Stefansson Collection on Polar Exploration at Dartmouth College and, second, to suggest that, in his choice of photographs for publications and lectures, as much as in his words, Vilhjalmur Stefansson (1879–1962) developed and promulgated a view of Eskimo people which remains the prevailing popular image of Eskimos throughout much of the world today.

One of the most articulate proponents of Arctic exploration and understanding in this century, Stefansson contributed to an appreciation of the region both through his own work and through his outstanding collection of the works of others. His credentials as an explorer are substantial. When he came out of the north in 1918 at the close of his Canadian Arctic Expedition, he had spent all but eighteen months of the previous twelve years in the Arctic. His contributions were widely lionised. In January of 1919 he was awarded the Hubbard Gold Medal of the National Geographic Society. Photographs show him flanked by Admiral Robert E. Peary and General Augustus W. Greely, who presented him to the Society's members and gave speeches in his praise at the ceremony.[1]

But of even more lasting impact than his work as an explorer is the contribution Stefansson made in the years between his last expedition in 1918 and his death in 1962 – his work as a writer, lecturer and constant booster of interest in the Arctic. His more than thirty books and monographs, substantial contributions to nearly fifty others, and 375 published articles have been among the best known sources of information and opinion about the Arctic in this century.[2] The Stefansson Collection on Polar Exploration, begun by the explorer himself as a personal research library, was acquired by Dartmouth College in 1951. It has since grown to more than 3000 monographs, some 50 ft (15.25 m) of vertical file materials, and well over 200 manuscript collections.[3] Though it is a well-used source of research for northern scholars, perhaps the least explored element in this outstanding collection is the more than 15,000 photographs it includes. Particularly rich in work from the period of 1890 to 1930, the Stefansson Collection contains important groups of images from as late as the 1950s.[4] The range of the individual manuscript collections in the Stefansson Collection which contain Arctic photographs is a veritable *Who's Who* of polar exploration.[5]

A particularly important body of work is a group of more than 500 Robert E. Peary photographs acquired in 1985, which joined other photographs already contained in the Peary papers at Dartmouth. Peary took most of these photographs himself, using an Eastman No.#4 Kodak.[6] Most of the images were published in his books and magazine articles. The photographs are of particular interest, however, as they are Peary's working copies and are frequently annotated in his hand. The majority of the pictures were cropped for publication, and in some cases black, brown and/or white ink was used to enhance, delete or modify the images to achieve a desired effect. In addition to these photographs used for Peary's publications, seventy-eight of the pictures in the collection are apparently unpublished and are perhaps unique.[7]

But primary among the Stefansson Collection's photographic archives are the pictures

TOP
Fig.1. Stefansson
dragging a slain seal
to camp.

ABOVE
Fig.2. Two Inuit
women and a child.

tinted lantern slides which are now in the Stefansson Collection. He used these slides in his many public lectures, as well as in classes at Dartmouth College throughout the 1950s (fig.1).

The lantern slides are rarely identified as to photographer. Stefansson was regularly, often justifiably, criticised for his appropriation of the images of others without attribution or permission, from the official Canadian Arctic Expedition photographs themselves[9] to the work of other photographers throughout the Arctic. The debate over Stefansson's conduct in this regard, like the debate over his conduct of the various expeditions he led in the Canadian Arctic,[10] is outside the scope of this brief paper. It is clearly fair to say that the Geological Survey of Canada should have a great deal of honour for its contribution not only to the explorer's expeditions but also to the stock of photographs on which he could draw in order to promulgate his view of the Arctic and its people.

For my purposes here, however, it is important to turn to Stefansson's choice of photographs to use. It is in his selection of images for his lantern slides that we can perhaps most clearly see him consciously forging a particular view of the Arctic and of its native inhabitants – a view emphasising the 'friendly' aspects of the land itself and the capable, industrious and ingenious character of its indigenous peoples. Quite in contrast to then-prevailing views of Eskimos as either ignoble or noble primitives, or solely as members of cultures under siege by the forces of acculturation, Stefansson depicted the Inuit as exemplary in their adaptation to a land that in their eyes, and his, was not hostile but welcoming.

If we examine a few representative examples of various groups of the lantern slides, we can clearly see the themes which preoccupied him both as an explorer and as a chronicler of Arctic life: anthropological documentation, skilful adaptation, technological innovation and the Arctic as a 'friendly' place, not barren but teeming with life.

The most conventional of Stefansson's lantern slides are those which were seemingly taken for purposes of anthropological documentation. This is especially true of the early images. In a photograph of two Eskimo women and a child (fig.2), from Stefansson's first expedition to Herschel Island via the Mackenzie River in 1906–7,[11] his emphasis is clearly on the Eskimos' ornate parkas. Every element of the photograph, from composition to facial expression to body language, makes clear the lack of personal connection with the individuals depicted. In this regard it is not markedly different in character from sketches,

taken on the 1913–18 Canadian Arctic Expedition (CAE), sponsored and paid for by the Canadian government and led by Stefansson himself. More than 2500 photographic images from the CAE document every aspect of the enterprise, including personnel, flora and fauna, ice and geological formations, and native peoples encountered by the expedition from Alaska through the central Canadian Arctic. Photographs were taken by Stefansson, by the expedition's official photographer George Hubert Wilkins, by ethnographer Diamond Jenness and by others. Most are not identified by photographer. Supply and requisition lists identify several cameras used on the expedition, including a naturalist's Graflex 4×5 equipped with a Graflex focal plane shutter and Zeiss lens, and with tripod and accessories; two Kodak 3a cameras ('one for myself and one for Mr Wilkins', says a note in Stefansson's hand);[8] and a Kodak Vest Pocket model. Kodak supplied their cameras and film to be tested under Arctic conditions.

Stefansson used the images from this and other expeditions as illustrations for his publications, and as the basis for a set of more than 700 hand-

watercolours and engravings made by artists accompanying Arctic expeditions during the preceding two centuries.

Another extensive group of lantern slides documents Stefansson's fascination with the so-called 'White Eskimos' or 'Blond Eskimos' of Victoria Island, a fascination dating from the 1906–7 expedition. At Herschel Island Stefansson heard accounts, from both whaling captains and from Mackenzie Eskimos, of people on Victoria Island who were clearly Eskimo in dress and culture, but who made extensive use of copper implements and included persons with light hair, blue eyes and other European features. Fired by the possibility that they might be either remnants of the lost Greenland colony or survivors of Sir John Franklin's lost expedition, Stefansson became determined to visit and investigate the colony.[12] It was thus that he came to encounter the Copper Inuit in his second expedition, from 1908 to 1912 (fig.4).

However motivated by such tales Stefansson may initially have been, the kind of ethnological documentation to which he increasingly turned, and which we see documented in his choice of images to be made into lantern slides, focused on means of Arctic subsistence and technological innovation in Arctic travel. In adopting and championing traditional Eskimo modes of subsistence and travel to an unprecedented degree, he set out to change the way Arctic exploration was undertaken and ended by changing our perception of both Eskimo people and the Arctic itself. His choice of images underscores his passionate verbal defence of traditional Eskimo methods, and in the process he leaves us with an impression of Eskimo people as capable, adaptable and technologically innovative people.

Modes of travel for Arctic explorers had been evolving steadily during the century which led up to Stefansson's expeditions. Up through the early nineteenth century, exploration of the Arctic took place largely through summer incursions by ship. Edward Parry's attempts to dig in and weather the Arctic winter while awaiting spring, and John Ross's adoption of sleds for necessary winter travel as early as 1819 were evidence of slowly changing attitudes. The major change in approach came with John Rae, who in his 1846–54 journeys was the first European explorer to shed the fear of winter and extend the capacity of the exploring party to travel in the Arctic, but even he waited for April to begin his surveys. Just a generation before Stefansson, Admiral Peary took this evolution toward Eskimo means a step farther, preferring winter as the easiest time to travel.[13]

But Peary, too, was hampered by the need to carry large quantities of food for both men and dogs. Stefansson chose to provision his expeditions by hunting while travelling, in the way of the Eskimos. He felt both his own good health and that of his Eskimo companions testified that raw or underdone meat provided all the necessary nutrients for indefinitely extended travel and subsistence in Arctic conditions. His lantern slides depict such traditional activities not in some general, picturesque sense but in terms of how these activities are accomplished. Seals are depicted being shot, being harpooned and being skinned. Methods of skinning bear and caribou are also documented. Successful hunting is depicted not just with modern means and equipment but with their traditional counterparts as well (fig.3).

While documenting those methods, the explorer's lantern slides subtly reinforce his image of the Arctic as a place of plenty, a welcoming environment for persons familiar with the means of procuring its wealth. We see that not only in the number of successful subsistence activities depicted but in the number of summer

TOP
Fig.3. Copper Inuit with drawn bows.

ABOVE
Fig.4. Victoria Island Inuit.

scenes he chose to make into slides and use in his lectures and publications (fig.5).

Stefansson not only made use of traditional Eskimo methods but introduced his own innovations based on their means. He was always convinced that the development of methods was more important than geographic discoveries. Stefansson's delight in technical innovations is evident in the number of photographs of such contrivances as a sail rigged to aid the locomotion of his sled and of his innovative method of using a tarpaulin to convert a sledge to a boat for crossing open water on the Arctic pack ice.

It is easy to tell when Stefansson was especially fascinated with an innovation or process and eager to talk about it, because there will be a whole series of images illustrating the procedure in his lantern slides. Fig.6 is the final one in a series of slides showing the process of conversion of the sled to a boat and successful crossing of an open lead.

We see this same kind of fascination with Eskimo dwellings, not just their form and function but the way they are built. A series of slides shows both a diagram of a timber-and-sod house and photographs of Eskimos excavating and erecting the framework of such a dwelling.

But the dwelling that fascinated Stefansson more than any other by far was the Eskimo snow house (fig.7). It is perhaps his most ubiquitous image. Though Stefansson was far from the first to document such dwellings photographically, his efforts to demonstrate the technological brilliance and extraordinarily adaptive design of this indigenous Arctic architecture fall little short of an obsession. Several images from his first, 1906–7 expedition show the beginning of his involvement with snow houses, but fully 10 per cent of his Arctic lantern slides document snow houses in one form or another.

Some of these images are simply by-products of the attempt to document the way of life of the Copper Eskimo, who did, after all, make extensive use of snow houses as both short- and long-term dwellings for up to eight months of the year.[14] But Stefansson's use of the images is far from incidental. From a diagram to a model to a series of nineteen slides showing the building of a snow house in the Arctic (fig.8) to a variety of particularly impressive examples of joined snow houses, Stefansson was able to demonstrate the ingenuity and suitability of the form in great detail.

Nor did his fascination with the form dim with time. Under Dr Stefansson's direction, 'How to Build An Igloo' became an annual demonstration on the Dartmouth campus in the 1950s as an internal part of the Northern Frontier Studies Program, and in fig.10 we see him in Hanover in 1962, the year of his death, with his wife Evelyn calling attention to their 'Iglu' licence plate (fig.10). The snow house image as a symbol of the Arctic seems even to have outlasted the explorer's presence at Dartmouth College. I was delighted to discover, while working at Dartmouth just this February on choosing images for this paper, that the current issue of the *Dartmouth Alumni* magazine not only features as its cover article the college's ongoing commitment to Arctic Studies, but that they chose as their cover illustration an image which Stefansson would in all likelihood have enjoyed – an image of an Eskimo seated before his snow house.

It is probably fair, then, to lay at the great explorer's feet some responsibility for the continuing stereotype that Eskimos live in igloos. But it is fair to give him a large measure of credit as well. What we can see in his photographs just underscores what we have long seen in his writing – a tremendous admiration for the way of life of Eskimo people (fig.9), whose ingenuity, adaptive character and powerful will enabled them to find the Arctic not a wasteland, but a welcoming and nurturing environment. Vilhjalmur Stefansson began this century trying to show us that we had much to learn from the Eskimos, a lesson we could perhaps do worse than to heed today.

## Acknowledgement

I would like to thank my friend Philip Cronenwett, Curator of Manuscripts and Special Collections Librarian at Dartmouth College, for his suggestions, willing assistance in gaining access to needed information, and unfailing support in the preparation of this paper, as in all other projects I have had the good fortune to work with him on at Dartmouth College.

## Notes

1. For a note on the ceremony and the text of the introductory speeches by Peary and Greely, see *National Geographic*, April 1920, pp.338–140, 342. This was Admiral Peary's last public appearance.

2. For a comprehensive list of Stefansson's publications, see Robert Mattila, *A Chronological Bibliography of the Published Works of Vilhjalmur Stefansson (1879–1962)* (Hanover, NH: The Stefansson Collection, Dartmouth College Library, 1978).

3. For an excellent, concise overview of the development of the Stefansson Collection before and since the death of the explorer, see Philip Cronenwett, 'The Stefansson Collection', *Northern Notes*, No.1 (November 1989).

4. Important holdings from the 1950s range from a group of 200 photographs of Alaska by Sally Carrighar to an extensive body of photographs and slides from Operation Deepfreeze, taken in 1956–8.

5. Examples include the collections of Clarence Leroy Andrews, Belmore Browne, Richard Evelyn Byrd, James Crawford, Lincoln Ellsworth, Augustus W. Greely, Ernest Leffingwell, Fridtjof Nansen, Albert Operti, William Stickney, Storker Storkerson and Sir George Hubert Wilkins.

6. This and other information on the Peary photographs at Dartmouth is drawn primarily from the Stefansson Collection's John Schwoerke's 'Notes from the Special Collections: The Peary Photographs', *Dartmouth College Library Bulletin*, Vol.26, No.2 (April 1986).

7. Ibid., p.83.

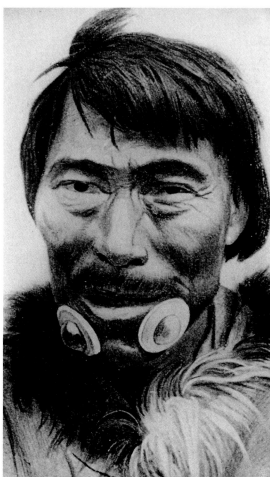

ABOVE
Fig.8. One of a sequence of nineteen slides showing the building of a snow house in the Arctic.

LEFT
Fig.9. Inuit man wearing labrets. Stefansson's first (1906–7) expedition.

8. Stefansson MSS 98, Box 4, Folder 6.

9. I am grateful to Dr Jim Burant, Chief of Art Acquisition and Research at the National Archives of Canada, for bringing to my attention one of the most extraordinary, detailed criticisms of this sort – a nine-page memorandum from R. M. Anderson, Chief of the Division of Biology at the Department of Mines at the time of the memo, to Charles Camsell, Deputy Minister of the Department of Mines in Ottawa (National Archives of Canada, RG45, Geological Survey of Canada, Vol.67, File 4078 I). In this 21 January 1924 memorandum Anderson, long at odds with Stefansson over accusations made by the expedition leader against his conduct and that of other members of the scientific staff on the CAE, argues

Fig.10. Vilhjalmur and Evelyn Stefansson at their home, Hanover, New Hampshire, showing the 'Iglu' licence plate on Stefansson's Peugeot. March 1962.

vehemently against the granting of Stefansson's request that he be supplied with a complete set of the photographs taken by members of the Geological Survey staff. Noting that Stefansson had already received the expedition pictures taken by George H. Wilkins, the official expedition photographer, as well as a number of other photographs, and had used them in several publications without attribution, Anderson expresses extreme concern over the self-serving uses to which Stefansson might turn the full collection of photographs. The request was nonetheless granted.

10. For a discussion of these and related issues, one may turn to the voluminous biographical literature on Stefansson. Some of the more important recent examples include William R. Hunt's *Stef: A Biography of Vilhjalmur Stefansson, Canadian Arctic Explorer* (Vancouver: University of British Columbia Press, 1986); G. Edgar Folk and Mary A. Folk's *Vilhjalmur Stefansson and the Development of Arctic Terrestrial Science* (Iowa City, Iowa: University of Iowa, 1984); Alexander Gregor's *Vilhjalmur Stefansson and the Arctic* (Agincourt, Ontario: Book Society of Canada, 1978); and Richard J. Diubaldo's *Stefansson and the Canadian Arctic* (Montreal: McGill-Queen's University Press, 1978).

11. Stefansson's account of this expedition is his engaging *Hunters of the Great North* (New York: Harcourt, Brace, and Company, 1992).

12. Ibid., pp.54–6.

13. One of the best concise summaries of Stefansson's contribution to methods of polar exploration, and the evolution in Arctic travel which preceded his innovations, is the address given in his memory by Edward Weyer Jr at the Explorer's Club in New York on 31 March 1963. A condensed version of his address was published in *The Explorer's Journal*, Vol.41, No.2 (June 1963), pp.2–9.

14. For a review of snow-house use by the Copper Eskimos, see Diamond Jenness, 'The Life of the Copper Eskimos'. *Report of the Canadian Arctic Expedition, 1913–1918*, Vol.12A (Ottawa, 1922), pp.65–76.

Robert J. Christopher

# Through Canada's Northland: The Arctic Photography of Robert J. Flaherty

When we consider how we imagine the Arctic, the cinematic work of Robert J. Flaherty (1884–1951) leaps to mind. Even as we reflect, somewhere in the world – in a cinema club, a school or university classroom – Flaherty's *Nanook of the North* is being screened. Since its release in 1922 this film has shaped world perceptions of the peoples and landscape of the Arctic. After the worldwide circulation of *Nanook* publicity photographs, such a picture as that of Nanook the harpooner (fig. 1), his arm cocked like a Sunday quarterback, constitutes a master image of our social memory. Given the iconic presence of this and other *Nanook*-related photographs in our imaginings of the north, they can also obscure Flaherty's career as a visual artist before 1922 and eclipse earlier but equally relevant Arctic images.

This paper proposes that we can revisit now-obscured Flaherty images of the north if we examine the genesis of that film through the prism of photographs he took and the expeditionary diaries he kept during the decade and more preceding *Nanook*'s release.[1] Just as diaries can serve as narratives of self, photographs can be narrative histories of visual perception. If we examine narratives in which picture-taking is recorded, then we can enhance our understanding of the historical context in which those photographs were produced and disseminated. Through these autobiographical resources we may reconsider Flaherty's progress as a visual artist so that we regard *Nanook* not just as a classic unto itself, but the climax of his extended effort to imagine the Arctic. In addition to diaries, we can also draw upon the visual resources of the nearly 1,500 pre-1922 photographs ascribed to Flaherty and currently housed in a number of North American and European archives.[2]

Flaherty's early mental images of northern native peoples are evoked vividly in an unpublished autobiographical narrative he wrote in the late 1930s, 'The Islands that Were Not There'.[3] 'Islands' is Flaherty's most ambitious effort to write a narrative of his upbringing, education and early career as a explorer. Its greatest value lies in the recollections of his early years, such as when, travelling with his father in 1896 to gold fields in western Ontario, he recalls that among the river boat passengers 'the traders and trappers interested me most. They might have stepped out of the very books by Parkman or Ballantyne that I had pored over ever since I had learned to read.' (*Butler* 48: 27, Ch.2.) Robert Ballantyne's *Ungava* (1858) was the standard Arctic adventure fare of its time, but the romance of the north had its darker side, one which Flaherty describes when he relates how his family, now reunited, lives in 1898 on 'The Isle of the Golden Dog' in the Lake of the Woods area, Ontario. About two miles (3 km) from the Isle there stood an encampment of tepees

whose inhabitants, of course, were Indians. They used to paddle over often to visit our island and trade with us whatever they might have – big birchbark baskets heaped with blueberries in the early summer, and with raspberries later on . . . None of them ever seemed to smile very much. Their furtive faces were depressing. Their terrible poverty was only too evident in the hopeless-looking rags of the white man's clothes which they wore. They were indeed a far cry from the Noble Red Man I had conjured in my mind. (*Butler* 48: 27, Ch.2.)

This polarisation of imagined nobility and denigrated reality was for Flaherty a cross-cultural shock. He is both imaginatively engaged and culturally disassociated, a dissonance intensified by

his observation that 'It made my mother uneasy to have them there, they coughed so much.' These recollections of native peoples, tinged with images of disease and helplessness, could be taken as the foundation of Flaherty's working credo to make the 'conjured' image the ascendant one and to favour the heroic, celebrating in the process a mode of existence predating the more diminished moment, the culture of the furtive face. The vitality of this credo, these passages suggest, is grounded in these earliest experiences of distressed cross-cultural encounter, the outcome of which is a life-long compensatory tendency to transform, visually, denigration to nobility.

When interviewed in 1979, Flaherty's sister, Frances Ruttan, recalled that the two most important material objects in her brother's life were his violin and his camera, and, in regard to the camera, that 'he loved pictures and he always carried a camera with him as he was growing up, as a young man he always carried a camera, took pictures everywhere.'[4] She also recalls that her father had a camera, and the son, she suggested, probably got his from the father. Though early snapshot cameras probably did circulate among the Flaherty family, his sister recalled that Flaherty still favoured the older-style plate camera with tripod.

He was always interested in very good, old pictures, you know, famous artists and all that and he had

his room that he had just filled with 'em but then he began to carry a camera with him all the time. I don't know just why. He took pictures of everybody, his friends, he'd take them downtown to the ice cream parlor, anywhere. It was a big camera, on a tripod which was awkward to carry in those days. He never was without a camera as he grew up and got to be 17, 18, 19 years old.

By 1906 Flaherty was experimenting with photographs in the service of a narrative recorded in a diary of a canoe trip to northern Ontario, 7 September–7 October 1906 (*Butler* 18: 11). The work took the form of a widespread Victorian conceit, a diary-album whose thirty-five photographs are interspersed among a narrative aimed at a privileged reader. In this instance Frances Hubbard, the woman who would marry him in 1914, was the reader as insider, privy to the guarded allusions he makes to their shared sights, moods and intimacies. The photographs, now badly bleached, are of the travel snapshot variety, depicting scenes, notable landmarks and campsites. Despite the conventionality of its genre, Flaherty was attempting to use photography as an expressive medium, exploring its capacity to heighten remembrance by associating images with a narrative of charged recall and shared union.

Sixteen in the first year of the new century, Flaherty was by 1910 beyond the apprenticeship nurtured by his father, Robert H. Flaherty (1856–1923). He was a seasoned prospector and outdoorsman who had benefited from his father's flourishing career as a mining engineer. In 1910 Flaherty senior was hired to head the mining department of Mackenzie and Mann and the younger Flaherty's career prospered by association when in 1910 he was retained to examine the iron ore potential of the Nastapokas, an island chain off the eastern coast of Hudson Bay. William Mackenzie (1849–1923) and Donald Mann (1853–1934) had developed a partnership as railroad contractors into a transportation empire that included the Canadian Northern Railroad. It was the ambition of Mackenzie and others to bring the harvests of the prairies by rail to the shores of Hudson Bay and create a less costly transportation route to European markets. If iron ore mined in the Bay could also be shipped to European markets, then that would greatly enhance the value of the Hudson Bay route. It was this tide of capitalist euphoria which carried Flaherty north and he reached Moose Factory by canoe on 4 September 1910.

Though it was his experience as a prospector that qualified him for the Mackenzie and Mann assignment, Flaherty ensured his own readiness to take photographs. Prior to departure, the first notes in his journey diary are reminders to acquire a supply of $4 \times 5$ in ($10 \times 13$ cm) plates, a lens, toner, and a selection of contact and printing papers. There is a diary section reserved for entries about exposure times and the locations of photographs such as those taken on the Taylor and Gillies islands of the Nastapokas, two formations which received his scrutiny and whose geology he photographed repeatedly.

That the taking of photographs was a significant aim of the journey is evident from the diary entry he makes three days after reaching Moose: 'Took and developed very good photographs of the place and people.' (*Butler* 18: 11, 7 September 1910.) Over the next few months there are intermittent entries where picture-taking is mentioned. By the first week of 1911, having reached the most northern arc of his journey, there is a great cluster of picture-taking on and about the Nastapoka islands: 'After a mile of our travel this a.m. came on an igloo encampment. Took photographs and visited four igloos and distributed sweets and tobacco. The men all off seal hunting. Had tea in one of the camps. Most interesting camp. Wish I had a hundred films.' (*Butler* 18: 11, 3 January 1911.) Reversing direction on 9 January, heavy sledging and eagerness to 'get south' result in no further diary entries of picture-taking.

Fig.2. Down-river canoe passage, Northern Ontario. 1910.

The number of photographs Flaherty took greatly exceeds the number of diary references to picture-taking. Within two months of his return in March 1911 to Toronto, Flaherty filed for copyright registration an album of 102 photographs under the title: 'Through Canada's Northland'.[5] In both title and content Flaherty's album follows the by-then established tradition of expeditionary photography which catered to the immense craving Europeans and Americans had for photographic images of exotic and far-away cultures. The expeditionary imperative made photography the ideal format for depicting otherness in exotic settings. The setting itself, in turn, could have its intrinsic appeal, especially when it evoked the awesome and the majestic.

Within the context of these larger influences of expeditionary photography, Flaherty's wish to document a journey makes transportation in all its modes an important subject. The photographs take us through the journey's stages of progress, beginning with the down-river canoe passage (fig.2). The pictorial effect is not simply descriptive of a river passage; it also references the world outside the frame, as the backward glance of the oarsman urges us to acknowledge the presence of the recording photographer. In the world of the north, waterways eventually flow to snowscapes, so the sled loaded, unloaded and, at times, upturned to have its runners iced is a ubiquitous vehicle. There can no sled journey without the dog, so the 'husky', in or out of traces, is either featured or present in one out of six photographs. The landscape is ever present in this journey, most often as background but on occasion the subject itself as when Flaherty depicts the sinewy progress of a river or the dramatic mists of the Nastapoka Falls.

RIGHT
Fig.3. Captioned as
'Fur Buyer of
Revillons, Fort
George' in *Canadian
Courier* (13 May
1911). 1910–11.

BELOW RIGHT
Fig.4. Cree woman
wearing trade shawl.
1910–11.

But the album is more than a narration of a scenic northern journey. It also depicts a world of emergent cultures, of a Euro-Canadian presence whose commercial settlements and transportation networks reach out to Montreal, Paris and London. Included in the album, therefore, are the sturdy, white buildings of the Hudson's Bay Company, one in particular displaying two ceremonial cannons, relics of the earlier struggle between the English and the French for control of the Bay. These buildings are the administrative centre of a trading company whose ships, like the *Sorine* which Flaherty photographed at Charlton island, unload the annual cargo of supplies for the network of James and Hudson Bay trading posts, and take aboard the principal harvest of the Arctic, the furs whose acquisition two traders (fig.3) affirm as they discerningly examine a fox pelt. There are other hoped-for mineral harvests – the nominal purpose of Flaherty's journey – so there is the need to record the gathering of science as he does in several photographs of jasperlite formations on Taylor island.

This presence of culture in transition is sustained in what proves to be the majority vision of the album, northern peoples in all their varieties and identities. It is a culture of polarities, part-indigenous, part-Western, its hybrid identity often signed by clothing and objects of utility. An emblematic photograph of this bipolar culture is that of a Cree hunter which Flaherty later captioned as 'Labrador Cree and Montreal Pipe'. Clothing serves as a primary indicator of cultural transition, as in the photograph (fig.4) of a Cree woman wrapped in trade cloth. A group photograph, reminiscent of an Edwardian family album, suggests the child as the focal centre amidst a group of adults dressed in a medley of clothing. The bipolar nature of culture can be not only that of dress but of parental identity, as Flaherty records in the portrait of a woman of mixed race whose clothing and associated objects suggest Western customs and commerce.[6]

Flaherty also accelerates the indicators of cultural transition by inverting them so as to frame himself as the insider. To do so, he surrenders the camera so that he might manipulate it to make himself the object of its documentation and, in so doing, becomes as camera-conscious as the native sitters. He wants to ally himself with the young through a grouping (fig.5) which suggests paternal protection, an alliance Flaherty favoured in a career of films featuring young males guided by wise adults. The north is a culture of new skills so the veteran canoeman wants to demonstrate his newly acquired adeptness (fig.6) in a native craft. Dressed in native garb

and gazing dramatically (fig.7) into the vastness, Flaherty exudes a confident self-presence in a wintry landscape.

As Flaherty travels north along the eastern coast of Hudson Bay he increasingly comments on a north–south fault line, one that separates the trees from the rocky barrens and the Indian from the Eskimo. He writes in an entry for 22 December 1910:

We are into Hudson Bay now and the character of

LEFT
Fig.5. Flaherty posing
with Cree children.
1910–11.

BELOW
Fig.6. Flaherty
demonstrating his
kayaking skills.
1910–11.

BELOW LEFT
Fig.7. Flaherty
exuding confidence
wearing Arctic outfit.
1910–11.

'Huskie' is all that an Indian isn't, and then some.
They have the ingenuity of the Jap, the strength
that is par with any man's, are fearless, open and
frank and (important!) grateful for kindness shown
(not so the Indian, damn him!). This trip is
accumulating interest in every mile. (*Butler* 18: 11.)

country is changed to high rugged and barren hills
and rocky country. It is more interesting than to
southward. I am glad to be rid of that monotonous
country. Huskie just making the patch shoeing as I
write. He mixed moss and flour and water into a
dough, to be put in the broken gap and allowed to
freeze. In a.m. it will be planed down and iced with
warm water as is usual in iceing the earthen
shoeing. A wonderful and ingenious affair. The

Flaherty's bluntness displays residual resent-
ments about experiences with Indians and an
affinity with an indigenous people only hitherto
conjured. There is a trend in the entries as
Flaherty travels further above the tree line, a
trend that suggests he is more likely to encounter
an authentic, less acculturated people than the
Indians. This more favoured status of the Eskimo
finds its expression in photography where

Fig.8. Captioned as 'Omarolluk, the head driver on the sledge expedition' in *The Geographical Review* (August 1918), 120. Great Whale River, 1910–11.

Flaherty attempts to depict more heroic, self-sufficient individuals, less tainted by Western markers. The image of the Eskimo face in a cowl of fur fascinated Flaherty. In these full-frame portraits a sitter such as Omarolluk, his sledge driver (fig.8), gazes upon us from within a surround of angular and textured skins. He also uses a group photograph to depict the range of reactions subjects have to the camera, one going so far as to shield her face from its intruding eye (fig.9) while another, pipe in mouth, stares nonchalantly. Flaherty also gives us a photograph of Nero Fleming and his wife (fig.10) where their awkwardness before the camera is offset by a gaze that is direct and assured, standing with solidity in clothing free of Western tokens. But Nero is a man of two worlds, a skilled provider who also serves as a lay catechist, as we see him here (fig.11) book in hand – presumably a Bible – standing in the church at Great Whale River, a

church which also serves as a school room.[7] It is the one instance in the album where Flaherty allows his journeying eye to acknowledge the influence of the missionary whose cultural impact is second only to that of the trader. This photograph of Nero in a church at Great Whale River dramatises the multiple religious and educational forces at work in the lives of the Eskimo. The church itself stands as the institution prepared to lead them out of their old ways, and the map and Anglican creed on the wall signify that through the word knowledge of God and the larger universe will prevail.

In the study of Flaherty's career as a photographer the 1911 album is a milestone of great value. Its undisputed provenance allows us to make more informed judgments about the dates, locations and contexts of his photographs. These are matters which have proven most difficult to resolve, given the absence of a reliable inventory of the Flaherty photographic canon. Though Flaherty never found a publisher for the 1911 album, his effort to obtain copyright registration suggests he viewed the album as a first harvest. What the album does do decisively is to provide us with an anthology of Flaherty's photographic styles during a specific period of his development as a visual artist. It thus helps us define the early boundaries of his visual sightings and guides our understanding of how, after 1911, Flaherty altered his picture-taking interests and techniques.

In summer 1912, when Flaherty left on the second Mackenzie sponsored expedition, his equipment included a $5 \times 4$ Eastman plate camera and a $4 \times 5$ Graflex roll-film camera. The context for photography-taking remained largely opportunistic. The diaries Flaherty kept for the subsequent Mackenzie expeditions of 1913–14 and 1915–16 now mention the inclusion of a motion picture camera.[8] These diaries also reveal that many of the activities which had earlier received Flaherty's still-photography attention will now migrate to the domain of motion pictures. While the movie camera studies action, the still camera studies character. The diaries for both expeditions reveal Flaherty's continuing interest in the portrait photography he had first experimented with in the 1911 album.

When Flaherty arrived at the Revillon Frères post at Port Harrison in mid-August 1920, he had been away from the north for four years, a period during which there is little evidence that he engaged in any photographic activity. This journey, his final one to the Arctic, would allow him to reinvent himself as a film-maker. In pursuit of that goal, Flaherty made photography an instrumental part of planning, designing and executing

the film he would first call 'Nanook of the Barren Lands'. Realising that co-operation from those featured in the film would be essential, he not only sought to retain them through compensation but sought through photography to help them

grasp the relationship of a picture to their self-identities. He later recalled that process in a 1930s autobiographical narrative:

My task now was to make Nanook understand what I intended to do. My first difficulty was that he didn't even know how to read a picture. The first pictures I showed him meant no more to him than so many curious marks. It was only when I showed him some photographs of himself which I had made as tests – I had him look at himself in the mirror, and then at the photographs – that I got him to understand what a picture meant.[9]

The 1920–21 photographs are on the whole less reliant on subjects and activities as found. Calculation prevails and takes the form of photogenic test shots, particularly of children, and the building of cinema identities for those selected to play parts of Nanook and Nyla in the film's drama.

To the extent that Flaherty succeeded in reinventing himself as a film-maker, he later did not so much set aside his still camera as much as he passed it to his wife Frances. In subsequent films, starting with *Moana* (1926), Frances with Robert's urging and co-operation pursued the practice of photography in the service of film-making through the use of the still camera as a location, casting and shot-planning instrument.[10] This emphasis has had the outcome of obscuring the distinctiveness of Frances' photographic

ABOVE
Fig.9. Inuit group.
1910–11.

LEFT
Fig.10. Nero Fleming and his wife, Great Whale River.
1910–11.

Fig.11. Nero Fleming, lay reader at the Anglican Mission Church, Great Whale River. 1910–11.

talents since the public products of her work, almost always publicity stills, were associated with – and often credited to – the work of her husband.[11] Flaherty's withdrawal from still photography and the dominance of the *Nanook*-related photographs essentially eclipsed his pre-1920 work. By endeavouring to reconstruct selectively Flaherty's pre-1920 photographic work through autobiographical sources, we can highlight a body of visual cross-cultural docu-

mentation of impressive scope in the history of Arctic photography. We can also reconstruct the stepping stones by which the photography of exploration, ethnography and portraiture provided Flaherty with the contexts in which to search for a visual understanding of the peoples and places of the north. It was a process that brought him to the door of *Nanook* and in large measure gave him the acuity to cross its threshold.

## Notes

1. These diaries are among 'The Robert J. Flaherty Papers' at Columbia University. Subsequent references to this microfilmed collection will be noted as *Butler*, followed by box and reel nos.

2. With the exception of the contributors to the 1979 Vancouver Art Gallery exhibition and catalogue, *Robert Flaherty Photographer/Film-maker: The Inuit 1910–1922* (1979), Flaherty's early photography remains unexamined. The most comprehensive collection of pre-1922 Flaherty photographs are in the archives of the successor firm, Revillon of Paris, to the Revillon Frères Fur Trading Company. An inventory of these 1,200 or so photographs was prepared by Dr Michèle Therrin in 1984. This inventory and the albums are on microfilm at the National Archives of Canada in Ottawa.

   Another significant archive is that conveyed by Frances Flaherty to the School of Theology at Claremont where it formed the core of the Robert and Frances Flaherty Study Center. This collection, numbering about 1,500, is currently on deposit at the National Archives of Canada.

   The most recent resource to come to light is an album of 102 photographs, to be discussed shortly, entitled 'Through Canada's Northland', which Flaherty deposited for copyright registration in the British Library in May 1911.

3. The 'Islands' TMS (*Butler* 48: 27) totals about 225 pages of 22 chapters. The first three chapters cover, roughly, the period 1884–1904.

4. Frances Flaherty Ruttan, Flaherty's youngest sister, was interviewed in July 1979 in Thunder Bay, Ontario, by Susan Boyd-Bowman on behalf of the Vancouver Art Gallery exhibition noted earlier. Quotations from this interview are cited with the kind permission of the Vancouver Art Gallery.

5. Flaherty's registration (no.23989), dated 22 May 1911, appears in *The Canada Gazette* 44: 48 (27 May 1911), p.4010. The copy of the album Flaherty deposited in Ottawa is now lost but a second copy was deposited in the British Library. That copy survives (Canadian Copyright Collection 23989/1–102) in the form of modern transparencies, the original collection of prints currently misplaced. For a history of these copyright deposits, see Patrick B. O'Neill, *Checklist of Canadian Copyright Deposits in the British Museum, 1895–1923*, Vol.5, Halifax: Dalhousie UP, 1989. For an anthology of photographs selected from the entire copyright deposit, including fourteen by Flaherty, see Patricia Pierce, *Canada: The Missing Years, 1895–1924*, Don Mills, ON: Stoddart, 1985.

6. The shots of the Nastapoka Falls, the *Sorine*, the group family photograph and that of the woman just noted are included in Pierce's anthology, *Canada: The Missing Years*, pp.40–43.

7. Flaherty speaks often in his diaries of Nero leading services when they travelled together on Hudson Bay expeditions. Charles K. Leith, a University of Wisconsin geologist, met Nero Fleming in 1910–11 and wrote of him in his *A Summer and Winter on Hudson Bay* (1912), pp.159–62, saying among other things that Nero devotes 'his spare time and Sundays to missionary work under the direction of Revd W. G. Walton of Fort George' (p.160). In *Canada's Wonderful Northland* (1917) William T. Curran includes a photograph of Nero leading the congregation with the caption 'Eskimos at Service, Great Whale River'. That the Flaherty photograph is of the church interior at Great Whale River is confirmed by another Curran photograph with the caption 'Interior of Church, Great Whale River Post', which appears (p.32) in his earlier *Glimpses of Northern Canada* (1907) and depicts the identical interior, including map and creed in Inuit syllabics on the wall. Leith (*Summer*, p.154) also photographed Nero, who sports a moustache.

8. The moving picture camera Flaherty had was a Bell and Howell for which he received two weeks of instruction in Rochester, probably the only formal schooling Flaherty ever received in camera operation. Bell and Howell did a testimonial on the camera, dated 24 March 1915 (*Butler* 16: 10), quoting Flaherty's experience: 'I have been fully satisfied with it and believe that for our particular work in Baffin's land where the wooden box cameras warp very quickly, due to intense cold and dry air, your camera is quite the instrument to use. We left here with very little knowledge of motion picture work and had to thresh a good deal of the subject out when we erected our Wintering station in the North, but we have been quite successful and have secured some very interesting film – 14,000 ft [4,250 m]. It is hoped that this film may go well toward defraying the expenses of the expedition.'

9. 'How I Made the First Motion Pictures with Nanook of the North', *Sunday London Referee* (2 September 1934). Flaherty published the autobiography in eight *Referee* instalments, the first 22 July, the last 9 September.

10. Writing to her parents in November 1923 from Safune, Samoa, Frances reports: 'Making bromide enlargements has given us, strangely enough, the clue to the right density and hence the right exposure for all our negatives. And the fun of it is that Bob knew no more of these things than I and we are going every inch of the way together. And the way I have "jumped" into the graflex Bob says proves I am a "born photographer." And there you are. Could anything be more promising for our future?' (*Butler* 11: 6.)

11. The photographic work of Frances H. Flaherty (1883–1972) is largely an unexamined subject. Film critics, such as Cecile Starr, who knew her in her lifetime, did attempt to acknowledge her contributions: 'Women on the Verge . . . Pioneer documentary film-makers that history ignored', *International Documentary* (Fall 1990), pp. 15–19. She receives brief notice in Naomi Rosenblum's *A History of Women Photographers* (1994), 302. A notable exception to this trend is the inclusion of eleven Frances Flaherty Samoa photographs in the recent exhibition and catalogue, *Picturing Paradise: Colonial Photography of Samoa, 1875–1925*, ed. Casey Blanton, Daytona Beach, Florida: Southeast Museum of Photography, 1995.

Alan Rudolph Marcus

# Reflecting on Contested Images

Geert van den Steenhoven, a Dutch legal anthropologist from the University of Leiden, arrived in the Canadian Arctic in August 1955 at a remote site known as Ennadai Lake, situated in the Keewatin District of the Northwest Territories. His mission was to live with a small band of Inuit known as the Ahiarmiut for six weeks and to write a report on them for the Canadian federal government. The Ahiarmiut were among the best-known Inuit in Canada, having been the subject of Farley Mowat's polemical book, *The People of the Deer* (1952). They were considered by outsiders to be among the most 'primitive' Inuit in the Canadian Arctic. Dependent almost entirely on the caribou (*tuktu*) for their sustenance, the Ahiarmiut were known to still hunt with spears in the 1950s.

To Steenhoven's surprise, he soon found himself joined at Ennadai by a journalist and photographer from *Life* magazine. They were there to do a feature story on the Ahiarmiut, who had been chosen by the magazine as the Canadian Inuit most representative of primitive man. Though Mowat's book focused considerable attention on the Ahiarmiut, it did not contain photographs. Thus the *Life* international edition of 2 April 1956, whose cover displayed a large photograph of an Ahiarmiut father, mother and new-born child, presented many in the outside world with their first real glimpse of these people (fig.1). Given that the photograph has an innate power to authenticate, I will seek to show that the way in which the article and its pictures were culturally framed was emblematic of Western views, offering a rationale for intervention, with potentially unforeseen results.

This family trio at once evokes a timeless image, that of the Madonna and Child, with Joseph or one of the angels or saints looking on. It is reminiscent of such Italian Renaissance paintings as the *Madonna di Loreto* by Raphael, or Tommaso's *Madonna and Child with Angel*. Indeed, through the picture's composition and the way photographer Fritz Goro posed his subjects, the intertextual echoing of familiar Christian iconography serves to elevate the birth scene and transpose it into an Inuit nativity tableau.[1]

The photo-artist's ethnocentric animation of the scene provides interpretative pathways from which to view the photographs as sites of intersection. Thus a tender and private moment is exhibited in a public arena. A heading on the cover informs the reader that these are 'Stone Age Survivors'. The article is one of a series which chart mankind's evolutionary development into a modern industrialised society. For Western audiences the article's framing of difference may evoke sympathy for a people existing in such harsh conditions, or an allure of the exotic 'Other'. Their ennoblement could present an attractive ideal, a state to be desired and recaptured for its apparent simplicity, suggesting an earlier paradise lost.

The article and the manner in which the photographs are presented serve to lionise primitivism, while using it as a benchmark for the distance covered by Western civilisation and the process of progress. The article finishes by making romanticised and ill-informed remarks about the Inuit way of life, stating that 'the Caribou Eskimo is a modern Mesolithic Man – the harvester of wild bounty, consumer of temporary abundance . . . but, lacking a concept of time, he is unwilling or unable to take present action for future needs.' The implication is therefore that in their innocence and apparent ignorance of

Fig.1. An Ahiarmiut family. (Photographer: Fritz Goro)

knowing how to pursue long-term planning, it is astonishing that the Inuit managed to thrive, or even to survive at all.

At the top of the *Life* cover there is an additional title which promises: 'In color: long-range missiles'. While this may seem in odd juxtaposition to a story on primitivism, in fact, it figures quite coherently in the unfolding narrative behind the headlines. The reader is presented with a series of lenses, offering multiple layers of meaning. The child on the cover is the atom of a family, the family is a nuclear unit, and the family of the 1950s existed here under the uncertain umbrella of a nuclear nightmare with its associative Western intrusions into their world.

Due to Cold War tensions and the militarisation of the North American Arctic in the 1950s, the long-range ballistic missiles displayed in this issue of *Life* posed a threat to the life of the newborn child, this 'survivor of the stone age'. The featured Inuit family provided a symbolic image which sprang from an enduring iconographic

people, and the juxtaposition between the Western representation of their way of life and what we learn actually transpired as a result of Western intervention is unsettling. The family trio depicted were the Ahiarmiut hunter Anowtelik, his wife Akjar, and their new-born son. At the time the picture was taken they were living in their ancestral lands around Ennadai Lake.

Like the *Life* photographer, Geert van den Steenhoven turned his camera's gaze on the Ahiarmiut, but his selection process is notable for the important differences it reveals. Steenhoven took a series of colour slides and black and white photographs during his stay, which included the photograph of Anowtelik in a kayak (kayam) on Ennadai Lake in fig.2. In contrast to the romanticised *Life* photograph of Anowtelik in animal skins, he is seen here in his daily summer clothing, which includes a second-hand army jacket and hat. Steenhoven's photograph (fig.3) of Anowtelik's wife Akjar (on the left) further illustrates the dichotomy within their material culture at the time, where Akjar is clothed in a traditional caribou outfit, while her friend Ookanak wears Western garb. Steenhoven lived with Anowtelik's extended family group, which was headed by a highly respected hunter called Owlijoot. In the course of my research (as presented in greater depth in Marcus 1995) I had the opportunity of interviewing Steenhoven, Anowtelik, Owlijoot and other members of the Ahiarmiut.

The group were initially referred to as *Ahiarmiut* (inland people) by those Inuit who lived on the Hudson Bay coast. They have called themselves by that group name for as long as people can remember, though originally they may have identified themselves as *Tahiriarmiut* (people of the lakes) (Csonka, personal communication). The size of the population has been contested in the literature (Mowat 1952; Porsild 1952; Burch 1986), and prior to 1920 they may have numbered approximately 400 people. In the 1920s to 1940s starvation and epidemics reduced the band to less than sixty souls (Csonka 1991). By 1955 there were only fifty-two Ahiarmiut left living in the area of Ennadai Lake, 285 miles (460 km) north-west of Churchill, Manitoba. The nearest permanently inhabited point was the Hudson's Bay Company (HBC) trading post at Padlei, 140 miles (225 km) north-east of Ennadai. This area was occupied by a band of Caribou Inuit known as the Paallirmiut. To the south of the Ahiarmiut were the Chipewyan Indians of the northern forests.

The Ahiarmiut migrated between seasonal camps at periodic times in the year. During the

TOP
Fig.2. Anowtelik at Ennadai Lake, 1955.

ABOVE
Fig.3. Akjar with her baby Igyekah, and Ookanak. Ennadai Lake, 1955.

representation of the Inuit. They were a people fixed in a generic white Arctic space and frozen in time. This perception was most notably situated in images such as those from Robert Flaherty's depiction of Inuit life in the classic film *Nanook of the North* (1922). Nanook was a stereotype of the stoical, resourceful, self-reliant Inuit hunter. Yet, the ubiquitous image of the Inuit as a primitive, child-like people has arguably served to obscure unwitting deeds carried out by the *qallunaat*, the white man, and by officialdom. The question then arises: can one hide behind a photograph, behind an image, a stereotype, or will in time more images emerge which better inform the viewer?

The *Life* picture and its accompanying article presented the Ahiarmiut as a people bound to ancient traditions, hunters in harmony with their environment, living on the fringe of Western civilisation in a bountiful Arctic Eden. The Ahiarmiut family featured on the *Life* cover were, of course, more than symbolic, they were real

winter they lived in dwellings with walls made of snow blocks and capped with a roof of caribou skins, all supported by wooden tent poles. Inside there were one or two sleeping platforms, with a stove (in the 1950s made from a ten-gallon fuel drum) raised on a stone platform and a chimney poking through the roof. Willow twigs and moss provided fuel for the stove. The dwellings were comfortable and during the winter the indoor temperature could average 54°–63°F (12°–17°C). In the summer the families would live in conical, poled tents, made of caribou skins and canvas (see fig.4). Cooking would be done outside over an open fire, protected by a windbreak of spruce boughs.

As long as caribou meat was available, the adults ate almost nothing else. Ptarmigan, water fowl, fish and berries would supplement their diet, depending on the season. The caribou migration would usually pass the Ennadai region in May, travelling in a north-westerly direction. The second annual migration occurred in September and October, when the caribou travelled in a south-easterly direction. In the autumn migration the men would employ their traditional hunting strategy of approaching the caribou when they were swimming across narrow crossing points at lakes and then spearing them from kayaks. The caribou were so numerous on their migrations in 1954–5 that one official reported that in the average year the danger of excessive killing was greater than the possibility of obtaining too few caribou for the group requirement (Houston 1955: 3). Some of the caribou were cached when killed, others were simply gutted and left on the ground. The skins were used for clothing and housing, but most were left on the carcasses. The winter dress, including parkas, pants, stockings and boots, was made from caribou skins.

*Life* magazine's iconographic representation of the Ahiarmiut as the archetypal Caribou Inuit was significant for several reasons. Although the inland Keewatin Inuit were first mentioned in the anthropological literature in 1888 by Franz Boas, it was not until members of the Fifth Thule Expedition encountered them in 1922 that Birket-Smith (1929a) and Rasmussen (1930) gave them the name 'Caribou Eskimos'. Birket-Smith (1929b) speculated that these were the original Eskimos, building on earlier hypotheses about the origin of the Inuit in the interior of North America, more specifically the interior of the area west of Hudson Bay (Rink 1875; Boas 1888; Hatt 1916; Steensby 1917). Thus at the time of the *Life* article the white perception was still largely informed by the mythical notion that the Caribou

Inuit were 'the sole survivors of the original stage of Eskimo development' (Arima 1984: 458). This view had already been disputed (Mathiassen 1930), although later research remained contradictory about their origins (Harp 1962; Taylor 1965; Burch 1978 and 1986).

From Steenhoven's pictures we see another view of the Ahiarmiut, one which was out of keeping with the noble savage context of the *Life* article. Indeed, they wore caribou-skin clothing and hunted with spears, but as Steenhoven's photographs demonstrate, they also wore cast-off army clothing, and would hunt with rifles when there was sufficient ammunition. The army jackets seen in fig.5 came from a radio station which was built in 1949 at Ennadai Lake and manned

Fig.4. Owlijoot's camp. Ennadai Lake, 1955.

by the Canadian Army Signal Corps. Summer dress included imported southern clothing obtained by trade with the station personnel. No other government, mission or trading agents were resident in the area.

Ennadai Lake is actually a Chipewyan place name meaning 'the lake of the enemies'. The Ahiarmiut referred to the lake as *Qamanirjuaq* (big lake). Like other Inuit bands, they had assigned a dense web of place names to the region in which they hunted and foraged. *Atiqturniarvik* was the name they gave the spit of land protruding into the lake which the whites had appropriated for their radio station. As in the symbolic reference on the *Life* cover to the Cold War, the Ahiarmiut were now witnessing its agents descending into the epicentre of their homeland. The irony between the magazine's juxtaposition of 'stone age survivors' and the military was to become abundantly clear.

The Ahiarmiut's encounter strategy with the radio station personnel entailed making contact

Fig.5. Pongalak, his wife Ootnooyuk, son Kiyai, grandson, and daughter-in-law Alikaswa. Ennadai Lake, 1955.

once the buildings had been constructed and the whites were established in their dwellings. In August 1949 the station's log recorded the 'first Eskimos visit station – six people, led by Ohoto, asking if they could earn some money – came walking and left same day – came from a place two sleeps to the north' (Steenhoven 1955). They settled nearby, probably because the personnel were friendly and there was the opportunity to obtain goods and make use of items discarded by the station. In addition, they were given jobs moving fuel drums, hauling water, and other chores in exchange for rations. The army personnel at the station admitted that the Ahiarmiut were of great assistance to them. A Department official recorded that the Ahiarmiut had provided moral support to the whites by showing them how to live in the country and dress for cold weather, and provided a much needed interest beyond the cramped life within the station (Houston 1955: 9).

However, the new radio station at Ennadai had a direct and profound impact on the lives of the Ahiarmiut which, as I shall explain, led to a series of attempts to remove them. The federal Department of Northern Affairs and National Resources (hereafter referred to simply as 'the Department') had responsibility for administration of the Canadian north. The Ahiarmiut were under the jurisdiction of the Department's Northern Service Officer (NSO) and the RCMP detachment in Churchill, but in practice the Officer in Charge (OIC) of the radio station usefully acted as an informal trader. He collected

their fox skins of his own volition and forwarded them by air to Churchill. He also distributed goods, including those in lieu of family allowances, and relief rations if necessary. The OIC arranged for the weekly allocation of goods at what were called 'tea days', which subsequently became an integral social occasion. While well intentioned, the effect of this practice meant that the Inuit could live no farther than one day's travel from the station, whereas they would have preferred to live at sites somewhat more distant away, where fishing was known to be better (Steenhoven 1962: 11).

When the radio station was opened, federal officials initially took a dim view of Inuit interest in camping nearby. The omnipresent threat of starvation, coupled with the Ahiarmiut's growing dependency on the radio station, was perceived by officials as problematic. The Department decided to act and in May 1950 relocated the entire Ahiarmiut group of forty-seven people by air from Ennadai Lake to Nueltin Lake, 60 miles (100 km) to the south-east, where it was hoped they might work for a proposed commercial fishery scheme. The project failed, and within a matter of months the Inuit found their way back to their homeland at Ennadai.

In 1955, at the time that Steenhoven and the *Life* team stayed with the Ahiarmiut, the band comprised thirteen families, divided roughly into two groups: one loosely under the leadership of Owlijoot (see fig.6), an *isumataq*, or respected elder, and the other under Pongalak (individual on far left in fig.5), who was a shaman (*angatkuq*).

Fig.6. Owlijoot. Ennadai Lake, 1955.

They lived in camps within a radius of 15 miles (24 km) of the radio station. After the establishment of the station the Ahiarmiut changed their pattern of migration, by now making only minor seasonal moves of perhaps 5 miles (8 km) between their winter and summer camps (Houston 1955: 2). Staying with Owlijoot's camp, Steenhoven (1962: 12) recorded that it was cheerful and peaceful, with caribou herds around almost all the time he was there. Owlijoot (forty-three years old) and his step-son Anowtelik (twenty-three years old) were described by Steenhoven (personal communication) and by officials as being among the best Ahiarmiut hunters (Houston 1955: 5).

In the halcyon summertime of 1955 everyone who visited the Ahiarmiut reported on their fine and healthy condition. By the time the *Life* article was published the following year, government perceptions of the Ahiarmiut had changed dramatically. The 1955–6 caribou migrations did not come sufficiently close to the community to provide enough animals to harvest. The station personnel were thus having to take an increasingly active role as intermediaries between the government and the Ahiarmiut. Additional relief supplies and foodstuffs were flown in to the station's air strip, and the personnel also provided occasional medical assistance.

The Department decided that the status quo should come to an abrupt end, and that action should once again be taken to relocate the Ahiarmiut away from the vicinity of the radio station. This time they would have to be moved further afield to prevent a replay of the earlier imbroglio at Nueltin Lake when they were able to return to their homeland. Thus, with much optimism the Department issued a press release in May 1957 announcing the resettlement from Ennadai under the banner 'Eskimos Fly to New Hunting Grounds'. An excerpt read:

A community of some of Canada's most primitive citizens has moved – but they did it the modern way. Eskimo hunters and huskies left their ancient ways for a day to travel in the comfort of an aircraft to new hunting grounds. (Canada 1957)

The entire Ahiarmiut band of fifty-nine Inuit and their six dogs were moved in May 1957. Referring to the relocatees as 'settlers', the press release uncharacteristically named the individual in charge of the operation. It stated that with the co-operation of the RCMP and the HBC the move was made under the supervision of NSO Bill Kerr. The Department publicly described the relocation as a consensual project, portraying the Inuit as 'volunteers' who moved because game was scarce in their home district. Irrespective of any subterfuge, the Department wanted to give the impression that this was a self-motivated migration and that officials were merely providing the transport.

However, the Inuit have stated that they had no input into the site selected for them. They were relocated northwards from Ennadai to a place called Henik Lake, where there were no white people and no other Inuit living in the immediate area. The nearest outpost was the HBC trading post about three days' journey away at Padlei. An underlying quixotic notion suggested that in this virgin Edenic land with its redemptive properties they might be reborn. The 'stone age survivors' were expected to become self-reliant 'Nanooks' once again, to conform to the image constructed of them in the *Life* article – stereotypes of Inuit as primitive man. It later transpired that they were moved without their informed consent. Their kayaks were left behind because there was not enough room on the plane for them. Apparently, officials did not consider why there were no other Inuit inhabiting the area.

The Ahiarmiut had little idea why they were moved from Ennadai. They articulated the event in terms that 'they had been sent away' (*aulaktitaujuvinitt nunamut ungasiktualukmut*), and regarded the move as punishment for their reliance on the Ennadai station personnel. There was indeed a possible punitive element associated with the operation (Marcus 1995: 138–44). Appropriately, the first principle of establishing a reformatory setting is isolation of the 'offender'

Fig.7. Ungmak, Shikoak, and Ootuk, next to the radio station. Ennadai Lake, 1955.

from the external world and everything that motivated the offence (Foucault 1977: 236). In this case, they had been isolated from their lands, the radio station, and ready access to provisions for the misdeed of relying too much on the whites.

When the Department official with field responsibility for the operation, NSO Bill Kerr (1955), discussed the relocation with the Ahiarmiut, they told him that the Padlei area was a poor country for game and that they would be hungry there. Thus they already had some knowledge of the place and its resources. In fact, there is a range of hills between the Ennadai and Padlei regions which the Ahiarmiut called *Huinnakuluit* ('the bad ones'), where there were historically known to be few caribou (Csonka 1991: 307–8). These hills extend to Henik Lake, and serve as a natural boundary between the Paallirmiut hunting area and *Ahiarmiut nunaat* (the country of the Ahiarmiut).

Ancestral land use and occupancy were bound up with an Inuit sense of identity (Brody 1976: 185). Inuit associations with the landscape not only endowed it with meaning, they were vital for survival. Knowing the place names was equivalent to knowing the good places to hunt and trap. Their 'memoryscape', as Nuttall (1992) refers to it, provided an orientational knowledge for hunting and foraging activity, as well as a binding sense of collective ties with a particular area. That nexus was removed when the people were moved to a place they had only a vague knowledge of. Toponymic knowledge of a region is a necessary

survival strategy, and relocation severed the Inuit from their associational knowledge of a familiar landscape, a homeland. This act resulted in a loss of hunting knowledge and a loss of cultural and intellectual security. The Ahiarmiut could no longer use their mental images of the landscape to ensure their survival.

The *Life* article presents various supplemental images featuring the Ahiarmiut within their familiar Arctic landscapes. However, images of the 'other' may serve to endear the audience, to alienate further or to recapture the temporally bound ethos of the culture. If the intention of Goro's photographs was to illustrate a utopic, pristine microcosm of society, it belied the tragedy that was to befall its subjects. An image of paradise lost was forever frozen in time.

After the relocation of the Ahiarmiut away from the *quallunaat*, the photographs ceased, the Keewatin winter closed in, and within eight months, eight members of the this small group were dead – dead from starvation, from desperation, from exposure, from neglect – from not having lived up to a popular, pictorially informed stereotype. Just as the *Life* photographer had conformed his Ahiarmiut subjects to an imaginary narrative construct for Western consumption, so too had officials imagined that the group could conform to a new construct. Their ability to survive those expectations, however beneficent by design, was put to the ultimate test, and among those who failed it and perished were Pongalak and his son Kiyai (fig.5), and Ungmak and Ootuk (fig.7). The deadly outcome had another considered effect. Due to the Inuit deaths in the Keewatin that winter in early 1958, the government decided to suspend any further relocation experiments of this nature. A policy reversal focused instead on resettling all Canadian Inuit off the land and into purpose-built communities. The cogent argument they came to accept was that it was no longer tenable to have Canadian citizens perishing from starvation, even if they were Inuit, stereotype or no stereotype.

**Note**

1. Fritz Goro formerly worked as an art director and designer in Berlin and Munich. He was born in Bremen, Germany, in 1901, was educated in Berlin and studied at the Bauhaus school. Goro emigrated to the United States in 1936 and, based in New York, became a leading freelance science photographer (Naylor 1988: 377–8).

Henrietta Lidchi

# Filmic Fantasies in Arctic Lands: Photographing the Inuit of North-West Greenland in 1932

My interest in Photography took on a more cultural turn. I decided I liked Photography *in opposition* to the Cinema, from which I nonetheless failed to separate it.
(Barthes 1984: 3)

The following essay will consider, briefly, the content and the context of production of a series of photographs taken in north-west Greenland in 1932. In so doing, it will seek to focus on the images in particular but will seek equally to draw on this experience to examine the relationship between photography and cinema.

On 24 May 1932 the Universal–Dr Fanck–Greenland Expedition set sail from Hamburg. On board the ss *Borodino* was a German-speaking film crew sponsored by the Universal Pictures Corporation (through its German arm, Die Deutsche Universal) and contracted to make three films in north-west Greenland: a German and an American version of an Arctic adventure entitled *SOS Eisberg/SOS Iceberg* respectively and a comedy *North Pole, Ahoy!* (Gallagher 1992: 86–7; Sorge 1935: 91, Ch. VI). The five-month expedition gave rise to numerous artistic products: three films (among the first feature films to be made in Greenland), several thousand photographs and four illustrated personal memoirs of the expedition (Fanck 1933; Sorge 1935; Udet 1935; Riefenstahl 1933a, 1992). The expedition was unusual in that it yielded a plethora of inter-linked but distinct visual records. The photographs differed from the cinematic images to the extent they were taken both for private and public consumption and denoted a series of encounters: those between the film crew, the landscape of Greenland and the native communities in north-west Greenland. But like the film, of which they were the product, these pho-

tographs constitute a partial truth (Clifford 1986). Insufficient testimonies of a set of personal encounters, they have to be embedded within the published accounts and compared to the filmic images produced concurrently.

## *SOS Eisberg* – the film in context

In April 1932 Carl Laemmle, the Head of Universal Pictures Corporation, invited Arnold Fanck to Hollywood. He wanted to discuss possibilities of a German/American[1] co-production to be set in Greenland, under the 'protection' of the Danish explorer Knud Rasmussen. In the 1920s and 1930s high dramas set in far-flung places and using local extras were increasingly popular. One favoured exotic location was the Arctic, and Fanck was known for his filming of snow and ice (Gallagher 1992: 86; Fienup-Riordan 1995: 57).

By 1932 Fanck, a geologist and champion skier, was a respected and popular film-maker who had enjoyed considerable success with *Die weiße Hölle vom Piz Palü* (*The White Hell of Piz Palü*) (1929). Fanck had created a genre of landscape and nature films: the 'mountain film', which sought to reproduce the magnificence of snow and ice on screen. Whereas contemporary German expressionism was studio-bound and oppressive in feel, mountain films were idealistic and mythical, staged in the great outdoors amongst *real* snow and ice, and up *real* mountains. Dramas focusing on the conflict between man and nature were played out against the magnificent backdrop of alpine settings in Switzerland, Austria and Germany and enacted through the vehicle of alpine sports. In later films, as in *SOS Eisberg*, aerial stunts were an increasingly important feature, consistent with a new fascination for aerial photography (Trace 1972: 34; Roh 1989: 161; Newhall 1978: 79). In Fanck's films the stunning photography and the daredevil feats of physical endurance (enacted in the main above 12,000 ft/3,700 m) were frequently unhampered by a good script or fine acting (Trace 1972: 31; Gunston 1960: 5). *SOS Eisberg*, which was Fanck's last important film, was no exception. He choose Greenland because he argued that he had exhausted the potential of other Alpine locations.[2] In this 'uncharted' territory Fanck felt he could film 'real' icebergs and reproduce the danger, the beauty and the majesty of Arctic scenery which he believed no other medium except film could capture (1933: 9–13).

Fanck's integrity as a film-maker depended on his refusal to fake adventure, so actors and crew for *SOS Eisberg* had to be drawn from an already established retinue of highly trained professionals, most of whom were former alpine sportsmen (Hans Schneeberger, Richard Angst, Max Holsboer – see Appendix).

The 2,000-ton tramp whaler ss *Borodino* was due to arrive in Uummannaq by early June 1932 (by way of Qeqertarsuaq/Godhavn to greet the authorities) and stay for a period of five months or so, returning to film indoor scenes in Berlin (Sorge 1935: 33). On landing in Uummannaq the ice was found to be too treacherous and unsuitable for Ernst Udet's planes: he could neither land nor take off. So the expedition and filming moved to other sites. Udet was restationed on Illorsuit.[3] During June the expedition moved between Uummannaq and Nuliarfik. In July it moved to Nuugaatsiaq with Knud Rasmussen to film the 'Eskimo' sequences (Sorge 1935: Ch. II). Ernst Sorge travelled between these locations and two glaciers – the Rinks and Umiammakku – where he took scientific measurements relating to fjords and glaciers and filmed some of the more dangerous sequences of icebergs disintegrating, or 'calving' (Loewe & Sorge 1933; Sorge 1935: Ch. XII). Ultimately, Fanck's dedication to authenticity was too risky for the American backers[4] who forced Fanck to return to Germany in October 1932 and complete filming in the Bernina Alps under the co-direction of the American, Tay Garnett.

The storyline of the German film, as scripted, was a fictional reinterpretation of the ill-fated Wegener expedition of 1930–31 of which both Sorge and Loewe were members and in which the leader of the expedition, Alfred Wegener, perished. The key elements of the mountain film were adapted for the Arctic landscape, blizzards gave way to icebergs moving and breaking down, rescue parties valiantly made their way across the frozen landscape, human passions were prompted by desperation, cold and lack of food. The plot was straightforward. Four members of an expedition return to Greenland to rescue their leader. Encountering and overcoming many dangers, they find him badly injured. They are, however, out of radio contact, and without food. Rescue comes fleetingly in the form of the plucky wife of the leader, Ellen Lorenz, but her plane crashes. It arrives decisively when the 'Eskimos' recruited from a nearby settlement arrive as a large flotilla of kayaks guided by Ernst Udet in his aircraft.

Filmed in Nuugaatsiaq under the direction of Knud Rasmussen (fig.1), the twelve-minute 'Eskimo' sequence (the last eighth of the film), in which the kayaking scene is the highlight, acts as a major dramatic break. It is the only sequence in the film where there is action rather than staged melodrama (although it is clear that the Inuit are not actors, but are being directed to behave in a certain way). The villagers run out of their houses on hearing the approach of the plane, and look up in wonder and astonishment. The hubbub of the dogs and the crowd, the rushing towards the drenched explorer and then the bounding into the beached kayaks, all give life and movement to the film (fig.2).

The continuous four-minute kayak sequence was filmed in a day in a complex operation involving a hundred kayakers recruited (with their families) from nearby settlements.[5] One cameraman was positioned on land, the other on the boat to get close-ups (fig.3), whilst Ernst Udet circled with a camera in the plane. Knud Rasmussen marshalled the kayakers from the bank near Nuugaatsiaq (fig.1) and the process yielded 2,000 m/6,500 ft of film (Fanck 1933: 26; Sorge 1935: 84–6).

*SOS Eisberg* was not a box office success. It did, however, earn critical praise for the quality of its photography, for its evocation of the ominous and beautiful Arctic landscape, and for its final breathtaking sequence.

## *SOS Eisberg* – the affiliated photographic images

Photography is a practice much prone to theoretical musings. This is, in large part, due to its ascribed transparency: to the promise that the photograph is true to the reality that it represents. André Bazin, for instance, argues that, however poor the quality, however blurred, fuzzy, discoloured or even lacking in documentary value a photograph may be, it must share, by the very act of becoming a photograph, the being of the object or subject of which it is a reproduction; in this manner photographs are 'sticky', because,

LEFT
Fig.1. 'Rasmusen praßt Rettung': 'Knud Rasmussen directs the rescue'. (Photographer Ferdinand Vogel)

BELOW RIGHT
Fig.2. Still from kayak rescue scene; photograph uncaptioned in collection. (Photographer: Richard Angst)

BELOW LEFT
Fig.3. 'Film aufnahme der Eskimos': 'Filming the Eskimos', showing the placement of the camera on the motorboat. (Photographer: Richard Angst)

like amber, they preserve what they perfectly entrap (Nichols 1991: 151). But though photographs might capture a historical event – 'what has been' (Barthes 1984: 85) – they simultaneously fail to disclose the historical or ontological status of that which they represent (Nichols 1991: 151). So although photographs are invested with historical authenticity, they are slippery and ambiguous, refusing to disclose important information about those events depicted within. Ambivalent and many sided, and by turn art, record and document, images may rise above, and be distinct from, textual description, but they can be mute and can drift in the absence of a textual

anchor. To interpret photographs, recourse must be made to the tangled web of memories and written histories that surround them.

The photographs produced as a consequence of the 1932 Universal–Dr Fanck–Greenland Expedition to north-west Greenland are difficult to read in the absence of textual description. As the remains of a corpus which seems to have at one time numbered several thousands, the surviving photographs (in their hundreds) constitute a very particular record, ignoring certain aspects of the expedition and highlighting others. The collection housed in the National Archives in Washington, for example, has a particular narrative. The thirty images taken by the publicity stills photographer Ferdinand Vogel are accompanied by a caption list and a deteriorating press

release. These exemplify the extraordinary risks the crew undertook and situate the crew within the landscape ('The North Pole as studio. Icebergs as scenery') and amongst 'friendly' people of north-west Greenland ('Esquimos [*sic*] as extras').[6] The photographs are mostly posed. A significant number depict the crew embracing or smiling at young local women (see Fanck 1933: T.38, T.54). Ernst Udet, in particular, is shown with Inuit women in their best clothes, enjoying, we are to suppose, the full extent of his legendary charm (Sorge 1935: 18, 64–5). Others depict the stars on board the ss *Borodino*, and the polar bears (Fanck 1933: T.28, T.29, T.30).[7]

The Stiftung Deutsche Kinemathek in Berlin, in contrast, has a more varied collection which includes revealing photographic and textual materials. In this collection, the personal legacy of cinematographer Richard Angst, there are significant written items: the original script (109 pages and in German, which differs in significant areas from the final film);[8] the original production documentation relating to the further use of film footage (with associated accounts);[9] and production comments and correspondence to and from Carl Laemmle when the production of the film ran out of Universal's control. This material is fascinating because it provides a fuller production history of the film, and thus of the associated visual images. It fails, however, to provide specific enlightenment as to the motives of the three photographers whose images form part of the collection: the official photographer Ferdinand Vogel, the cinematographer Richard Angst, and Gisela Lindeck, who was later to become Hans Schneeberger's wife.

In this collection there is evidence of what might be called a documentary vision. Richard Angst collected and assembled the largest proportion of pictures taken by himself and others on large and smaller cards, the larger may have been used for display, the smaller may have been an album at one time. These display, or album, photographs seem preoccupied with reportage: with reflecting what was encountered from a degree of intimacy. The subjects are varied and thus provide some form of narrative of the expedition. There are images of the crew, of arriving at and leaving Inuit villages, of the villages themselves, of the village cemetery, and of the animals on board the ship, and the usual pictures of icebergs and crew members with young local women – *Dorfschöne*, or 'village beauties'. The other loose photographs seem to be quite dissonant. The photograph entitled 'Eskimo Frauen' (fig.4) in particular is an ambivalent portrait when compared to the other images of women. These two women are

not in their Sunday best, and they are not smiling at the camera but confronting it and drawing away. So this assembled record presents a more diverse and thus complex view of the expedition, one interpreted by the short captions. Angst's photographs are captioned below, while Vogel's are numbered and have captions added to the negatives. These are simple, factual interpretations.

Although Angst collected these photographs, his do not feature as prominently in this collection or in the published texts (Fanck 1933; Sorge 1935; Udet 1935) as those of those of Ferdinand Vogel, Ernst Udet and Ernst Sorge. His preoccupation (as a photographer) seems rather to record himself in Greenland or show how he set up the cameras (Sorge 1935: 17, 32–3; Fanck 1933: T.49; fig.3). That Vogel (figs 1, 4–7) has a greater range of subject matter and Lindeck (figs 8, 9) seems more concerned with composition is confirmed by the published texts (Fanck 1933; Sorge 1935).

Among Vogel's photographs are those, already mentioned, that have documentary value, often not reproduced in the associated texts. Others, more widely reproduced, are publicity shots such as the one in which Knud Rasmussen consults Inuit men over a map (fig.6). This is one of a number of photographs which purposely denote Knud Rasmussen's involvement, though they more usually depict Rasmussen with the German crew members (Fanck 1933: T.35). This assemblage of Vogel's photographs indicates that he was not confined to a repertoire of images that glorified the landscape or promoted certain fixed

ideas about contact between the crew and the native communities near to whom they resided. Vogel's large uncaptioned portraits of the Inuit are both reflective and arresting (figs 5, 7). The portrait of the 'village beauty' (fig.5) is carefully framed and quite ambivalent: the subject has a circumspect relationship with the camera.

Lindeck's work is the most puzzling. She is a shadowy figure not mentioned in detail in the associated reminiscences (indeed omitted in Riefenstahl's most recent autobiography [1992:

112]), and her work focuses on people rather than place. It has in turn both a quality of intimacy and ease (fig.8) and great aesthetic value (fig.9).[10] She is the only photographer of the party to have taken a photograph of a native Greenlander aiming a camera at her (in the Stiftung Deutsche Kinemathek collection; see also Fanck 1933: T.9). The formal qualities of her portraiture, like those of Vogel, might cause one to speculate as to the artistic movements that influenced her.

So the fragmentary collections in the National Archives and Stiftung Deutsche Kinemathek point us towards the importance of the *context* of interpretation and, in so doing, towards the role of accompanying *texts*. On one hand, photographs can be better understood when placed within the context of personal memoirs of the expedition. Fig.10, for instance, clearly represents a community cutting up a whale. To place it properly, however, reference must be made to the relevant texts which reveal that at an early point during the expedition's stay in Uummannaq a Danish government steamer brought a whale to the community which temporarily halted the villagers' work with the crew (Riefenstahl 1992: 109; Sorge 1935: 42–4). On the other hand, the aesthetic qualities of photographs can be undermined by clumsy captioning: portraits by Vogel and Lindeck (like figs 7, 8 and 9) are used by Sorge (1935: 17, 32–3; 20, 96–7) and Fanck (1933: T.18, T.19) as illustrations of 'native types'. Although the majority of the subjects in the portraits are unidentified, anonymity does not jar quite as much in an uncaptioned image as it does in one judged to be representative.

### Text, context and image
The films and the photographs, it can be argued, provide a linked testimony of two encounters:

ABOVE LEFT
Fig.5. Portrait of a woman; photograph uncaptioned in collection. (Photographer: Ferdinand Vogel)

ABOVE
Fig.6. Knud Rasmussen consulting Inuit men over a map; photograph uncaptioned in collection. (Photographer: Ferdinand Vogel)

LEFT
Fig.7. Portrait of a man; photograph uncaptioned in collection. (Photographer: Ferdinand Vogel)

ABOVE
Fig.8. Inuit man and children; photograph uncaptioned in collection. (Photographer: Gisela Lindeck)

ABOVE
Fig.8. Inuit man and children; photograph uncaptioned in collection. (Photographer: Gisela Lindeck)

RIGHT
Fig.9. Portrait of a youth; photograph uncaptioned in collection. (Photographer: Gisela Lindeck)

ABOVE RIGHT
Fig.10. 'Fleisch, Fleisch': 'Meat, Meat'. (Photographer: Ferdinand Vogel)

1. That between the mainly European crew and the landscape of north-west Greenland. The crew were particularly struck by the Arctic landscape of Greenland, describing it as unimaginably beautiful and magnificent, but equally dangerous, treacherous and fiendish (Fanck 1933: 26–7; Sorge 1935: 82–3). This ambivalent relationship gave rise to some extraordinary still photography.[11]

2. That between the mainly European crew and the Inuit communities of Uummannaq, Illorsuit and Nuugaatsiaq, near to whom they resided and with whom they worked, who prompted different reflections and representations.

As a set of fragments, the photographs present a rich resource. Surviving in sparse and idiosyn-

cratic collections, these representations are embedded in the self-confessional and impressionistic memoirs written by Arnold Fanck (1933), Leni Riefenstahl (1933a, 1992), Ernst Sorge (1935) and the pilot Ernst Udet (1935). In these memoirs authors and photographers are not one and the same (Appendix), with photographers sometimes uncredited (Fanck 1933; Riefenstahl 1933a). Indeed authors make free use of other peoples' photographs, sometimes attaching different meanings to the same image. Captioned, but rarely analysed, the images serve principally as illustrations showing 'excerpts from the life of the expedition' or offering 'characteristic traits of the scenery of the fiords, and of their inhabitants' (Sorge 1935: 6). These images which are ascribed the role of evidence have their meaning and value fixed by the associated text (figs 6, 10). So, whereas the films are intended as dramatic constructions – seductive and scripted fantasies – the photographs have claims to objectivity and truth (fig.10).

In many ways it was fitting that in the film the kayak sequence received so much prominence and praise since the kayak acts as both a visual and a textual metaphor, a means through which the authors express ideas about the Inuit as a people. The expertise and the elegance of the kayakers serve to confront the European crew with their own limitations and that of their technology. For Sorge, though the plane, the boats and the kayaks are all equivalent means of rescue, only one – the kayak – is perfectly attuned to the Greenlandic environment (1935: 77–9, 84) (figs

2, 3). Only the 'Eskimos' and their kayaks can properly and expertly navigate the Arctic waters with its ice floes, fjords and icebergs (Sorge 1935: 65–7).[12] The final scene exemplifies dramatically what the crew already know: that the treachery and harshness of the Arctic environment are only surmountable by the people whose technology is adapted to it.[13]

So technology reflects culture, itself explained as an adaptation to the environment. Memoirs are replete with predictable and essentialist assertions as to the 'Eskimo' character. By turn pleasant, helpful, musical, cheerful, non-violent and without a rule of law, the Inuit are equally cautious, knowledgeable and wise, supremely adapted in character and habit to a treacherous and unyielding, but magnificent environment. As Fienup-Riordan remarks, this reflects the representation of the Inuit in heroic mode, where harshness is a property of the landscape, not the people (1995: 12–14). The German male crew members compare themselves to their Inuit companions and use photographs to fix the accuracy of these reflections visually. Photographs (figs 5, 6, 7, 8, 9) conveniently captioned might be read as evidence of these native characteristics.

But the qualities these authors choose reflect their own subjectivity. Udet (1935: 167–8) speaks of the Inuit's love of music, of the enjoyable 'Kaffeemiks' and dancing that the crew and local communities arranged (see also Sorge 1935: 137–8; Kent 1962: 297). Fanck talks of the Inuit's caution and coolness towards his schemes for staging and filming stunts on icebergs (1933: 36; see note 4). Sorge admires their skill, on which he relies during his expeditions (1935: 54, 167). Riefenstahl makes much of the 'Eskimos'' easiness of character and enthusiasm (1992: 109–10).

The questions of cultural difference are most illuminatingly voiced (and illustrated) in relationship to Knud Rasmussen, the polar explorer and ethnographer. Knud Rasmussen worked with the crew for a period of three weeks (in July). Ascribed the title of 'protector' of the expedition, he may have played the role of facilitator or mediator. Sorge offers an explanation by arguing that local knowledge and custom are fragile and can easily be contaminated by the harmful influence of 'civilisation' (1935: 54).[14] Rasmussen expressed his keenness to be involved, writing that it was important to ensure that someone with knowledge of the country and its people should be involved in one of the first full-length feature films to be recorded in Greenland (1933: 37–8). Rasmussen interrupted the Seventh Thule Expedition to take part, and left his assistant (Emma Landberg) with the party after his departure for north Greenland (Riefenstahl 1933b: 9).[15]

Knud Rasmussen's qualities are attributed to his hybridity, being of native descent on his mother's side and of Danish on his father's. He is quiet and wise, mixing the boundless charm and gentleness of the 'Eskimos' with the cultivation of the Danes (Fanck 1933: 47–8). Rasmussen acts almost as Fanck's conscience. As a director, Rasmussen is primarily concerned with people's safety: compassionate and caring like the Inuit in general. Unlike Fanck, he would not seek to film 'real' icebergs if this puts lives in danger, he would content himself with safe studio shots (1933: 26–8). He moves easily between both communities or cultures and this is illustrated photographically (Fanck 1935: T.35 and fig.6).

Knud Rasmussen is consistently praised, an essential figure who personally guaranteed the co-operation of the community of Nuugaatsiaq in the making of the film. Described as 'the uncrowned king of the Eskimos' (Udet 1935: 160), Rasmussen is said to be the only person who could persuade the people of the neighbouring communities to gather and stay at Nuugaatsiaq for the duration and forgo seal hunting (Sorge 1935: 84; Riefenstahl 1933b: 9), though the Inuit were paid to do so.[16] Sorge simply asserts the three weeks filming in Nuugaatsiaq were the happiest time of the expedition (1935: 84).

But questions of commonality and companionship are very interestingly gendered. This is, again, reflected and reinforced in the photographs. The male members of the crew emphasise their admiration for manly skills and traditional knowledge – the Inuit as Arctic hunter or gifted kayaker. For Udet the kayak is the means through which a bond is established with an elder of Illorsuit, Daniel ('the great hunter'). Udet recounts with great feeling how he was able to satisfy Daniel's last wish: by flying over Illorsuit and the fiords. Udet marvels at the ease with which Daniel adapts himself to the movement of the aircraft, knowing how to swing into the curve by virtue of a life tracing the waves in his kayak (Udet 1935: 173–5). So modern technology – as plane, boat or camera – is equally a point of commonality or identification. Fanck reflects on the ease with which the men from Nuugaatsiak repaired a motorboat. It leads him to comment that they did so 'in total silence and as casually as they would mend a kayak' (1933: 54). He reflects that the 'Eskimo' are an 'exceptional people, an incomprehensible mixture of primitiveness and intelligence' (1933: 54). The Inuit are said to have become easily habituated to the camera, quickly understanding what was expected of them (Riefenstahl 1933b: 9). Sorge marvels at their superior understanding of lighting contrasts and praises their patience (1935: 85).

So it is often the case that men are named and form emotional bonds or relationships of respect; with women, the similarities and differences are more superficially articulated. In the texts and associated pictures women, young women in particular, are represented or written of solely in terms of their attractiveness (Sorge 1935: 51). Captions emphasise the fact that they are 'darlings', 'village beauties' or more surprisingly little 'peaches' (Sorge 1935; Udet 1935; Fanck 1933: T.38, T.54). Though clearly other photographs were taken of women, of older women in a more ambivalent mode, these were not published or publicised. The exceptions are the photographs credited to Sorge (1935). In Sorge's book there are many pictures of a young girl called Dorothy, pictured on her own or with her friends (1935: 20, 96–7). Photographs credited to 'Sorge' were equally taken by Gerda Sorge, who befriended Dorothy and sought, therefore, to take photographs of someone with whom she was acquainted and who was not too dissimilar in age from herself.[17]

By embedding these images within the associated narratives, we gain some understanding of their meaning, but equally a feeling of the different sets of relationship that the crew, authors and photographers had with the Inuit communities near whom they lived.[18] On the other hand, these photographs should not be seen solely as evidence or illustration. They were not created in an aesthetic vacuum. In order to make sense of some of these works as art, one needs to move levels, to make reference to other arenas such as the national artistic context in which Vogel and Lindeck, in particular, can be seen to be operating.

The 1920s and 1930s inaugurated many experimental movements in photography, especially in Germany. Photographers sought to escape French impressionist photography and play with realism to heighten the artistic merit of the photograph (Mellor 1978). The work of Vogel and Lindeck (figs 6, 7, 9), in particular, contains powerful examples of new types of photography, reminiscent of the 'worker-photographers' (*Arbeiter-Fotograf*) but equally the New Objectivity (*Neue Sachlichkeit*) movement more generally (Eskilden 1978). This advocated realistic portraiture which captured the subject faithfully and without affectation. Undertaking to represent people with a small 'p', this movement argued that people should be portrayed truthfully, without sentiment or sentimentality (Macpherson 1978: 65). The words of the art critic Paul Renner, written

in 1930, provide a convincing reading of one of Vogel's pictures (fig.6) (1989: 167–8).

The new photography . . . refuses to sacrifice richness of tonal gradation to a cheap painterly effect. It does not want to change or prettify anything . . . It does not shrink from producing human skin with all its pores and hairs, all its charming irregularities and spots. It doesn't change the human skin into an insipid sculpture of wax and soap. It does not ask the subject to look into the lens and smile. It despises all forms of coquetery between the photographer and the imaginary viewer of the photograph.

So these more ambivalent, starker, portraits can be re-contextualised. It is not sufficient to read them solely in relation to the accounts of the expedition; reference can also be productively made to the artistic influences which may have affected the photographers. An understanding of contemporary aesthetic movements allows some insight into the meaning and the motive behind Lindeck's work in particular, since there is no other means of 'reading' her work. Lindeck's images acquire their worth not as illustration, but as artistic products to be seen in relation to the larger context of the expedition, the cultural encounters which they represent and the artistic movements of the time.

## Conclusion

This paper has sought to investigate the articulation of film and photography through exploring narratives (memories and histories) and contexts. In so doing it indicated how the sophisticated medium of film relies on a simplistic narrative, in contradistinction to and subverted by its more entangled photographic counterparts. The photographs under investigation are artefacts, but they equally amount to a body of work or evidence that depicts a series of encounters that took place in north-west Greenland in the early 1930s.

As incidental documents, these images have survived the test of time and have become more substantial testimonials than the film. As a body of evidence, they are contextualised and multiply interpreted by several authors, thus they articulate in a more complex, but also sometimes more unwitting way the vision and the ideals of the participants involved in the expedition. They are partial truths significant in their omissions. But they are, equally, lasting documents which perfectly capture the moments they represent. They can, therefore, be used as a powerful, and contemporary, source of memories.

One of the last surviving members of the expedition, Gerda Scholz-Sorge (formerly Gerda

Sorge), returned to Greenland in 1982 accompanied by a copy of her husband's book (Sorge 1935). On taking this to the old people's home in Uummannaq she met and shared memories of the photographs with those who had originally witnessed their taking[19] but whose testimonies have never formed a significant element of the written record. There are still, therefore, more memories and 'other' histories that could be disclosed.

## Acknowledgements

The author would like to thank Gerrit Thies and the Stiftung Deutsche Kinemathek for kindly providing the photographs and other materials for this paper. She would also like to thank Gerda Scholz-Sorge for making time to share her memories of the expedition and Astrid de Boer for facilitating this important meeting. Henriette Classen of the Nunatta Atuagaateqarfia, Det Grønlandske Landsbibliotek, Nuuk, provided much assistance in obtaining rare publications, as did the library staff of the Museum of Mankind. Dirk Weiken very helpfully made available his copies of film material. Mads Graverson of the Royal Danish Embassy generously arranged for material to be brought over from the Rigsarkivet, Copenhagen. Many thanks are due to the unpaid translators Tim Wells, Julie Rolls, Hans Rashbrook and Anais Thomas who generously gave of their time and intellectual energies. Inge Kleivan provided essential reference material and editorial advice while Jonathan King and Elizabeth Edwards helped in the revising of this paper.

## Appendix: *SOS Eisberg* members of the expedition

| | |
|---|---|
| Dr Arnold Fanck (A) | – Leader/Director |
| Dr Knud Rasmussen | – Protector |
| Leni Riefenstahl (A) Sepp Rist Dr Max Holsboer Gibson Gowland Walter Riml Gustav Lantschner | } Actors |
| Ernst Udet (A/P) | – Stunt pilot/actor |
| Dr Fritz Loewe* Dr Ernst Sorge (A/P)* Manfred Kraus* Franz Kelbl* | } Scientific advisors and radio/motor boat operators |
| Werner Klinger | – Assistant Producer |
| Emma Landberg Elizabeth Kind | } Production Secretaries |
| Karl Buchholz | – Director of Photography |
| Franz Schriek | – Airman |
| Erich Baier | – Mechanic |
| Hans Schneeberger Richard Angst (P) | } Cameramen |
| Walter Traut Luggi Foeger | } Assistant Cameramen |
| Ferdinand Vogel | – Still Photographer |
| Zoltan Kegl | – Sound Recordist |
| Charles Metain | – Assistant Sound Recordist |
| Giuseppe Marinucci | – Cook |
| David Zogg Fritz Steuri Hans Ertl | } Mountaineers |
| Dr Karl Georg Fuhrman | – Medical Officer |
| Karl Herbig | – Animal Keeper |
| Andrew Marton Yarmilla Marton Louis Adlon Jr | } Comedy Crew |
| Ellons Illing Gisela Lindeck (P) Else Loewe Gerda Sorge (P) | |

*Former members of Alfred Wegener Greenland expedition*

P = photographer

A = author

## Notes

1. In the 1920s and early 1930s the German film industry was thriving, ranked 'second only to Hollywood in size, technical sophistication and world influence' (Thompson & Bordwell 1994: 105).

2. According to notes from an interview in Berlin (1 March 1996) with Gerda Scholz-Sorge, widow of Ernst Sorge.

3. The coastal land of Greenland was divided at this point into three sub-provinces: North Greenland, South Greenland and East Greenland. Each one included several 'colony-districts' (*kolonidistrikter*, sing. *kolonidistrikt*), which included one colony (*koloni*), several outposts (*udsteder*, sing. *udsted*) and smaller settlements. The administrative centre was Qeqertarsuaq/Godhavn in North Greenland and Nuuk/Godthåb in South Greenland. Whereas Uummannaq was a *koloni*, Nuugaatsiaq and Illorsuit were *udsteder*.

4. A particularly spectacular incident was described by the *New York Times* (21 August 1932, p.9). Flying too low, Udet crashed into an iceberg. Saved by the Inuit in their kayaks, he was then taken to the iceberg on which Angst, Schneeberger and Fanck were filming. Within minutes the iceberg disintegrated ('calved'), throwing crew and equipment into the water below and causing the film crew's ship nearby to capsize. The Inuit rescued ten men and two women, but much equipment was destroyed. Fanck in his account reveals the extent to which the crew were shocked at their close encounter with death (1933: 36–9). He states that the Inuit were horrified at the danger the crew willingly undertook. As a consequence Knud Rasmussen tried to convince Fanck to confine his effects to studio models (Fanck 1933: 36–9).

5. Information from Scholz-Sorge (n.2 above).

6. National Archives, Washington, Still Pictures Branch, Peary Collection, catalogue number 302-NT-542-H.

7. Three polar bears and two seals were taken from Hagenbeck Zoo in Hamburg to Greenland. None of the animals survived the journey. The polar bears were shot, the seals expired during the journey or soon after (Riefenstahl 1992: 104; Sorge 1935: 27–30, 206; Sorge 1996).

8. Written materials 4.3–85/03–0 'SOS Eisberg', Stiftung Deutsche Kinemathek, Sammlung Richard Angst (Richard Angst Collection).

9. This correspondence indicates that Arnold Fanck was thinking of using the surplus footage taken for *SOS Eisberg* – of which there was quite a substantial amount – to make three documentaries. Interestingly, it also states that extra footage was allocated to Knud Rasmussen's film *Palos Brudefærd* ('Palo's Wedding'), made in 1933, released posthumously in 1934. Written materials 4.3–85/03–0 'SOS Eisberg', Stiftung Deutsche Kinemathek, Sammlung Richard Angst (Richard Angst Collection).

10. In Sorge (1935: 18, 48–9) Lindeck's photographs do include pictures of the village dogs and general filming.

11. Taken mostly by Ferdinand Vogel and Ernst Udet. The latter took the aerial photographs (Fanck 1933: T.12, T.13, T.50, T.51).

12. Kayaking also stands metonymically for a range of skills attributed to the Inuit. The 'Eskimo' are said to possess an acute sense of hearing – always aware of the approach of a motorboat or Udet's plane (Fanck 1933: 61, 63–4). They are passionate and excellent hunters – the only ones who readily chase and are capable of 'lassooing' (*sic*) the frequently escaping polar bears (Riefenstahl 1992: 119).

13. Information from Scholz-Sorge (n.2 above).

14. Fienup-Riordan argues that this common representation of Inuit culture as fragile is based on a premise of it being authentically primitive and essentially civilised (1992: 14–15).

15. There is a lack of clarity concerning Rasmussen's role. Correspondence in Rigsarkivet (National Archives), Underingsministeriet (Foreign Office), 1909–45, file no.8.X.17, indicates a degree of suspicion about the German film crew's motives which it argues only the involvement of Knud Rasmussen can dispel.

16. Information from Scholz-Sorge (n.2 above).

17. Information from Scholz-Sorge (n.2 above).

18. Udet seemed to have a close relationship with the people of Illorsuit. He alone lived within the community, away from the rest of the crew, although near the American illustrator Rockwell Kent (Udet 1935: 166, 173–5; Sorge 1935: 19, 64–5). Other members of the crew lived at a distance from the settlements as they did not wish to share the living conditions of the local communities (the dogs, however, did not keep away) (Sorge 1935: 154; Riefenstahl 1992: 115–16, 118; Scholz-Sorge, n.2 above). The crew themselves were not spared some unflattering representations by those other Europeans who knew the communities of north-west Greenland (Freuchen 1954: 237; Kent 1935: 316–17; Kent 1962: 265; Kleivan 1987: 182).

19. Information from Scholz-Sorge (n.2 above).

Stephen Loring

# In Torngak's Realm:
# The Nineteenth-Century Photography of
# Moravian Missionaries in Labrador

## Introduction

Labrador – for many *qallunaat* the name has been synonymous with a bleak and barren landscape, an ice-scoured wilderness, isolated and forlorn. While it was among the first lands in the New World to be visited by Europeans, it remained among the last to be mapped. Prior to the inroads of the missionaries it was inhabited by malevolent spirits, by Torngak. It was, in the celebrated words of Jacques Cartier – who despaired of ever finding a harbour – the 'land that God gave Cain'. Yet this Cain's Land, this realm of Torngak, was home for small bands of scattered Inuit families whose knowledge and skills had made that land their home.

Following an initial disastrous attempt in 1752, the United Brethren, the Moravian Church, was successful in establishing a mission to the Inuit of Labrador in 1771 (Davey 1905; Hiller 1966, 1971; H. Kleivan 1966). The first settlement at Nain soon expanded to include 'Christian Inuit communities' at Okak (1776), Hopedale (1782) and Hebron (1830). During the later nineteenth century additional mission stations were established so that the Moravian hegemony extended along the entire Labrador coast between Hamilton Inlet and Ungava Bay (fig.1).

In Labrador, as throughout the non-literate world, one consequence of the successful European invasion is the domination of a history that relies on documents rather than oral tradition; documents that justify an ideology of colonialism and which shape, manipulate and interpret perceptions of the past. Western scholarship, its science and letters, has for the most part marginalised the voice of indigenous peoples. This lopsided view of culture and history has had a devastating impact on recent genera-tions of northern villagers, who, having suffered from having much of their cultural heritage defined by outsiders, are only now asserting the primacy of their voice and the voice of their ancestors.

Historical research pertaining to Labrador's indigenous Inuit and Innu populations brings one up against two extraordinary archives: (1) the records of the Hudson's Bay Company, incorporated in 1670 and active in Labrador since the late eighteenth century, and (2) the records of the Church of the United Brethren – the Moravian Mission. Much of what is known about the recent history of the Inuit people of Labrador is derived from the writings of Moravian missionaries. Fortunately, part of the Protestant work ethic that the Moravians embraced was a compulsion for documentation. Consequently, the Moravian Archives (at Bethlehem, Pennsylvania, London and Herrnhut, and in the National Archives of Canada and the Provincial Archives in St John's, Newfoundland) contain an incredible treasure trove of written and visual materials: the *Periodical Accounts*,[1] diaries, station reports, ecclesiastical musings, shipping inventories, letters, store accounts and photography, which – coupled with the duration of these records (now for over 200 years) – provide an extraordinary picture of the social dynamics, subsistence strategies and nature of Inuit participation and involvement with the Moravians, thus providing a very rich perception of the past, biased as it is by the structure of Moravian beliefs and practices.

Throughout the Moravian tenure in Labrador there was a persistent controversy over the problem of combining the Moravians' primary evangelical objectives with their very lucrative entrepreneurial and trade initiatives. The

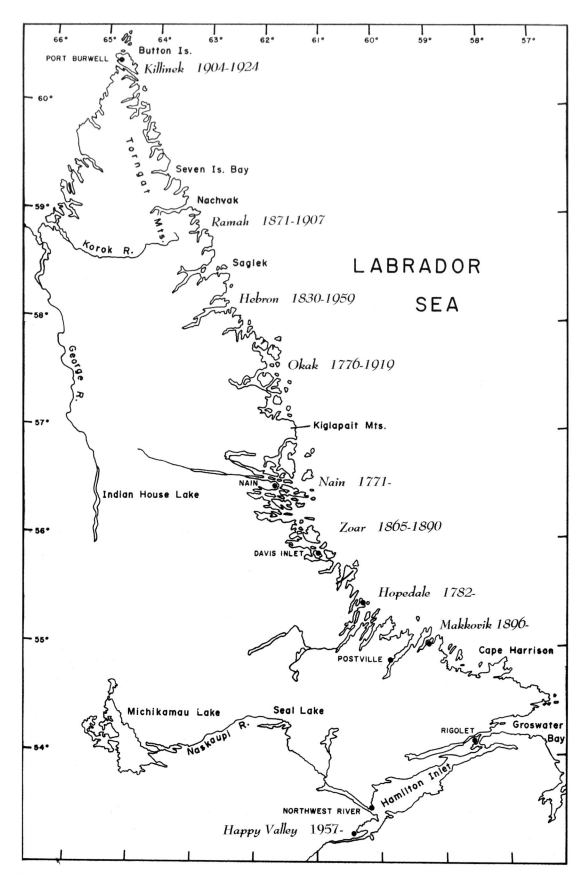

Fig.1. Labrador with mission stations and dates.

Moravians strove forcefully to present this trade as a necessary inconvenience tangential to their primary purpose of saving souls. In order to proselytise for Christ, the Moravians had first to attract and then anchor the nomadic Inuit to the Christian communities they desired to create in the wilderness. This they were only able to do by acquiescing to the demands of the Inuit to provide them with European manufactured products, food items and raw materials. As the

Christian communities grew and became more linked to a global world economy, the Moravians sought to justify their mercantile interests to their European supporters by elaborating on their need to continue the struggle against the heathen elements in Inuit society. In so doing, the Moravians 'constructed' a dichotomy between the orderly hard-working 'Christian Inuit' of the mission villages and the 'Heathens' – the feral, wandering hunters of the north. With the advent of photography the Moravians were provided with a new means to present themselves and their work to Christian charities and philanthropists in Great Britain and Europe.

## The Moravian Church

The United Brethren, or Moravians, are a Protestant missionary sect that originated in central Europe during the late fifteenth century. In 1722 a number of Moravians congregated about the estate of Count Zinzendorf at Herrnhut near the German–Polish border, and formed the nucleus of the modern Church. Communal life at Herrnhut emphasised diligence, work, orderliness, punctuality and frugality. It became the social model to which the Moravians believed all human societies should aspire. The certainty of their moral and spiritual belief sustained them in their confrontations with indigenous and non-Western peoples throughout the non-Christian world. The Moravians were one of the first Protestant Churches to promote a foreign mission enterprise beginning in the West Indies in 1732, and expanding thereafter to maroon communities in Nicaragua and Dutch Guiana, to Greenland, Labrador, eastern North America, India, Tibet, South Africa and Alaska.

## Moravians in Labrador

### LESSONS IN POWER AND AUTHORITY

The Moravians' zeal, which sustained them in the wilderness of Labrador, was founded in their belief in their ability, with God's help, to transform the barrenness and anarchy of the heathen's country into a land of Christian piety and order. The Inuit proved to be formidable adversaries. Through tact, diplomacy, intrigue and aggression the Inuit had in the two centuries prior to 1750 gained considerable experience in dealing with Europeans, and had acquired a strong desire for European manufactured products and raw materials. During this early contact period in Labrador, historical records and archaeology point to the emergence of a group of powerful native leaders who were able to consolidate their authority along two lines of control: one eco-

nomic, as 'trading captains' or 'big men', powerful family heads who controlled access to European products; and the other religious, in the form of the powerful shaman-sorcerers, or *angakkuk*, who interceded with the powers of the spirit world. Often, prominent Inuit 'leaders' would be both. It is exactly along these lines, access to trade goods and as an intermediary between humans and the spiritual world, that the Moravian agenda in Labrador would have coincided with traditional trends of authority.

Prior to the arrival of the Moravians there existed a state of internecine raiding, murder and anarchy along the southern Labrador coast where European and Inuit cultures collided. This situation precluded the expansion of British interests in their North Atlantic fishery. The Governor of Newfoundland, Sir Hugh Palliser, acting with the belief that the missionaries' influence might prove the means to pacify the Inuit, was instrumental in arranging for a royal land-grant and trading concession in northern Labrador in 1769.

The Moravians established their first Labrador mission at Nain in 1771 and from that time forward the Moravian and Inuit identities have been closely entwined. Except for the annual voyage of their supply vessel, the *Harmony*, and the chance visit from fishermen and explorers, the Moravians were completely cut off from their European homeland. No one can doubt the power of the faith that sustained them in their self-imposed exile.

The early years of the Labrador mission were fraught with tension as the memory of native treachery remained:

All accounts agreed in representing them as heathen of the worst stamp, treacherous, cruel and bloodthirsty in their dealings, with scarcely a trace of religion of any kind, enslaved by the darkest superstition, and entirely ruled by the powerful influences of their sorcerers. (PA28:1, 1871)

In the Labrador of the Moravians the wild barren land was a mute testament to the wilderness of men's souls. In order to win conscripts for Christ, the Moravians had to challenge the authority of the traditional leaders. While the battle for souls may have taken place on a spiritual plane, the battlefield resided on earth, and had much to do with access to resources. Throughout the nineteenth century, as the Inuit become more desirous and more dependent on European supplies and more acquiescent to the advantages of seasonal residence at the mission village, there is a transition from the nomadic, independent life that characterised traditional Inuit society to one that coincided with the Moravian precepts of a Christian community.

RIGHT
Fig.2. Nain,
Labrador, c.1790.

BELOW
Fig.3. Nain,
Labrador, c.1880.

## THE GROWTH OF CHRISTIAN COMMUNITIES

The architecture and landscaping of the mission stations was a powerful demonstration of Christian confrontation with the forces of chaos in the wild lands that surrounded them; mission stations imposed order on the wilderness. This physical transformation was a bulwark against the despair at the slow progress of Christianity among the Inuit; it was also a very tangible testimony to the existence, promise and potential of the mission. That these Moravian views sometimes clashed with those of the Inuit is no surprise: 'At first [they were] opposed to our idea of building the huts in a straight line, they eventually acquiesced in our wish and were finally quite pleased with the appearance of the row of . . . houses, covered with sod.' (PA26:365–6, 1866.)

Moravian Archives have extensive visual materials documenting the growth of the Christian communities in Labrador: originally (in the eighteenth and early nineteenth centuries) drawings, maps and plats (fig.2), and later on photographs (fig.3). Interestingly, there are very few drawings or representations of the Inuit in the early Moravian documents. With photography it becomes possible to testify to the success of mission activities by bringing the faces of the Inuit attached to the mission villages to the Moravian authorities and supporters in Europe.

The mission at Nain had not been established long before the Moravians realised that the varied resources on which the Inuit depended necessitated a high degree of mobility. However, not only did a wandering, rootless existence threaten

LEFT
Fig.4. 'A good catch of seals', vicinity of Hebron, prior 1900. Photograph by Br. Townley. A missionary stands in his spotless woollen 'dickey' while beside him a group of Inuit men (dirty and wet) pause in their work to be photographed. Two women (left) ignore the camera. Photograph purchased by E. B. Delabarre, summer 1900.

BELOW
Fig.5. Working in the blubber yard, Hebron, c.1900.

the pastoral idyll that the Moravians envisioned for their 'flock', but it was readily apparent that once removed from the missionary presence the Inuit would revert to their 'traditional', i.e. 'heathen', ways. The Moravians sought to control these tendencies and practices with the opening of additional mission stations. This expansion had several objectives: (1) it sought to extend the missionary influence to areas which the Inuit had recourse to move to; (2) it sought to counter the necessity for Inuit to travel down the Labrador coast to intercept European traders and fishermen; and (3) it provided a buffer for the 'civilised' or 'Christian Inuit' from their heathen, barbarous relatives in the north.

By 1824 Nain and Hopedale were Christian communities. Part of the Moravian strategy of control was to encourage the Inuit to maintain a relative degree of sedentariness, to keep them apart from the disruptive influences of their northern relatives. The Moravians thus encouraged changes in Inuit subsistence activities.

Around 1800 they introduced the use of nets for catching seals (Brice-Bennet 1981). Strung across narrow inner island passages, large numbers of migrating harp seals could be captured. While Moravian accounts presented this 'industry' as a means to assure a winter food supply for both the Inuit and their dogs, the excess blubber, rendered into oil, was a principal component of the Moravian trading economy (figs 4 and 5). The Moravians also encouraged the Inuit to adopt a summer cod fishery. Surplus dried cod was traded with the mission. Trade, primarily in dried fish and seal oil, but to some degree including furs and handicrafts, was critical to the economic well-being of the mission.

THE MISSION ECONOMY

From their inception the Moravian missions in Labrador were set up to cater to both the spiritual and material needs of the Inuit. The Moravians had a trading monopoly along the Labrador coast but sought to deflect the criticism this invoked by trying to separate two spheres of activity in Labrador. Trade was placed under the control of the 'Brethren Society for the Furtherance of the Gospel Among the Heathen' in London, which oversaw the financial management of the Labrador Mission. But this responsibility was a dilemma and set in place a source of conflict that was never resolved (Williamson 1964). The Moravians were frustrated by the Inuit resistance to frugality and to storing (away) food and resources against a future period of want, as well as their resistance to sustained employment. The Inuit, on the other hand, never divorced the store from the mission, so they were astonished at the meanness and the hypocrisy of the mission traders during times of starvation and the unsympathetic attitude towards debt accumulation which flew in the face of both the Moravians' Christian tenets and intrinsic Inuit custom.

There was however, as usual, great liberality on the part of those who had been successful; they willingly divided the spoil with their less-favoured countrymen. It is an old custom, which, like several others somewhat similar in character, is kept up and watched over with jealous care, to divide all the animals captured among the natives who frequent the same hunting-ground. (PA25:310, Nain 1864)

The mission's trading agenda was controversial not only in Labrador but in Europe as well.

Our only aim in carrying on this trade is, however, to benefit the poor Eskimoes, and raise funds for carrying on the missionary work to the glory of God: the trade forms a sort of outward bond of union between us and the natives, which is valuable, especially as long as God's Spirit has not wrought a spiritual union. (PA:16, Nachvak 1868)

The expense of running the Labrador missions was offset both by Christian philanthropy, principally through the London Society for the Furtherance of the Gospel, and by the 'Labrador trade' which depended on Inuit labour. Products from Labrador included a fine grade of oil, baleen (in the eighteenth century), furs, fish and handicrafts. The seal fishery was of paramount importance for both the Inuit and the Moravians, as the meat fed people and dogs, the skins were used in traditional clothing, and the blubber was made into oil for export. The late autumn/early winter migration of harp seals could be extraordinarily productive,[2] and by 1870 enough cod and salmon were being caught and dried to warrant a separate ship being sent 'down north' to collect this product.

CONFLICTING WORLD VIEWS

In 1861 the Moravian Brother Reichel estimated the Inuit population along the entire Labrador coast at 1500, of which 1163 were under the influence of the Moravian Brethren (Gosling 1910: 3030). The approximately 350 unaccounted persons mostly comprised the small scattered family groups who lived and hunted in the Torngat Mountain region of northern Labrador between Saglek and Cape Chidley. These were the heathen Inuit who were so dreaded by the Moravians.

A missionary stationed at Ramah in 1872 described the Inuit perception that linked the spiritual and pragmatic:

I have had occasion often to observe, during the winter, that these heathen Eskimoes fancy that by becoming Christians they would be better off in temporal matters, and more successful in their struggle for maintenance. Many a time I told them that our Saviour had promised to remember the temporal wants of His people, for He only entertained thoughts of love and benevolence towards them; but that His chief desire was, that their souls might be saved for the life to come; that our Saviour well knew what was good and beneficial for us, and that if we had all our hearts could wish in worldly things, we should probably often forget Him, and be content if our souls perish with hunger. (PA28:354, 1871)

Throughout the nineteenth century the Moravians persisted in presenting the Inuit of Labrador as essentially two discrete populations, the Christian Inuit settled in their vicinity, and the heathens – the Northlanders – from northern Labrador and Kangivia (Ungava) who lived in their isolated camps scattered along the coast.

**Inuit identity: Christian and heathen**
The construct of the 'Christian Inuit' that emerges from the pages of the *Periodical Accounts* incorporates a number of attributes: the Christian Inuit were devout (fig.6), clean, hard-working and industrious. Attached to one of the mission stations, they dressed in clothing made from cloth and wool (fig.7), and lived in their own single-family homes, with glass windows and stoves:

The walls are papered with bright colours and adorned with pictures, and each house has its clock, mirror, and petroleum-lamp. Few chairs are to be seen, as boxes can be used for this purpose or the table. The clothing, too, has become European. (PA30:146–7, 1876)

They were provident:

Under the influence of Christian teaching some improvement has taken place, and there are not a few who, by careful economy, have become owners of good boats, and log-houses with pictures and looking glasses on the walls, and iron stoves to warm them. (PA28:63, 1871)

They were exposed to the refinements of civilised society – school and church – and musically adept. Fond of liturgical music, hymns and chorales, they formed choirs, string quartets and

Fig.7. 'Old Ruth in her best dress.' Okak, c.1905. From, *Among the Eskimos of Labrador*, Samuel King Hutton (1912).

OPPOSITE ABOVE
Fig.8. A heathen Inuit man and his two wives, from Ungava, visiting a mission station in northern Labrador, c.1880.

traffic ... when one of the heathen, dissatisfied with the price offered for a seal-skin full of holes, and disappointed at not obtaining a present for himself and his company, became angry, and seizing Br. Ribbach's hand, exclaimed in a threatening tone, 'Now, you are in my power! Will you give me a present or not?' ... this is another proof how mistaken is the notion of those, who think that the Esquimaux are naturally a harmless and good-natured race. They are as savage as they were ninety years ago, unless they are converted by the power of God, or restrained by fear, or by the desire to be richly rewarded for their submissive conduct; and hence we have no hesitation to declare our firm belief, that the Esquimaux residing from Saeglek to the North of the Ungava Bay, if tempted by their natural covetousness, and disappointed in their expectations, are quite capable of murdering an European for the sake of a trifle. (PA24:546, 1862)

The heathen were idolatrous, they wore amulets and were subject to the power of the *angakkuk*. Dirty and unkempt, the women carried their infant children naked in their hoods (PA23:86 1858). They were nomadic:

You must continue to bear in mind, that the roving habits of the Esquimaux retard their progress in civilization, and even those who have become obedient to the faith, must necessarily retain the manners and customs received from their fathers, in as these are fixed by the nature of the country.' (PA24: 468, Nain 1863)

They were lazy and improvident in that they refused to put aside food against future contingencies.[3] They wore the skins of animals, ate uncooked food, were polygamous (fig.8), lived in sod- and earth-covered semi-subterranean huts (fig.9) heated by seal-oil lamps and stoves. Their dead were buried under rocks on the hillside.

This dichotomy between the pacified Christian and the wild nomadic heathen pervades the Moravian documentation including the photographic record. And while the *Periodical Accounts* present these two groups as distinct and separate entities, a careful reading suggests that by the latter half of the nineteenth century we are dealing with more or less a single population, a portion of which changes their identity as they alternate between residence at one of the mission stations and prolonged encampments in the country beyond mission influence. There were many reasons for Inuit families to sever periodically their ties with a particular community. People would leave for opportunities at better hunting,[4] to live with relatives and to escape from the tensions of the community. Certain infractions of village morals, primarily related to sexual impropriety

brass bands that played 'in a very creditable manner' (PA30:148, 1877). Their dead were buried in churchyards.

On the other hand, there were the 'Heathen Eskimos' whose annual winter visits to the mission stations are a re-occurring lament in the pages of the *Periodical Accounts*. Ostensibly, these visits were to renew kin relations and acquire European manufactured products, but they also provided the northern Inuit groups with an opportunity to observe the social and economic consequences of an intimate association with the Moravians.

While the Moravians dreaded the disruptive influences of the northern visitors on their normally complacent congregation they also saw in it a challenge to the furtherance of their mission in Labrador:

A company of heathen, from Nachvak, with their sorcerer, arrived here in a boat, for the purpose of

and/or drinking, could incur the wrath of the Moravians and lead to temporary expulsion, and an instant shuffle in the rolls of Christian and heathen head-counts.

Through the *Periodical Accounts*, and other related publications, the work of the Moravians was made known to a wider audience. The profitability of the Labrador mission was predicated on both the revenue generated by the trading enterprise and by the munificence of benefactors. In order to continue to garner such support the Moravians needed the heathens as a cause to rally around. As late as 1898 a mission plea specifically recognises the heathen cause: 'It will require £300 a year . . . to provide this clergyman . . . for the heathen Esquimaux. Out of the fabulous wealth of England can it not be found?' (Pilot 1898:45.) The Moravians could not accept a world inhabited by northern spirits subordinate to the power of the shamans, and they struggled to bring salvation and Christianity to Labrador. Yet the mission documents continue to propagate and foster the notion of two discrete Inuit identities long after most 'heathen' elements had been abandoned.

## Moravian photography in Labrador

The earliest extant photographs from Labrador are not Moravian, they appear to be those taken by Mr P. C. Duchochis for the US Eclipse Expedition to North Aulatsivik Island during the summer of 1860. In addition to a series of the eclipse (alas clouds interfered at the critical moment), there are a number of scenes of expedition members at their observatory and camp in the Torngat Mountains. Duchochis took additional photographs of the Inuit whom the expedition met near Nain and at Domino in southern Labrador but these have not been located.

Notions of the sublime and the beautiful inherent in the grand scenery of the Labrador coast had two of America's foremost landscape painters of the Luminist school converge on Labrador:

BOTTOM
Fig.9. 'Old Tuglavi's Iglo', Killinek Island 1908. 'Tuglavi is a famous old heathen chief, now in his second childhood, and this is his house. It is a gloomy little hut of turf and stones, floored with trampled mud.' From *Among the Eskimos of Labrador*, Samuel King Hutton (1912).

Frederic Church in 1859 (Noble 1862), and William Bradford, who made his first voyage to Labrador in 1861 (Packard 1885).[5] The Bradford expedition of 1864 employed a photographer, William Pierce, who arranged for a group of Inuit to pose for him in Hopedale. Other early photographers in Labrador include H. N. Robinson, who produced a series of forty-six stereoviews 'Labrador Life and Scenery' in 1876 (Darrah 1971:147; Vernon Doucette, personal communication), and Lucien M. Turner, a naturalist and ethnographer from the Smithsonian, who photographed both the Inuit and the Innu of northern Quebec and Labrador during his stay at Fort Chimo (Kuujjuak) between 1882 and 1884. I am unaware of other pioneering photographers working in Labrador, but given the interest in the region, inspired both by the work of the Luminist painters and by the Arctic explorations of Elisha Kent Kane, Isaac Israel Hayes and Charles Francis Hall, some are likely to exist.

The most expansive collection of historic photography pertaining to the Inuit of Labrador is situated at the Archiv der Brüder Unität in Herrnhut, Germany, which houses a collection of approximately a thousand photographs from Labrador c.1870–1935. There are to my knowledge no early photographs (daguerreotypes or calotypes) at Herrnhut; the earliest images appear to date from around 1870.

In the back of the *Periodical Accounts* for 1875 (vol.29) there is an advertisement for 'Labrador Views, photographed from Nature' by H. Linklater, the captain of the Moravians' supply vessel the *Harmony*. Also on sale (for the benefit of the mission) were photographs of a 'Group of Native Men', and a 'Group of Native Women on board the *Harmony*', as well as photographs of the plucky mission ship itself.

In the *Periodical Accounts* there are occasional references to Moravian photographers, which coupled with some contextual evidence in the photographs themselves, provides insight into where and when and by whom the photographs were made. While the earliest photographer appears to be Linklater, his opportunity to photograph was limited by the short time he had available while the *Harmony* made its hurried round to mission stations during the short summer voyage. The first conscientious Moravian photographer appears to be Brother Hermann T. Jannasch who began taking photographs in Nain sometime around 1880. He carried his camera with him on a winter sledge journey to Hopedale in 1887–8. He is described as 'the photographer among our Labrador missionaries, and we have to thank him for some excellent pictures of per-

sons and places in that cold land' (LaTrobe 1888–9). Jannasch's pictures were very popular, being sold by the Moravians at their London office as prints, stereoviews and cartes-de-visite. Jannasch's *oeuvre* was clearly substantial and it is likely that much of the Herrnhut collection from Nain in the nineteenth century is his work.

Other Moravian photographers are identified with other missions: (1) Samuel King Hutton, missionary and doctor, served in Okak from 1902 to about 1910 and produced an extensive corpus of photographs that appear widely in Moravian publications (including his own book: Hutton 1912) at the turn of the century; (2) a Mr Bohlmann, stationed at Hebron in 1906, is responsible for an interesting series of photographs (approximately 105), detailing, among other subjects, Inuit house construction and wage labourers at the station; (3) the southern region of missionary activity, at Makkovik, is documented by Walter W. Perrett who photographed the erection of the church there in 1896–7, as well as informal aspects of mission life (picnics and frolics in the snow); and (4) among a number of more informal pictures and snapshots taken after 1920, there is a group of approximately ninety-five pictures taken by Revd Paul Hettasch in Nain between 1926 and 1931 and a few by his son Seigfried between 1930 and 1940. These later photographs are more candid then earlier images, they tend to be informal views of people in the village (fig.10) and may in part be a response to a circular issued by church leaders in Herrnhut in 1925 requesting views of mission activities worldwide (MR489:9151). They also suggest a growing familiarity on the part of the Inuit with the presence of cameras as well as the technological advances in cameras and film that negated cumbersome equipment and formal posing.

While the Herrnhut collection has limited documentation, some prints are annotated and there are sometimes chronological clues that can be used in ordering the collection, such as the building sequence at the different mission stations (e.g. the Ramah mission, established 1871, closed 1907); the presence of boats and expeditions (e.g. Donald MacMillan and the *Bowdoin* 1927–8); and the tenure of identified missionaries (e.g. Walter Perrett arrives in Labrador in 1892).

Taken as a corpus of work the Moravian photograph collection reveals several themes. First of all, there are relatively few landscapes and hardly any natural history subjects. By and large the Moravian landscape is a cultural phenomenon. Surrounded by the unrelenting wilderness and their isolation, the Moravian photographers looked inwardly upon themselves and their community. There are numerous photographs of the mission stations, often with the *Harmony* in the background. Nain, Okak and Hebron are well documented, Hopedale and Makkovik a little less so, Ramah and Burwell poorly. There appears to be but two photographs taken at Zoar. Missionaries and their families – often posed on the church steps – are a popular subject: solid, sober, middle class. By far and away the most common theme is the Inuit.[6] Photographs of subsistence activities include men in kayaks and with dogteams and sleds, men preparing to go hunting, women fishing and gathering wood, and people standing beside recently butchered animals (walrus, beluga whales, seals, bear) and at their summer fishing camps. But the largest set of photographs are of the Inuit in the communities, posed singly and in groups. The anonymity of these village pictures – few of the individuals are named – serves to epitomise the Moravian ideal of what their aspirations for the Inuit were. Within a few generations the Inuit have been brought from the darkness into the light and set firmly on the road to Christian morality and responsibility.

The formality in many of these group photographs is apparent (frontispiece). Intended for the edification of church members and a lay audience far across the sea, the photographs are for the most part conventional portraits that have been constructed for the purpose of presenting the success of the Moravian labours in making a Christian land out of the wilderness.[7]

It is harder to discern what the Inuit thought of the camera beyond its troubling capacity to intrude. There is at least one obligatory story of the camera as soul-catcher, as told by the Moravian doctor Samuel Hutton during a visit to Port Burwell in 1908:

It is not to be wondered at that superstition is strong among these Killinek folk, so lately utterly heathen, without knowledge of Christianity or of civilisation. The first glimpse I had of it was in the fear that some of them had of being photographed.

I chanced to meet a young man whose face was a perfect picture of the heathen Eskimo type, and to my delight he was willing to pose then and there for his portrait.

I got an excellent likeness of him from the front and then made ready for a side view. But he would have no more. 'Tâva,' he said (that is completely finished). I tried to coax him. Would he have it done if there were other Eskimos with him? He hesitated. 'Imakka' (perhaps), he said. 'Then go and fetch that group of men to stand with you.'

Off he trotted, and I saw him palavering with the men. Presently he started back; but stopped at a fair

Fig.10. 'Keeophas & Jeremias, 4-year-old eskimo children carry water.' (Photographer: S. Hettasch, Nain, 1930)

distance and shouted 'They cannot come: the lady has their ghosts in her box,' pointing to a lady who was wandering on the beach with a kodak, and who had apparently just photographed the group. Then he fled to his tent on the hillside! (Hutton 1912: 41–2)

There is little doubt in my mind that this narrative, presented as a quaint tale of superstition, masks a disturbing tendency of camera-wielding *qallunaat*, outsiders and visitors for the most part, to act as if their camera was a licence to violate polite behaviour and personal privacy.

I do not know when people in the Labrador communities began to take photographs themselves. The Torngasok Cultural Centre in Nain and the Them Days organisation in Goose Bay/Happy Valley have both initiated projects based on archiving the images from family photograph albums. Should these become available I suspect the perception of Inuit culture would vary dramatically from that presented by the Moravians. It seems surprising that, given the alacrity with which the Labrador Inuit adopted European inventions, no Inuit appears to have attempted photography at an early date. Some sense of the historical narrative nature of photography was long apparent to the Inuit, as the Moravians had been using magic-lantern slides for religious instruction since at least 1865 (PA25: 543). During the winter of 1877–8 Inuit visiting the mission station at Ramah (established 1871) were shown magic-lantern slides which 'filled these visitors of ours with astonishment, for which they could find no words' (PA31:29). Hutton used his own photographs mixed with images from Bible stories to provide lessons in morals and 'sanitary reform': 'The magic lantern was a great help in this direction: the people shouted with glee to see their own faces on the screen, and sat quietly listening while I told them some Bible story or talked of better houses and ideal home life.' (Hutton 1912:317.)

## Conclusions: a picture is worth a thousand words

There is a tower of rock set upon the summit of the highest hill above the abandoned station at Hebron.[8] Here the missionaries sometimes stood gazing seaward, anxious for the first sight of the *Harmony*. Even on the fairest summer's day the landscape is stark and imposing – and melancholy: the cemetery with its fallen fence and toppling monuments, the weather-beaten facade of the mission building, the garden, walk-ways and Inuit houses all overgrown (figs 11 and 12). No one standing next to these navigation beacons and gazing over such a wild romantic scene can doubt the remarkable dedication and piety of the brethren for their work and their beliefs, nor gain some inkling of the thoughts and aspirations of those stern, sober, self-exiled missionaries.

The introspective power of historical photography is well known, as is its propensity for misrepresentation and selectivity. When the corpus of Moravian photography is considered as a whole, one is struck by the paternalism and social control the images imply, especially those where the Inuit are posed, dressed in clean clothes (often the formal Church dress: white cloth *sillapâks* and dickeys), stiffly and in rows: in front of their houses, in groups of Church 'helpers', in choirs and in brass bands. The Inuit are domesticated. Rarely in these photographs is there a flicker of levity or mirth. There is no denying the power of these photographs to entrance and delight us with their window into the past, especially when so much of that past has been denied its descendants. Not surprisingly, the photographs tell us as much about the photographers as they do about their subjects. As a body of work, one can't help but be struck by the ideology of domination that these images convey. There are few smiling faces, few home interiors, few camp scenes, few relaxing moments. There is little evidence to suggest that there was much Inuit consultation in the construction of this collection. It was designed to be a Moravian story. While not unexpected, it is disturbing, nevertheless, to find a Moravian photographer exhibiting the tourists' stereotypical hubris at an encounter with an exotic native, albeit one who was a much respected village elder:

I gave up trying to draw any information out of him after I had tried to take his portrait. I armed myself with a ship's biscuit, and went in search of Tuglavi. I found him near his iglo, and offered him the biscuit.

He took it with a most delighted 'Thank-you': 'Nakome-e-e-ek,' he said, 'nakomek.'
'Adsiliorlagit-ai' (let me take your photograph).
'Sua?' (what?)
'Will you let me make a likeness of you?'
'Atsuk (I don't know). May I eat the biscuit?'
'Yes, presently; just stand over here.'
'Nerrilangale' (let me eat it), and he turned his back on me.
'All right; just turn round and stand still a moment.'
'Nerrilangale, ner-ri-langa-le-e-e-e'; and the poor old man broke down into sobs and ambled off home munching his precious biscuit. (Hutton 1912: 39–40)

I don't know which is more disturbing: the callous disrespect of an eminent Inuit elder or the inherent language of racism and paternalism that is paraded in the quaintness of Hutton's remarks.

Through archaeology, oral history, and the reassessment of archival materials, the potential for a new dynamic multi-vocal 'history' of the Inuit people of Labrador is possible – a history that celebrates the extraordinary accomplishments of the ancestors through the experiences, observations and memories of both native and non-native eyes. I was struck by the comments of an Inuit elder from Keewatin whose thoughts were recorded several years ago in an issue of *Inuktitut* that dealt with cultural patrimony:

The *qallunaat* are different in this way too. Since they have recorded their history, they seem to know a lot. They can refer to books to check their history. The only thing they really believe is what has been written. I think because they know they can look things up, they depend on the written word and have shorter memories. Older Inuit have good memories of what happened years ago. Many of them can still easily recall an incident that occurred years ago. Long ago, we didn't have a system of writing or the necessary materials to record what happened in past times. Because things were not written down on paper, many people today will not believe what we tell them about our past. *The things that we talk about actually happened but they are accepted only as legends.* (Nutarakittuq 1990: 41, emphasis added.)

Much of the post-colonial critique of photography as it applies to people is framed within the context of 'taking' photographs (Brumbaugh 1996). Many museums are now redefining their commitment to native communities, by providing the means by which community members can

participate in the construction and interpretation of their past. Old photographs, the visual patrimony of the past, are a language that government and development interests can see and hear. The old photographs speak loudly: this is Inuit land, this is the land of their ancestors and their inheritance.

That the Inuit past belongs to them seems obvious, that it has – in some respects – been denied them is also apparent. The challenge and hope for the future is that archaeologists, anthropologists and historians, with their arcane skills and knowledge, learn to surrender the supremacy of their voice in order to hear the voice of the people whose life and land it is. In Labrador, as elsewhere in the Arctic, not to listen dooms the *quallunaat* to a history of the north that is as one-sided, as inherently silent and false, and as unforgiving as the black-and-white photographic legacy left us by the Moravians.

## Acknowledgements

I must thank the conference organisers and volume editors Jonathan King and Henrietta Lidchi for their patience, humour and elan at bringing this all together. To every academic there falls, from time to time (too infrequently, alas), these alchemical convergences of people and ideas that are exactly right. So, obviously, I must, and do, thank my fellow conference participants for their inspiration and insight.

My knowledge of the Moravian collections must be considered superficial, limited as it is by having spent just a week at the Archiv der Brüder Unität in Herrnhut in July 1995. More intensive research is needed. In Herrnhut my work in the archives was greatly facilitated by the linguistic accomplishments and the enthusiasm of my good buddy Joan Gero, and the extraordinary generosity of the archivist Ms E. v. Ungern and her staff, whose many considerations on my behalf I very gratefully acknowledge. Stephan Augustin, the curator/director of the Völkerkundemuseum Herrnhut, and Hans Rollman at Memorial University in St John's Newfoundland have guided me further than either suspects.

Finally, I would be remiss were I not to acknowledge my deep respect for the integrity of the Moravian brethren who laboured in Labrador. While their beliefs and behaviour and struggles are as foreign to me as those of the Inuit were to them, I am thankful for their archival legacy and I am in awe at the power of their vision.

## Notes

1. The *Periodical Accounts*, published annually between 1790 and 1960 by the Society for the Furtherance of the Gospel, contained abstracted accounts of mission letters and diaries from Moravian mission work worldwide.

2. The *Periodical Accounts* for 1860 contain the following passage: 'The flesh of these animals is the chief food of the Esquimaux. From 3000 to 4000 of them are taken on an average in a year at our four stations. It is affirmed, that the number of those caught along the whole coast, partly in nets, partly in kayaks, exceeds a million. Their number is said to be now decreasing, in consequence of which, more attention is paid than formerly to fishing. Cod, salmon and trout are the principal fish.' (PA24:275–6, 1862)

3. 'The rule is, to part with their fish and blubber and furs to any trader, who can supply them with various European articles of food, without bestowing a thought on the possible exigencies of a failure of their native food supplies in the long winter. This childish thoughtlessness is a source of great concern to the missionaries, and introduces much unpleasantness and difficulty in business transactions.' (PA28:63, 1871)

4 The Inuit hunter 'is unhappy, and feels unjustly treated, if any obstacle is placed in the way of his return to his natural pursuits. An equivalent in money or goods for the proceeds of the hunt, would not be a substitute to him for the loss of his favourite employment.' (PA25:92, Hebron 1863)

5. William Bradford led seven summer cruises to Labrador and Greenland between 1861 and 1869. On his most ambitious trip, to Greenland in 1869, Bradford was accompanied by Mr Dunmore and Mr Critcherson, two photographers from Boston, whose work, along with the earlier photographs by Pierce from Labrador, appear in Bradford's *The Arctic Regions* (1875). For more on Bradford see Condon (1989), and Wamsley and Barr (1996).

6. There were only ten images of the Innu (the Montagnais-Naskapi) in the Moravian Archive collection at Herrnhut.

7. In 1895 photographs of mission work begin to appear regularly in the *Periodical Accounts*, whose editors mined the Herrnhut archives for visual material from the world wide arena of Moravian missionary activity.

8. The dwindling population and the expense of keeping open this northernmost station caused its abandonment in 1959 and the relocation of the Inuit population south to Nain.

Simeonie Keenainak

# The Native Photograph

**Simeonie**

There was my father and his father and his brothers, they were the only people living at that time. I was born in December in the middle of the winter, I was born in a *qarmaaq*, as some of you will understand. Because I noticed a lot of you people are studying us, studying Inuit problems, so I will say I'm Inuit. My mouth and eyes may not look Inuit because my grandmother's mother was the daughter of a whaler. So I was born there and my *amuliak* cleaned me when I was born, and she in my culture, when the boy's born or the girl's born, is the first lady who cleans a baby. She used to tell the mother of the child what a boy was going to be good at when he grew up. So my grandmother, the lady who cleaned me up, told my mother that I was going to be a good hunter, plus I would be able to face another man without being afraid. That's what she said to my mother, and when I was a boy I felt I was born to be a hunter like Zebedee said yesterday, a boy was born to be a hunter, so I was one of them. The only good I had when I was a boy was as a hunter. I played like a hunter, and my father was the only hero, with my uncles, but my father was the hero I got, because I didn't know any other world, I didn't know that there were places like the south or white people. I never saw a white person until I was seven years old, so being a hunter was the only goal I had and when I grew up I was a hunter and I was good at it, and I achieved that, because it was the only goal I had. I liked animals, because all the hunters do, not just to kill them, but also to watch them along a landscape line. So that was that. I was hunter until I was twenty four years old, and then I was asked to work for the Royal Canadian Mounted Police, to be a guide for their patrols, and interpreter. I already spoke English

at that time, because I went to the Hamilton, Ontario for TB like many Inuit kids born up to then. So that was going on. I was really happy to work with the RCMP, because the RCMP were the first white people I saw in my camp. They went to our camp every year to patrol our camp, counting births, to make sure everything was all right there I guess. That was their job at the time, there was no crime, and a couple of years later, after I joined, my boss told me I was going to have to be a policeman, like the policemen that I worked with. So they wanted to send me down to Regina. So I was there like other RCMP. That went on for twenty one years, I was a Mountie for twenty one years, I went to different communities like round Baffin Island, that's how I get to know people from other communities like Mr Qulaut.

I worked with a guy named John Nicholls from Newfoundland, he was a mountie in Igloolik when I was there, in 1987 I think it was, or 1986, one or the other. He told me 'Simeonie, you like outdoors very much and you like the scenery and you like animals', he said 'Why don't you buy a camera, because you won't do what you do now, all the time, because you're going to be old, you might get ill in the future, so you can look up your pictures, and see what you did, what you enjoyed most in your life.' So then I bought a K1000, everybody had one, a Pentax K1000, that old automatic, I mean manual, so I had that and I take pictures, and the more I take I find photography got into me, like everybody else I guess. So I have collections of pictures of wild life as you can see, a little bit in the hall there, polar bears especially, because polar bears are a very important animal in our area, so I love to take polar bear pictures, and scenery, and people with traditional clothes. So I am still taking pictures

Fig.1. This snow house was shot in Igloolik, 1979, when I was an RCMP officer patrolling the land, that's what the Mounties do sometimes.

OPPOSITE ABOVE
Fig.2. People fishing in front of our house, in the middle of August or about then, in 1989. The char *iqaluk* feeds in salt water on the little shrimp, then it goes to the lakes to spend the winter, and comes down to the sea again in the spring. We used the *kakivak*, or leister, to spear the fish before we had fishing rods.

OPPOSITE BELOW
Fig.3. Black guillemot, *pitsiulaaq*, taken in July 1979, in Igloolik, in open water: the ice did not go away for a long time that year.

now but when some of you people talked about native photographers that have passed away I was thinking, I told myself, 'Am I going to be like them, you know, I'm not going to be known and go and die!' So that was in my mind. I really enjoy taking pictures like everybody else in this room I guess. You know I learned a lot here because I didn't know what we can do with pictures, I know I've seen some pictures of my great grandfather that I don't remember too well, I saw that, and so for that reason the pictures, my pictures some day are going to be our history because I take what the people do like hunting and that's how people were living for years and years, so I'm going to keep on doing it until I can't go out any more I guess. I really appreciate what I heard from you people, because I learned a lot from it. I never thought that I was going to gain something too much from what I did, so I got the idea of what to do with my work, and not just that. I wanted to see that everybody learnt a little more about it, but I don't have time. A lot of our history came from here, like religion and the whalers, all came from here, so I'm proud of it, to have even stepped out in London, England. I asked Zebedee to help me explain what we do he's a really good speaker. Zebedee, Mr Nungak, could you help me?

## Additional comments from Zebedee Nungak

And hold your applause for him, because it's his speech! I just wanted to, at his invitation and with the permission of Mr King, first of all thank the organisers of this conference for having invited us. It has heightened our awareness of the importance of the photograph as a historical record, as it is historical gold, if I can describe it that way. Its documentary value and the fact that people will continue to make sure that this sort of thing is preserved, not only preserved but circulated,

talked about and so on, is very important. When somebody asked me yesterday what should we do, or what can we do, to get more circulation of this historical gold, as I call it, I said somewhat in jest 'If you can submit to our absolute and every dictatorial order of what to do about it, we'd all live happily ever after!' I was being facetious, but attending this conference has given us an appreciation of the value of photography, especially Arctic photography. We have been given a very good appreciation of the problems the early photographers encountered in coming up with those images.

Now I want to fast-forward a little bit to what Simeonie does. Simeonie is a very accomplished photographer, widely known in Canada, not only in the north but elsewhere as his reputation as a photographer expands. As a hunter, we develop a very keen sense of observation and a hunter like him is there all year round. He is not there for the time period of an expedition. He is not there for an archaeological dig, he is there all year round living the life, using that keen sense of observation we all develop as hunters; and a hunter with a camera, I can see now, I can see more clearly now, is a producer of archival and historical gold. And so I will be back in my home land encouraging more of our people, who are there all year round doing what they do, to get more cameras and take more pictures, and appreciate the value of these pictures, so Simeonie won't have to wait till after he's thirty or forty years dead not only to get the recognition but to demonstrate the value of his work while he's still able to enjoy the benefits of it! So I think we all thank you for reflecting that back to us. Besides being a former RCMP officer and an accomplished photographer, Simeonie is also an excellent accordion player! So we were just in a music shop at noon and we played a few duets on a button accordion, some jigs and reels, and we had some Londoners' toes tapping.

So, thanks again, I know that there's only four of us Inuit. I'm sorry if I don't count the one from Alaska who was here, but we are accustomed to being a minority in such gatherings but we don't rant and rave about it. We appreciate what we can get out of attending these things, we take back to our respective communities the things we have learned and the insights we have gained in attending your forum. Perhaps at some future gathering you will be in the minority and the Simeonies and the Zebedees will be in the majority, but I have no quarrel with the equation here. As we say, we truly appreciate having observed the tremendous work that has gone on in this field of activity. Thank you very much.

Fig.4. This picture was taken round end of August, I'm not sure of the exact date. This is a big chunk of ice *gugbuck*, couple of years old ice, near Pangnirtung, 12 or 13 miles into Cumberland Sound.

Fig.5. Owl, *uppik*, taken 1½ miles from Pang, behind in the mountains. This was photographed during the first week in September; I would say that the bird was born in July. He's just beginning to fly, and, having to rest I was able to get close to him, using a zoom lens.

Fig.6. A young bull caribou, *tuktu*, shot by my wife, Daisey, perhaps in 1989. We might bury the meat under rocks, cache it, and then pick it up in the winter. The meat won't spoil. It is the right time of year to use the fur for a *qulittaq* [parka], and for parka trim, meat, and also to make sleeping mats for use out on the land.

Fig.7. Polar Bears are
great swimmers under
water: they often
swim that way to
catch their prey. This
is a female, no young
ones, around mid-July
1991, in Cumberland
Sound, towards
Blacklead Island,
photographed on a
fishing trip with
Daisey and my son
Patrick.

BELOW
Fig.8. I took this
picture in 1991, the
bears were just
coming out of the
water onto the ice.
They weren't
hunting, just
travelling in
Cumberland Sound.

Hugh Brody

# In Conclusion:
# The Power of the Image

Two days of looking at and hearing about Arctic photographs might promise to be a repetitive or scholastic undertaking and not, therefore, in the spirit of the place where the photographs originate. Questions can all too quickly arise that are about aspects of technology or photographic history, or about the nature of archives and collections, or, finally, about where the funds will come that can sustain the accumulation and analysis of photographs and photographers. Apprehensions of this kind, however, overlook the extraordinary power of still images.

As we listen to and learn from expertise about Arctic photographers and photography, we may begin to lose contact with the remarkable and obvious ways in which photographs are silent and unreliable. Silence and unreliability are part of what holds our attention when a picture is first seen, and are, moreover, at the heart of a photograph's extraordinary power.

The silence is obvious enough. Photographs make no noises, say no words. They seem, rather, to wait for someone to provide the story, the facts, that can transform the images into a mysterious aspect of oral history. A family snapshot is the starting point for our being told who the person is, who his or her relatives are, when the picture was taken, and what was happening at that moment – the lives and events hinted at by the single image, even a single face. More formal photographs – records of people in a photographer's studio or, more likely in the case of the Arctic, pictures of groups on a shoreline or ships at anchor – are self-evident records of some particular moment. The record is a fragment of history that urges historians to widen the frame and explain. Photographs in this way urge a breaking of their silence.

So relatives and specialists and experts project an image and talk. Those who can sit and listen, especially in a darkened room with a large screen, have the privilege of access to the photograph. At the same time, those who watch also long for the voices of those speaking to stop. We want to experience the photographs for what they are, in their real silence. We want to be allowed to experience what happens in the brain when we look at a photograph including that strange attempt to get the story for ourselves. We like to say, without prompting, 'Ah, there's so-and-so's wife, or child.' We take keen pleasure in *knowing*, and then reaching what we do not know and wish to ask. There is, perhaps, an archetypal way of looking at photographs which begins with their silence and goes on to the questions that come to mind, as if we wish to begin with the puzzles, and wish, for a time, to be left with them, before breaking the silence.

During the silence, as the questions begin to form, many things take place in the mind at the same time. The photograph registers as a family album – there is recognition of who; at the same time the eye picks out the indications of when and where, often, in the case of Arctic images, searching for ethnographic clues and details; also, there is a sense of the image as a whole, as a set of shapes and balances of light, as art; and there can, simultaneously, be thoughts about the technology – how that was done, the lenses that might have been used, the conditions under which this was taken. Or, more generally, there is also the wonder that this tiny moment – some fraction of a second – has been caught and preserved for all time. The brain fills with these and other thoughts and impressions; we experience wonder, enjoy recognition, and also think, 'Why has that woman got bulging boots?' This range of activity occurs in the mind in an overlapping interplay of thoughts; it takes place in the silence, because of the silence. Here is one source of the photograph's power.

The second source of power that a conference about Arctic images may remind us of is the unreliability of photographs. You can't quite trust them. Consider the example of pictures used by Bishop Fleming, on the one hand, and Makivik Corporation on the other.

Fleming illustrated his writings about the Arctic with photographs that contrasted, as Fleming saw and invited others to see, the pagan with the Christian, the darkness of savagery with the light and enlightenment of progress. On one side of a page shown to us by Geller (this volume) is an Inuk woman and her child. They are dressed in furs and somehow exude the unease that conveys the distance of aboriginal Inuit life. Their expressions are somehow withdrawn – they display, at the very least, unease about the photographer and, at the most, some sense of their non-Christian condition. On the facing page there is a picture of two boys in school uniforms, with ties and jackets, smiling cheerfully. The pictures speak to the immense distance that the Inuit can travel, thanks, presumably, to the work of the missionaries. These photographs serve Fleming's purposes: to show the need of the Inuit and the successful work of the missions, and therefore inviting his audience and readers to support the missionary endeavour in the far north.

Fleming assumed that everyone who looked at these photographs would see a before and after. Before the mission, after the mission. Before Christianity, after Christianity. But Fleming cannot trust his photographs, because he cannot trust us. Even in the 1920s he probably could not be sure that people looking at his images would get it right. It is quite possible that they would look at the pictures, even guided by Fleming's captions and speeches, and say to themselves – albeit privately, albeit as they pushed their five pounds into the mission box – 'I much prefer the picture on the left!' Also, it would be the picture on the left, the picture of the woman and her child, with the uneasy look in her eyes, dressed in furs, that could well excite the imagination, and make Fleming's reader or listener long to go to the north, to be in the north, to know about the north. Not with a view to helping change the Inuit into pre-school children with blazers and ties; rather, with a wish to experience the wonder and beauty of Inuit life on Inuit terms.

Fleming cannot be sure, therefore, that he will have the effect he intends. His photographs, like all photographs, are rogue creatures, constantly meeting and combining with those who look at them in different, unpredictable ways. Similarly, Makivik's pictures are not to be relied upon.

Makivik is the Corporation set up by the Inuit of Arctic Quebec with funds they received as a result of the James Bay Settlement of the 1970s. Using extensive capital funds, Makivik has put in place much northern development, under the direct management of Inuit. To illustrate this work, Zebedee Nungak shows photographs of an aeroplane in the Inuit airline, a shrimp boat bought and operated by Inuit as part of an ocean-going shellfish development, the annual convention of the Arctic Quebec Inuit Association at which decisions are discussed and resolved in Inuit communities, and even the negotiating table at the Canadian Constitutional conference, at which Inuit (along with other aboriginal leaders) can be seen in the foreground with Trudeau – then prime minister of Canada – a small figure, at the same table, in the background.

Zebedee Nungak speaks of this work by Makivik's *angunasunirq aipungak* – the secondary hunt. The pictures show the Inuit seeking and finding modern game and new resources, which they must now be sure to collect. They hunt for their economic place in the modern world, and for their rights within Canada.

Yet Makivik cannot trust the photographs, any more than could Bishop Fleming trust his. Those who look may not see these new economic and political activities as might be expected of them. Even now there are questions in the minds of those who consider the images. Is Makivik capturing resources? Or are its activities the way in which Inuit resources are captured? Do the negotiators at the Constitutional Conference win rights for their people? Or does the Trudeau government have a way of ensuring that all agree to his government's view of the world? In this 'secondary hunt' who is the hunter and who the hunted? And in fifty years time – with the distance that is now between us and the work of Fleming – what will the questions be to which the Makivik photographs give rise? Just as Fleming could not know where his juxtaposition of photographs would sit in history, neither does Makivik.

This unreliability of the image is, of course, a reason for delight, as much as it is a source of power. The human mind takes advantage of the silence to reach its own thoughts, and to ask its own questions. A power of photographs is that, in their silence and stillness, they propose so much, and reveal nothing.

# Appendix

# Discussions

## Discussion 1

*The discussion followed the session of the conference which featured papers by Pamela Stern, Nicholas Whitman, Douglas Wamsley, Dorothy Harley Eber, Peter Geller, and Zebedee Nungak and Stephen Hendrie. William C. Sturtevant acted as discussant and spoke of the value of photography as a historical record. Comments were then made on the accessibility of historical texts and photographs and the access of native people to historical photographs in institutional locations. Picking up on previous discussions the session ended by considering the work of Peter Pitseolak and Archibald Lang Fleming.*

WILLIAM C. STURTEVANT
I was impressed in Pamela Stern's paper with her rather brief allusions to postures and to style changes in clothing. It seems to me that a major use of photographs is to trace the history of such things.

PAMELA STERN
Yes, what has always struck me is that things have changed so much. That's what people talk about, and particularly people at Holman. When they look at this sort of photograph they go, 'Oh it's so different!' They saw the beach where the community sits now, it's empty. A lot of the children and young adults at Holman never saw the community before it existed. It was an amazing thing for them. And I don't know if people at Holman would see the same similarity that I saw, but I look at the photographs and say, 'I've got a slide, it looks just like that'. It was a revelation to me to realise that while the whole thing has changed and the actual implements have changed, people

are doing a lot of the same things. Bernadette Driscoll arranged for some women from Holman to view the Diamond Jenness clothing collection at the Canadian Museum of Civilisation just prior to the opening of a recent exhibit. Three women from Holman, three generations, went down to Ottawa, viewed the collection and videotaped their review of it. They went back to Holman with the videotape and their review, and several hundred photographs of the collection. What's come out of this is that a group of women in Holman have started a skin-sewing workshop, organised by one of the older women who went down with the group. This group of women of all ages is meeting once a week and sewing skin clothing, which had very much dropped out of use in the last ten years. I've got slides from fifteen years ago showing lots of children wearing skin boots and fur mitts, and then pictures from five years ago where nobody's wearing them. And all of a sudden they're wearing them again.

WILLIAM C. STURTEVANT
From an anthropological or historical point of view these are records. Both your slides and the modern photographs are historical documents. In another fifty to a hundred years one will be able to look at them and learn something about the nature of our own times. The technological changes in photography are also relevant, in that one can use the nature of the prints and the negatives to date the photographs. One can then sometimes date what's shown in the photographs, using these dates to caption photographs. In my own experience such photographs are very useful for genealogies. Everyone is interested in old pictures and especially in old family pictures. If

one then enquires about who's who and how they are related, one can develop family genealogies that you can't really develop in any other way.

[*The discussion then moved to consider historical texts and photographs of early expeditions to the Arctic.*]

ZEBEDEE NUNGAK
I have a fascination with the early expeditions and I try to get my hands on every book I can of those early expeditions, but the little bit that is available to the general public is so miniscule. For example, I am entirely familiar with the titles and the authors of those early expedition photographers and reports of their expeditions either in the polar regions or in the Northwest Passage regions, but you can't just go down to the corner bookshop and pluck them out of a shelf. I suppose it's because they're not bestsellers so they're not widely circulated and you have to be a researcher or an academic to gain access to wherever they may exist, which is a real pity for people like me who have a burning curiosity to see, for example, Hayes' photographs from his expedition in the 1850s.

DOUGLAS WAMSLEY
The difficulty in those photographs is that they're not published, and it takes a great deal of work going through journals as well as the published books to find out first that they actually took photographs, then you've got to find out where those photographs are located. It's time-consuming and haphazard, but there are some wonderful images that were produced at that time. For example, the Hayes photographs and the Inglefield photographs, which recently just came to light, go back to the 1850s and 1860s, and they are very early records of Greenland Eskimos that are really worthy of anthropological study. To me, that's the value of those photographs. Someone can go through that and say, 'Haven't things changed from that period to the early 1900s or even today,' and that's a whole study in itself.

ZEBEDEE NUNGAK
I would be curious even just to get my hands on the book that they wrote even if there were no photographs. I'm intensely interested in how some of them failed so spectacularly in their endeavours. I've read anything I can get, the period books, the polar Greenland books, but it's very difficult to get actual accounts and even more difficult to get them with photographs. It's not just polar buffs like me, but the public in general, who would be well served to have that sort

of material more widely available to get an appreciation of the time and of the conditions under which those things were done.

DOUGLAS WAMSLEY
(In terms of) failing spectacularly, two of the photographs were of Hans Hendrik, who was on the Hayes expedition. He was instrumental in saving those expeditions from spectacular failures, unlike some of the other ones like the Franklin expedition. He certainly deserves a lot more recognition with respect to his efforts and endeavours on both those expeditions and on the Nares expedition later. He's a relatively unknown figure among those expeditions.

ZEBEDEE NUNGAK
And it's not only him. You describe the role which he played, then there's the ones who saved the *Polaris*, Joe [*Ipirvik*], then there's the people who helped Peary and Hensen, who get no credit. It warps the historical account of what happened because people who had a very vital and important role in those activities are not given the due that they should.

DOUGLAS WAMSLEY
You're right. For instance, the Hall expedition: Hall died on the expedition and the remaining members retreated, and on the way back half of them were caught on an ice floe for six months and it was only through the hunting of Joe [as I know him] that they were able to survive for that length of time until the ice floe drifted far enough south to be picked up by the whaler.

[*The discussion then moved on to consider access of native people to institutionally housed collections.*]

EILEEN NORBERT
I just wanted to bring up something that you said earlier. Many folks here are talking about people who made a name taking photographs, such as yourselves. They, or people who are influential enough, should bring those photographs back to the communities, so that people enjoy them. It is very important for museums, for anybody who speaks for us to return to us the photographs.

ZEBEDEE NUNGAK
Hear, hear! I might add that in our region when our Inuit cultural institute Avataaq started a project to repatriate or retrieve some photographic records, first they researched what was in the hands of the government, the A. P. Low expedition, the expedition that was government spon-

sored. Then they did an inventory of all living or deceased *qallunaat* who had been in our community as traders, missionaries, whatever they were, and wrote to them or their estates. They wrote to 585 sources and within two years got over 300 sources sending them their collections and from those records they have been able to do family histories. In fact I myself found a photograph of my great grandmother, a photograph taken in 1939 about a few weeks before she died, taken by a Roman Catholic Oblate priest. So those have a value beyond being mere photographs. The people who are active in such an 'obscure' activity should be aware that these are very important to the people and the regions and the communities in which they were taken for historical purposes, as well as for comparison and historical study and whatever.

PHILLIPA OOTOOWAK
I'd like to follow up on the matter of returning historical photographs to communities in the north. In Pond Inlet (Mittimatalik), members of the local Library Board and I have been working on the creation of a photohistory collection of the Pond Inlet/North Baffin area. The albums put together so far are located in the local Library and are viewed by residents and visitors alike. Since the original project in 1993, a number of small collections have been donated to the Library and several other possible sources located that need to be followed up. This is very encouraging, though two problems have arisen. First, a suitably secure location is required to store these photographs (preferably humidity-controlled) and this includes responsible staffing of such a facility. Few northern communities have access to this kind of space. Second, in order to make the photographic collections accessible to the public they should be catalogued, identified, labelled and displayed in a suitable manner. This requires trained personnel, time and funding, all of which are scarce commodities in the north today. A collection of photographs stored in boxes on some shelf, however valuable, is no more accessible to the public locally than if stored in a southern institution. It is all too easy to hand round a set of uncatalogued photographs to interested people and hear, 'I'd love a copy of that, can I just borrow it to make a reprint?', and so often the collection then becomes incomplete.

So in our experience, it would be wonderful for many reasons to have local access to original or reprinted materials in the individual communities where photographs were taken, and we should all work towards this end. However, until more communities have suitable, secure facilities

and more funding is made available for these types of projects, northerners will have to continue to rely on southern institutions for the safe storage of archival material that originated in the north.

UNIDENTIFIED MALE PARTICIPANT
Access is the really big issue, and I think this era will be looked back on as the pre-digitised era, and it'll seem primitive in fifty or a hundred years. It should be possible in the future to call up images on screen, to be able to peruse any collections in the world. This is the ultimate situation, and I don't think it's unreasonable to expect that could happen in our lifetime.

J. C. H. KING
Can I ask Mr Nungak how you see metropolitan institutions such as the Smithsonian Institution and the National Archives of Canada responding to questions of access?

ZEBEDEE NUNGAK
Submit to every dictatorial order from the likes of me about what to do! But I know that's a useless statement, because whenever I bring up or broach the subject of such things, our governments plead poverty, and it is very difficult to properly conduct an operation such as this without a substantial amount of money. It's a specialised field of activity. There's got to be all manner of connected activity to do justice to preserving and cataloguing and disseminating and so on. So I think there is room for a good head-on, square-in-the-face dialogue about what to do about this between native leadership and institutions who have the capability and the resources to provide those things to the people that rightly should have access to them.

[*The discussion then moved on to consider Peter Pitseolak as a visual artist, and Archibald Lang Fleming's work in relation to the circulation of photographs.*]

WILLAM C. STURTEVANT
Peter Pitseolak was an innovator in his own community, but not an innovator in the method, the idea, the technique of using photographs as a base for drawings. How did he learn to be such a good photographer?

DOROTHY HARLEY EBER
He got a camera through the Hudson's Bay Company, I believe, and he observed people taking pictures. He asked how to develop from the son of one of the Bay managers, and learnt in the

simplest manner through trial and error. Of course, he was passionately interested. He told me with regard to developing, 'I watched a man do it, but I knew he wasn't doing it well.' Mostly it was trial and error. He and Aggeok got the developing fluid – the different waters, they called them – and developed sometimes out on the land in hunting igloos. They printed back in Cape Dorset in their hut, where they used oil lamps. Of course, today it's Tom Humphry at the Notman Photographic Archives who prints Peter Pitseolak's negatives and makes enlargements, and he does get spectacular results with his expertise from even very exposed negatives.

WILLIAM C. STURTEVANT

Do you think that the influence of Houston and his pupils shows in the sequence of development of Pitseolak's artistic style? The later drawings perhaps show the influence of Houston-style watercolours. The earlier ones seem to me to be quite naive-realist (using the phrase in a technical sense) based on photographs, but later ones seem to me to be more Houston-like. He was evidently influenced by the other kinds of art that were going on at the time.

DOROTHY HARLEY EBER

He was probably influenced by the evolution of the print-making programme in Cape Dorset and the fact that it began to enjoy considerable success, though in what ways he was influenced I am not really sure. I don't think he was ever much influenced by Houston. As I said, Houston told me he was never much interested in Peter Pitseolak's work because he appeared to be so much influenced by the south. Peter Pitseolak was well aware of this and believed that Houston and the Co-op did not favour the 'real'. Perhaps they neglected him a bit – they didn't use a great number of his drawings, but these were not always easy to use. The small lithographs I showed in my presentation do appear to me to be particularly successful, but they were done long after Houston left Cape Dorset (he left in the early sixties), in the late sixties perhaps and early seventies. The original works were not watercolours – they were rendered in some other medium. As far as I know, he only used watercolours in the Tweedsmuir series and in the series he did for Houston.

NELSON H. H. GRABURN

Archibald Fleming took genealogies and a complete census of every living Inuk in the whole area when he went around by dogsled. It would be absolutely marvellous to put that together with the photographs, because he did the whole of what was then Frobisher Bay, Lake Harbour, up the coast to Cape Dorset, and presumably he took photographs in the same area.

PETER GELLER

Yes, this material was taken during the period when he was an active missionary, not later when head of the Arctic missions. Some of those photographs exist in albums and aren't all that well identified, though a lot more have turned up recently in the collections of the General Synod Archives of the Anglican Church of Canada (in Toronto). On the question of the use of photographs by Inuit themselves, we need to consider the fact that people weren't just going away and taking those images away and showing them in London, Toronto, Ottawa and elsewhere. Fleming, in the early part of his career (in 1913), was projecting lantern slides to Inuit audiences. In many ways there was an attempt to try and get photographic representation, based on Western intellectual traditions. It has a long history, it doesn't just start with when Peter Pitseolak gets the camera and is taking pictures, it's a long history of exchange that I think we could do more work on.

ROBERT J. CHRISTOPHER

I am just beginning to understand how these photographs are circulated, especially when there were two photographers in the same community at the same time as Fleming was there. Flaherty reports in his diary that he goes to the opening of the church that Fleming has built, that Flaherty was taking photographs and that Fleming was taking photographs. One has to do all of this to understand the circulation of photographs. Meaning is also invested at the level of projecting the images in a lantern slide show. It may not be important who took the picture as the author of the show, Fleming or whoever might be presenting the slide show and would have been the authority. In different contexts it would mean different things.

WILLIAM C. STURTEVANT

To conclude, I thought there was an interesting similarity and difference between two presentations. In the first case it was Fleming. The viewer was being told what messages were to be read out of the pictures, and I thought that although Fleming was only a half century or so ago one really needs to hear his words in order to see in the pictures what he saw in the pictures or what he wanted his audience to see. Whereas in the second one it's close enough to our own times so that we can really understand without the explanations of what to see in the pictures, without having to put ourselves in another time and place in order to follow the purpose of the images.

## Discussion 2

*This discussion followed the session of the conference which featured the papers by Jim Burant, Donny White, Jonathan King, Inge Kleivan and Ann Christine Eek. Elizabeth Edwards acted as discussant, and spoke of the properties of photography as a medium, including its linkage with archaeology and cinema. The discussion then focused on the relationship between photography and art.*

ELIZABETH EDWARDS

I will start with a few introductory remarks, largely about photography because the Arctic is not my area of specialisation. What has struck me is the complexity of the making of the historical photographic record. What I find particularly interesting and exciting is that ten or fifteen years ago a gathering like this would not have been possible. The basic research quite simply was not being done in sufficient volume to bring a group like this together. It's a great credit to everybody's hard work that we're all here. And we're slowly getting to grips with the data: its content, its form, its tensions and its meaning.

I'm going to take one step back perhaps and make a few historiographical points which perhaps we ought to consider. This would underline just about everything everyone said today, because I think the richness of the material we've seen this afternoon and, indeed, this morning should silence anyone who sees photography as a secondary way of recording history. It seems to me that photography along with film is *the* historical source of the late nineteenth and twentieth century and it's going to become more so. So it's time historians, and I use that in the broadest terms, got to grips with what photography has to tell us. I'm rather overcome by the enormity of it all.

We have all assumed throughout that photography is relevant to history. Now this seems a very stupid question to ask but I think we should step back and say, 'Why do we think this?' This is tied up with our cultural expectancy of the medium itself. Photography changes the way we think about the past because photographs are naturally sites of historical intersections. All photographs we've seen today have been sites of social and historical intersections. They are the histories of everybody here. They are conduits which are variously inscribed histories. They are

constructions of memory, and often torpedos into memory. I was struck by somebody who commented that photographs had given the community something that they had forgotten about themselves; it is changing the relationship between people and their past. I think photographs are unlike any other historical source, at least in the Western tradition. They're not a linear narrative, they give information in a totally different way, conflating layers of meaning. Photographs introduce access to a past which may not mesh comfortably with more conventional ways in which we are used to telling history, and I think we have to address these problems at the theoretical and intellectual level in addition to our emotional response to images. Because images talk very different forms of visual dialect, we are seduced by their surface appearance. Despite the appearance, these very basic statements link to our historical imaginations, yet they are statements which I think belong to very different layers of history. We often put them side by side when perhaps we should be taking an archaeological approach to them.

Another thing that has come up very strongly is the interplay between the private and the public making and consumption of photography, and photographs moving between these different spaces. This, after all, is what we're talking about when photographs go back to the communities. They're moving from the public space – the archive, the anthropological, the historical document – into the private sphere, where they are seen as having a completely different set of meanings. We should look perhaps at the idea of consumption and images as performance, because sometimes it is very difficult to look at photographs and quite simply remain passive. There is something active within them.

Finally something else comes into play: the idea of the photograph as a material culture object, and a cultural object in its own right. This is why photographs fascinate me and film and video don't. It's the material culture side of it. One can hold a photograph in one's hands and stick it on a wall, and put it in a frame and tear it in half in a temper, or cut it up with kitchen scissors, or send it to someone, or weep over it, put it under your pillow at night. I don't know anyone who does that with a video tape! And we should be looking at the very materiality of the image, as a cultural object, in all our deliberations on photography and its historical meaning in all sorts of different communities. And we've seen all sorts of different visual dialects which move over these different spaces, in different ways, becoming public and private, becoming family, coming out of government photography, anthropological photography, expedition photography. You name it, it's capable of moving through these different spaces.

J. C. H. KING

I would like to comment on the relationship between archaeology and photography. The most obvious similarity is in the use of the word 'lens', because when you're excavating you excavate different stratigraphic layers, and archaeologists say that you have lenses of ash, or lenses of this or that coloured earth, and of course the whole point about the lens is that it is layered on top of things. What we've been looking at today is a series of lenses in the archaeological sense, about the images produced by a different kind of lens.

ELIZABETH EDWARDS

I agree. The exciting thing about pictures is that one can take these two different axes of meaning, a horizontal axis, if you will, which is the appearance and primary data – what the picture is of in purely evidential terms – then you have a vertical axis, which is archaeological.

PETER GELLER

It occurs to me, for the historical record there is a real relationship between the two forms: still photography and moving images. Many of the people I encountered in my research tended to try and exploit both still and moving images as much as they possibly could, in order to construct the image of the north, of the Arctic, of Inuit. This included both professional photographers or film-makers (like Richard Finnie) and amateurs like Archibald Lang Fleming, although the professional/amateur distinction is itself a construct. Then in terms of consumption, there is a real interchange between lantern slide shows and motion pictures.

ELIZABETH EDWARDS

You're right. In the immediately pre-cinematic period of the early 1890s there existed technology that could project lantern slides fairly fast and which could be used with sound recordings. It must have been an incredible experience for people who had not seen moving images. These were not moving in the way we would understand cinema today, but a very fast turnover of images was being used to create a realistic cinematic approach.

[*The discussion then moved onto questions of public accessibility.*]

JOHN MILLER

Instead of thinking of these images as images to preserve and put away in our private collection, or maybe print for people in books, I'm more interested in their ability to allow people to hang them on their walls, to enjoy them as works of art. And I'd be interested in knowing whether any of the individuals or any of their institutions make, or are taking steps towards making, these images more publicly available?

WILLIAM C. STURTEVANT

Quite commonly people who aren't in the business, as it were, assume, we assume, that the photographs (and also the objects) that you see on exhibit and in the museum shop are what you have access to. It's not true: what one must do is ask to look behind the scenes. Where is the archival collection? Once you ask that, you will be given access to the collections during normal opening hours, and one can then usually order prints. It's not that museums are hiding things, it's that we don't have enough space and time to put all our collection out on public exhibit. One must ask for what's behind the scenes, what's in store.

[*The discussion then moved on to the relationship between art and photography.*]

JOHN MILLER

I have not heard the word 'art' used here at all, and now I've been here virtually a whole day and I have a feeling that if most of these had been hand-drawn you'd say, 'Oh that's art', but if you looked at a photograph of exactly the same situation you'd say, 'That's part of a chronology', or it's just a different kind of dimension. To what extent does the public accept that photography is art?

JAMES H. BARKER

The point I wanted to make has to do with my own work. I think of myself as an art photographer who happens to be working with people, and it has been very clear in the marketing of the book [*Always Getting Ready*, 1993] and the exhibit that goes along with it that the exhibit is only accepted by natural history museums and not art museums because it is about people. And yet a lot of people have said, 'Your work is very creative, it's very artistic.' Book stores refused to place it with art books; they put it only with ethnographic books. There is a conception here very clearly that art is being aesthetic.

HUGH BRODY

We need to ask the questions: What does it mean

to take a photograph? What are the photographers doing? Are they making art? With Geraldine Moodie, for example, I have a strong sense of a fierce aesthetic preoccupation. The photographers that have been talked about today, were they art makers rather than some form of ethnographic technocrat?

ELIZABETH EDWARDS

I think our problem is that we have tended to ghetto-ise ethnographic pictures. Once you declare 'These are art' you have to put on white gloves and go to the Getty to see them. As I was trying to say earlier, they move to all sorts of different spaces, and just because some have deep anthropological, scientific or community value, it doesn't mean to say they cannot be aesthetically pleasing as well. A lot of early photographers were on the kinds of contracts that allowed them to go along with the expedition and could keep a certain percentage of royalties when they got back to pay off the bills. So naturally they had half an eye on the market, but they were simultaneously creating scientific documents. Jack Hiller's work in the Southwest amongst the Zuni and the Tewa peoples is a perfect example. Wonderful documents at one level, but on the other hand they're very, very pictorialist in an almost prescient way.

PETER GELLER

I want to raise the issue of the collection of photographs and the construction of the image of the Inuit. I was absolutely fascinated when working with Fleming's collection (some of which is held at the General Synod Archives of the Anglican Church of Canada in Toronto) by the fact that you have a page of photographs which was labelled 'Eskimo life in the winter', with pictures of igloos, people lined up, and then the next page over was an unbelievable page with a collection of photographs of all these chaps wearing cloth caps and sweaters and rubber boots, and running an oil-rendering operation, again at Lake Harbour. The same people in both sets of photographs, and yet one is probably used to market the image of the Inuit, and the other set of photographs I've never seen used anywhere.

So you have to be very careful in talking about the distribution of these pictures because photographic albums are a very mixed bag. We have to be very careful in considering what we create in our selective reproduction of images.

JIM BURANT

Talking about the historiography of visual documentation, Low used sixty-three (photographs) in his book, produced three albums, one for the

Geological Survey and a couple that went to other people. But most of the negatives (80–140) have never been printed, or at least were never printed until an archivist came along and said, 'Hmm, that's interesting, we'll put it in our photographic catalogue'. Archivists have to make decisions about what it is that gets reproduced out of holdings and put in catalogues, so we're making a judgement. When talking about art/photography we are being asked to make a further judgement – about which ones are the most aesthetically pleasing.

## Discussion 3

*This discussion followed the session of the conference which featured the papers of Chris B. Wooley and Karen Brewster, Bill Hess, Robert Stapleton, Eileen Norbert, Nelson Graburn, Diane Brenner and Molly Lee. Aldona Jonaitis acted as discussant and started by considering Walter Benjamin's analysis of photography. The session sought to address the difference between native and non-native photography, and how photographers work with/in their communities. Questions of dissemination and access were also addressed.*

ALDONA JONAITIS

The problem of photography is that it does purport to represent 'reality' and in many cases that's exactly true. But the reality that the photograph represents is limited by its borders, the framing. I want to briefly mention that in *The Work of Art in the Age of Mechanical Reproduction* (written in the 1930s) Walter Benjamin (1985) argued that photography does not have that 'aura' which emanates from authentic expression of community values in the form of a unique artwork, because a photograph can be reproduced over and over again. The talks today suggest the very opposite of Benjamin's ideas. These photographs of native people, and photographs by native people of themselves do have an aura of authenticity and a profound significance to the cultures from which they came. And in a very ironic twist on Benjamin, they do inspire community values, particularly when they are returned to the communities, as in Eileen Norbert's talk about display of the photographs in various villages. So the role of photography in culture is really changing. We also need to consider both what is in a photograph and what is left out. Claude Lévi-Strauss once wrote that sometimes what is not there is more important than what is there. And one final question – what is the difference between a native representation of his or her culture and a non-native representation?

EILEEN NORBERT

Well, I think the photographs that my grandfather took were part of his life. They were different, in that sense, from an anthropologist's or others. You know, I've seen very, very many photographs of beautiful people sitting dressed in their best clothes, and I think that's a big difference with a total stranger taking photographs. You don't see too many photographs a long time ago of hunts. If you saw the whole collection that my grandfather has, there are wonderful, wonderful hunting scenes, women working on skins. You depict the hard life that people did, and you don't see those kind of photographs, I don't think, from an outsider. You know, I really enjoy Bill [Hess]'s photographs because I see a real similarity: his photographs depict what is really important to people up in Barrow. My grandfather took a lot of pictures of what was important to us. My people were mainly walrus and seal hunters, although they were whalers also, but not to the extent that Barrow is a whaling community.

CHRIS B. WOOLEY

I noticed a big difference between the photographs that Dr and Mrs Henry Greist had taken and Marvin Peter's photographs, which were taken a little bit later. It seems more a question of boundaries. He was an insider, he was a family member, he took pictures of his own friends and family, and those are the pictures that were important to him and to his people. By contrast, there are some portraits in the Greist collection which just don't have the same feel, the same 'relaxed' nature about them. With Bill Hess and contemporary photographs, he's a member of the community and you know the boundaries are not as strong there. I guess he is taking those views from the inside. It's a question maybe not so much of native or non-native, although that is important, but of access and familiarity. Furthermore, in the Greist photographs there's lots of 'exotica'; with Marvin Peter's there are hundreds of photographs of just people. And that's what's important to Marvin, to the people. I didn't show as many of those 'people photographs' because I wanted to show a wide range of what's in the collection, but there are more photographs of people than of other subjects.

UNIDENTIFIED MALE PARTICIPANT

There are the agendas by photographers who come from the south to work in the north. With Pitseolak, for instance, the hunting scenes, the traditional clothing or whatever, they're a lot more relaxed. Southern photographers, however, would have people put on winter parkas out of season and so on. You see continuity to the lifestyle with the native photographers.

NELSON H. H. GRABURN

Well, I entirely deny that! You said Peter Pitseolak didn't have an agenda, he had an incredible agenda – frustrated his family, all these people had to perform for him. They got really mad at him and shouted at him. Is that relaxed? I think the only difference is, if you're there in the summer for a week, all right, you put the winter parka on in the summer, but if you're there throughout the year then you don't have to pretend anything, just get photographs. First of all, if you're a human being, if you want to remember people and take photographs of stages in their life, kids and so on, you take some snapshots. You like photographs, and those will be nostalgic for you, in the same fashion as for others. In addition, of course, you might want to take somebody throwing a harpoon or a subject that you're not going to see down south, but I think as far as I can tell most anthropologists who have been in the place any length of time want to have some continuity with the people. Early on when I took photographs, I wanted to show what Eskimos looked like when they're out hunting or something – that is a stereotype. Then they are individuals. If you take photographs of individuals as individuals, then everybody should appreciate them more and more. Especially if you are a member of the community as your grandfather was, then you'd know all the individuals. If you don't know all the individuals then you can't take photographs of individuals, you're taking generic 'Eskimo' or something like that. So I think that's the difference. It's whether you're taking photographs of people you know as individuals or you're taking a shot of natives doing something. So, I would cut it up in an entirely different way. Peter Pitseolak did individuals, but he also had an agenda which drove people crazy.

He knew everything was changing, he wanted to record all the old stories, natives that he knew and a lot of us had that feeling. I remember dragging along a tape recorder and putting the microphone on the runners of a sled because I knew that in ten or twenty years that sound would never be heard again, the sled sound, and I think Peter Pitseolak was doing exactly that. He was always saying, 'This is like history.' The present is history. He knew what was being recorded was going to be history very soon, and thank goodness he did.

BILL HESS

In my own case, the driving factor for me to be getting out and getting the photographs is that I've wanted to experience that life myself. If I hadn't been a photographer I would have been out there trying to do it one way or another, a camera was a good way in. There's a big barrier that often separates native Alaskan peoples and non-native, it's a very easy barrier to cross, and that is food. If you go into people's homes anywhere you go they'll generally offer you something to eat, and if you don't take it they're going to be offended and you're going to have a little bit of a harder time with them. An awful lot of people come to the north and when they're presented with Inupiat food they say, 'Well, no, I can't eat that', and they kind of expect people to understand. But there have been many times in my career when I have not known people and I have been trying to get to know them, I've been real edgy and then there's a plate of *muktuk* sitting on the table and I just go pick up a piece and eat it, and the barriers begin to fall. Just like that. And that may sound simple, but it's true.

People were talking about asking people to put on parkas, and what have you. You notice that some of the photographs I have were portraits: I give them the choice of what they want to wear, and people – even though they're in their homes and it's warm, or even if it's summer or whatever – they like to put on their parka because that parka is like their best dress.

DOROTHY HARLEY EBER

When I worked with the Geraldine Moodie pictures and with those of whaling master Captain Comer, it was very, very interesting to discover that the native people at that time kept swapping parkas because some parkas were prettier than others. And everybody wanted to be in a more handsome parka. At first, I thought I was going to be able to identify the people by their costume. But then Inuit informants would say, 'Oh that's my grandmother, she's dressed up in Nivisinaaq's parka', so that approach was not too useful. Of course, the photographers may have encouraged, or asked, for this sort of swap, [but] I don't know.

UNIDENTIFIED MALE PARTICIPANT

Can I ask Bill Hess about the relationship – of trust – that has been built up between yourself and the people that you're photographing over the years.

BILL HESS

That's a hard one to answer. In those photographs is a lot of what I've gone through. I have all kinds of names that people have given me and one of them is *Pukuk*, which means essentially a person who's always getting in the way. But they say it affectionately, so I don't mind. But when I first went out whaling, this was in a very tense time, when the quota was very severe and the feelings that people had towards the outside world, and people from the outside world, were angry. Feelings were really hurt.

Every time I held the camera in my hand and took a picture, for every minute I did that, I had about three hours of swinging a pick, chopping ice, making coffee, doing the work of a boy, essentially, working my way in. And that was how, when they saw that I would be willing to swing that pick, when they'd seen that I'd be willing to wash the dishes, make the coffee, and then I didn't do this just one day and then leave, I stayed for a couple of weeks and no photograph opportunity even arises in that couple of weeks, then gradually they start to say, 'He's willing to do what we have to do'. Well, over years it's just like anything else, you get to know people and then as they know you, you build up relationships and they get comfortable with you.

EILEEN NORBERT

I just want to add to what Bill had to say on trust. With our people when outsiders first come into our community, we sit back and watch them. If they do something to upset us that will hurt us or the community, we don't trust them. I've known Bill for some years now and I could understand why the people in Barrow trust him and embrace him as somebody like ourselves. I think that element of trust is very important. Even myself, you know I'm from Nome, but I worked for the Department of Fish and Game with the Subsistence Division. I lived up in Kotzebue and I was doing a socio-economic study up on the upper Kobuk, and Ambler and Shungnak. That was a real different experience for me because those folks up there are inland Inupiat, which is rather different from the coast, and that was the first time I was ever in that situation. People did the same to me even though I was Inupiat: they waited to see how I would be. One day I had to eat five meals! My latest one was ten or eleven that night and I was so full, but you cannot refuse, as Bill says, you know, and somebody even said, 'Gosh, you'll eat anything!', but I always have to try everything myself when I go into a community, because even among us Inupiat there are very different dishes. People tend to lump us together, but I just want to clarify a little further on why people trust Bill.

*[The discussion moved on to questions of circulation and access.]*

JIM BURANT

Although we discussed how these photographs have been taken, nobody has really talked about where these photographs appeared, where they are published, and how widely they are disseminated commercially.

MOLLY LEE

They're on their way north. I discovered Gladys Knight Harris's photographs about ten years ago. I wrote to the Alaska Historical Commission to have them reproduced, had a small number of them reproduced in microfilm and wondered why they'd never been used. She used them herself to convey the real Eskimos to people around Los Angeles in talks to other photography schools, to white people basically. She sent some up I believe to the people, but as far as I know not many. I couldn't understand why they'd never been used. It's because they were lost. This time it's not going to happen, and they're going to end up in the community. So that's what I know about it.

BILL HESS

As I said when I began, I made a magazine that is funded by the North Slope Borough and covers the North Slope Borough and is primarily for its people. So the record I make is first and foremost for the Inupiat and then if it should go beyond that, then that is fine, but it is made first and foremost for the local population.

EILEEN NORBERT

In my case, the project that I did, the University of Alaska Archives has a copy. I have all the original negatives of course. Before my family agreed to share their personal photographs, they signed a statement that they wanted assurance that their photographs would not be used for anybody's personal monetary gain, that if they were to be used they had to get their permission first. So there's that stipulation on using the photographs in my grandfather's collection, in my family collection. When I did the project, KAMIRAK, the non-profit organisation that I worked for, I also made a complete set for their records. The other thing that I made sure was done was that for all the communities that photographs came from, we made 8 × 10 copies and sent them to the tribal councils for their records. I think they were very proud of these old photographs of their community, of people in their community. If you go into the community hall you'll see them up on the wall. They're enjoyed by all.

CHRIS B. WOOLEY

Marvin Peter's photographs are one collection of many that form part of the Inupiat History, Language and Culture Commission (IHLC). It's a canvassing of archives and museums around the country to try to return images from the region to the IHLC offices so they could be used in publications, for enjoyment, also for preservation and use in the local community. So this one collection is part of a much larger, ongoing project.

ROBERT STAPLETON

I've come into a situation in my life, twenty years of working in Alaska, I've been on several sides of the fence on this issue of where the work goes, where it's been published and what happens to it. I've worked for *Time Life* and *Sports Illustrated*, *People* magazine, *Newsweek*. I've illustrated books, I've done assignments for all major newspapers in the United States, I've worked for State Arts Councils. What I've learned over the years basically is that this concept of giving back to the community is important. I'm currently living in Nome, and working on a project where I compare the contemporary lifestyle with the images made by Edward Curtis in 1927, 1928, 1929. One of the things I intend to do is work closely and have conversations with Eileen about this and that. I'm going to make presentations to each IRA council and communities where I am going to make images, and as part of that presentation and agreement I give photographs to each person that I photograph, and a series of the images would be given to each community.

NELSON H. H. GRABURN

A forum like this makes you think very hard about this, because what are, to me, literally research shots are [also, of course] snapshots of people from twenty or thirty years ago. These have now become more important, especially to the villages where the people live. I don't have duplicates of everything. The vast majority of the individual snapshots were sent back to the communities. If I did a photograph in 1959 and sent it to someone in 1959, that doesn't mean it still exists today, even though I sent it back once. In the case of Saluit, I did make a permanent bank of images in the form of slides – which they could use for video or any purpose in the community, or they publish what they want – in addition to 18 × 24 prints, photographs of older people who weren't alive. I thought they were going to put them on the wall in the school or the community hall. I found that they'd sold them at cost to the individuals who wanted them! By the end of the month they'd all gone.

They went back to people's houses. So most of them had gone back, but that doesn't mean there's some permanent archive. I've used them for slide talks, obviously, particularly those of Inuit art, and for teaching. The only person who has ever used my photographs as an archive and a serious research album is Jonathan King for the *Living Arctic* exhibition.

## Discussion 4

*This discussion followed the session that featured papers by Kesler E. Woodward, Robert J. Christopher, Alan Rudolph Marcus, Henrietta Lidchi, Stephen Loring and Simeonie Keenainak. Paula Richardson Fleming acted as discussant, responding to questions about access of native people to archival sources and possibilities for sharing information and photographs. The question of the circulation of images was also tackled. The discussion ended with a short focus on Simeonie Keenainak's work.*

PAULA RICHARDSON FLEMING

At conferences there is an understating of how much wealth of information is out there, an undercurrent that there are major repositories – the haves – and native peoples who need access to this historical gold. Unfortunately it is sometimes seen that we (the institutions) are stonewalling and that's not the case. I would like to make a few positive comments about what is being done and what can be done. Many repositories have archivists who are knowledgeable and who really want to help. It's not just in shoeboxes in corners, people know what's there. At the Smithsonian Institution we have a specially funded Native American programme, which provides funding to bring people from specific tribes to the institution to research what documents, what images are there, to provide for their own photographers, to make photographs. Then all these photographs, 100 per cent, nothing held back, is sent back to the tribes for them to do completely as they wish, no strings attached. We've put a lot of catalogue information on the internet, I'm under no illusion that everyone has that, but it's out there. Increasingly we hear about people putting images on CD-ROMS. This is a bit of silicone snake oil, it sounds like that's the best thing to do but it isn't: it's extremely time-consuming and it's costly. The National Anthropological Archives (NAA) has well over 350,000, by the time you had put 50,000 captioned images on CD-ROM you might end up with obsolete equipment. So we have to deal with discrete units, and funding is a problem. At the NAA we work with tribes that show an interest; there is

little point getting funding money for a group who do not hold this as a priority. Native people need to get involved, to get informed, and they need to work jointly with the archivists so that we can get the photographs back. It's a group effort.

JIM BURANT

The Federal Government of Canada has been talking about devolving native records back to the community, either through the Assembly of First Nations or any other native groups, Métis or Inuit. They are trying to look at archival training for people in their communities in order to take care of such references that might go back to the communities. So that's one concern that is being expressed. But as an archivist, like you, I don't want to see records go back to the community and then sit inadequately stored in a cabinet, not available to everybody in the community. There is a second thing, the Federal Government in Canada has launched a project called School-net, which involves getting communities to start digitising images. That's the only growth area in the Canadian Federal Government; there is tremendous fiscal restraint.

JAMES H. BARKER

Zebedee has made a formal request. Are you going to help him?

PAULA RICHARDSON FLEMING

I've taken the first step: getting Zebedee's business card and starting to give him some information already. At the National Anthropological Archives (NAA) we start by letting the people know what is there, and we've produced a guide to the major collections. At least one copy is sent to every known tribal group and tribal organisation that we could find listed. This should inspire our native colleagues to see the kind of records that are there. We can only give the information out; we can't give the support to come and research. Though we are hoping that our information will get people to write back and inspire some to come and to help us get funding.

CHRIS B. WOOLEY

To make an analogy with hunting, there are some skills we need to learn for finding out the right questions to ask, how to make the approach, and then sift through the possibilities. Archivists help you learn skills for finding out how to narrow down your scope, so look for the assistance of the professionals who know the collections. I can vouch for the responsiveness of both the Canadian Archives and the Anthropological

Archives in helping the North Slope Borough people get photographs.

PAULA RICHARDSON FLEMING

The NAA has to work very personally with people on the Tribal Programme, like we do in effect with anyone new to the archives. It's a complex vintage system of describing things and even with new technology there's a lot of material that you have to dig through. It's still a joint effort because while we're teaching native people how to access the records, they're finding images and telling us what they are. It's a nice two-way street.

ZEBEDEE NUNGAK

I'd just like to thank you for concentrating on something that I thought I could at least come away with from this conference. I am sitting on top of quite a few resources as a boss of one organisation, and if I could be guided towards sources, organisations, people to whom I can delegate somebody from my staff, from my corporation, to devote attention to that, to dig out, to pursue and so on. I don't expect the 'historical gold' from all these plethora of sources to come down and fall on my lap, without me doing anything. I know I have to do something to get at things. I recognise that it's, by necessity, a co-operative effort, that you're not going to deliver this stuff to my office and I am not instantly going to gain access to all I might want for the people of my territory.

DIANE BRENNER

The Arctic Study Centre, associated with the Smithsonian but also in Anchorage, prepares workshops for people organising native cultural centres in Alaska. Part of that programme of coming to town and learning about how cultural centres work and how museums work is coming to the library or archives to see what kinds of things are there. To start the conversation up, these are the photographs and this is how you get them, and it's a training process.

JAMES H. BARKER

I wanted to address this problem of getting pictures back to villages. As a photographer, I always feel guilty because I simply can't make enough 8 × 10 prints to get back.

This January, Molly Lee and a couple of others were involved in putting the exhibit *The Living Traditions of Yup'ik Masks* (1996), at Tooksok Bay, Yup'ik village. To have some images to go along with this, I took a bunch of prints and had high-quality xeroxes made cheaply. We put them on the wall, and started to

find people wanting these and I said, 'Sure, they don't cost much'. I suddenly realised that we tend to look at images with an over-degree of preciousness. We can really allow an awful lot of stuff, inexpensively now but adequately produced, to get out there. People want pictures of their relatives, friends and that sort of thing. Sure, I don't know what the lifetime of xeroxes is, but a lot of people need them because people are dying and it's very easy to do.

GEORGE QUVIQ QULAUT

What I specifically have to say is the importance of the photographs and how we should be able to get them. I think one of the most important authorities, of course, our elders, are passing away very, very rapidly and every time an elder passes away part of our tradition and culture dies with us. Because of this, it is very, very important to get as many old photographs as possible. I have some friends in Rankin Inlet who actually xeroxed images and sent them through faxes to be identified. That work was very, very important because no matter how poor it was, some of these elders were able to identify some of these photographs and then we would relay it back and say this is the person, is so and so, thanks to modern technology. Once they are identified we can appreciate whether we should have the actual photographs, better quality photographs, for exhibiting in schools and, most importantly, in cultural centres.

BILL HESS

I'm going to follow on James (Barker) here because what he's said is the problem I've always had too, is that you photograph all these people, and they want images and you want to get them back, but it's impossible. But in the last few years, I've gone to completely digital format, in that instead of making prints I scan my film and set it all up in the computer. Now what I have discovered is once I've done that I can spit these things out on a laser printer as fast as possible and they look a little better even than xerox, and I dig these things out for people who write and it makes a big difference.

STEPHEN LORING

There's a flip side to the information-giving which is when native people come to the museum. For example, I've been working with people from Nunivak Island. We have a large collection of photographs that were taken in the same summer that Edward Curtis was on the island. An anthropologist from the Smithsonian made a corpus of several hundred photographs.

Up until last September these were captioned 'Eskimo woman and child', 'Eskimo man', 'Eskimo man, woman and child', and we had 200 examples of this. I took these photographs back to Nunivak Island and within ten days everybody was identified. That information came back, and became part of the records.

The Smithsonian has community scholar awards that enable the northern native researchers to travel to Washington to do their own research at the National Anthropological Archives. Their insight and knowledge allows us to correct and enrich the documentation of the collections.

[*The discussion moved on to questions of circulation of imagery.*]

UNIDENTIFIED MALE PARTICIPANT
We've been watching a lot of slide presentations, and I've seen pictures in other collections where there's no attribution. It seems to me that, historically, there's been a circulation of images, a circulation of documents, and sometimes it's not very clear who originated this work. There are two sides to this: one, that we need to trace the originators; and secondly, that the construction and circulation of particular pictures allow them to become the normative pictures for the Inuit.

KESLER E. WOODWARD
It is really difficult to figure out who the originators of some images are. The other thing, the conscious and subconscious construction of the image is not the product of any single person. The reason I focused on Stefansson was that there were all these wonderful photographs in the collection at Dartmouth. When I started delving, I noticed the Smithsonian *Handbook of North American Indians*. In the section on Copper Inuit it said these people match probably more closely than any other Eskimo group the popular conception of Eskimos. I thought, 'Well, it's sort of the other way round': it is because of Stefansson's photographs and Diamond Jenness's – very probably the most extensive ethnology of any Eskimo group – that that came to be.

ROBERT J. CHRISTOPHER
You're right about the wide circulation of images among photographers. I've found that Flaherty either collected or subsumed under his name a number of photographs by A. A. Chesterfield. The question of ownership of early Arctic photographs is a tricky one. I think photographers weren't into the notion of authorship as authors were. The notion of copyright authorship is actually more a twentieth-century phenomenon with a strong literary tradition. On the other hand I know that Flaherty worked hard to copyright his photographs, but that it all broke down. Copyright protection was not very intensive in photographs. People were borrowing and stealing images without proper attribution. There was a lot of circulation and photographers didn't have the protection that authors did. People just lost sight of rights. After a while, you forgot whose collections they were from. Photographs came into people's handling collections, or they were made into postcards, or were copied by someone else who wanted them, so I think there was a merry-go-round of ownership and that we're all going to have to spend a long time sorting out the questions of attribution. It is going to be difficult to do, given the range of archival resources.

ELIZABETH EDWARDS
Actually research can be done. We [the Pitt Rivers] did an exhibition last year called *Picturing Paradise*, about photography in Samoa. This was a German, American and British research collaboration. What we did, particularly at the German and American end, was actually trawl the archives looking for the duplications of the images. We came upon layers and layers of different kinds of information, of sitters, of photographers, of dates, and of different ways of printing the images, images which were missing. What we found in this research was the first thing that has to go is the researcher's ego. It has to be truly co-operative, no private work, sitting on your footnotes, you've really got to work together. But the richness of the material that came out was quite astonishing. In many ways the exhibition depended on countless local researchers. The whole lot was purposely sent back to Samoa. It just needs massive collaboration and patience. *Picturing Paradise* was a four-year project on the documentation of the images.

[*The discussion then moved on to consider the work of Simeonie Keenainak.*]

GEORGE QULAUT
Simeonie, I know that over the years you have been taking photographs of wild animals and hunting techniques, and I know for a fact that you use your photographs to teach the students. I also know that you are an extremely good carver, especially with soapstone and ivory. Do you take photographs of your work?

SIMEONIE KEENAINAK
Do I take pictures of my carvings? I try to take pictures of every one of them. The other ques-

tion that you ask, since I have been in the job for over a year now, I don't really have any books for teaching, but I have them [photographs] in my classroom just to show which animal is used for what, how you can recognise the animal, and things like that, which animal looks like this. I like to use my pictures for my teaching.

GEORGE QULAUT
And the reason why I ask you that question is because yesterday, if not this morning, you told me about when you showed your work especially with the polar bears, they helped to identify a polar bear that was very, very mean.

SIMEONIE KEENAINAK
Yes, that's another point. I show the kids, my son, which animal is not friendly. One time I showed one elder my albums, my four great albums, and he looked at them just like ordinary looking at them, and he told me, 'This polar bear wasn't friendly, isn't it?'. I said, 'Yes, how did you know that?' He said, 'When a polar bear look at you, you notice the ears are dark, this kind of polar bears are not friendly.' He was right, every time I would get near that polar bear he would charge, so he would know exactly what the animals look like, but I'm not like him, but I could pass that on to the kids with my pictures.

# Bibliography

Agnes Dunbar (Moodie) Chamberlin Collection. 1886-1937. Documents and Material relating to Geraldine Moodie and her study of plant life and photography. Toronto: Thomas Fisher Rare Book Library, University of Toronto (MS Coll. 112).

Aldrich, H. 1889. *Arctic Alaska and Siberia, or, Eight Months with the Arctic Whalemen.* Chicago: Rand-McNally.

Alloula, M. 1986. *The Colonial Harem*, trans. M. and W. Goldzich. Minneapolis: University of Minnesota Press.

Amundsen, R. 1907. *Nordvestpassagen*. Oslo: Aschehoug and Co.
— 1908. *The North West Passage – The Voyage and the Exploration of the Gjoa 1903-1907*, 2 vols. London: Archibald Constable and Company Ltd.

Anderson, J. W. 1939. 'Trading North of Hudson's Bay', *The Beaver*, Outfit 270 (3), December 1939, p.43.

Anon. 1995. 'World War II in Alaska', *Alaska Geographic*, 22: 4.

Arima, E. 1984. 'Caribou Eskimo' in *Handbook of North American Indians, volume 5: Arctic*, ed. D. Damas, pp.447-62. Washington: Smithsonian Institution Press.

Arndt, K.L. 1985. 'The Russian-American Company and the smallpox epidemic of 1835 to 1840.' Paper delivered to the Annual Meeting of the Alaska Anthropological Association. Anchorage.

Ballstadt, C., Hopkins, E. and Peterman, M., eds. 1985. *Susanna Moodie, Letters of a Lifetime.* Toronto: University of Toronto Press.

Banta, M. and Hinsley, C.M. 1986. *From Site to Sight: Anthropology, Photography, and the Power of Imagery.* Cambridge, MA: Peabody Museum Press.

Barker, J.H. 1993. *Always Getting Ready.* Seattle, Washington, London: University of Washington Press.

Barr, S. 1993. *Spirit of Exploration - Roald Amundsen's Polar Expeditions*, exhib. cat. (in conjunction with *The Grieg Jubilaeum: Norway Celebrates the Arts*). San Francisco.

Barr, W. 1990. 'Comment', *Arctic Anthropology*, 27: 1, pp.113-14.

Barthes, R. 1981. *Camera Lucida: Reflections on Photography.* New York: Hill and Wang.
— 1984. *Camera Lucida*, trans. R. Howard. London: Fontana.

Beattie, J.H. 1989. Hudson's Bay Company Archives Photographic Collection, Provincial Archives of Manitoba (Mimeographed information pack). Winnipeg: Hudson's Bay Company Archives.

Becker, H. 1978. 'Do Photographs Tell the Truth?', *Afterimage*, 5: 8, pp.9-13.

Belcher, E. 1855. *The Last of the Arctic Voyages.* London: Lovell Reece.

Bell, M. 1972. 'Thomas Mitchell, photographer and artist in the high arctic, 1875-76', *Image*, 15, pp.12-21.

Bell, R. 1901. *Geological Survey of Canada Annual Report*, 14. Canada: Parliamentary Papers.

Bellman, D., ed. 1980. *Peter Pitseolak (1902–1973)*. Montreal: McCord Museum.

Benjamin, W. 1985. *Illuminations* (trans. H. Arendt). New York: Shocken Books.

Bernier, J.E. 1909. *Cruise of the Arctic, 1906-7: Report on the Dominion Government Expedition to Arctic Islands and the Hudson Strait.* Ottawa: King's Printer.

Bertelsen, A. 1943. 'Grønlandsk medicinsk Statistik og Nosografi', *Meddelelser om Grønland*, 117: 4.

Berton, L. 1961. *I Married the Klondike.* Great Britain: McClelland and Stewart Limited.

Berton, P. 1987. *Why We Act Like Canadians.* Markham, Ontario: Penguin Books Canada.

Bessels, E. 1879. *Die Amerikanische Nordpol-expedition.* Leipzig: Verlag von Wilhelm Engelmann.

Birket-Smith, K. 1924. 'Ethnography of the Egedesminde District with Aspects of the General Culture of West Greenland', *Meddelelser om Grønland*, 66.
— 1929a. *The Caribou Eskimos. Material and Social Life and their Cultural Position. I. Descriptive Part*, Report of the Fifth Thule Expedition, 1921-24, vol.V, part I. Copenhagen: Gyldendalske Boghandel Nordisk Forlag.
— 1929b. *The Caribou Eskimos. Material and Social Life and their Cultural Position. II. Analytical Part*, Report of the Fifth Thule Expedition, 1921-24, vol.V, part II. Copenhagen: Gyldendalske Boghandel Nordisk Forlag.

Black, Mrs G. 1939. *My Seventy Years.* London: Thomas Nelson and Sons.

Blanton, C., ed. 1995. *Picturing Paradise.* Daytona Beach: Southeast Museum of Photography.

Blasdale, M.J. 1990. *Artists of New Bedford.* New Bedford: Old Dartmouth Historical Society.

Boas, F. 1888. 'The Eskimo', *Proceedings and Transactions of the Royal Society of Canada for the Year 1887*, 5: 2, pp.35-9.
— 1888. 'The Central Eskimo' in *Sixth Annual Report of the Bureau of American Ethnology for the Years 1884-1885*, pp.399-669. Washington: US Government Printing Office.

Bockstoce, J.R. 1977. *Steam Whaling in the Western Arctic.* New Bedford: Old Dartmouth Historical Society.
— 1986. *Whales, Ice and Men.* Seattle and London: University of Washington Press.

Bomann-Larsen, T. 1995. *Roald Amundsen – en biografi.* Oslo: J. W. Cappelen Forlag A/S.

Bonsall, A. 1902. 'After fifty years' in *The White World: Life and Adventures within the Arctic Circle Portrayed by Famous Living Explorers*, ed. R. Kersting, pp.39-50. New York: Scribner and Co.

Bradford, W. 1873. *The Arctic Regions, Illustrated with Photographs taken on an Art Expedition to Greenland.* London: Sampson Low, Marston, Low and Searle.

Brice-Bennet, C. 1981. 'Two opinions: Inuit and
Moravian Missionaries in Labrador 1804-1860.'
Unpublished MA thesis, Department of Anthropology,
Memorial University of Newfoundland, St John's.

Brody, H. 1976. 'Land occupancy: Inuit perceptions' in
*Inuit Land Use and Occupancy Project*, ed. M. Freeman.
Ottawa: Department of Indian and Northern Affairs.
— 1987. *The Living Arctic: Hunters of the Canadian
North*. Vancouver: Douglas and McIntyre.

Brown, M. 1994. 'Photographs bring Old Gjoa back to
life.' Article in an unknown local newspaper, 24 January
1994. Northwestern Territories.

Brown, J.S.H. 1981. 'Mission Indian progress and
dependency: ambiguous images from Canadian Methodist
lantern slides', *Arctic Anthropology*, 18:2, pp.17-27.

Bruemmer, F. 1993. *Arctic Memories: Living with the
Inuit*. Toronto: Key Porter.

Brumbaugh, L.P. 1996. 'Shadow Catchers or Shadow
Snatchers? Ethical issues for photographers of
contemporary Native Americans', *American Indian Culture
and Research Journal*, 20: 3, pp.33-49.

Bugge, Aa. 1965. 'Kallihirua: Polareskimoen, Canterbury',
*Gronland*, 13: 5, pp.161-75.
— 1966. 'Polareskimoen, Canterbury: Supplerende
Oplysninger vedr. Kallihirua', *Gronland*, 14: 1, pp.17-22.

Bunyan, I. *et al.* 1993. *No Ordinary Journey: John Rae,
Arctic Explorer 1813-1893*. Edinburgh: National Museums
of Scotland.

Burch, E. 1978. 'Caribou Eskimo Origins: An Old
Problem Reconsidered', *Arctic Anthropology*, XV: 1,
pp.1-35.
— 1981. *The Traditional Eskimo Hunters of Point Hope,
Alaska: 1800-1875*. North Slope Borough.
— 1986. 'The Caribou Inuit' in *Native Peoples, The
Canadian Experience*, ed. R. Morrison and C. Wilson,
pp.106-33. Toronto: McClelland and Stewart.

Bush, A.F. and Mitchell, L.C., eds. 1994. *The Photograph
and the American Indian*. New Jersey: Princeton University
Press.

*Calgary Herald*. 5 October 1945. Alberta: Calgary.

Canada (Department of Northern Affairs and National
Resources). 1957. Press release: 'Eskimos Fly to New
Hunting Grounds', 24 May 1957. National Archives of
Canada (NAC) RG22/335/40-8-14/1.

Carver, M.N. 1979. *Home Economics as an Academic
Discipline: A Short History*. Tucson: University of
Arizona, College of Education, Center for the Study of
Higher Education, topical paper 15.

Cato, C.M. 1909. 'Voyage of Auxillary Barque "Pelican"
of London, to Montreal, Labrador and Hudson's Bay, via
Peterhead. Commenced Saturday May 15th 1909. Ended
at London Jan. 3rd 1910', MS in the Archives of the
Department of Ethnography. London: British Museum.

Chalfen, R. 1987. *Snapshot Versions of Life*. Bowling
Green, OH: Bowling Green State University Popular
Press.

Clifford, J. 1986. 'Introduction: Partial Truths' in *Writing
Culture: The Poetics and Politics of Ethnography*, ed.
J. Clifford and G.E. Marcus. Berkeley: University of
California Press.

Clifford, J. and Marcus, G.E., eds. 1986. *Writing Culture:
The Poetics and Politics of Ethnography*. Berkeley:
University of California Press.

Cohen, E., Yeshayahu, N. and Almagor, U. 1992.
'Stranger-Local Interaction in Photography', *Annals of
Tourism Research*, 19, pp.213-33.

Cole, D. and Müller-Wille, L. 1984. 'Franz Boas'
Expedition to Baffin Island 1883-1884' in
*Études/Inuit/Studies*, 8:1, pp.37-63.

Cole, D. and Lockner, B., eds. 1989. *The Journals of
George M. Dawson: British Columbia, 1875-78*. Vancouver:
University of British Columbia Press.

Collier, J. and M. 1986. *Visual Anthropology: Photography
as a Research Method*. Albuquerque: University of New
Mexico Press.

Collins, H.B. 1946. 'Wilderness exploration and Alaska's
purchase', *The Living Wilderness*, December 1946.
— 1988. 'The man who buys good-for-nothing things' in
*Inua: Spirit World of the Bering Sea Eskimo*, ed.
W.W. Fitzhugh and S.A. Kaplan, pp.29-37. Washington:
Smithsonian Institution Press.

Condon, R. (with Julia Ogina and the Holman Elders)
1996. *The Northern Copper Inuit*. Norman: University of
Oklahoma Press.

Condon, R.G. 1989. 'The history and development of
arctic photography', *Arctic Anthropology*, 26: 1, pp.46-87.

Condon, R.G. and Ogina, J. 1990. 'The Holman
Photohistorical Project: the methodology of community
based oral history research.' Paper presented at the
Seventh Inuit Studies Conference, Fairbanks.

Cook, T. 1980. 'Canada's Arctic Islands: a centennial
perspective', *The Archivist*, 7: 5, pp.1-4.

Cooke, A. and Holland, C. 1978. *The Exploration of
Northern Canada, 500-1920: A Chronology*. Toronto:
Arctic History Press.

Copland, A.D. 1985. *Coplalook: Chief Trader, Hudson's
Bay Company 1923-39*. Winnipeg: Watson and Dwyer
Publishing Ltd.

Corner, G.W. 1972. *Doctor Kane of the Arctic Seas*.
Philadelphia: Temple University Press.

Cotter, H.M.S. 1933. 'Chief Factor and Photographer',
*The Beaver*, Outfit 264 (3), December 1933, pp.23-6, 66.

Cox, W. 1993. Guide to the Edward William Nelson and
Edward Alphonso Goldman Collection, *c*.1873-1946 and
undated. *Guides to Collections*. Smithsonian Institution
Archives.

Csonka, Y. 1991. 'Les Ahiarmiut (1920-1950) dans la
perspective de l'histoire des Inuit Caribous.' Unpublished
PhD dissertation. Québec: Université Laval.

Curran, W.T. and Adams, H.P. 1907. *Glimpses of
Northern Canada, the Land of Hidden Treasure*. Montréal:
Cambridge Corporation Ltd.
— and Calkins, H.A. 1917. *In Canada's Wonderful
Northland*. New York and London: G.P. Putnam's Sons.

Curtis, E. 1907-30. *The North American Indian: being a
series of volumes picturing and describing the Indians of the
United States and Alaska*, ed. F.W. Hodge, 20 vols.
Norwood, Mass.: Plimpton Press (Johnson reprint, New
York, 1970).

Dall, W.H. 1870. *Alaska and its Resources*. Boston: Lee
and Shepard.
— 1875a. 'On further examinations of the Amaknak Cave,
Captain's Bay, Unalaska', *Proceedings of the Californian
Academy of Sciences*, 5, pp.196-200.
— 1875b. 'Alaska Mummies', *American Naturalist*, 9: 8,
pp.433-40.
— 1877. 'On succession in the shell-heaps of the Aleutian
Islands' in: 'Tribes of the Extreme Northwest',
*Contributions to North American Ethnology*, ed.
J.W. Powell, 9 vols, 1: 2, pp.41-91. Washington: US
Government Printing Office.

— 1878. 'On the remains of later pre-historic man obtained from caves in the Catherina Archipelago, Alaska Territory, and especially from the caves of the Aleutian Islands', *Smithsonian Contributions to Knowledge*, 22, Publication 318, pp.1-40. Washington.

— 1884. 'On masks, labrets, and certain aboriginal customs …' *Third Annual Report of the Bureau of Ethnology*, 1881-1882, pp.67-203. Washington: US Government Printing Office.

Danzker, J.B. ed. 1979. *Robert Flaherty, Photographer/Filmmaker: The Inuit 1910-1922*. Vancouver: Vancouver Art Gallery.

Darrah, W.C. 1971. *The World of Stereographs*. Gettysburg: Darrah Publishing.

Davey, Revd J.W. 1905. *The Fall of Torngak*. London: S.W.Partridge.

Davis, C.H., ed. 1876. *Narrative of the North Polar Expedition, U.S. Ship 'Polaris', Captain Charles Francis Hall Commanding*. Washington: US Government Printing Office.

Davis, K.F. 1981. *Désiré Charnay Expeditionary Photographer*. Albuquerque: University of New Mexico Press.

Diubaldo, R.J. 1978. *Stefansson and the Canadian Arctic*. Montréal: McGill-Queen's University Press.

Domville, W. 1852-3. 'Private Journal Kept on Board HMS "Resolute", Cap. H.Kellett, Feb.-Nov. 1852 and some rough notes for 1853'. London: National Maritime Museum, JOD/67.

Driscoll-Engelstad, B. 1995. 'Silent echoes: the displacement and reappearance of Copper Inuit clothing.' Paper presented at the annual meeting of the American Anthropological Association, Washington, DC.

Dumond, D.E. 1996. 'Poison in the cup: the South Alaskan smallpox epidemic of 1835' in: 'Chin Hills to Chiloquin: papers honoring the versatile career of Theodore Stern', *University of Oregon Anthropological Papers*, ed. D.E.Dumond, 52, pp.117-29. Eugene, Oregon.

Dunmore, J.L. 1869. 'The camera among the icebergs', *The Philadelphia Photographer*, 6, pp.412-14.

Dyson, G. 1986. *Baidarka*. Edmonds, Washington: Alaska Northwest Publishing Company.

East, K. 1996. Howard, Mary. Personal Interview. Eastend, Saskatchewan, January 1996.

Eber, D. 1977. 'How it really was', *Natural History*, (February), pp.70-75.

— 1989. *When the Whalers Were Up North*. Montreal: McGill-Queen's University Press.

— 1994. 'A feminine focus on the last frontier: Geraldine Moodie's hidden treasures', *Arctic Circle*, Spring, pp.16-21.

Edwards, E. 1992a. 'Introduction' in *Anthropology and Photography 1860-1920*. New Haven: Yale University Press.

— ed. 1992b. *Anthropology and Photography, 1860-1920*. New Haven: Yale University Press.

— 1997. 'Beyond the Boundary: a consideration of the expressive in photography and anthropology' in *Rethinking Visual Anthropology*, ed. M.Banks and H.Morphy. London: Yale University Press.

Eskilden, U. 1978. 'Photography and the Neue Sachlichkeit Movement' in *Germany: The New Photography 1927-1933*, ed. D.Mellor. London: Arts Council of Great Britain.

Fabian, J. 1983. *Time and the Other*. New York: Columbia University Press.

Fanck, A. 1933. *S.O.S. Eisberg Mit Dr Fanck und Ernst Udet in Grönland (Die Grönland-Expedition des Universal-Films S.O.S. Eisberg)*. München: Verlag F.Bruckman AG.

Fienup-Riordan, A. 1990. *Eskimo Essays: Yupik Lives and How We See Them*. New Brunswick, New Jersey: Rutgers University Press.

— 1995. *Freeze Frame. Alaska Eskimos in the Movies*. Seattle: University of Washington Press.

Fitzhugh, W.W. 1983. 'Introduction' in "The Eskimo about Bering Strait", by E.W.Nelson. *Bureau of American Ethnology Annual Report*, 19, pp.7-106 (reprint of 1899 edn). Washington: Smithsonian Institution Press.

— 1988a. 'Baird's naturalists: Smithsonian collectors in Alaska' in *Crossroads of Continents: Cultures of Siberia and Alaska*, ed. W.W.Fitzhugh and A.C.Crowell, pp.89-96. Washington: Smithsonian Institution Press.

— 1988b. 'Persistence and change in art and ideology in western Alaskan cultures' in *The Late Prehistoric Development of Alaska's Native Peoples*. Alaska Anthropological Association Monograph, 4, pp.81-105. Aurora Press.

— 1993. 'Art and iconography in the hunting ritual of North Pacific peoples' in *Proceedings of the 7th International Abashiri Symposium*, pp.1-13. Abashiri: Abashiri Museum of Northern Peoples.

Fitzhugh, W.W. and Kaplan, S.A., eds. 1982. *Inua: Spirit World of the Bering Sea Eskimo*. Washington: Smithsonian Institution Press.

— 1983. *Inua: Spirit World of the Bering Sea Eskimo*. Washington: Smithsonian Travelling Exhibition Service.

Fitzhugh, W.W. and Selig, R.O. 1981. 'The Smithsonian-Alaska connection: 19th-century explorers and anthropologists' in *The Alaska Journal: 1981 Collection*, compiled and edited by V.McKinley, pp.193-208. Anchorage: Anchorage Northwest Publishing Company.

Fleming, A.A. 1934. 'Old and New', *The Beaver*, Outfit 164 (4), March 1934, pp.36-7.

Fleming, A.L. 1928. *Dwellers in Arctic Night*. Westminster and Toronto: Society for the Propagation of the Gospel in Foreign Parts; Missionary Society of the Church of England in Canada.

— 1957. *Archibald the Arctic*. London: Hodder & Stoughton.

Fleming, P., Richardson and Luskey, J.L., eds. 1993. *The Shadow Catchers: Images of the American Indian*. London: Laurence King.

Folk, E.G. and Folk, M.A. 1984. *Vilhjalmur Stefansson and the Development of Arctic Territorial Science*. Iowa City: University of Iowa Press.

Ford, G. 1850-54. *Journal of an Arctic Voyage, HMS 'Investigator'*. California: Karpeles Manuscript Library, Santa Barbara.

Foucault, M. 1977. *Discipline and Punishment*. London: Allen Lane.

Freuchen, P. 1954. *Vagrant Viking: My Life and Adventures*. London: Victor Gollancz Ltd.

Gallagher, J. 1992. 'S.O.S. Iceberg: Arctic Wastes, Antic Adventures', *American Cinematographer*, 73: 11, pp.86-91.

Geller, P. 1993. 'The "True North" in Pictures? Photographic Representation in the Hudson's Bay Company's *Beaver* Magazine, 1920-1945', *Archivaria*, 36, pp. 166-88.

— 1996. 'Conference Report: Imagining the Arctic', *Rupert's Land*, 1, pp.12-13.

Gilbert, G. 1980. *Photography: The Early Years*. New York: Harper and Row.

Gjessing, G. and Krekling-Johannessen, M. 1957. *De hundre år – Studies Honouring the Centennial of Universitetets Etnografiske Museum, Oslo 1857–1957* 5. Oslo: Forenede Trykkerier.

Goldman, E.A. 1935. 'Edward William Nelson – Naturalist, 1855-1934', *Auk*, 52: 2, pp.135-48.

Gosling, W.G. 1910. *Labrador: Its Discovery, Exploration and Development*. London: Alston Rivers.

Graburn, N.H.H. 1963. *Lake Harbour, Baffin Island: The Decline of the Eskimo Community*. Ottawa: Government of Canada NCRC-63-2.
— 1964. *Taqamiut Eskimo Kinship Terminology*. Ottawa: Government of Canada NCRC-64-1.
— 1967. 'The Eskimos and "Airport Art"', *Transaction*, 4, pp.28-33.
— 1969. *Eskimos without Igloos*. Boston: Little Brown.
— 1974. 'A Preliminary Analysis of Eskimo Art and Symbolism', *Proceedings of the International Congress of Americanists (Rome 1972)* 22, pp.165-70.
— 1976a. '*Nalunaikutanga*: Signs and Symbols in Eskimo Art and Culture', *Polarforschung*, 46, pp.1-11.
— 1976b. 'Canadian Eskimo Art: The Eastern Arctic' in *Ethnic and Tourist Arts*, ed. N. Graburn, pp.39-55. Berkeley: University of California Press.
— 1977. 'Tourism: the Sacred Journey' in Smith 1977, pp.17-31.
— 1978a. '"I Like Things to Look More Different than that Stuff Did": An Experiment in Cross-Cultural Art Appreciation' in *Art in Society*, ed. J. V. S. Megaw and M. Greenhalgh, pp.51-70. London: Duckworth.
— 1978b. 'Inuit Pivalliajut: The Cultural and Identity Consequences of Commercialization of Canadian Inuit Art' in *Consequences of Economic Change in Circumpolar Regions*, ed. L. Muller-Wille et. al., pp.185-200. Edmonton: Boreal Institute, paper no.14.
— 1980. 'Man, Beast and Transformation in the Canadian Inuit Art and Culture' in *Manlike Monsters on Trial*, ed. M. Halpin and M. Ames, pp.193-210. Vancouver: University of British Columbia Press.
— 1983. 'Inuit Art' in *Arctic Life: Challenge to Survive*, ed. M. M. Jacobs and J. B. Richardson III, pp.175-93. Pittsburgh: Carnegie Museum of Natural History.
— 1987a. 'Severe Child Abuse among the Canadian Inuit' in *Child Treatment and Child Survival*, ed. N. Scheper-Hughes, pp.211-25. Boston: D. Reidel.
— 1987b. 'Inuit Art and the Expression of Eskimo Identity', *American Review of Canadian Studies*, 17: 1, pp.47-66.
— 1993a. 'Ethnic Arts of the Fourth World: the View from Canada' in *Imagery and Creativity: Ethnoaesthetics and Art Worlds in the Americas*, ed. D. S. and N. E. Whitten, pp.171-204. Tucson: University of Arizona Press.
— 1993b. 'Will the Language of Inuit Artists Survive?' *Inuit Art Quarterly*, 8: 1, pp.18-25.
— 1993c. 'The Fourth World and Fourth World Art' in *In the Shadow of the Sun: Perspectives on Contemporary Native Art*. Ottawa: Canadian Museum of Civilization, Canadian Ethnology Service, Mercury Series 124.
— 1996a. 'British Museum Hosts Arctic Photography Conference', *Museum Anthropology*, 20: 3, pp.154-6, and in *American Anthropologist Newsletter*, 37: 8, p.8.
— 1996b. 'Introduction: The Alaska Commercial Company Collection' in N. H. H. Graburn, M. Lee and J-L. Rousselot 1996, pp.1-18.

Graburn, N.H.H. and Lee, M. 1989. 'The Arctic Culture Area' in *Native North Americans: an Ethnohistorical Approach*, ed. D. L. Boxberger, pp.23-64. Dubuque: Kendall-Hunt.

Graburn, N.H.H., Lee, M. and Rousselot, J-L. 1996. *Catalogue Raisonné of the Alaska Commercial Company Collection*. Berkeley: University of California Press.

Graham-Brown, S. 1988. *Images of Women: The Portrayal of Women in Photography of the Middle East 1860-1950*. New York and Columbia University Press.

Green, D. 1984. 'Classified Subjects', *Ten8*, 14, pp. 30-7.
— 1986. 'Veins of Resemblance: Photography and Eugenics' in *Photography/Politics: Two*, ed. P. Holland, J. Spence and S. Watney. London: Comedia/Photography Workshop.

Greenhill, R. and Birell, A. 1979. *Canadian Photography 1839-1930*. Toronto: Coach House Press.

Gregor, A. 1978. *Vilhjalmur Stefansson and the Arctic*. Agincourt: Book Society of Canada.

Greist, H. n.d. Photograph collection on file. North Slope Borough Planning Department, Barrow.

Greist, M. n.d. *Nursing Under the North Star*. White County Historical Society, report on file at North Slope Borough Planning Department, Barrow.

Gunston, D. 1960. 'Leni Riefenstahl', *Film Quarterly*, 14: 1, pp.4-19.

Hansen, G. 1912. *Gjoa-ekspedisojonen 1903-1906*. Copenhagen: Udvalget for Folkeopplysningens Fremme.

Harp, E. 1962. 'The Culture History of the Central Barren Grounds' in *Prehistoric Cultural Relations Between the Arctic and Temperate Zones of Northern America*, ed. J. Campbell, Arctic Institute of Northern America Technical Paper no. 11, pp. 69-75.

Harris, G.K. 1947-9. Notebooks from Alaska Trip. Unpublished manuscript deposited at the Department of Archives and Manuscripts, Southwest Museum, Los Angeles.

Harris, K. 1996. Telephone interview with Molly Lee, 7 April.

Harris, L.E. 1994. 'Protecting your art: a lawyer interprets Canada's copyright law', *Inuit Art Quarterly*, 9: 1, pp.13-16.

Hatt, G. 1916. 'Moccasins and their relation to Arctic footwear', *American Anthropological Association Memoir*, 3, pp.147-250.

Hayes, I.I. 1867. *The Open Polar Sea: A Narrative of a Voyage of Discovery Toward the North Pole in the Schooner 'United States'*. New York: Hurd and Houghton.
— 1872. *The Land of Desolation*. New York: Harper and Brothers.

Herchmer, L. 1897. Official Report of the Commissioner of the NWMP, Appendix N. Ottawa: House of Commons (Sessional Paper no.28).

Hiller, J. 1966. 'The Moravian expedition to Labrador, 1752', *Newfoundland Quarterly*, 15: 2, pp.19-22.
— 1971. 'The Moravians in Labrador, 1771-1805', *Polar Record*, 15: 99, pp.839-54.

Holtved, E. 1967. 'Contributions to Polar Eskimo Ethnography', *Meddelelser om Gronland*, 182: 2.

Hooper, C.L. 1883. *Report on the cruise of the U.S. Revenue Steamer* Thomas Corwin *in the Arctic Ocean, 1881*. Washington: US Government Printing Office.

Houston, J. 1955. Ennadai Lake, Northwest Territories – 1955. Department of Northern Affairs and National Resources Report. Department of Indian Affairs and Northern Development Library, Hull.

Huntford, R. 1987. *The Amundsen Photographs*. London: Hodder and Stoughton.

Hutton, S.K. 1912. *Among the Eskimos of Labrador*. London: Seeley Service.

Hunt, W.R. 1986. *Stef: A Biography of Vilhjalmur Stefansson, Canadian Arctic Explorer*. Vancouver: University of British Columbia Press.

Huyda, R. 1980. *Camera in the Interior*. Toronto: Coach House Press.

*Illustrated London News*. 1851. 'The Portraits', *The Illustrated London News*, 13 September 1851, p.330.
— 1852a. 'Sir Edward Belcher's Arctic searching squadron', *The Illustrated London News*, 17 April 1852, p.306.
— 1852b. 'The Arctic searching expedition', *The Illustrated London News*, 24 April 1852, p.322.

Ipellie, A. 1992. 'The Colonization of the Arctic' in *Indigena: Contemporary Native Perspectives*, ed. G. McMaster and L-A. Martin, pp.39-57. Vancouver, Toronto and Hull: Douglas and McIntyre and Canadian Museum of Civilization.

Jacknis, I. 1984. 'Franz Boas and Photography', *Studies in Visual Communication*, 10: 1, pp.2-60.

Jacobsen, J.A. 1977. *Alaskan Voyage, 1881-1883. An Expedition to the Northwest Coast of America*, trans. E. Gunther. Chicago: University of Chicago Press.

James, W.C. 1985. *A Fur Trader's Photographs: A. A. Chesterfield in the District of Ungava, 1901-4*. Kingston and Montreal: McGill-Queen's University Press.

Jenness, D. 1922. 'The Life of the Copper Eskimos', *Report of the Canadian Arctic Expedition 1913–1918*, 12A, Ottawa.
— 1928. *The People of the Twilight*. New York: The Macmillan Co.
— 1964. *Eskimo Administration: II: Canada*. Montreal: Arctic Institute of North America.

Kane, E.K. 1856. *Arctic Explorations: the Second Grinnell Expedition in Search of Sir John Franklin, 1853, '54, '55*, 2 vols. Philadelphia: Childs and Peterson.

Kent, R. 1935. *Salamina*. New York: Harcourt Brace and Company.
— 1962. *Rockwell Kent's Greenland Journal*. New York: Ivan Obolensky, Inc.

Kerr, W. 1955. Memorandum to the Chief of the Arctic Division, 4 July 1955. National Archives of Canada/RG22/335/40-8-14/1.

King, J.C.H. 1987. *Arctic Hunters: Indians and Inuit of Northern Canada*. London: British Museum Publications.

King, R.E. 1994. 'The Pribilof Islands in the 1870s: the stereo-photographs of Dr. Hugh H. McIntyre', *Alaska History*, 9: 1, pp.38-45.

King, W.F. 1905. *Report on the Title of Canada to the Islands north of the Mainland of Canada*. Ottawa: Government Printing Bureau.

Kleivan, H. 1966. *The Eskimos of Northeast Labrador: A History of Eskimo-White Relations*, 1771-1955. Oslo: Norsk Polarinstitutt.

Kleivan, I. 1958. 'Træk af John Møller liv og virke', *Grønland*, 6: 8, pp.303-13.
— 1987. 'Rockwell Kent - en engageret amerikansk kunster i Grønland i 30'erne', *Tidsskriftet Grønland*, 6-7, pp.175-90.
— 1996. *John Møller: En grønlandsk fotograf. Fotografier fra perioden 1889-1935/John Møller: Kalaaleq assiliisoq. Ukiuni 1889-1935 assilisat*. København.

Koldewey, C. 1874. *The German Arctic Expedition of 1869-70 and Narrative of the Wreck of the 'Hansa' in the Ice*. London: Sampson Low, Marston, Low and Searle.

Krech, S. III. 1989. *A Victorian Earl in the Arctic*. London: British Museum Publications.

Kunnuk, S. 1995. 'Judas Ullulaq: It appears that I will live to be an old man, in which case you still will find me carving', *Inuit Art Quarterly*, 10: 2, Summer 1995.

Lantis, M. 1954. 'Edward William Nelson', *Anthropological Papers of the University of Alaska*, 3: 1, pp.5-16.

LaTrobe, B. 1888-9. 'With the *Harmony* to Labrador, Notes of a Visit by the Editor', *Periodical Accounts*, 34, pp.396-411, 432-49, 475-93.

Lee, M. 1996. 'Context and contact: the history and activities of the Alaska Commercial Company, 1867-1900' in *Catalogue Raisonné of the Alaska Commercial Company Collection. Phoebe Apperson Hearst Museum of Anthropology*, ed. N.H.H. Graburn, M. Lee and J-L. Rousselot, pp.19-38. Berkeley: University of California Press.

Lee, M. and Graburn, N.H.H. 1986. 'Alaska Commercial Company Commerce and Curios, 1868-1904', an exhibition presented by the Lowie Museum of Anthropology, 15 November 1986 – 30 June 1987. Berkeley: Robert H. Lowie Museum.

Leith, C.K. and Leith, A.T. 1912. *A Summer and Winter on Hudson Bay*. Madison: Cartwell Printing Co.

Levere, T.H. 1993. *Science and the Canadian Arctic: A Century of Exploration 1818-1918*. Cambridge: Cambridge University Press.

*Life*. 1956. 'A Mesolithic Age Today: Caribou Eskimos illustrate its culture', *Life Magazine*, 27 February.

Lindsay, D. 1993. *Science in the Subarctic: Trappers, Traders, and Naturalists*. Washington: Smithsonian Institution Press.

Lippard, L.R. 1992a. 'Introduction' in *Partial Recall: Photographs of Native North Americans*, ed. L.R. Lippard. New York: The New Press.
— ed. 1992b. *Partial Recall: Photographs of Native North Americans*. New York: The New Press.

Loewe, F. and Sorge, E. 1933. 'Scientific work in Greenland - Universal-Dr Fanck-Greenland Expedition 1932', MS housed at the Royal Geographical Society, destined for publication in *Forschungen and Fortschritte*, 10 February 1932.

Low, A.P. 1906. *The Cruise of the Neptune, 1903-1904; Report on the Dominion Government Expedition to Hudson Bay and the Arctic Islands on Board the D.G.S. Neptune*. Ottawa: Government Printing Bureau.

Lowry, S. 1994. *Natives of the Far North: Alaska's Vanishing Culture in the Eye of Edward Sheriff Curtis*. Mechanicsburg, Pa.: Stackpole Books.

Lutz, C.A. and Collins, J.L. 1993. *Reading National Geographic*. Chicago: University of Chicago Press.

Lyman, C.M. 1982. *The Vanishing Race and Other Illustrations: Photographs of Indians by Edward S. Curtis*. New York: Pantheon.

Mack, G.E. 1938. 'The Nascopie', *The Beaver*, Outfit 169 (2), pp.5-9.

Macpherson, K. 1978. '*As Is*: A review of Helmar Lerski, *Köpfe des Alltags* (1931)' in *Germany. The New Photography 1927-1933*, ed. D. Mellor. London: Arts Council of Great Britain.

Marcus, A. 1995. *Relocating Eden: The Image and Politics of Inuit Exile in the Canadian Arctic*. Hanover: University Press of New England.

Markham, C.R. 1876. *The Threshold of the Unknown Regions*. London: Sampson Low, Marston, Searle & Rivington (4th edn).

Mathiassen, T. 1930. 'The Question of the Origin of Eskimo Culture', *American Anthropologist*, 32: 4, pp.591-607.

Mattila, R. 1978. *A Chronological Bibliography of the Published Works of Vilhjalmur Stefansson (1879–1962)*. Hanover: Dartmouth College Library.

McClintock, F.L. 1852-4. *The Private Journal of F.L. McClintock*. Cambridge: Scott Polar Research Institute, MS 1.
— 1859. *The Voyage of the 'Fox' in the Arctic Seas: A Narrative of the Discovery of the Fate of Sir John Franklin and His Companions*. London: John Murray.

*Medicine Hat News*. 1897. Medicine Hat, Alberta, Thursday 28 January.

Mellor, D. 1978. 'London-Berlin-London: a cultural history of the reception and influence of the New German Photography in Britain 1927-1933' in *Germany. The New Photography 1927-1933*, ed. D. Mellor. London: Arts Council of Great Britain.

Merrifield, R.R. 1993. *Speaking of Canada*. Toronto: McClelland and Stewart, Inc.

Metz, C. 1985. 'Photography and Fetish', *October*, 34, pp.81-90.

Minotto, C., Psutka, M., Burant, J., and Houston, J. 1977a. 'To Photograph the Arctic Frontier, Part I', *The Archivist*, 4:2, pp.1-4.
— 1977b. 'To Photograph the Arctic Frontier, Part II', *The Archivist*, 4:3, pp.1-4.
— 1977c. 'To Photograph the Arctic Frontier, Part III', *The Archivist*, 4:4, pp.1-5.
— 1977d. 'To Photograph the Arctic Frontier, Part IV', *The Archivist*, 4:5, pp.3-6.
— 1977d. 'To Photograph the Arctic Frontier, Part V', *The Archivist*, 4:6, pp.6-8.
— 1978. 'To Photograph the Arctic Frontier, Part VI', *The Archivist*, 5:1, pp.1-4.

*Die Mission in der Polarländern*, 1867. *Missions-Bilder*, vol.5. Calw and Stuttgart: J.F. Steinkopf.

Møller, J. 1928. 'Nûngme piniarnikut avdlatigutdlo inûtigssarsiorneq/Grønlandske Erhverv i Godthaab' in *Niuvertoqarfiup Nûp oqalugtuagssartaisa ilait/Træk af Kolonien Godthaabs Historie 1728-1928*, ed. K. Honoré, pp.103-24. Nûk/Godthaab.
— 1961. 'Nûngme tarrarssugkanik ássilissat qanganitsat autdlarnerneqarnerat/Fotografiapparatets As indførelse i Grønland', *Atuagagdliutit/Grønlandsposten*, 3, pp.15-16 (Greenlandic text reprinted from *Atuagagdliutit*, 7, 1930).

Moodie, G. 1895. Letter to Catherine Parr Traill, 8 May 1895, in Traill Family Collection. Ottawa: National Archives of Canada, MG 29 D81 V.1.

Moodie, J.D. 1905. Copy of Daily Diaries. Medicine Hat: Medicine Hat Museum and Art Gallery (Geraldine Moodie Collection).
— 1908-9. Portions of Daily Diaries. Medicine Hat: Medicine Hat Museum and Art Gallery (Geraldine Moodie Collection).

Mowat, F. 1952. *People of the Deer*. Boston: Little, Brown.

MR. Moravian Records, Microfilm collection, National Archives of Canada, Record Group 489: Records from Nain.

Muir, J. 1917. *The Cruise of the* Corwin: *Journal of the Arctic Expedition of 1881 in Search of De Long and the* Jeannette, ed. W.F. Bade. Boston: Houghton Mifflin.

Murdoch, J. 1892. 'Ethnological results of the Point Barrow Expedition' in *9th Annual Report of the Bureau of American Ethnology for the Years 1887-1888*, pp.19-441. Washington.

Murray, T.B. 1856. *Kalli, the Esquimaux Christian, A Memoir*. London: Society for Promoting Christian Knowledge.

Nares, G.S. 1875-6. *Nares Family Papers. Entry Book. Captain George S. Nares' Correspondence*. Ottawa: National Archives of Canada.
— 1875-7. *Nares Family Papers. Private Remark Book, No.1*. Ottawa: National Archives of Canada.

Naske, C. and Slotnik, H.F. 1987. *Alaska: A History of the 49th State*. Norman: University of Oklahoma Press.

*National Geographic*. 1920. 'The National Geographic Society's Notable Year', *The National Geographic Magazine*, 37:4, pp.338-42.

National Photography Collection. 1979. 'To photograph the Arctic frontier' in *Robert Flaherty: Photographer/Filmmaker*, ed. J.B. Danzker, pp.74-80. Vancouver: Vancouver Art Gallery.

Naylor, C. 1988. *Contemporary Photographers*. Chicago: St James Press.

Neaf, W. 1975. *Era of Exploration*. New York: Albright-Knox Art Gallery.

Neatby, L.H., ed. 1977. *My Life Among the Eskimos: the Baffinland Journals of Bernhard Adolph Hantzsch 1909-1911*. Saskatoon: Institute of Northern Studies.

Nelson, E.W. 1882. 'A sledge journey in the delta of the Yukon, northern Alaska', *Proceedings of the Royal Geographical Society and Monthly Record of Geography*, n.s. 4: 667.
— 1887. *Report on natural history collections made in Alaska between the years 1877-1881*. Washington: Arctic Series of Publications, US Army Signal Service III.
— 1899. 'The Eskimo about Bering Strait', *Bureau of American Ethnology Annual Report*, 19, pp. 1-518. Washington: Smithsonian Institution.

*New York Times*. 1932. 21 August, p.9.

Newhall, B. 1964. *The History of Photography*. New York: New York Graphic Society.
— 1978. 'PhotoEye of the 1920s: The Deutsche Werkbund Exhibition of 1929' in *Germany: The New Photography 1927-1933*, ed. D. Mellor. London: Arts Council of Great Britain.

Newman, P.C. 1991. *Merchant Princes*. Toronto: Penguin Books Canada Ltd.

Nichols, B. 1991. *Representing Reality*. Bloomington/Indianapolis: Indiana University Press.

Noble, Revd L.L. 1862. *After Icebergs With a Painter: A Summer Voyage to Labrador and Around Newfoundland*. New York: D. Appleton and Co.

Nutarakittuq, E. 1990. 'Recollections and comments', *Inuktitut*, 72, pp.26-41.

Nuttall, M. 1992. *Arctic Homeland*. London: Belhaven Press.

Oldendow, K. 1957. *Bogtrykkerkunsten i Grønland og mændene bag den. En boghistorisk oversigt*. København. (Abridged English edn: *Printing in Greenland*, Copenhagen, 1959.)

O'Neill, P.B. 1989. *Checklist of Canadian Copyright Deposits in the British Museum*, 5. Halifax: Dalhousie University Press.

PA. 'Periodical Accounts Relating to the Missions of the Church of the United Brethren, Established Among the Heathen, 1790-1960'. London.
— (vol.28) 1871. 'Retrospect of the History of the Mission of the Brethren's Church in Labrador for the past hundred years', pp.1-19, 53-72.
— (vol.30) 1877. 'Report of the Visitation of the Mission in Labrador, by Br L.T. Reichel, in the summer of the year 1876', pp.145-55.

Packard, A.S. 1885. 'Notes on the Labrador Eskimo and their former range southward', *American Naturalist*, 19, pp.471-81, 533-60.

Perry, A.B. 1903. Report of the Commissioner of the NWMP, pp.71-9. Ottawa: House of Commons (2-3 Edward VII, Sessional Paper No.28).
— 1907. Report of the Commissioner of the RNWMP, pp.1-15. Ottawa: House of Commons (6-7 Edward VII, Sessional Paper No.28).
— 1908. Report of the Commissioner of the RNWMP, Part IV. Ottawa: House of Commons (7-8 Edward VII, Sessional Paper No.28).

Petersen, C. 1857. *Erindringer fra Polarlandene*, ed. L.B. Deichmann. Copenhagen: P.G. Philipsens Forlag.
— 1860. *Den sidste Franklin-Expedition med 'Fox', Capt. M'Clintock*. Kjøbenhavn: Fr Woldikes Forlagsboghandel.

Pierce, P. 1985. *Canada, the Missing Years, 1895-1924*. Don Mills: Stoddart.

Pierce, R. 1977. 'Edweard Muybridge, Alaska's first photographer', *Alaska Journal*, 7: 4, pp.202-10.

Pilot, Revd W. 1898. *A Visit to Labrador*. London: Colonial and Continental Church Society.

Pinart, A. 1875. *La caverne d'Aknanh, Ile d'Ounga (Archipel Shumagin, Alaska)*. Paris: E. Leroux.

Pinney, C. 1992. 'Underneath the Banyan Tree: William Crooke and Photographic Depictions of Caste' in Edwards 1992b. *Anthropology and Photography 1860-1920*. New Haven: Yale University Press, p. 1601.

Pitseolak, P. and Eber, D. 1975. *People from Our Side: An Eskimo Life Story in Words and Photographs*. Edmonton: Hurtig.

Porsild, A. 1952. 'Review of "People of the Deer"', *The Beaver*, June 1952.

Pridchard, J.C. 1855. *The Natural History of Man*, ed. and enlarged E. Norris, 4th edn, 2 vols. London: H. Ballière.

Psutka, M. 1976. *Wakeham Expedition to Hudson Strait and Cumberland Sound, 1897*. Ottawa: National Archives of Canada manuscript report.

Public Archives of Canada. 1977. *Arctic Images: The Frontier Photographed, 1860-1911*. Ottawa: Public Archives of Canada.

Rasmussen, K. 1925. *Myter og Sagn fra Grønland III: Kap York-Distriktet og Nordgrønland, København*. Gyldendalske Boghandel Nordisk Forlag, pp. 138-9.
— 1930. *Observations on the Intellectual Culture of the Caribou Eskimos*. Report of the Fifth Thule Expedition, 1921-24, VII: 2. Copenhagen: Gyldendalske Boghandel Nordisk Forlag.
— 1933. 'South-east Greenland - the Seventh Thule Expedition, 1932 - From Cape Farewell to Umivik', *Geografisk Tidsskrift*, 36, pp.35-41.

Ray, D.J. 1984. 'The Hudson's Bay Company and Native People' in *Handbook of North American Indians, 5: 'Arctic'*, ed. D. Damas. Washington: Smithsonian Institution Press.

RCMP Records. Documents relating to J.D. and Geraldine Moodie, 1895-1917. Ottawa: National Archives of Canada (RG 18 A.1).

Renner, P. 1989. 'The Photograph (1930)' in *Photography in the Modern Era: European Documents and Critical Writings, 1913-40*, ed. C. Phillips. New York: The Metropolitan Museum of Art/Aperture.

Richards, E.A. 1949. *Arctic Mood*. Caldwell: Caxton Printers.

Richardson, J. 1847-8. *Contents of Sir John Richardson's Account Book of the Richardson-Rae Overland Expedition*. Urbana: University of Illinois.
— 1851. *Arctic Searching Expedition: A Journal of a Boat-voyage through Rupert's Land and the Arctic Sea, in Search of the Discovery Vessels under Command of Sir John Franklin*. London: Longman, Brown, Green and Longmans.

Riefenstahl, L. 1933a. *Kampf in Schnee und Eis*. Leipzig: Hesse and Becker Verlag.
— 1933b. 'Min Filmsrejse til de Arktiske Egne' *Tidens Kvinder*, 14 February, pp.8-9.
— 1992. *The Sieve of Time: The Memoirs of Leni Riefenstahl*. London: Quartet Books.

Rink, H. 1866. *Eskimoiske Eventyr og Sagn oversatte efter de indfødte Fortælleres Opskrifter og Meddelelser*. Kjøbenhavn: C.A. Reitzels Bog-Handel.
— 1875. *Tales and Traditions of the Eskimo*. London: Henry S. King and Company.

Rivinus, E.F. and Yousef, E.M. 1992. *Spencer Baird of the Smithsonian*. Washington: Smithsonian Institution Press.

Robeson, G.M. 1873. *Report to the President of the United States of the Action of the Navy Department in the Matter of the Disaster to the United States Exploring Expedition Toward the North Pole, Accompanied by a Report of the Examination of the Rescued Party, Etc.* Washington: US Government Printing Office.

Roh, R. 1989. 'The Value of Photography (1932)' in *Photography and the Modern Era: European Documents and Critical Writings, 1913-40*, ed. C. Phillips. New York: The Metropolitan Museum of Art/Aperture.

Rosenblum, N. 1994. *A History of Women Photographers*. New York: Abbeville Press.

Rosse, I.C. 1883. 'Medical and anthropological notes on Alaska', *Cruise of the Revenue Steamer* Corwin *in Alaska and the N.W. Arctic Ocean in 1881*. Washington: US Government Printing Office.

Ross, W.G. 1976. 'Canadian sovereignty in the Arctic: the Neptune Expedition of 1903-4', *Arctic*, 29: 2, pp.87-104.
— ed. 1984a. *An Arctic Whaling Diary: The Journal of Captain George Comer in Hudson Bay, 1903-1905*. Toronto: University of Toronto Press.
— 1984b. 'George Comer, Franz Boas, and the American Museum of Natural History' in *Études/Inuit/Studies*.
— 1985. *Arctic Whalers, Icy Seas: Narratives of the Davis Strait Whale Fishery*. Toronto: Irwin Publishing.
— 1990. 'The uses and misuse of historical photographs: a case study from Hudson Bay, Canada', *Arctic Anthropology*, 27: 2, pp.93-112.

Rowley, S. 1988. *Inua: Spirit World of the Bering Sea Eskimo*, exhib. cat. for European tour, Washington: United States Information Agency.

Russack, R. 1975. 'Dr. Isaac Hayes', *Northlight. Journal of the Photograph Historical Society of America*, 2:2, pp.5-7, 11.

Ruvigny and Raineval, Marquis of, 1906. *The Moodie Book*. Privately printed.

*Saskatchewan Herald*. 1891/1895. Battleford, Saskatchewan District, Friday 12 April 1891 and Friday 28 June 1895.

Savours, A. 1963. 'Early Eskimo Visitors to Britain', *Geographical Magazine*, 36: 6, pp.336-43.

Schwoerke, J. 1986. 'Notes from the Special Collections: The Peary Photographs', *Northern Notes*, 1.

Sciberling, G. 1986. *Amateurs, Photography, and the Mid-Victorian Imagination*. Chicago: University of Chicago Press.

Sekula, A. 1986. 'The body and the archive', *October*, 39, pp.3–64.

Sexton, T. 1982. 'The images of Charles H. Ryder', *Alaska Journal*, 12: 3, pp.32–41.
— n.d. 'A guide to the photographs of Edward W. Nelson.' Undated MS in possession of the Arctic Studies Center and National Anthropological Archives, 12pp.

Silversides, B.V. 1994. *The Face Pullers: Photographing Native Canadians 1871–1939*. Saskatoon: Fifth House Publishers.

Smith, V. 1977. 'Eskimo Tourism: Micro-Models and Marginal Men' in *Hosts and Guests: The Anthropology of Tourism*, ed. V. Smith, pp.51–70. Philadelphia, University of Pennsylvania Press.

Smith, V., ed. 1977. *Hosts and Guests: the Anthropology of Tourism*. Philadelphia: University of Pennsylvania Press.

Sontag, S. 1977. *On Photography*. New York: Farrar, Strass and Giroux.

Sorge, E. 1935. *With 'Plane, Boat, and Camera in Greenland: An Account of the Universal Dr. Franck Greenland Expedition*. London: Hust and Blackett Ltd.

Starr, C. 1990. 'Women on the Verge ... Pioneer documentary film-makers that history ignored', *International Documentary*, (Fall), pp.15–19.

Steenhoven, G. 1955. Notes of Interest, the N.W. Territories and Yukon Radio System. Steenhoven private collection.
— 1962. 'Leadership and law among the Eskimos of the Keewatin District, NWT.' Unpublished PhD dissertation, University of Leiden.

Steensby, H. 1917. 'An Anthropogeographical Study of the Origin of the Eskimo Culture', *Meddelelser om Gronland*, 53:2, pp.39-228.

Stefansson, V. 1922. *The Friendly Arctic*. New York: The Macmillan Company.
— 1926. *My Life with the Eskimo*. New York: The Macmillan Company.
— 1992. *Hunters of the Great North*. New York: Harcourt, Brace and Co.

Svensson, T.G. 1995. 'Ethnic Art in the Northern Fourth World', *Études/Inuit/Studies*. Quebec.

Taber, C.R. 1991. *The World is Too Much with Us: 'Culture' in Modern Protestant Missions*. Macon: Mercer University Press.

Tagg, J. 1988. *The Burden of Representation: Essays on Photographies and Histories*. Amherst, MA: University of Massachusetts Press.

Taylor, W. 1965. 'Fragments of Eskimo Pre-History', *The Beaver*, Spring Issue, pp.4-17.

Thompson, K. and Bordwell, D. 1994. *Film History: An Introduction*. Madison; University of Wisconsin.

Thorleifsen, D., ed. 1995. *Ilinniarfissuaq ukiuni 150-ini. Ilinniarfissuup 1995-imi ukiunik 150-iliilluni nalliuttorsiornerannut atatillugu atuakkiaq/Festskrift i anledning af Ilinniarfissuaqs 150-års jubilæum i 1995.* (Summaries in Greenlandic, Danish and English.) Nuuk: ilinniarfissuag Atuakkiorfik.

*The Times*. 1853. 'The American Arctic Expedition', *The Times*, 2 November 1853, p.8.

Tippet, M. 1994. *Between Two Cultures: A Photographer Among the Inuit*, with photographs by Charles Gimpel. London: Viking/Penguin.

Trace, M. 1972. 'Upon that Mountain', *Silent Picture*, 14, Spring, pp.31-7.

Trafford, D. 1968. '*Takurshungnaituk*: Povungnituk art', *North*, 15, pp.52-5.

Traill, C.P. 1906. *Studies of Plant Life in Canada*. Toronto: William Briggs.

Turner, L. 1894. 'Ethnology of the Ungava District, Hudson Bay Territory' in *11th Annual Report of the Bureau of American Ethnology for the Years 1889-1890*, ed. J. Murdoch, pp.159-350. Washington.

Tyrrell, J.B. 1898. *Across the sub-Arctics of Canada*. London: T. Fisher Unwin.

Udet, E. 1935. *Mein Fliegerlieben*. Berlin: Im Deutschen Verlag.

Van Valin, W. 1941. *Eskimoland Speaks*. Caldwell: Caxton Printers.

VanStone, J. 1978. 'E.W. Nelson's notes on the Indians of the Yukon and Innoko Rivers, Alaska', *Fieldiana: Anthropology*, 70. Chicago.

Walsh, H., ed. 1934. *Stewards of a Godly Heritage: A Survey of the Church's Mission Fields in Canada*. Joint Committee on Summer Schools and Institutes of the Church of England in Canada [no city].

Wamsley, D. and Barr, W. 1996. 'Early Photographers of the Arctic', *Polar Record*, 32: 183, pp.295-316.

Washburne, H.C. and Anauta. 1940. *Land of the Good Shadows: The Life Story of Anauta, an Eskimo Woman*. New York: John Day, reprinted AMS Press Inc., 1976.

Weinstein, R.A. and Booth, L. 1977. *Collection, Use, and Care of Historical Photographs*. Nashville: American Association of State and Local History.

Whitman, N. 1994. *A Window Back: Photography in a Whaling Port*. New Bedford: Spinner Publications.

Whymper, F. 1869. *Travel and adventure in the territory of Alaska: formerly Russian America - now ceded to the United States – and in various other parts of the North Pacific*. New York: Harper and Brothers.

Williamson, H.A. 1964. 'The Moravian Mission and its impact on the Labrador Eskimo', *Arctic Anthropology*, 2: 2, pp.32-6.

Wooley, C. and Martz, M. 1995. 'ATG: Alaska's Patriotic Militia', *Alaska Geographic*, 22: 4, pp.66-71.

Young, A.W. 1876. *Cruise of the 'Pandora': From the Private Journal kept by Allen Young*. London: William Clowes & Sons.
— 1879. *The Two Voyages of the 'Pandora' in 1875 and 1876*. London: E. Stanford.

Zagoskin, L.A. 1967. 'Lieutenant Zagoskin's travel in Russian America, 1842-1844: the first ethnographic investigations on the Yukon and Kuskokwim valleys of Alaska' in *Anthropology of the North: Translations from Russian Sources*, 7, ed. H.N. Michael. Toronto: published for the Arctic Institute of North America by University of Toronto Press.

Zaslow, M. 1971. *The Opening of the Canadian North, 1870-1914*. Toronto: McClelland and Stewart, Ltd.
— 1975. *Reading the Rocks*. Ottawa and Toronto: Energy, Mines and Resources, Canada: MacMillan & Co.
— 1981. 'Administering the Arctic islands 1880-1940: policemen, missionaries, fur traders' in *A Century of Canada's Arctic Islands, 1880-1980*, ed. M. Zaslow. Ottawa: The Royal Society of Canada.

# Photographic Acknowledgements

Every effort has been made to trace and contact the owners of the copyright in the photographs reproduced in this book. The Editors and the Publishers apologise for any inadvertent errors or omissions and will be pleased to make the necessary amendments in any future editions or reprints if contacted in writing by the copyright holders.

**Introduction, pp.10–18**
1 Ausstellung i. Unitäts-Archiv, Herrnhut, Germany, 1995; 2 The Trustees of the British Museum; 3 Makivik Corporation, Montreal, Québec; 4 Stephen Loring.

**Qulaut, pp.19–23**
1 Jorgen Meldgaard; 2 & 6 John MacDonald; 3 Tessa MacIntosh (Government of the Northwest Territories; 4, 5, 8 & 9 George Quviq Qulaut; 10 Pat Qulaut.

**Sturtevant and Kleivan, pp.24–8**
1 Courtesy of the Trustees of the British Museum; 2 Department of Eskimology, University of Copenhagen, Denmark.

**Whitman, pp.29–35**
1–9 Whaling Museum, New Bedford, MA.

**Wamsley and Barr, pp.36–45**
1, 2 & 4 National Maritime Museum, Greenwich, London; 3 Douglas Wamsley's private collection; 5 Scott Polar Research Institute; 6 Photographic History Collection, National Museum of American History, Smithsonian Institution; 7 Arctic Institute, Danish Polar Center, Copenhagen; 8 & 9 National Archives of Canada, neg. nos NL–18943, C4588.

**Stern, pp.46–52**
1, 2 & 4 Canadian Arctic Expedition, Courtesy of the Canadian Museum of Civilization; 3 & 5 Richard G. Condon; 6 & 7 Courtesy of the Canadian Inuit Art Information Centre of Indian and Northern Affairs Canada.

**Eber, pp.53–9**
1, 4, 6 & 9 Peter Pitseolak Collection, Notman Photographic Archives, The McCord Museum of Canadian History, 2 The Hudson's Bay Company Archives, Provincial Archives of Manitoba, 1987/363-M-145/9; 3 & 5 Collection of The Canadian Museum of Civilization; 7 Courtesy of Galerie Elca, London, Montreal and Feheley Fine Arts, Toronto; 8 & 10 Courtesy of the West Baffin Eskimo Cooperative.

**Geller, pp.60–68**
1 *The Arctic Mission*, 1932; 2–6 Archibald Lang Fleming, *Dwellers in Arctic Night*, 1928, Plates 1, 27, 7, 31, 46, Missionary Society of the Church of England in Canada, Toronto; 7 *Fellowship of the Arctic*, 1929; 8 Archibald Lang Fleming, *Arctic Advance* (n.p. 1943), 13.

**Nungak and Hendrie, pp.69–76**
1, 2 & 5–9 Makivik Corporation, Montreal, Quebec; 3 & 4 *Taqralik* Archives.

**Burant, pp.77–87**
All photographs courtesy of National Archives of Canada (NAC).

1 GSC Neg. No. 2808, Geological Survey of Canada Collection, Acc. No. 1970–088, NAC PA-53548; 2 Geological Survey of Canada Collection, Acc. No. 1970–088 NAC PA-51465; 3 Bell Neg. No. 11–84, Robert Bell Collection, Acc. No. 1963–058, NAC C-20323; 4 GSC Neg. No. 2099, Geological Survey of Canada Collection, Acc. No. 1970–088, NAC PA-53581; 5 William Wakeham Collection, Acc. No. 1975–235, NAC C-84690; 6 Neg. No. APL 1565–97, Geological Survey of Canada Collection, Acc. No. 1970–088, NAC PA-51460; 7 RCMP Neg. No. 6275-2, Royal Canadian Mounted Police Collection, Acc. No. 1976–245, NAC C-1817; 8 Neg. No. APL 17 1903–4, Lorris Borden Collection, Acc. No. 1969–068, NAC C-88422; 9 Lorris Borden Collection, Acc. No. 1969–068, NAC C-88435; 10 GSC Neg. No. 2883, Geological Survey of Canada Collection, Acc. No. 1969–120, NAC PA-38301; 11 GSC Neg. No. 2790, Université d'Ottawa Collection, Acc. No. 1973–029, NAC C-24520.

**White, pp.88–97**
1 Courtesy of Medicine Hat Museum & Art Gallery #PC 696.9; 2 Courtesy of Medicine Hat Museum & Art Gallery #PC 395.77; 3 Courtesy of the Old Timers Museum, Maple Creek; 4 Courtesy of Medicine Hat Museum & Art Gallery #PC 395.78; 5 Courtesy of RCMP/GRC Ottawa #4705–1; 6 Courtesy of the National Archives of Canada #C89344; 7 Courtesy of Joan Eldridge, Victoria; 8 RCMP/GRC Ottawa #4659; 9 Courtesy of Medicine Hat Museum & Art Gallery #P422.1.

**King, pp.98–105**
All pictures courtesy of The Trustees of the British Museum.

1 fl4/99: MM 034321/104; 2 f4v/22: MM 034321/22; 3 f9v/62: MM 034321/65; 4 fl2/84: MM 034321/88; 5 fl4/97: MM 034321/102; 6 fl5v/115: MM 034321/123; 7 f23/186: MM 034321/199; 8 f21/162: MM 034321/171.

**Kleivan, pp.106–15**
All pictures courtesy of The National Museum and Archives of Greenland, Nuuk.

1 11x1064; 2 11x2800; 3 11x859; 4 11x1081; 5 11x961; 6 11x852; 7 11x1524; 8 11x2102; 9 11x1632; 10 11x1326.

**Eek, pp.116–24**
Etnografisk Museum, University of Oslo.

**Fitzhugh, pp.125–42**
3–5, 7–10 & 12–15 © Smithsonian Institution.

**Wooley and Brewster, pp.143–7**
Marvin Peter Family Collection.

**Hess, pp.148–55**
All pictures © Bill Hess.

**Norbert, pp.156–9**
Charles Menadelook Family Collection.

**Graburn, pp.160–67**
1 Courtesy of Dorset Fine Arts; 2–10 Nelson Graburn Collection.

**Lee, pp.168–74**
All pictures courtesy of the Southwest Museum, Los Angeles. Gladys Knight Harris Collection.

1 Neg. #26950; 2 #42371; 3 #26919; 4 #26954; 5 #26842; 6 #26855; 7 #27198; 8 #26728; 9 #26832; 10 #26795.

**Woodward, pp.175–80**
Author's note: all the lantern slide titles used in the captions are merely descriptive, and are taken from the February 1987 Index to the Stefansson Lantern Slide Collection, Special Collections, Dartmouth College. The only change I have made from the Index wording is to change 'Eskimo' to 'Inuit', to conform to contemporary usage in relation to Canadian Inuit.

As noted in the text, Stefansson rarely acknowledged the original photographers and/or sources of the photographs he used in his lantern slides (or those he used as illustrations in his published works). Images 1–8 were apparently made from original photographs taken on his Canadian Arctic Expedition, 1913–18, originals of which are in the Geological Survey of Canada holdings at the National Archives of Canada. All photographs reproduced in this paper are courtesy of Special Collections, Baker Library, Dartmouth College.

1 Lantern slide #61. Stefansson Lantern Slide Collection; 2 #6; 3 #129; 4 #166; 5 #466; 6 #335; 7 #266; 8 #252; 9 #1; 10 Photo. Adrian Bouchard.

**Christopher, pp.181–9**
1 With the kind permission of the Robert and Frances Study Center at Claremont and the National Archives of Canada; PA-121984. Reproduced in *My Eskimo Friends* (1924), p.146, with caption 'Nanook the Harpooner'.

2–4, 6–11 Reproduced with the kind permission of the Trustees of the British Library; 2 Canadian Copyright Collection 23989/31; 3 23989/49; 4 23988/57; 6 23989/33; 7 23989/48; 8 23989/32; 9 23989/87; 10 23989/46; 11 23989/97.

5 With the kind permission of the Thunder Bay Historical Museum Society: 972.255.175pp.

**Marcus, pp.190–96**
1 *LIFE* Magazine © Time Inc. Reprinted with permission; 2–7 Geert van den Steenhoven.

**Lidchi, pp.197–206**
All pictures reproduced with kind permission of Deutsche Kinemathek, Sammlung Richard Angst (Richard Angst Collection), 4.2–85/03-0.

1 Production Still (No. 522) *SOS Iceberg* (Deutsche Universal Film AG); 4 Production Still (No. 239) *SOS Eisberg* (Deutsche Universal Film AG); 10 Production Still (No.22) *SOS Eisberg* (Deutsche Universal Film AG).

**Loring, pp.207–20**
2 Moravian Archives, London, 1991; 3 Ausstellung i.Unitäts-Archiv, Herrnhut, Germany, 1995; 4 United States National Archives, Office of Polar Archives, Record Group 401 (74); 5 Ausstellung i.Unitäts-Archiv, Herrnhut, Germany, 1995, #7204; 6 William Brooks Cabot Collection (A-71), National Anthropological Archives, National Museum of Natural History, Smithsonian Institution, Washington DC; 7 From *Among the Eskimos of Labrador*, Samuel King Hutton (1912), Seeley, Service & Co., London. 8 Ausstellung i.Unitäts-Archiv, Herrnhut, Germany, 1995, #6221; 9 From *Among the Eskimos of Labrador*, Samuel King Hutton (1912), Seeley, Service & Co., London; 10 Ausstellung i.Unitäts-Archiv, Herrnhut, Germany, 1995, #7157; 11 Ausstellung i.Unitäts-Archiv, Herrnhut, Germany, 1995, #7190; 12 Stephen Loring.

**Keenainak, pp.221–5**
All pictures © Simeonie Keenainak

# Index